REINCARNATION

THE MISSING LINK IN CHRISTIANITY

REINCARNATION
THE MISSING

LINK IN CHRISTIANITY

Elizabeth Clare Prophet

with ERIN L. PROPHET

SUMMIT UNIVERSITY 🦢 PRESS®

REINCARNATION: *The Missing Link in Christianity*
by Elizabeth Clare Prophet with Erin L. Prophet.
Copyright © 1997 by Summit University Press. All rights reserved.

Library of Congress Catalog Card Number: 96-072012
ISBN: 0-922729-27-1

SUMMIT UNIVERSITY ❧ PRESS®
Summit University Press and ❧ are registered trademarks.

This book is set in Sabon.
Printed in the United States of America

The paper used in this publication meets the requirements of the American
National Standards Institute Z39.48-1992 (Permanence of Paper).

*To the followers of Christ
who are ready to drink
the full cup of his message*

CONTENTS

ILLUSTRATIONS

Maps

PREFACE

IN HIS FIRST LETTERS TO ME, "MARVELOUS MARV," as he sometimes signed his name, asked me to pray for his release from prison. He felt he had much more to accomplish in life.

Marvin Baker was a carpenter and heavy equipment operator. He was doing sixty years for killing an acquaintance during a drunken argument. He began reading my books soon after entering prison and felt that they gave his life purpose. He wrote, "I had searched all of my life for that missing element and I have truly found it."

Two of the most important themes in my books are reincarnation and the soul's opportunity to become one with God. While he was in prison, I advised Marvin to enter into communion with the divine spark in his heart and to seek union with God. Marvin made this his top priority. He underwent a transformation, became a mystic and had some amazing spiritual experiences, all the while looking forward to his release. He thought a competent attorney could get him out.

But in 1995, he was diagnosed with throat cancer. Despite several operations—his tongue and voice box were removed—the cancer spread to his lungs and he died in April 1996. He was fifty-four and left behind three grown children whom he desperately wanted to help and guide.

By most standard Christian interpretations, Marvin, as a murderer unreconciled with the Church, would be forever denied the chance to return to God. He would be consigned to either eternal separation from God or eternal pain in hell.

But Marvin was a good soul who made a bad mistake. He wasn't that far removed from many of us who could say, "There but for the grace of God go I." What Marvin needed was a second chance at life—not in heaven or hell but on earth. In order to atone for the murder, Marvin needed not only to serve time in prison but also to find and serve the man he killed. The only way Marvin can serve that one is to be reborn in circumstances that will bring them together.

Reincarnation forms a pivotal part of my belief system because it allows us all another chance. Most of us have not committed crimes as serious as Marvin's in this life. But many of us need further opportunities in which to resolve painful situations and complete our learning experience.

I like to see earth as a schoolroom. We each have our own lessons to learn: like getting along, loving, forgiving. The graduation requirement is that you achieve union with God—the same God who dwells within each heart. In this book, we will explore how to progress through the grades and graduate. And why we need reincarnation if we don't make it in this life.

Reincarnation is opportunity—both to learn from our mistakes on earth and to pursue God. It is *the* key to understanding our soul's journey.

I invite you to journey with me as we explore how reincarnation once fit in with Christian concepts like baptism, resurrection and the kingdom of God. We will also see how Church Fathers removed reincarnation from Christian theology and why reincarnation could resolve many of the conflicts plaguing Christianity today.

I offer this research as an adjunct to your own reading and communion with God. As you search for the heart of Jesus' message, I am certain you will find the answers within—for they are already written in your own heart.

In prison, Marvin designed a card for me, hand-drawn by one of his friends, with a picture of an open window looking out on a rising sun. It represented his hopes, not only for getting out of prison but also for getting out of the prison of human existence by returning to God, the Sun, the Source of all life. I write this book for Marvin and for all of you who, like him, have been looking for the missing link in Christianity.

Elizabeth Clare Prophet

FOREWORD

FOR ME, REINCARNATION AND CHRISTIANITY HAVE
always gone together. As a child, I used to listen to
my father, Mark Prophet, explain why he believed
that Jesus taught reincarnation.

The spiritual organization he had founded, The
Summit Lighthouse, was headquartered in a large
brick mansion in Colorado Springs. When several
hundred people would show up for meetings, they
overflowed out of the chapel (the mansion's former
living room) and down the red flagstone hallway,
where they sat three across in white stacking chairs,
as if on some kind of celestial railroad.

I would sit and look into the gilt-edged mirror
that hung in the hall and listen to my father bless
the Communion—long, complicated blessings in
his rich, deep voice. He reached a crescendo with
a phrase I would hear often: "from GLO-ry UN-to
Glo-ry..." I didn't hear much else until the Communion trays were passed and I held the bread
crumb in my mouth while it dissolved in a sip of
tangy grape juice.

My godmother, a former Baptist Sunday school
teacher, made sure I learned the Bible. She had

joined The Summit Lighthouse soon after I was born, and she saw no contradiction in the message: reincarnation *and* Christianity.

When I was six, we went on a pilgrimage to the Middle East, taking in the holy sites of Jerusalem along with the pyramids of Egypt. At the time, standing on tiptoe to peer at one of the Dead Sea Scrolls in a glass case, I little guessed that I would one day be looking to them for clues about the meaning of Christianity.

After my father died, my mother, Elizabeth Clare Prophet, moved The Summit Lighthouse to the former site of a Catholic seminary in the Santa Monica Mountains near Los Angeles. Periodically she would play a tape of that Communion blessing during devotional services. "From GLO-ry UN-to Glo-ry."

My father was raised as a Christian. He never stopped quoting scripture even though he later studied Eastern teachings and developed a mystical interpretation of Christianity, including the idea that Jesus taught reincarnation.

As I began to read the Bible for myself, many things about my parents' message puzzled me. If Jesus taught reincarnation, why are there so many places in the Bible that talk about the resurrection of the dead? Is it possible to believe in both? I thought about the contradictions and conflicts in the Bible, and I could see room for both interpretations.

One June morning in 1986, when I was in my senior year in college, another piece of the puzzle fell into place. I sat down in the back of the large yellow-and-white striped tent at our California headquarters and listened to my mother's first lecture on Gnosticism. She has since spoken frequently on the subject, quoting from ancient manuscripts written by people who called themselves Christians but who had been dubbed Gnostics because they sought *gnosis,* or knowledge, of God. It turned out that the Gnostics believed in reincarnation. I read everything I could find about them. I wanted to get to the bottom of Christianity.

My mother talked a lot about mysticism and the ancient mysteries. I used to think they were detective stories. As I came to learn, mysticism is the experience of direct contact or union with God. My parents taught that Jesus' primary message was that each of us is a son of God who has the ability to walk in Jesus' footsteps and become one with God.

In his Communion blessing, my father was referring to a verse from Corinthians that reads, "And all of us, with unveiled faces, seeing the glory of the Lord as though reflected in a mirror, are being transformed into the same image *from one degree of glory to another.*"[1] In other words, we are meant to be transformed into the image of Christ. As you will see in the following chapters, in the history of world thought mysticism and reincarnation are often linked.

After I earned my degree in journalism in 1986, I went to work for my mother as a writer and editor at the Royal Teton Ranch, her spiritual community in Montana. Six years later, I left the ranch, wanting some time to think about my beliefs and goals.

As I made new friends and attended different churches, I discovered a gap between people's spiritual needs and what they are being offered in church. Along with many of my friends, I find Christianity's take on life incredibly bleak. If we really have only one shot at eternity in either heaven or hell, what happens to those of us whose lives are cut short by war or cancer? And if Jesus can simply wipe away all of our past mistakes, is there a point to our actions on earth?

Questions like these led me to a new appreciation of mysticism, which says that salvation is an internal experience of God rather than a world-ending event. I saw that reincarnation offers a satisfying alternative to orthodox Christianity. And so I decided to work with my mother on a book that would present her ideas about Jesus, reincarnation and the inner meaning of Christianity in the context of new research about the historical Jesus.

In this two-year project, I have learned that scholars' picture of both Christianity and Judaism at the time of Christ is evolving at a rapid pace, thanks in large part to the discovery of the Nag Hammadi texts (1945) and the Dead Sea Scrolls (1947). Scholars have concluded that much of the Gospels can't be taken as gospel. Instead, they believe that in the early centuries of Christianity, there were conflicting interpretations about what Jesus taught and that the New Testament manuscripts reflect a spectrum of ideas.

Some scholars say that there is no "bottom" of Christianity, no "true" teachings of Jesus to be discovered, because Christianity was as diverse at its inception as it is now. This may be so. But today, when Christianity no longer works for many Christians, it's time to reexamine some of the early ideas that didn't make it into the mainstream.

For me, the greatest thrill of this project has been to realize that the twin concepts of reincarnation and mysticism were present in several forms at the time of Christ. And that means that my parents' view of Jesus—that he was a mystic who taught reincarnation—may be just as plausible as the orthodox view. I have enjoyed helping my mother present her theology, which takes into account both new research and essential spirituality.

ERIN L. PROPHET

Note: Since gender-neutral language can be cumbersome and at times confusing, we have used the pronouns *he* and *him* to refer to God or to refer in general to the individual. We have used these terms for readability and consistency, and they are not intended to exclude females or the feminine aspect of the Godhead. God is both masculine and feminine. We do, however, use the pronouns *she* and *her* to refer to the soul because each soul, whether housed in a male or a female body, is the feminine counterpart of the masculine Spirit.

PART 1

What
Reincarnation
Means to
Christians

CHAPTER 1

❦

A Martyr for Infinite Worlds

Since the soul is not found without
body and yet is not body, it may be in
one body or in another, and pass from
body to body.

Giordano Bruno
Venice trial, 1592

LIGHTED TORCHES PIERCED THE PALE FEBRUARY morning. Spectators jostled each other to see the procession. It would be a slow half mile from the Tower of Nona, where the prisoner had been confined, to the Field of Flowers, an open square where he was to be executed.

The fifty-two-year-old philosopher shuffled his way over the tufa stones that paved the streets of Rome. Barefoot and chained by the neck, he wore a white sheet decorated with crosses and splashed with devils and red flames.

Monks of the Brotherhood of Saint John the Beheaded walked with him, urging him to repent. Periodically they presented the crucifix to his lips, giving him every opportunity to obtain salvation.

Pilgrims from all over Europe packed the square. Drawn to Rome by the Church's yearlong jubilee celebration of 1600, they were eager to see the burning of a notorious heretic. Some spat and jeered as the guards stripped the small, thin man and tied him to an iron stake surrounded by bundles of wood. After he once more refused to kiss the cross, they gagged him, then piled more wood mixed with straw around the stake, heaping it up to his chin. The monks sang litanies while the officials of Rome gave him one last chance to recant, then lit the pile.

As the flames licked his beard and his lungs filled with smoke, did Giordano Bruno regret the course that had led him to the stake? As his skin began to crack and his blood hissed in the flames, did he wonder if the pain would continue for an eternity in hell? Or did he hold firmly to his dream of viewing other suns, innumerable heavenly worlds, and of journeying on "through all infinity"?[1]

Burnings at the stake were less frequent in 1600 than in medieval times. Only twenty-five heretics had been burned in Rome during the entire sixteenth century. How did Bruno, formerly a Dominican monk and for many years a wandering philosopher, come to receive the Church's ultimate punishment?

He was burned for his heretical views, among them the idea that the human soul could return to earth in a new body after death and could even move on to inhabit an infinite number of worlds besides earth. He also held to an idea that often occurs alongside reincarnation—the idea that man can become one with God during his soul's journey on earth. For him, religion was the process by which the divine light "takes possession of the soul, raises it, and converts it into God."[2] One does not have to wait until the end of the world for divine union to take place, Bruno believed. It can happen today.

In Bruno's view of human potential, we can find the seed

In 1600, after he was condemned by the Inquisition, Giordano Bruno was executed in Rome. This eighteenth-century engraving depicts a public execution similar to the scene of Bruno's burning. In the foreground, priests present crosses to the condemned, urging them to repent and so avoid the fires of hell.

of why Christianity ultimately rejected reincarnation: it undermined the authority of the Church. Under Bruno's system, salvation was not linked to a person's relationship to the Church but to his direct relationship with God. And it was on this point, as much as on reincarnation, that he collided with the Inquisition.

Bruno had been a thorn in the Church's side almost from the moment he was ordained a Dominican priest at Naples at the age of twenty-four. The son of a professional soldier, he did not fit in well with monastic life. He was a thinker and an avid reader with an irascible temper and a penchant for angering the authorities.

As a young monk, Bruno had too many of his own ideas.

He defended the fourth-century heretic Arius, of whom we will hear more later, and he read the forbidden works of the Dutch humanist philosopher Erasmus. When his contraband copy of Erasmus was discovered hidden in the monastery's outhouse, Bruno found himself in serious trouble. For his heresies, Church officials at Naples prepared an indictment against him and he fled Italy in 1578.

He spent the next fourteen years wandering France, England, Germany and Switzerland. Passionate, fierce and sarcastic, Bruno was repeatedly forced to flee after stirring up trouble with inflammatory remarks and writings. He attacked the Oxford fellows for their support of Aristotle and ridiculed French academics. He was put on trial in Geneva for pointing out "errors" in a Calvinist theologian's lecture.

Both the Catholic and Protestant churches excommunicated him (even though he probably never became Protestant). Yet he dreamed of reconciling Catholics and Protestants through philosophy. He took issue with both of their theologies and called himself "a citizen and servant of the world, a child of Father Sun and Mother Earth."[3]

Bruno was one of the most brilliant men of his day. He instructed the French king Henry III in the art of memory, taught philosophy at the University of Toulouse and mingled with the literary circle that surrounded England's Queen Elizabeth I. His prolific and unusual writings gained a small but ardent following.

He was either far ahead of or far behind his times. His ideas about the universe presaged some of the discoveries of twentieth-century physics. But Bruno was not a scientist.

In the nineteenth century, intellectuals revered him as a martyr to scientific inquiry and freedom of thought, largely for his defense of Copernicus' sun-centered view of the solar system. Bruno even shared enemies with the Copernicans—one of his inquisitors, Cardinal Robert Bellarmine, would also question Galileo about his observations that the earth revolved around the sun. However, Bruno did not share Copernicus' scientific world view.

It was mysticism and philosophy that brought Bruno to his vision of innumerable worlds. Bruno agreed with Copernicus that the earth could not be the center of the universe. But, as he saw it, neither was the sun. He believed the earth was only one among an infinite number of worlds.

At a time when most people thought the stars were permanently pasted to the sky, Bruno detailed his revolutionary beliefs: "There is a single general space, a single vast immensity which we may freely call *Void;* in it are innumerable globes like this on which we live and grow. This space we declare to be infinite. . . . In it are an infinity of worlds of the same kind as our own."[4]

Giordano Bruno (1548–1600) carried on a lone battle with the Church. He fought for, among other things, the right to believe in reincarnation.

For Bruno, the idea of infinite worlds opened the door to the idea of infinite human possibility. If there are infinite worlds, then why can't there be infinite opportunity in which to explore them? A person, whether in or out of a body, Bruno wrote, "is never completed." He has the opportunity to experience life in different forms. "Even as infinite space is around us, so is infinite potentiality, capacity, reception, malleability, matter."[5]

THE BEAST TRIUMPHS

The Church would later claim that Bruno was not burned for his defense of Copernicus or for his doctrine of infinite worlds but rather for his "theological errors"[6] and belief in magic. But trial records reveal that both infinite worlds and reincarnation were at issue. The two ideas appear in his original indictment, which also accused Bruno—still officially a monk—of boasting of his female conquests and joking about the final judgment.[7]

Gaspar Schopp, an eyewitness at Bruno's Rome indictment and sentencing, tells us that among Bruno's heretical doctrines were "those of an eternal universe and innumerable worlds," as well as "a libel concerning the Triumphant Beast—which is to say the Pope."[8]

He was referring to Bruno's *The Expulsion of the Triumphant Beast*. Since it was the only one of Bruno's works mentioned at his sentencing, it must have hit a raw nerve with the Church. But the "triumphant beast" was not the pope. Bruno meant the "beast" to represent the evil side of man's nature, qualities such as superstition and ignorance. He argued for a religion based on reason, through which man could purge himself of this "beast" within.[9] Incidentally, the *Expulsion* contains Bruno's most elaborate writings on reincarnation.

Bruno used two tactics in his defense. He recanted his

"errors" and "heresies," and he tried to argue his points "as a philosopher" rather than as a monk. At his trial in Venice in 1592, he said that reincarnation was, if not proven, "at least likely," according to the opinion of the fifth-century-B.C. philosopher Pythagoras. Bruno said: "I have held and hold souls to be immortal.... Speaking as a Catholic, [I say] they do not pass from body to body, but go to Paradise, Purgatory or Hell. But I have reasoned deeply, and, speaking as a philosopher, since the soul is not found without body and yet is not body, it may be in one body or in another, and pass from body to body."[10]

But Bruno's philosophical window dressing could not hide his very real differences with the Church. He admitted to doubting the principles behind the Trinity, especially the incarnation of the Son, and challenged the doctrine that souls are created "out of nothing" and therefore are not a part of God.[11]

This doctrine, which is fundamental to Church teaching, will come up in later chapters as we examine how and why the Church denied reincarnation. It is at the root of the conflict between orthodox Christianity and mysticism.

Bruno argued that the soul originates in God and is immortal. He believed that human bodies are simply formed and re-formed from the same matter and that death is "nothing else than division and reunion."[12] In support of his belief, he quoted the Old Testament book Ecclesiastes: "There is nothing new under the Sun."[13]

The Venetian Inquisition might have been willing to listen to such arguments. But Bruno had come to the attention of the Roman Inquisition, which engineered his transfer to Rome in 1593. There he faced Cardinal Robert Bellarmine for the first time, along with a panel of eight other cardinals. Bellarmine, later Saint Robert, was a formidable opponent. His tombstone was to read, "With force I have subdued the brains of the proud."[14]

The Inquisition's first method of subduing Bruno was to leave him alone in prison. For the greater part of seven years, there is no record of his life. We do know he was deprived of food, books and writing materials, and he may have been tortured, as were most accused heretics at the time.

Around 1599, Bellarmine brought matters to a head. He presented Bruno with a list of eight "heretical propositions" taken from his work and required him to renounce them. A year passed, during which Bruno may have considered retracting some of the statements. But by December, Bruno hardened his position, perhaps sensing that the Church had no plans to release him whether he recanted or not. He refused to retract, saying that he had nothing to renounce. It was the beginning of the end.

On February 8, 1600, Bruno was led into the church of Saint Mary over Minerva. Guards forced him to his knees, but he held himself erect, facing the cardinals with defiance. The words that echoed in the church did not come as a surprise. The Inquisition sentenced him as "an impenitent and pertinacious heretic" and expelled him once again from the "holy and immaculate Church," telling him he had become "unworthy" of its mercy. The indictment condemned Bruno's writings "as heretical and erroneous" and placed them on the "Index of Forbidden Books."[15]

To exonerate themselves, the cardinals attached to his indictment a meaningless disclaimer asking the secular court to be lenient with Bruno and not to put him "in danger of death" or "mutilation."[16] The secular authorities knew exactly what to do. Bruno was to be burned.

Before he was led from the hall, Bruno, never renowned for tact, gave his parting shot to the inquisitors: "Perchance you who pronounce my sentence are in greater fear than I who receive it."[17] The guards turned him over to officials of the governor of

Rome, who locked him in the Tower of Nona, a prison on the Tiber River. He had another eleven days to live.

Bruno's trial is an important chapter in the history of reincarnation in Christianity, significant in that it juxtaposes a fiery and independent thinker with one of the world's most powerful institutions. The chestnut-bearded philosopher was part of an ancient reincarnation tradition in the West, one that developed alongside Christianity, sometimes inside the Church and sometimes apart from it.

In the upcoming chapters, we will examine reincarnation in Christianity today and explore why some Christians from the first and second centuries to the present have clung to the belief.

❦

CHAPTER 2

Unanswered Questions

I'll be right back.

Johnny Carson
epitaph of choice

WHAT IS HAPPENING TO CHRISTIANITY? Millions of Americans, Europeans and Canadians believe in reincarnation. Many of them call themselves Christians, yet they persist in a belief that the Church rejected fifteen hundred years ago.

By conservative estimates, over one-fifth of American adults believe in reincarnation[1]—and that includes a fifth of all Christians.[2] The figures are similar for Europe and Canada.[3] Another 22 percent of Americans say they are "not sure" about reincarnation,[4] indicating that they are at least open to the belief.

The percentage of Christians in America who believe in reincarnation is about the same as the percentage of believers in the general population, according to a 1990 Gallup poll. An earlier poll gave the breakdown by denomination. It found that 21 percent of Protestants (including Methodists, Baptists and Lutherans) and 25 percent of Catholics held the belief. For clergy who got out their calculators, that comes out to an eye-popping 28 million Christian reincarnationists![5]

Reincarnation is starting to rival some of the fundamental tenets of Christianity. In Denmark, a 1992 survey found that 14 percent of the country's Lutherans believed in reincarnation, while only 20 percent believed in the Christian doctrine of resurrection. Younger Lutherans were even less inclined to believe in the resurrection. In the eighteen-to-thirty age bracket, only 15 percent believed in the resurrection, while 18 percent believed in reincarnation.[6]

These shifts in Christian beliefs mark a trend toward what some scholars are calling a post-Christian religion in the West. It's a shift away from traditional Church authority and toward a more personal faith based on contacting the God within.

Like the Protestant Reformation, it emphasizes personal contact with God over church membership. But unlike Protestantism, it discards some of the principles that have characterized Christianity since the fourth century—things like hell, the bodily resurrection and the idea that we have only one life to live on earth. Some Christian denominations are trying to make room inside of Christianity for reincarnation and related beliefs. Others remain opposed to the concept.

What most Christians don't know, however, is that reincarnation isn't new to Christianity. Today, the majority of denominations would answer no to the question: "Can you believe in reincarnation and still be a Christian?" But in the second century, the answer would have been yes.

During the first three centuries after Christ, numerous Christian sects flourished, some of which taught reincarnation. Although orthodox theologians attacked the belief from the second century on, the reincarnation controversy continued through the mid-sixth century.

Among the reincarnationist Christians were the Gnostics, who claimed to possess Christ's inner, more spiritual teachings, which had been hidden from the general population and reserved for those who could understand them. The Gnostics' religious practice centered around enlightened spiritual teachers and the personal experience of God rather than membership in an organized church.

The orthodox, however, taught that salvation could be granted only through the Church. This tenet gave their views strength and longevity. When the Roman emperor Constantine became a supporter of Christianity in 312, he backed the orthodox view, perhaps because he thought it would lead to a stronger, more organized society.

Between the third and sixth centuries, the authorities of church and state gradually eliminated the reincarnationist Christians. But their beliefs returned to the features of Christianity like a stubborn wart. Reincarnation beliefs traveled to the areas of present-day Bosnia and Bulgaria, where they surfaced in the seventh century with the Paulicians and in the tenth century with the Bogomils. The beliefs also traveled to medieval France and Italy, where they formed a central part of the Cathar sect.

After the Church wiped out Catharism with a thirteenth-century crusade followed by a campaign of inquisition, torture and burnings, belief in reincarnation was kept alive through the nineteenth century in the secret traditions of the alchemists, Rosicrucians, Kabbalists, Hermeticists and Freemasons. Reincarnation continued to crop up inside the Church as well. In nineteenth-century Poland, a Catholic archbishop, Monsignor Passavalli (1820–97), grafted reincarnation onto his faith and openly embraced it. He influenced other Polish and Italian priests, who also took up reincarnation.[7]

The idea that 25 percent of Catholics in America today believe in reincarnation might raise Vatican eyebrows. But there is anecdotal evidence of a silent minority of reincarnationist Catholics to back up the statistics. I have met many Catholics who accept the belief. And one former Catholic pastor in a major Midwestern city told me, "I know many, many Catholics and Christians of other denominations who believe in reincarnation."

CHRISTIANITY'S FUNDAMENTAL PROBLEM

Why do some Christians believe in reincarnation?

For one thing, it provides an alternative to the all-or-nothing view of heaven or hell. Although 95 percent of Americans believe in God and 70 percent believe in life after death,[8] only 53 percent believe in hell.[9] The 17 percent who believe in life after death but don't believe in hell probably can't accept that God would cause anyone to burn forever or would even, as the current Catholic catechism defines it, exclude someone from his presence eternally.

Those who don't believe in hell must ask themselves, "Does everybody go to heaven, then? What about murderers?" To many, reincarnation seems a better solution than hell. For Christianity has had difficulty answering the question "What happens to someone who dies neither good enough for heaven nor bad enough for hell?"

We often read stories in the newspaper that seem to defy standard Christian explanations. For example, stories about seemingly decent people who commit murders in the heat of passion and then take their own lives. According to many Christians, including Catholics, they would go to hell. Although murder is a serious crime, do those who commit it really deserve eternal punishment?

Here's a recent example. James Cooke, an employee of the

In this picture, The Last Judgment, *sinners endure devils' torment while the righteous join the saints in heaven. Today, many Christians question the fairness of eternal punishment in hell.*

city of Los Angeles, retired to rural Minnesota with his wife, Lois, and their two adopted teenage daughters. He got along well with his neighbors and took a job milking cows.

In September 1994, sixty-three-year-old James discovered that Lois had told the police that he was molesting their daughters. James killed all three—shooting Lois in the back and the two girls, Holly and Nicole, as they slept in their beds. He then shot himself. In his suicide note he apologized for the killings but did not admit to molesting the girls.[10]

Where does the soul of Mr. Cooke go when he gets to the other side? Hell or heaven? Will God really send him to burn in hell for all time? Will he ever get a chance to make up for his final desperate acts?

If there is no hell or if God doesn't put him there, will he go to heaven? Assuming Holly, Nicole and Lois went to heaven, will they have to share their lives with their murderer for all eternity? The first alternative lacks mercy; the second lacks justice. Only reincarnation offers a satisfactory solution: Mr. Cooke must return and give life to those he deprived of life. They must reembody to complete their life plans and he must serve them to make up for the pain he caused them.

All four need further opportunity on earth. So do many others who die prematurely. Christianity draws a blank on some questions like: "Why does God allow babies and children to die? What about teenagers killed by drunken drivers? Why do they live at all if their lives are so brief?" "Why, God—why did you give me Johnny, only to allow him to be taken by leukemia?"

What are priests and ministers to say? Their training offers such bland answers as "It must be part of God's plan" or "We cannot understand His purposes." They may suggest that Johnny or Mary was here to teach us about love and has now gone to be with Jesus in heaven.

Reincarnation is an attractive solution. But the Church's continued opposition to it has forced many Christians to carve out their own faith. They are left in a kind of spiritual limbo— between beliefs that satisfy a soul need and a Church that still refuses to consider them.

Take actor Glenn Ford, who, under hypnosis, recalled lives as a cowboy named Charlie and as a member of King Louis XIV's cavalry. "It [reincarnation] conflicts with all my religious beliefs," he fretted. "I'm a God-fearing man and proud of it, but this has got me mixed up."[11]

The United States is a country of God-fearing people, many of whom call themselves Christians. Yet the conflicts embedded in Christianity don't go away. While Christianity may motivate and inspire many people, there are an equal number of people who are disenchanted. They can't understand a Christianity that says non-Christians will burn in hell and a God who "lets" our loved ones die.

Reincarnation is an appealing option for people who have asked themselves searching questions about God's justice. And it has appealed to many of our great minds.

OUR REINCARNATIONIST HERITAGE

The list of Western thinkers who accepted or thought seriously about reincarnation reads like *Who's Who*. In the eighteenth and nineteenth centuries it included French philosopher François Voltaire, German philosopher Arthur Schopenhauer, American statesman Benjamin Franklin, German poet Johann Wolfgang von Goethe, French novelist Honoré de Balzac, American transcendentalist and essayist Ralph Waldo Emerson and American poet Henry Wadsworth Longfellow.

In the twentieth century it included British novelist Aldous Huxley, Irish poet W. B. Yeats and British author Rudyard Kipling. Spanish painter Salvador Dali claimed he remembered living as Saint John of the Cross.

Other Western greats have given credence to reincarnation by writing about it or having their characters express reincarnationist ideas. They include British poets William Wordsworth and Percy Bysshe Shelley, German poet Friedrich Schiller, French novelist Victor Hugo, Swiss psychiatrist Carl Jung and American author J. D. Salinger.

Yeats referred to reincarnation in "Under Ben Bulben," a poem he wrote the year before he died:

> Many times man lives and dies
> Between his two eternities,
> That of race and that of soul,
> And ancient Ireland knew it all.
> Whether man die in his bed
> Or the rifle knocks him dead,
> A brief parting from those dear

Is the worst man has to fear.
Though grave-diggers' toil is long,
Sharp their spades, their muscles strong,
They but thrust their buried men
Back in the human mind again.[12]

When he was twenty-two, Ben Franklin drafted an epitaph for himself predicting that he would reincarnate. He compared his body to the worn-out cover of a book with "its contents torn out." He predicted that the contents would "not be lost" but would "appear once more in a new and more elegant edition revised and corrected by the Author."[13]

THE STREAM RESURFACES

These thinkers reflected a new openness to reincarnation that had begun with the Enlightenment. During the late nineteenth century, reincarnation gained increased popularity in the West through the Russian-born mystic Helena P. Blavatsky and her Theosophical Society. While she emphasized Eastern religion and philosophy, Blavatsky also embraced esoteric Christianity. William Q. Judge, one of the society's cofounders, was fond of calling reincarnation "the lost chord of Christianity."[14]

Theosophy opened the door for a number of other groups to teach reincarnation in a Christian context. Among them are Rudolf Steiner's Anthroposophical Society and Charles and Myrtle Fillmore's Unity School of Christianity.

Edgar Cayce, the "sleeping prophet," was a devout Christian who came to believe in reincarnation and popularized it for millions of people. He started out as a psychic diagnostician who gave health readings while in a self-induced hypnotic sleep. Although Cayce had never studied medicine, his readings proved accurate and his remedies effective. The cures included everything from drugs and surgery to vitamins and massage.

Cayce first mentioned reincarnation in a 1923 reading. Referring to the subject of the reading, Arthur Lammers, he said, "He was once a monk."[15] Cayce never remembered what he said in his trances, so when his stenographer read those words back to him, they plunged him into turmoil. Didn't reincarnation conflict with scripture? he wondered.

Cayce had accepted a literal interpretation of the Bible, which, by 1923, he had read once for each of his forty-six years. He knew about reincarnation but considered it a Hindu superstition. After the Lammers reading, Cayce read the Bible straight through again to see if it condemned the idea. He decided it didn't and continued his past-life readings. Ultimately he came to accept reincarnation and predicted his own reincarnation in twenty-second-century Nebraska.[16] Cayce's work has influenced millions of Americans, many of whom will never go back to the orthodox Christian view of life.

Sandbox recollections

Like Cayce, I came to my belief in reincarnation through an unconventional experience. When I was four I remembered a past life. It happened one spring day while I was playing in my sandbox in the picket-fenced play yard my father had built for me. It was my own little world inside the larger world of our backyard in Red Bank, New Jersey.

On that day I was alone, letting the sand slip through my fingers and watching fluffy clouds roll by. Then gradually, gently, the scene began to change. As though someone had turned the dial on a radio, I was on another frequency—playing in the sand along the Nile River in Egypt.

It was just as real as my play yard in Red Bank and just as familiar. I was idling away the hours, splashing in the water and feeling the warm sand on my body. My Egyptian mother was nearby. Somehow this too was my world. I had known that river forever. And the fluffy clouds were there too.

How did I know it was Egypt? How did I know the Nile? Knowing it was part of the experience. Perhaps my conscious mind made the connection because my parents had put a map of the world over my toy chest and I already knew the names of most of the countries.

After some time (I don't know how long), it was as though the dial turned again and I was back at home in my little play yard. I wasn't dizzy or dazed. I was back in the present, very much aware that I had been somewhere else.

So I jumped up and ran to find my mother. She was standing at the kitchen stove cooking. I blurted out my story, then asked, "What happened?"

She sat me down and looked at me and said, "You have remembered a past life." With those words she opened another dimension. The picket-fenced play yard now included the whole world.

Instead of ridiculing or denying what I had experienced, she spoke to me in terms that a child could understand: "Our body is like a coat we wear. It gets worn out before we finish what we have to do. So God gives us a new mommy and a new daddy and we are born again so we can finish the work God sent us to do and finally return to our home of light in heaven. Even though we get a new body, we are still the same soul. And the soul remembers the past even though we do not."

As she spoke, I felt as if she was reawakening my soul memory. It was as though I had always known these things. I told her that I knew I had lived forever.

Over the years she was to point out to me children who were born maimed or blind, others who were gifted, some who were born into wealthy homes and some into poverty. She believed their past actions had led to their present inequalities.

She said that there could be no such thing as divine or human justice if we had but one life, that we could know God's justice only if we had the chance to experience many lives in which we could see the consequences of past actions returning to us in our present circumstances.

My experience in the sandbox brought me to a new level of awareness and I began to have many questions about God and the world. I begged to be taken to church. Mother, a native of Switzerland, had been brought up in the National Protestant Church and Father was reared a Lutheran in Germany, but they seldom went to church. Mother made me wait until I was five—I think the year between four and five was the longest year of my life!

Finally, Mother started me in the Methodist Sunday school. After coloring Easter bunnies and putting money in the collection plate, I was disappointed. I wanted someone who could answer my questions about Jesus. "Take me to another church," I said. My mother (or the neighbors) took me to services at almost every Protestant church in town. I also convinced her to take me to St. James Catholic Church whenever we were downtown.

As I continued my pilgrimage through the churches, I felt dissatisfied with the sermons I heard from the pulpit. I asked Jesus to explain to me the true meaning of his message and I began to receive answers in a clear and unmistakable voice I heard in my mind. Thus began a lifelong mystical communion with Jesus.

I came to believe that the ministers did not have the keys to the mysteries of God and of his kingdom because Jesus' teachings had not come down to us as he had originally taught them. I decided that I wanted to help people to understand his message.

To prepare myself, I studied the Bible and continued my search for a teacher. When I was nine, my best friend's mother began taking me to Christian Science Sunday school. I was immediately convinced that I had found the most advanced teaching on Jesus' message available in my hometown.

Unfortunately, Christian Science didn't allow room for rein-carnation either. Although I eventually joined the church, I never let go of that belief. I stayed in the church until I was twenty-two, even becoming a Sunday school teacher and usher in the Mother Church. I also worked for the *Christian Science Monitor* while I studied political science at Boston University. How-ever, I kept searching for deeper answers.

In 1961, in Boston, I met Mark Prophet, a teacher whose mystical Christianity included an intricate understanding of reincarnation. He became my teacher and husband. Together we built The Summit Lighthouse, the spiritual organization he had founded in 1958, which admitted both Eastern and West-ern ideas. One of the central concepts of our teaching is that Jesus was a mystic who taught reincarnation.

A NEW PERSPECTIVE

Back in the sixties, who would have expected that our ideas would be corroborated by ancient manuscripts dating from the second century or earlier? These texts, discovered at Nag Ham-madi, Egypt, in 1945, say that they preserve Jesus' secret teach-ings—among them, reincarnation.

When they were published in English in 1977, the Nag Ham-madi manuscripts touched off a storm of controversy among scholars and clergy. I first began interpreting them in 1986. But Mark and I had been teaching some of their central themes for decades.

In this book, we will explore the mystical teachings of the Christian reincarnationists along with ancient manuscripts and new archaeological discoveries such as the Dead Sea Scrolls.

First we'll examine what reincarnation means and how it provides the missing link in Christianity. Then we will look at the different kinds of reincarnation beliefs in Jesus' world, a world ruled by the Romans but dominated by Greek ideas, a world in which the Judaism of Jesus' parents mingled with the philosophy of Plato. We will see that Jesus could easily have picked up reincarnation from his environment if he had not already derived it from his own communion with God.

We will examine what the Bible says, and doesn't say, about reincarnation—who believed in reincarnation in Jesus' world and why they believed in it.

Then we will look at some early Christians who believed in reincarnation—Gnostics and others—and ask why the Church rejected their beliefs. To do this, we will examine the councils at which the Church decided that for all time to come reincarnation was not an acceptable belief for Christians. We'll also live through the stories of reincarnationist Christians in medieval France who were willing to die for their beliefs.

Finally, we will look at the Bible, the Dead Sea Scrolls and other scriptures and see how some scholars today are reaching the conclusion that Jesus may indeed have been a mystic who taught both reincarnation and the path of developing our relationship with the God within.[17]

We will reach a new perspective on the meaning of Christianity. Until now, many Christians have believed that the purpose of their faith is to ensure their place in the resurrection, often seen as a world-ending event. The Church teaches that those who die outside of God's good graces are forever excluded from the kingdom of God.

In this book, you will learn about another view. One that provides a mystical interpretation of the resurrection and gives everyone—from James Cooke and Marvin Baker to a child who died yesterday—another chance to live Jesus' message.

CHAPTER 3

Why They Believe

*"It's so silly," [Teddy] said. "All you do is
get the heck out of your body when you die.
My gosh, everybody's done it thousands and
thousands of times. Just because they don't
remember it doesn't mean they haven't done it.
It's so silly."*

J. D. Salinger
"Teddy"

LAUREL DILMEN COULDN'T HOLD BACK THE
memories that flooded into her mind. She remembered having lived as a woman named Antonia Michaela Maria Ruiz de Prado in the sixteenth
century. She said that Antonia had been born on
the Caribbean island of Hispaniola and had later
moved to Spain, where her life was filled with intrigue and romance.

She was imprisoned for several months by the
Spanish Inquisition, fell in love with her inquisitor,
became his mistress, followed him to South America and finally drowned near a small Caribbean

island. Antonia's traumatic death was burned into Laurel's mind. She remembered that Antonia's lover had tried to save her and that she had died in his arms. Antonia had realized she was dead only when she could no longer feel her lover's tears splashing on her face.

It sounds like an elaborate fantasy or a romantic novel—except that Laurel was able to recall over one hundred facts that she would not have known if she hadn't lived in sixteenth-century Spain.

Psychologist Linda Tarazi spent three years checking Laurel's story, which had come to Laurel during a series of hypnotic regressions in the 1970s.[1] To check the facts, Tarazi spent hundreds of hours in libraries, consulted historians and even visited Spain. Although she was unable to find evidence that someone named Antonia Ruiz de Prado had lived, Tarazi verified almost every other aspect of Laurel's story.

"Antonia" accurately gave names and dates that were available only in documents written in Spanish in the town of Cuenca, Spain—names like those of the two inquisitors at Cuenca, Ximenes de Reinoso and Francisco de Arganda, and the names of a couple arrested for sorcery, Andres and Maria de Burgos. Laurel had never visited Spain, and her command of Spanish was limited to tourist phrases picked up during a week in the Canary Islands.

Where did Laurel get the information? Genetic memory is ruled out because Laurel, of German ancestry, had no Spanish blood. Possession by a disembodied spirit is far-fetched, even more so than reincarnation. And the specific facts could hardly have come from her childhood or education.

A Chicago-area schoolteacher, she was brought up Lutheran. Her schooling was standard—no Catholic school—and her major at Northwestern University was education. It is unlikely that she is the perpetrator of a fraud. She has nothing to gain by the story, which hasn't been published outside of academic journals, and she refuses to allow her real name to be used.

What is the likelihood of Laurel knowing the building in Cuenca where the Inquisition sat in 1584? Even the government tourist office in Cuenca didn't know. Laurel described it as having been in an old castle overlooking the town. The tourist office said it had been in a building *in* town. However, in an obscure Spanish book, Tarazi found that it had been moved to just such a castle in December 1583, shortly before the date that Laurel said Antonia had moved to Cuenca.

Could Laurel have concocted "memories" from romantic fiction she had read? Tarazi quizzed her on the books, movies and television shows she had watched and even went so far as to review indexes of historical fiction. She found nothing that resembled Antonia's story.

Antonia's case seems improbable because it does sound so much like romantic fiction. Tarazi acknowledges that "parts of it may be just that."[2] However, it is also closer to life than fiction. For instance, although novels generally portray inquisitors as villains, Antonia described the ones she knew as more humane.

Tarazi confirmed her characterization. She found that during the time when, according to Laurel, Antonia had lived in Cuenca, the Inquisition there was rather moderate. No one was burned alive at the stake during Antonia's lifetime, although one person was drawn and quartered. Laurel's historical accuracy is more than uncanny.

Laurel's is only one among thousands of documented past-life cases that have contributed to the widespread belief in reincarnation in the West. When people hear stories like hers, it often reinforces a budding belief in reincarnation. Other contributing factors may be their own past-life memories, out-of-body experiences and near-death experiences. In this chapter, we will look at examples of all three kinds of experiences to further understand why people choose to believe they have lived before.

PERSISTENT MEMORIES

Much of the documented evidence about past lives comes from Ian Stevenson, the West's most prolific past-life researcher. A psychoanalyst and former chairman of the Department of Psychiatry at the University of Virginia Medical School, Stevenson has been researching past lives full-time since 1967.

That was the year Chester F. Carlson, inventor of the process used in Xerox machines, established an endowment to further Stevenson's work. Stevenson gave up his department chairmanship to direct the division of parapsychology within the university's Department of Psychiatry.

Stevenson prefers not to deal with hypnosis, saying it rarely produces something of "evidential value." (He cites Antonia's as one of those rare worthwhile cases.[3]) Instead, he prefers to work with people who have had spontaneous past-life memories, primarily children. He interviews them, documents their memories and then tries to independently verify the details of their previous existence. Stevenson has over twenty-five hundred cases on file, chiefly from India, Sri Lanka and Burma.

Some skeptics criticize Stevenson's cases because most are from Asian countries, where belief in reincarnation is widespread and parents may be more likely to encourage recollections of past lives. However, many Asian parents do not encourage their children's past-life memories. As Stevenson points out, they believe these memories are bad luck and lead to early death. In fact, in a full 41 percent of Stevenson's Indian cases, parents tried to stop their children from talking about their past lives, even using such methods as beatings and washing their mouths out with dirty water.[4]

Stevenson believes the reason there are fewer reported Western cases is this: Westerners don't know what to do with such memories when they come up. Their belief system gives them no framework. One Christian woman, whose child claimed to be the reincarnation of the woman's older sister, told Stevenson, "If my church knew about what I'm telling you, I would be expelled."[5]

The recollections of some of his subjects are amazingly accurate. They recall names, places and circumstances and even manage to perform skills, like drum playing, that they have not learned in this life but which their past-life personalities had learned. Although Stevenson does not believe any of his cases are good enough to scientifically prove reincarnation, he thinks there may be an ideal case out there that does the trick. One recent case in England appears to come close.

A MOTHER'S LOVE SURVIVES

"I know it's going to sound very strange, but I remember the family through dreams," said Jenny Cockell to the woman on the other end of the line.[6]

It was April 1990 and she was speaking to the daughter of Jeffrey Sutton, an Irishman whose mother had died after childbirth on October 24, 1932. She spoke awkwardly. It was her first contact with the family she believed she had abandoned in death nearly sixty years before.

It wasn't just dreams that had brought them together. The memories had been with her, waking and sleeping, since early childhood. She had first spoken of them before she was four. Rather than fading away, the memories continued and became more detailed as she grew older. Jenny was haunted by the sense that she must make sure her children were all right.

As a schoolgirl in England, she picked out on a map the town where she knew she had lived. It was Malahide, a small village north of Dublin. Although she had never visited Ireland, she drew a map of the town, marking the cottage where she remembered living with a husband and seven or eight children.

She knew her name had been Mary and that she had been born around 1898 and died in the 1930s in a white room with tall windows. She believed that her husband had fought in World War I and that his work had something to do with "timbers and being up high." She had happy memories of her marriage before her children were born. But her memories grew vaguer after that and she recalled "a sense of quiet caution."

Jenny grew up, attended college and became a podiatrist. She married and had a son and a daughter. As her children grew older, she once again became obsessed with the past and with finding out what had happened to the other family she remembered. In 1980, she bought a more detailed map of Malahide, which she compared with the map she had drawn in childhood. They were very similar.

Ruling out a genetic connection, she became convinced that her memories were genuine. Her only Irish relative was a great-grandmother who had been born on the west coast of Ireland (Malahide is in the east) and had spent most of her life in Malta and India. So she could not have been a source for memories of twentieth-century Ireland.

Jenny became convinced that she was "reliving a past life through reincarnation," as she wrote in her 1993 book *Across Time and Death*. It was the "*strength* of the emotions and memories," she wrote, that made her decide the past life was real. She decided to undergo hypnosis, which helped her remember specific incidents.

She remembered often passing a certain church, retaining a

clear enough image to later draw a picture of it. She also remembered her children having snared a rabbit. They called her to come out and see it. She did, and remembers saying, "It's still alive!" This recollection helped convince the eldest Sutton boy, Sonny, that she was indeed his mother reincarnated.

She visited Malahide for a weekend in June 1989 and made some astonishing confirmations. The church she had drawn was indeed there, looking remarkably like her drawing. Along Swords Road, where she remembered her cottage had been, the landscape was changed considerably. She didn't find a building on the spot she had marked for the cottage. However, the stone wall, the stream and the swamp were exactly where she had described them.

The trip gave her confidence to continue her search. She wrote to the owner of an old building she had seen on Swords Road. He wrote back, saying he recalled a family with a large number of children who had lived in a nearby house and whose mother had died in the 1930s. His second letter gave her the name of the family, Sutton—and painful news: "After her death the children were sent to orphanages."

She realized that there had been good reason to be concerned for their welfare. "Why had their father not kept the family together?" she wondered. She began an intensive search for the Sutton children. She got the first names of six of the children from a priest at a Dublin-area orphanage and then began writing to Suttons with the proper first initials. During her search, Jenny found Mary's marriage certificate and, most importantly, her death certificate. She had died in Rotunda Hospital in Dublin, which did have white rooms with tall windows.

At last, in answer to one of her many queries, she received the call from Jeffrey* Sutton's daughter. Although Jeffrey did not show much interest in her story, his family gave her the

*In her book, Jenny substituted "Jeffrey" for his real name to protect his family's privacy.

Is Jenny Cockell the reincarnation of Mary Sutton? Jenny is an English podiatrist whose persistent memories of a past life led her to search in Ireland for a cottage and children she remembered. In 1989, she found evidence that the family existed. The mother, Mary Sutton, had died in the 1930s. Jenny found and reunited the five surviving children. This 1927 photo (top) shows Mary and her daughter Phyllis Sutton, age two. This 1993 photograph (bottom) shows Jenny with Phyllis at the Dublin airport.

addresses and numbers of two of the boys, Sonny and Francis. The boys had lost contact with their sisters after the girls were sent to orphanages.

She gathered up the courage to call Sonny and found him receptive. He confirmed that the cottage had been in the place she remembered it and said he wanted to meet her and discuss the memories.

When she met Sonny, Jenny was instantly at ease. And, she wrote, "I came to discover just how accurate and detailed those memories were." She told him about the incident with the rabbit. "He just looked at me blankly and said, 'How did you know that?'" He confirmed that the rabbit had still been alive. "This was clearly the first piece of information that had really shocked him by its accuracy," Jenny wrote. "The incident was so private to him and his family, how could anyone else know about it?"

Sonny also confirmed Jenny's fears about Mary's husband. John Sutton, a scaffolder, had been a heavy drinker who was often violent. He had hit his wife and beaten the children with "a large, brass-buckled belt." After Mary died, government authorities took all of the children except Sonny away from their father, Jenny wrote, "as he was deemed unfit to look after them." Sonny was the only one who was left at home. John became more violent, beating him regularly until he ran away to join the army at age seventeen.

With Sonny's help, Jenny tracked down the rest of the eight Sutton children. Three had died, but in April 1993 the five surviving children were reunited with Jenny during the filming of a documentary in Ireland. "It was the first time the family had been together since 1932," Jenny wrote.

Although Sonny says he accepts reincarnation as the explanation for Jenny's recollections, the other children don't go that far. The surviving girls, Phyllis and Elizabeth, accept the explanation suggested to them by a priest—that their mother was working through Jenny to reunite the family.

Jenny is glad she followed up on her memories. "The sense of responsibility and guilt have fallen away," she wrote, "and I feel a sense of peace that I have never really known before."

FAULTY RECOLLECTIONS

Memories like Jenny's and Laurel's have helped to feed past-life beliefs among Christians. But past-life recollections can seldom be confirmed in the way that Jenny's and Laurel's were. For every set of confirmed recollections, there are hundreds more that cannot be confirmed. Some are simply vague and unverifiable. Others turn out to be inaccurate or, worse, mixed with scenes from novels or films. Consequently, many people regard them as fantasies.

The potential inaccuracy of memories from hypnotic regression came out all too plainly in a study conducted by Nicholas Spanos of Canada's Carleton University. His researchers induced a hypnotic trance in 110 of the school's undergraduates and instructed them to recall a past life. Thirty-five reported a past-life identity and twenty were able to name a specific year and country in which they had lived during the past life. But most gave inaccurate details. "When asked to name the leader of their country and whether the country was at peace or at war, all but one of these individuals either could not name the leader, named the wrong individual, were incorrect about whether their country was at peace or war in the designated year, or supplied historical misinformation," Spanos wrote.[7]

One subject, who claimed to have been Julius Caesar, said it was A.D. 50 and he was the emperor of Rome. Caesar was never crowned emperor and lived *before* Christ.

This study highlights some of the pitfalls of hypnotic regression. But inaccurate memories don't disprove reincarnation.

People don't always accurately remember events from their present lives. As with other skills, people's ability to recall events under hypnosis varies. Most subjects are better at remembering events that involve strong emotions rather than dry facts like names and dates. Others are good on the big picture but fuzzy on details.

Despite the historical unreliability of many past-life recollections, a growing number of psychologists are using regression to treat patients. They say it can help cure everything from phobias to chronic pain and can even improve relationships.

While hypnotic regression is seldom useful in proving reincarnation, its widespread popularity should be telling us something: People are not satisfied with the orthodox Christian way of looking at life. They turn to alternatives like reincarnation because they are looking for better answers.

OUT-OF-BODY EXPERIENCES

A few years ago I received a letter from a man describing an experience he had had while clinically dead. It happened in 1960 after a football accident and lasted seven minutes.

"During this time," he wrote, "I found myself transported through a dark tunnel into a bright white light. Standing in this light was a bearded gentleman who told me that there was more work to be done. Very soon after hearing this I awoke on the operating table to the amazement of the doctors and nurses present."

I recognized this as a description of a typical near-death experience, or NDE.

Since 1975, when medical doctor Raymond Moody published *Life After Life,* medical science has begun taking the NDE seriously. And in too many books and TV shows to keep track of, people have described how they were embraced by, saved by, transformed by and brought closer to and beyond the light.

Moody found that there are several common elements of the NDE, such as hearing a loud noise, journeying through a tunnel, meeting a being of Light and experiencing a life review. But the aftereffects are almost as interesting as the experience itself.

Beginning in 1977, Kenneth Ring, a University of Connecticut psychologist, systematically corroborated most of Moody's findings. One of his lesser-known findings is that people who have NDEs are likely to become more open to the idea of reincarnation. Thus NDEs may be one factor in the spread of the belief.

In 1980–81, a Gallup Poll found that 15 percent of American adults said they had had a "verge-of-death" experience, such as an experience of "continued life or an awareness after death."[8] Basing his calculations on the Gallup figures, Ring estimates that between 35 and 40 percent of the people who come close to death have an NDE.[9]

Ring also found that NDEers developed "a greater openness toward a reincarnation[ist] view of life after death."[10] A University of Connecticut study conducted by Amber Wells, a graduate student under Ring's guidance, further documented the belief shift.[11] Wells questioned fifty-seven NDEers about their reincarnation beliefs. She found that 70 percent of them believed in reincarnation, whereas only 23 percent of the general population and 30 percent of her control group held the belief.

Why do NDEers tend to take up reincarnation?

Ring found that some subjects based their shift on a specific piece of information given to them by their being of Light. For example, one NDEer told Ring that the being he saw during his NDE told him that his older son had experienced "14 incarnations in female physical bodies." He said this made his belief in reincarnation "a matter of personal knowledge."[12] Some NDEers have reported viewing souls waiting to be reincarnated. Other people attribute their belief shift simply to their general receptivity to new ideas that they developed after the NDE.

Perhaps NDEs turn people toward reincarnation because they give them the experience of being out of the body. This leads people to the natural conclusion that they are not their bodies. This can easily lead to the idea of leaving one body behind and taking up life in another.

An out-of-body experience that I had while in college helped to reinforce my understanding that although my soul inhabited my body, I was more than my body. It happened as I was walking to my job at the *Christian Science Monitor* in Boston. It was 4:30 or 5:00 in the morning and the streets were empty. All of a sudden I became aware that my soul had soared to a great height. The dawn was breaking and I was looking down at my body walking along the street. I could even see myself putting one penny-loafer-clad foot in front of the other.

From that vantage, I knew that I was a part of God and that I was looking at my lesser self, my mutable self, even while I was one with my immutable self. God was showing me that I had the choice to be one with my immutable self, my Higher Self, or to remain locked into my lower self with all of its mundane doings. I decided to take the high road and to embrace the part of me that is real and eternal. From that day on it would be impossible for me to forget that I am a part of God.

Past-life recollections, near-death experiences and out-of-body experiences show us that we don't need to be preoccupied with death. They are gifts that allow us to penetrate other dimensions of ourselves. They get us on track to pursuing higher reality, the one thing that is really important. They can give us an expanded sense of our destiny, not just on planet earth but in the many realms of God's consciousness.

The soul's opportunity to become one with God is a theme that will continue to crop up in our exploration of reincarnation.

CHAPTER 4

Gods in Ruins

Self-luminous is Brahman, ever present in
the hearts of all. He is the refuge of all, he is
the supreme goal....Attain him, O my friend,
the one goal to be attained!
Mundaka Upanishad

MARK PROPHET USED TO JOKE ABOUT A "come as you were" party he attended in Chicago. People were supposed to dress up as one of their past-life personalities. Everyone came dressed as royalty. "There were no bricklayers or street cleaners or anything like that," he recalled. "They had more kings and queens there...than all the stream of history ever had."

It's hard to bring up reincarnation without focusing on people's memories of who they were in the past. I have recalled lifetimes as both famous people and ordinary people. But remembering past lives—famous or infamous—isn't really why reincarnation is important to Christianity. Although some find that past-life memories help them understand their relationships or untangle their psychology, the real value of reincarnation is simply that it implies opportunity.

It means that if a person doesn't find God in this life, he can return to try again in another life. It means that the child who dies before she has a chance to live and the soldier cut down in the prime of life can return to take up where they left off.

Almost every belief system that teaches reincarnation also includes the idea that man has the potential to become God. This divine potential is described as a seed or spark within us that needs to be nurtured or fanned so that it can develop into full godhood. Reincarnation gives us the chance to pursue that development.

It's easy to understand the concept of becoming God if we think of our latent divinity as a seed. A seed can remain dormant for hundreds or even thousands of years. But when it is nurtured by light and water, it begins to grow and blossom.

"The real unfoldment of man is to be found in the implanted divine seed," said Mark Prophet. "And the seed is the seed of the Christ within us all. Every son of God has that divine seed implanted within him at the moment he is created."[1]

Mark found support for this idea in Genesis: "Let us make man in our image, after our likeness."[2] He taught that the divine image is the seed of divinity within our hearts. If you think of yourself as having a divine seed inside, then you will realize that at any time you can exercise the option to pursue and develop your godhood as Jesus did. Then you can realize that which has always been your true inner God-manifestation.

What does it mean to become God, to develop godhood? Why would someone want to do it? Mystics have described it as a process of returning to the state of primordial bliss that we knew before we ever made the choice to be separate from God. Their goal is not omniscience or superhuman powers but rather a feeling of oneness with all of life. The Native Americans call it *skanagoah*.

Today, some New Agers refer to all people as Gods and Goddesses. But that immediately raises the question: If we are Gods and Goddesses, how have we made such a mess of our world?

Ralph Waldo Emerson answered the question by describing man as "a god in ruins."[3] His vivid image accounts for both the human frailties that hinder us and the spark that gives us divine potential. We are *unformed* Gods and Goddesses. And we all have the opportunity to enter, portion by portion, into a mystical union with that divine spark. If we look at our lives as a process of reconstructing our God Self, then we can claim to be Gods in the making rather than Gods in ruins.

How does a God in the making act? Is he distant and removed? Does he have superhuman powers?

A God in the making may be hard to spot. Superhuman powers are not a prerequisite. Rather, Gods in the making have some or all of the qualities that we call Christlike or Buddhic.

They may be calm, peaceful, humble and helpful, devoted to loving and healing. Although they may have an otherworldly sense about them, they often retain the practicality with which to negotiate this world. They have learned to maintain an awareness of God while engaged in all of the mundane tasks of the day.

Like sculptors, they are molding their souls after the pattern of the indwelling God. This metaphor comes to us from the Neoplatonist philosopher Plotinus, who advised, "Never cease chiselling your statue until... you have become this perfect work, ... wholly true to your essential nature."[4]

I like to compare the process of divine union to mounting a golden spiral staircase. Bruno saw it as a journey through heavenly spheres. Plotinus described it as a journey within. Other mystical traditions also use the imagery of ascending a ladder or traveling through heavenly palaces. Later we will look at the

Jewish and Greek images of ascent to the divine and their parallels in Christian writings.

Mystics in every religion have outlined various ways of achieving union with God. Paul spoke of Christ being "formed" in us.[5] Early Christian saints practiced asceticism and sought divine visions. Hindus have used mantras, mudras and a variety of breathing techniques, yogic postures and rituals. Greek philosophers relied on the pursuit of knowledge. Bruno believed the key was "the reformed intellect and will"[6] as well as sharing in "the infinite love of the Divine."[7] In future chapters we will talk more about this process of divine union.

GOD WITHIN

The idea of an indwelling God is a central theme of both Hinduism and Buddhism, as is reincarnation. Taking a closer look at these ideas will help us to better understand the importance of reincarnation to Western spirituality.

In Hinduism, reincarnation is linked tightly with the Hindu concept of God. Although Hindus worship many deities, in the ultimate sense they worship them as aspects of a single, all-pervasive, impersonal God called Brahman.

This God is everywhere. It pervades everything, yet it can't be comprehended. It is transcendent, beyond the limits of possible experience. It does not conform to our definitions of time and space. One Hindu text describes God as "ever present in the hearts of all,"[8] existing inside of each person. Yet God is so large that all worlds exist inside of him.

The part of God that is inside of us is identical with Brahman and is called Atman. Another text compares Atman to "the smallest granule of millet"[9] but says it is also "greater than the sky, greater than space, greater than this earth, greater than all existing things."[10]

According to Hinduism, the goal of life is union with Atman/ Brahman. One Hindu sage tells us that Atman is "my own self"— the God within. He says that he will "merge into that very self."[11] One who achieves this merging, or divine union, can then access God's infinite power even while living in a mortal body.

Giordano Bruno echoed and elaborated upon this Hindu concept when he wrote that the purpose of reincarnation is to give us the opportunity to learn to transcend the human condition. Bruno believed that the soul can become one with the infinite, which is God, because everything is interconnected.

The earth is one with the heavens and the stars—and so are we, he wrote. "Every soul" has a "continuity" with "the spirit of the universe," existing not only where the body lives but also "diffused throughout immensity" so that "the power of each soul is itself somehow present afar in the universe." He explored ways in which we can realize that our souls are "continuous with the soul of the universe"[12] and thereby access a new form of existence.

Today, some physics experiments suggest that at the level of subatomic particles the universe is indeed interconnected. In other words, every point is one with every other point. And some physicists even go so far as to say that human beings may be able to access this state of interconnectedness.[13] Thus, science and mysticism may ultimately reach the same conclusions. We will explore this idea in Part 5.

KARMIC CHAINS

Although the soul contains a spark of the divine, the soul is not God. Through life on earth, souls have become entangled with ignorance, pain and suffering. They have created karmic ties that cause them to continually return to earth in new bodies. One Hindu text compares the universe to a wheel upon which are bound "all creatures that are subject to birth, death, and rebirth."[14]

Karma is a Sanskrit word meaning act, action, work or deed. In Hinduism *karma* evolved to mean the actions that bind the soul to the world of existence. "Just as a farmer plants a certain kind of seed and gets a certain crop, so it is with good and bad deeds," says the Mahabharata,[15] a Hindu epic. Because we have sown both good and evil, we must return to reap the crop.

Hinduism acknowledges that some souls are content to continue doing this lifetime after lifetime. They enjoy life on earth with its mixture of pleasure, pain, success and failure. They live and die and live again, tasting the bittersweet of the good and bad karmas they have sown.[16]

But there is another path for those who weary of the endless return: union with God. Each life, as French novelist Honoré de Balzac explained the concept, may be lived to "reach the road where the Light shines. Death marks a stage on this journey."[17]

Once souls have decided to return to their source, their goal is to purify themselves of ignorance and darkness. The process may take many lifetimes. The Mahabharata compares the process of purification to the work of a goldsmith purifying his metal by repeatedly casting it into the fire. Although a soul may purify herself in one life by "mighty efforts," most souls require "hundreds of births" to cleanse themselves, it tells us.[18] When purified, the soul is free from the round of rebirth, one with Brahman. The soul "achieves immortality."[19]

Buddhists, too, see the cycle of rebirth as a wheel—a wheel to which we are bound until we can break the karmic chains. Siddhartha Gautama (c. 563–c. 483 B.C.), the founder of Buddhism, began life as a Hindu. He borrowed from and expanded on the Hindu ideas about karma and reincarnation.[20]

The Dhammapada, one of the best-known Buddhist texts, explains karma as follows: "What we are today comes from our thoughts of yesterday, and our present thoughts build our life of tomorrow: our life is the creation of our mind. If a man speaks or acts with an impure mind, suffering follows him as the wheel of the cart follows the beast that draws the cart.... If a man speaks or acts with a pure mind, joy follows him as his own shadow."[21]

Today, the word *karma* is used as a fashionable substitute for *fate*. But belief in karma isn't fatalism. Karma, according to the Hindus, can cause people to be born with certain tendencies or characteristics, but it doesn't force them to act according to those characteristics. Karma does not negate free will.

Each person "can choose to follow the tendency he has formed or to struggle against it,"[22] as the Vedanta Society, an organization promoting Hinduism in the West, explains. "Karma does not constitute determinism," we read in *The Encyclopedia of Eastern Philosophy and Religion*. "The deeds do indeed determine the *manner* of rebirth but not the *actions* of the reborn individual—karma provides the situation, not the response to the situation."[23]

Buddhism concurs. Buddha taught that understanding karma gives us the opportunity to change the future. He challenged a contemporary teacher named Makkhali Gosala, who taught that human effort has no effect on fate and that liberation is a spontaneous event. For the Buddha, belief in fate, or destiny, was the most dangerous of all doctrines.

Rather than consigning us to an irreversible fate, he taught, reincarnation allows us to take action today to change the future. Our good works of today can bring us a happier tomorrow. As the Dhammapada puts it, "Just as a man who has long been far away is welcomed with joy on his safe return by his relatives, well-wishers and friends; in the same way the good works of a man in his life welcome him in another life, with the joy of a friend meeting a friend on his return."[24]

According to the Hindus and Buddhists, our karma requires us to continue reincarnating until we achieve divine union. The union with Atman may occur in stages while we are alive and be made permanent after death.

Early Christian reincarnationists may have gotten some of their ideas about reincarnation from Hinduism. For they, too, believed that the soul contains a part of God, a seed or spark, and has the potential to integrate with that spark and become God. They also believed that becoming God is a process.

A COLLISION COURSE

Christians who accept reincarnation also tend to believe that they are a part of God and are meant to return to their source. The Catholic and Protestant churches, on the other hand, teach that man is radically different from God and can become one with God only through grace. This difference is the key reason reincarnationist Christians like Bruno were on a collision course with the Church.

During the first few centuries of Christian thought, the Church Fathers excavated a great chasm between the soul and God. As explained by Catholic theologian Claude Tresmontant, the Church concluded that "the human soul is not...by nature from the divine substance...It is called to share the life of God, but by grace." For the Catholics, this grace can be accessed only through the Church. The Catholic view is that the soul cannot return to God since it has never been a part of God. "We are not parts of the divine substance, but creatures of God," writes Tresmontant.[25]

When the Church Fathers defined the soul as separate from God, it became impossible for them to accept the reincarnationist idea that the soul can unite with God. Their definition also threw up a roadblock for Christian mystics since mysticism is the search for either direct contact with God or union with God. (Christian mystics like Meister Eckhart and Saint Teresa of Avila treaded perilously close to the precipice of heresy when they talked about union with God.)

The collision between reincarnationist and orthodox Christians was made inevitable by their divergent world views. The orthodox were literalists. They held beliefs many Christians today have decided are untenable. For example, they believed that the Garden of Eden was a real place on earth you could journey to.

The reincarnationists, on the other hand, seldom took the Bible literally. They looked for hidden symbolism. For them, Eden was not so much a historical place as an eternal state in which souls were a part of God. Souls had somehow lost that state and had been placed on earth for the purpose of regaining it. Since the human body is finite and weak, the reincarnationists believed that souls may require more than one life to complete the process. For them, the idea of reunion with God thus went hand in hand with the idea of reincarnation.

The reincarnationists saw Jesus as a man who showed us how to become one with God. The orthodox, in contrast, saw Jesus as someone entirely different from us—to be worshiped, not emulated. Even though they teach that Christians should try to imitate Jesus' admirable human qualities such as humility and kindness, they do not believe that human beings have the capacity to become Sons of God.

I see all of us as sons of God who have the potential to become the Christ as Jesus did. Christhood is not something that was unique to Jesus. It was something he achieved through becoming one with the Logos, or divine Word. *Logos* is a Greek term for the part of God that mediates between Creator and creation. We, too, can become one with the Logos, in other words, become the Christ, and be called Sons of God.

From Pythagoras to medieval Jewish mystics, from second-century Gnostic teachers like Valentinus to third-century Christian theologians like Origen of Alexandria, we will see the same theme: infinite opportunity equals infinite possibility. If we have the time and space to become God, we also have the ability to do so. Reincarnation gives us that time and space.

Becoming God doesn't appeal to everyone. Some people are happy with life as it is. Reincarnation offers a way out for them, too—a chance to continue returning to earth until they have had enough of it and are ready to move on to the higher forms of existence offered by mystical union.

Even if you are content with your life, you may be on the road to union with God and not know it. If you've ever felt as if you were part of all of life, whether as a feeling of oneness with nature, with a loved one or with mankind, then you have started the process.

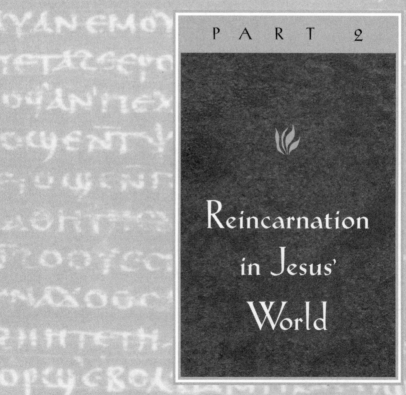

PART 2

Reincarnation
in Jesus'
World

CHAPTER 5

Reincarnation in Judaism

> If [a person] dies before his time, what
> happens to his unlived life, his joys and his
> sorrows, the ideas he did not have time to
> develop, the deeds he had no chance to do?...
> A human life cannot be lost. When a person
> dies before his time his soul returns to complete
> the span of life which he was given on earth,
> to finish the work he began, to feel the joys
> and sorrows he did not live to know.
>
> S. Ansky
> *The Dybbuk*

WHEN YOU SEE A GROUP OF HASIDIC JEWS
with their characteristic black hats, ear-
locks and long black coats, you are looking at
people who believe in reincarnation. But most of
us don't even know that it's found in Judaism. In
fact, reincarnation in Judaism goes all the way
back through the Middle Ages to before the time
of Christ, as we will discover in this chapter.

Hasidic Jews got their ideas about reincarnation

from the Kabbalists, medieval Jewish mystics. Hasidism is a form of Judaism that was founded in eighteenth-century Poland by Rabbi Israel Baal Shem Tov (c. 1700–1760). He took elements of Kabbalism and made them accessible to the common people in a movement that spread across eastern Europe. Reincarnation is a fundamental Hasidic belief. One Hasidic bedtime prayer asks forgiveness for "anyone who has angered or vexed me... in this incarnation or any other."[1]

The following Jewish mystical tale from the sixteenth century illustrates the belief in reincarnation. It seems that a famous Kabbalist rabbi, Isaac Luria (1534–72), once showed his students a stone in a wall in which he said there was a soul imprisoned. "It has suffered through the wheel of transmigration [reincarnation].... All that it needs is a prayer to set it free." The disciples began to pray for the soul to be set free from the round of rebirth. As they finished praying, the story concludes, "they heard a flutter of wings, although there was no bird to be seen anywhere."[2] The soul was free.

Both Kabbalists and Hasidic Jews tell us that every person has a divine spark imprisoned inside of him and that man's destiny is to liberate the divine spark and, as scholar Ben Zion Bokser puts it, to unite with "the larger unity of creation and Creator."[3]

The twin ideas of reincarnation and union with God have been a part of Judaism at least since the time of Christ. However, these ideas have often been suppressed or kept secret. Mysticism, which involves the search for either direct contact with God or union with God, could have easily been misinterpreted as a violation of the first commandment: "Thou shalt have no other gods before me."[4] And so the mystics ran the risk of being accused of blasphemy. Therefore the rabbis who practiced mysticism guarded their secrets as closely as they guarded the Tabernacle. They preserved the secrets and passed them down in an oral and written tradition that survived the centuries.

In the nineteenth century, however, mysticism was almost entirely obscured by rabbis who wanted their faith to appeal to those with a scientific world view. Then, in the twentieth century, scholars rediscovered mystical Judaism—along with its ideas about reincarnation and divine union. The Dead Sea Scrolls and other early Jewish manuscripts confirm that mysticism was an important part of early Judaism.

Gershom Scholem (1897–1982), a well-known Jewish scholar, believed that Jewish mysticism originated before Kabbalism and before the time of Christ. Some Kabbalists claimed that their tradition actually dated back to Moses. We may never be able to nail down its origins since much of the teaching was never written but was passed on orally and in secret. Nevertheless, we can uncover evidence of these mystical beliefs in early pre-Christian Judaism.

What we now know as traditional, or rabbinic, Judaism was founded by groups of rabbis who studied and explained the scriptures in the last centuries before Christ. What many scholars are now realizing is that at the time of Christ, mystical and rabbinic Judaism were one—the rabbis who founded traditional Judaism were also mystics.[5] Thus, if Jesus did teach reincarnation and divine union, as I believe he did, he could have absorbed those ideas from the great rabbis of his day.

The afterlife

Reincarnation is only one among several conflicting ideas in Judaism about the afterlife. One common view is that there is neither a soul nor an afterlife. People can be said to live on only through their descendants. The Old Testament's emphasis on genealogy—the "begats"—illustrates this idea. A modern version of this view is that the deceased live on through their reputations or in people's memories.[6]

A second idea is the Sheol of the Old Testament. It is said to be a place of forgetfulness and silence where disembodied spirits live apart from God with neither reward nor punishment. People believed that these spirits could be contacted, as when King Saul asked the witch of Endor to conjure up the spirit of the prophet Samuel.

A third afterlife belief is the resurrection—bodies will rise from the dead at some time in the future. At the time of Christ there was a smorgasbord of ideas about who would participate in the resurrection and where and when it would occur.

A fourth afterlife belief is reincarnation. In Judaism, reincarnation reached its most developed form in the writings of the Kabbalists. When we understand reincarnation in Kabbalism, we can more clearly trace it back to the time of Christ.

THE MYSTIC THREAD OF REINCARNATION

The earliest known Kabbalistic text, *Sefer ha-Bahir,* published around 1180,[7] treats reincarnation as a given. It uses a dialogue about reincarnation to explain misfortune:

Q: "Why are there evildoers who are well off and righteous who suffer evil?"

A: "Because the righteous man was... an evildoer in the past and is now being punished."[8]

Q: "Is one then punished for his childhood deeds?"

A: "I am not speaking of his present lifetime. I am speaking about what he has already been, previously."[9]

In other words, the *Bahir* is telling us that bad things happen to good people because they have done bad things in previous lives.

The early rabbis who interpreted Jewish scripture had instituted the practice of reading one word for another. The Kabbalists were thus relying upon an ancient system of agreed-upon inner meanings. The *Bahir* used this technique to "discover" reincarnation in the Old Testament. It tells us that the biblical term *generations* can be replaced by the word *incarnations.*

In this way, Kabbalists developed their own interpretation of the covenant God made with Abraham and his seed. God said, "I will establish my covenant between me and thee and thy seed after thee in their generations for an everlasting covenant."[10] They believed God made this covenant with the seed of Abraham not only for one life but for thousands of incarnations.[11]

For those who are skeptical of the Kabbalist view, the Old Testament offers a less esoteric reference to reincarnation. God tells the prophet Jeremiah that he knew him before he was conceived. "Before I formed you in the womb I knew you; before you came to birth I consecrated you; I have appointed you as a prophet to the nations."[12] This passage implies that Jeremiah's soul existed before his birth in the sixth century B.C.

JEWISH WISDOM TRADITION

Preexistence, the belief that the soul exists before the body, is often associated with reincarnation. This idea appears in the Jewish wisdom writings, which were composed between the first and sixth centuries B.C.

The Wisdom of Solomon, accepted as scripture by Roman Catholics but not by Protestants, alludes to the concept of karma and the preexistence of souls. The unknown author of the book, who presents himself as Solomon, writes: "I was, indeed, a child well-endowed, having had a noble soul fall to my lot; or rather being noble I entered an undefiled body."[13] Clearly, the author believes that the soul exists before the body.

Because the soul was "noble," she entered an undefiled body.

If the soul had never before been born in an earthly body, when and where did she become noble? The writer is implying that good karma from a previous existence follows the soul and that the momentums of personality, ego and character are cumulative.

In addition to the wisdom writings, the Jews also composed a large body of scriptures between 250 B.C. and A.D. 200. Many of them were written under the names of famous Old Testament figures like Enoch and Moses.

One, the *Testament of Naphtali,* was probably written during the third century B.C. The book purports to be the final words of Naphtali, who was the father of one of the twelve tribes of Israel. Naphtali says that God makes the body "in correspondence to the spirit" and "instills the spirit corresponding to the power of the body." In other words, he makes bodies to match the spirits that will inhabit them. Or, as Naphtali puts it, "From one to the other [from body to spirit] there is no discrepancy, not so much as a third of a hair."[14]

God knows the potential of a body before he puts a soul into it, says Naphtali: "Just as the potter knows the use of each vessel and to what it is suited, so also the Lord knows the body to what extent it will persist in goodness, and when it will be dominated by evil."[15] Again, the author is referring to the idea that the soul exists before the body. And, as we will see, there is not much of a leap from preexistence to reincarnation.

THE ESSENES AND THE PHARISEES

We find further evidence for reincarnation in Judaism when we examine two important Jewish sects at the time of Christ, the Essenes and the Pharisees. The Essenes probably founded the religious community whose ruins lie at Qumran on the northwest shore of the Dead Sea. This community existed from the second half of the second century B.C. until the Romans wiped it out during the Jewish Revolt of A.D. 66 to 70.

The first-century Jewish historian Josephus tells us that the Essenes lived "the same kind of life" as the followers of the Greek philosopher Pythagoras. And we know that Pythagoras taught reincarnation. According to Josephus, the Essenes believed that the soul is both immortal and preexistent. They also believed that the soul is separate from the body, he said. Souls are "united to their bodies as in prisons," but when "set free from the bonds of the flesh," they "rejoice and mount upward."[16]

As we will see in the next chapter, these beliefs are quite similar to the Pythagorean view of the soul. If the Essenes shared this view, they may also have shared the Pythagoreans' belief in reincarnation.

Josephus also implies that the Pharisees, the founders of rabbinic Judaism, believed in reincarnation.[17] He writes that the Pharisees believed that the souls of bad men are punished after death but that the souls of good men are "removed into other bodies" and they will "have power to revive and live again."[18] Some scholars believe that these are references to reincarnation, while others believe they refer to the resurrection of the dead.

The Pharisees were the most popular Jewish sect. The Sadducees, the other prominent Jewish sect in Palestine, did not emphasize life after death. But they did not represent the majority of Jews. New evidence from the Dead Sea Scrolls shows that the Pharisees dominated the Jerusalem Temple for a good part of the period between 164 B.C. and A.D. 37.[19] So if the Pharisees believed in reincarnation, that would mean that an important segment of Palestinian Jews did also.

After the Romans destroyed Jerusalem in A.D. 70 and the Jews were once more dispersed, the Pharisees were at the heart of rabbinic Judaism. If Josephus is correct about the Pharisees' belief in reincarnation, we can be fairly certain that it was a part of pre-Christian Judaism. And, as I said earlier, we also have evidence that the rabbis who founded rabbinic Judaism sought mystical union (see also chapters 22 and 23), which, as we have seen, is a companion belief to reincarnation.

DIVINE VISIONS

A few centuries before Christ, Jewish rabbis began secretly practicing an elaborate system of rituals designed to bring them a mystical vision of a divine being on a throne. This vision became a symbol for union with God. To achieve the divine vision, the rabbis fasted, purified themselves and spent hours repeating the names of God. They reported ascending through heavenly palaces as they journeyed toward brilliant beings of light. The system was known as *Merkabah* mysticism, or "throne-chariot" mysticism. It also became known as *Hekhalot,* or "palace," mysticism, after the heavenly palaces the mystics traveled through.

The system of *Merkabah* mysticism is based on the first chapter of Ezekiel, which tells us that the prophet saw a divine being come "out of the north" surrounded by a "great cloud with brightness." In the cloud is a vehicle, or chariot, powered by "four living creatures," cherubim. The divine figure is seated over the heads of the creatures on "something like a throne, in appearance like sapphire."[20]

The rabbis who composed the Talmud (working between the third and fifth centuries A.D.) knew about *Merkabah* mysticism and may have even been practitioners. However, perhaps fearing accusations of blasphemy, they did not teach it openly but reserved it for their closest disciples. The Kabbalist text the *Bahir* seems to be connected with *Merkabah* mysticism because it uses the term *Ma'aseh Merkabah,* literally "Workings of the Chariot."

As we will see, some passages in Christian scripture reflect

Merkabah and *Hekhalot* ideas. This indicates that Jesus or Paul may have known about the tradition. But can we be certain that it predated Christianity?

The prophet Ezekiel tells of his vision of a divine being on a throne-chariot, or Merkabah, *as shown in this seventeenth-century illustration. The throne and the radiant human form seated upon it are surrounded by a bright cloud flashing with fire. Ezekiel's vision came to symbolize for Jewish mystics the experience of becoming one with God. They practiced an elaborate system of rituals designed to allow them to have the same vision.*

The mystics claimed that their tradition had been passed down from Old Testament times. They said that Jacob's vision of a ladder going up to heaven and Moses ascending Mount Sinai to commune with Yahweh (the God of the Old Testament) were examples of mystical communion. However, we have no way to verify their claims. Much of the *Merkabah* literature was written after the Old Testament, between the end of the second century and the fifth or sixth century A.D.

Some scholars used to think that *Merkabah* mysticism could not date before the second century. Other scholars pointed to pre-Christian manuscripts that contained accounts of both divine visions and heavenly ascents. But the debate was pretty much resolved by the Dead Sea Scrolls, a group of ancient manuscripts discovered in 1947 by Bedouin shepherds.

More than eight hundred documents have now been discovered, most in fragments, in the caves near Qumran. They include biblical commentaries, prophecy, community rules and portions of every book of the Hebrew Bible.[21]

Most scholars believe that the scrolls belonged to the Essene community at Qumran. The Dead Sea Scrolls indicate that the Jewish mystical tradition went back at least to the first, if not the third, century before Christ.

Some of the hymns found at Qumran are similar to the *Hekhalot* hymns sung by the Jewish mystics. One text gives us unmistakable evidence of *Merkabah* mysticism. It is called *Songs of the Sabbath Sacrifice*. Scholars have dated it to the first century B.C., although it may have been copied from an earlier work. It tells of a vision of a divine being on a throne-chariot surrounded by brilliant light and angels. Analyzing this text, scholar Neil Fujita argues that it is likely that the Jews "embraced the mysticism connected with the chariot-throne of God...even before the establishment of the sect at Qumran in the second century B.C."[22]

Fragments of 1 Enoch, which is considered the oldest evidence of *Merkabah* mysticism, were also found at Qumran. The book is attributed to Enoch, "the seventh from Adam."[23] Genesis 5:24 says he "walked with God: and he was not; for God took him."[24]

Chapter 14, probably written in the third century B.C., describes Enoch's ascent to heaven. It contains the essential elements of the *Merkabah* experience—ascent into heaven and a vision of a divine being on a throne. "Its appearance was like crystal and its wheels like the shining sun.... And the Great Glory was sitting upon it."[25]

Qumran, Israel, on the northwest shore of the Dead Sea. Shown here are the openings of the caves in which the Dead Sea Scrolls were hidden just before the Romans invaded Palestine in A.D. 70. The scrolls were probably buried by the Jewish inhabitants of the nearby community, who were most likely Essenes. The scrolls demonstrate that mysticism—including the idea that humans could unite with a divine being— existed in Judaism before the time of Christ.

If *Merkabah* existed in the third century before Christ, as Enoch indicates, then it would certainly have been present in first-century Judaism. In Part 5 we will explore whether Jesus was familiar with it. In our search for evidence of *Merkabah* mysticism in early Christianity, we will examine the transfiguration, Paul's description of his ascent to the "third heaven," and Gnostic texts. If we can trace the twin ideas of divine union and reincarnation back to early Christianity, we may have the key to the heart of Jesus' message.

A NEW COVENANT

Before we examine Jesus' teachings on reincarnation, we will examine one of the most important influences on the Judaism of his day. In the long and difficult centuries between King David and Jesus, the Israelites were conquered several times. They absorbed ideas from their conquerors—first the Assyrians in the eighth century B.C., then the Babylonians and the Persians in the sixth century B.C. But the greatest influence on Judaism would come in the fourth century B.C.

By that time, many Jews had returned to Palestine from Babylon after the Persian king Cyrus, a tolerant ruler who had conquered Babylon, gave them permission to rebuild their temple. They found life difficult and made slow progress in their work. At this time, both the Jews in exile and those in Palestine undoubtedly gave thought to the ideas of reward and punishment. They could see that good deeds were not always rewarded and bad deeds were not always punished. Had God abandoned them?

They took comfort in the prophecies of Jeremiah, who had predicted that God would establish a new covenant, different from the one he had made when he brought them out of Egypt. "They broke that covenant," said the LORD through the prophet.

He offered a new covenant: "Deep within them I will plant

my Law, writing it on their hearts. Then I will be their God and they shall be my people. There will be no further need for neighbor to try to teach neighbor, or brother to say to brother, 'Learn to know Yahweh!' No, they will all know me, the least no less than the greatest."[26] A clearer description of the God within cannot be found in the Old Testament.

As the Jews sought the fulfillment of this promise, they may have begun to look outside their culture. And they may have found a new perspective after a blond, charismatic Macedonian turned the world upside down.

CHAPTER 6

Becoming God

I have flown out of the sorrowful
  weary Wheel.
I have passed with eager feet
  to the Circle desired.

Orphic tomb inscription
Fourth century B.C.

THREE CENTURIES BEFORE JESUS WAS BORN, A
Greek invader changed his world. When Alexander the Great conquered the lands between Greece
and India, including Palestine, he made Greek culture the standard of civilization.

Sweeping across the Hellespont, the strait that
forms the gateway to Asia, and defeating the Persian Empire and its six-hundred-thousand-man
army with his force of thirty thousand Greeks, he
invited comparisons to Greek heroes like Achilles.

He made way for philosophers like Plato and
Socrates to gain preeminence in the world of ideas.
And when, in 332 B.C., he conquered Egypt and Pal-
estine, he set the stage for the birth of Christianity.

Alexander the Great's empire barely outlasted his early death in 323 B.C. But his conquest paved the way for a Hellenistic age in which Greek language and culture dominated the known world. The Jews living in Alexandria, an Egyptian city Alexander founded, translated their scriptures into Greek and studied the ideas of Plato alongside those of Moses.

Alexander promoted both religious toleration and Greek culture. Although he spread Greek ideas, he respected the religions of those he conquered, creating an atmosphere in which cultures could safely mix.

The Romans, who conquered Palestine in the first century B.C., built on Alexander's foundations. It was into this Greco-Roman civilization that Jesus was born. And this was the milieu in which Christianity grew from an obscure Palestinian cult into the dominant religion of the Roman Empire.

GREEK INFLUENCE ON JUDAISM

By the first century, Greek language and culture dominated the civilized world. And within the broad stream of Greek religion ran the twin currents of reincarnation and union with God. Many scholars now believe that Jesus spoke Greek and therefore may have had the opportunity to be exposed to these ideas.

Just as former British colonies like India and Hong Kong

adopted the English language and culture, so the cities that Alexander conquered or founded used Greek. Many first-century Jews spoke Greek. We can see the influence even in the words the Jews used—*synagogues* for their places of worship and *Sanhedrin* for their highest court. Both words are of Greek origin.

Greek influence even penetrated into Jerusalem, where Jewish aristocrats lived in Greek-style houses and an amphitheater and gymnasium were built in the second century B.C. A major Greek-speaking city, Sepphoris (population thirty thousand), grew up just three and a half miles—an hour's walk—from Nazareth, where Jesus lived.

Sepphoris sat along a major roadway that came from Egypt, where Greek ideas flourished in the city of Alexandria. When the Romans conquered Palestine, they made Sepphoris the capital of Galilee. Coins and artifacts discovered at Sepphoris reveal that in the first century A.D. it was home to Romans as well as to Greek-speaking Jews.[1]

During Jesus' lifetime, Herod Antipas, the Jewish king who ruled on behalf of the Romans, was rebuilding and fortifying Sepphoris.[2] Jesus doubtless traveled there often and—like many Jews of his time—would have had the opportunity to be exposed to Greek ideas.

Some Jews were uncomfortable with the Greek influence, as evidenced by writings that sought to depict a schism between Jews who adopted Greek culture and those who didn't. Nevertheless, Greek ideas penetrated deeply into Jewish thought. The Greek concepts of an afterlife, paradise and an immortal soul—which appear only marginally, if at all, in the Old Testament—grew to full development in the Judaism of this time.

But there was hardly a consensus on the nature of the afterlife or the fate of the soul. Scholars have concluded that first-century Judaism was characterized by variety, not consistency.

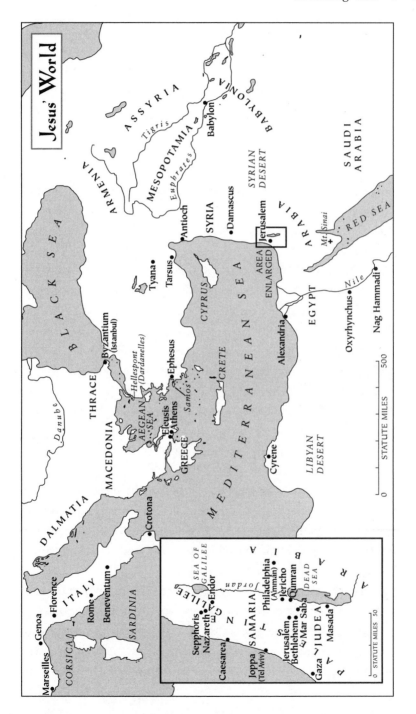

Thus Jesus was probably exposed to a variety of afterlife beliefs in Judaism.

In future chapters we will explore which of these he may have adopted. But first, let us examine some of the Greek ideas that may have influenced Jesus.

THE MYSTERIES

A procession winds its way from Athens toward the sea. Thousands of Greeks, Romans, Thracians and Egyptians alike pace solemnly, clothed in white robes. Men, women and slaves disregard rank as they walk on foot across a narrow bridge. It is the holiest festival of the year and they have prepared for it with fasting and ritual purification. As evening falls, they light torches and file into the great temple at Eleusis on the Aegean coast.

What are they doing?

They are participating in the Eleusinian Mysteries, secret religious ceremonies that have been practiced since the seventh century B.C. At night in the great Hall of Initiation, they reenact the quest of the earth goddess Demeter for her daughter, Persephone.

According to myth, Hades, lord of the underworld, kidnapped Persephone and carried her off to his kingdom. Bearing torches, Demeter wandered the world looking for her daughter until the god Hermes rescued her from Hades and returned her to the light of day. But Persephone was thereafter required to spend half of each year in the underworld, returning to earth in the spring.

The initiates found special meaning in this myth. For them it was not about agriculture or harvest but about the immortality of the soul. In one interpretation, Persephone represents the soul and Demeter represents the Divine Self. Each year as the celebrants reenacted the separation and union of Demeter and

Persephone, they may have been celebrating their own hoped-for reunification with their Divine Self—their own divinization.³

The Eleusinian ceremonies were a carefully guarded secret. Those who revealed even the faintest hint of their content were punished by death. But scholars' best guess today is that the purpose of the ceremonies was to induce an experience of oneness, or union, with God.⁴ For the Greeks believed that men could become Gods.

Alexander the Great was aware of these traditions, but he tried to take the prize by force. He ordered the Athenians to vote him a god and encouraged the rumor that he was the son of Zeus. Many of the rulers of the ancient world, including the emperors of Rome, followed his lead and deified themselves.

Alexander's "godhood" was based on his invincibility in battle and his external conquests. But the divinization of the mysteries was based on an internal conquest—the conquest of self.

By teaching people that they could achieve union with God, the mystery religions—and there were many that thrived in the Greco-Roman world—were not implying that there is more than one God. Although some mystery religions worshiped Isis, others the god Serapis or Mithras, they all believed that there is but one God and that the different gods were simply forms of the one universal and transcendent God. Mystery initiates believed that when they achieved deification, they, too, would be manifestations of the one God.

In the mystery religions, external wealth or power like Alexander's were not criteria for spiritual progress. What was important was pursuit of a course of study that included systematic teachings, rituals and initiations designed to lead to soul growth and a mystical experience of rebirth or union with God.

The goal of the mystery initiates—the perfecting of the soul through union with God—was the essence of spirituality for millions of people in the Greco-Roman world. Augustus, the

Persephone, daughter of the earth goddess Demeter, is abducted and carried off by Hades, lord of the underworld, who is also known as Pluto. In the Greek myth, Persephone is rescued and reunited with her mother, but she is required to return to the underworld for half of each year. This story was central to the secret ceremonies conducted each year at Eleusis; it may have symbolized the soul's separation from and reunion with the God within.

first Roman emperor (63 B.C.–A.D. 14), and some of the early emperors were initiates. At the time of Christ, many people were skeptical of Homer's capricious and spoiled gods. Though they participated in formal worship and sacrifice, they found fulfillment in the secret yet satisfying mystery rites.

GRECO-ROMAN REINCARNATION BELIEFS

The idea of reincarnation went hand in hand with the view that man can become one with God. Cicero (106–43 B.C.), a great Roman orator and philosopher as well as a mystery initiate, was familiar with reincarnation. He said that the ease with which children absorb difficult subjects could be taken as a "strong argument that men's knowledge of numerous things antedates their birth." The children, he wrote, learn "innumerable things" so quickly that "they seem not to be then learning them for the first time, but to be recalling and remembering them."[5]

Other great Romans accepted reincarnation. Virgil, the greatest Roman poet, who lived in the first century B.C., wove reincarnation into his *Aeneid*. He described how after death souls are purified of their sins, then sent to the fields of Elysium and finally called to the river Lethe, "where memory is annulled and souls are willing once more to enter into mortal bodies."[6]

Plato (c. 427–c. 347 B.C.), the most influential Greek philosopher, gives us the most detailed evidence for Greek reincarnation beliefs. He relates several stories that describe reincarnation,[7] including the following account of a near-death experience.

It seems a man named Er was killed in battle. His body did not begin to decay and, twelve days later, while lying on the funeral pile, it returned to life. Er told the story of what had happened to him during those twelve days. He remembered being brought before a group of judges, who told him that he was to act as a messenger and tell men on earth what he had seen.

He saw some souls going upward into heaven and others descending beneath the earth for punishment. Though this sounds much like the Christian view of heaven and hell, these souls did not remain forever in either location. Er reported that once their period of reward or punishment had been completed, they were sent back to earth into new bodies, "like stars shooting."[8]

LEAVING THE SORROWFUL, WEARY WHEEL

Where did Plato get his ideas? He was heavily influenced by Orphism, the first Western system to combine the ideas of reincarnation and union with God. As far back as the seventh century B.C., the Orphics, like the Hindus, taught that within each of us resides a divine particle.

They believed that this divine nature is buried in the body as in a tomb. They sought to release it through mystic initiations, secret rites and righteous living—during more than one lifetime if necessary.

Poems inscribed on thin, gold-leaf tablets buried in the hands of Orphic believers in the fourth century B.C. clearly spell out the Orphic belief in divinization. These tablets, which were discovered in southern Italy, were designed to coach the dead on how to behave on the other side.

They instruct the initiate that after death he should recite the following words before the goddess Persephone: "I also avow me that I am of your blessed race.... I have paid the penalty for deeds unrighteous.... I have flown out of the sorrowful weary Wheel. I have passed with eager feet to the Circle desired." The hoped-for response from Persephone is: "Happy and Blessed One, thou shalt be God instead of mortal."[9]

When the verse speaks of flying out of the "sorrowful weary Wheel," it is almost certainly referring to escaping the round of rebirth. And reaching the "Circle desired" indicates that the soul has arrived at the sphere outside the matter universe. What is this sphere?

The concept of heavenly spheres, found in the mystery religions, holds that the world is ruled by the seven planets: Sun, Moon, Mercury, Venus, Mars, Jupiter and Saturn. Each planet rules its own sphere. The Greeks believed that in order to attain divine union, the soul must pass through the seven concentric heavenly spheres, each one ruled by one of the planets, until it reaches the outermost sphere and escapes the matter universe altogether.

This journey is accomplished by giving up the negative energies or tendencies ruled by the planet. When the soul has

Some early Christians interpreted their faith in light of Orphism (which taught oneness with God and reincarnation), as demonstrated by this fifth-century ring. It depicts the Greek god Orpheus, reputed founder of Orphism, surrounded by a Christian inscription: "The Seal of John, the Pre-eminent Saint."

purified herself fully, she is released from the wheel of rebirth. The "Circle desired" would therefore be the outermost sphere, the realm outside the dominion of the planets.

But the "Circle desired" could have a further meaning. The Greek word translated as *circle* literally means "crown." Some mystery religions used attaining the crown to represent identification with, or becoming, God. Therefore, as one gives up the tendencies binding him to the matter universe, he is preparing himself to attain the crown, or union with God.

Pythagoras and the Dog

The Greek philosopher Pythagoras was also a student of Orphism. In his thought, too, we can clearly see the confluence of reincarnation and union with God. Pythagoras founded a school at Crotona, a Greek colony in southern Italy, around 530 B.C. He taught that the soul is separate from and exists beyond the body and that the soul is judged after death on the basis of its works and then migrates into another body. He is said to have accepted men and women of all races into a mystical brotherhood whose goal was union with God.

This sarcastic story about Pythagoras—told by his contemporary, Xenophanes of Colophon—shows his belief in reincarnation: "He [Pythagoras] was once passing by when a man was beating a dog, and they say that he took pity on the animal and said: 'Stop beating it. Indeed it is the soul of a friend of mine. I recognized it when I heard its voice.'"[10] Pythagoras and other Orphics believed that men could be reborn as animals.

Empedocles, a poet and statesman of the mid-fifth century B.C., encapsulated the Pythagorean tradition in his poem *Katharmoi* ("Purifications"). In it, Empedocles tells us that his fate is to wander the earth for "three times countless years, being born throughout the time as all kinds of mortal forms, exchanging one hard way of life for another."[11]

He believed he had experienced all forms of life: "For before now I have been at some time boy and girl, bush, bird, and a mute fish in the sea." As Empedocles explained it, the cycle of birth through plant and animal form is meant to culminate in the world of men. The most advanced souls are reborn as "prophets, minstrels, physicians, and leaders, and from these they arise as gods, highest in honor."[12] Again the two ideas appear: reincarnation and divinization.

Godlike powers were attributed to both Pythagoras and Empedocles. Iamblichus (c. A.D. 250–325) tells us that Pythagoras could predict earthquakes, stop hurricanes, calm the seas and even bilocate. Empedocles was called "windstiller"[13] and claimed to walk the earth as "an immortal god"[14] who could stop the wind, heal the sick and "bring the dead back to life."[15]

Although these stories sound far-fetched, it is not surprising that these teachers were thought to have achieved divine status. After all, they believed that all human beings could pursue and achieve divinity. Whether or not they really possessed these powers, the stories demonstrate that the Greeks did believe that the soul is immortal, that man can become divine and that divinity is achieved in stages.

A Greek-speaking Jesus would have had easy access to these ideas. And, as we will see in the next chapter, other Jews of his day sought to harmonize Greek ideas about the nature of the soul with their own scriptures. Their writings provide the strongest evidence that some Jews at the time of Christ believed in reincarnation and practiced mystical identification with God.

❧

CHAPTER 7

Moses Meets Plato

*It seems to me that Pythagoras, Socrates,
and Plato with great care follow him [Moses]
in all respects.*

Aristobulus
Second century B.C.

SEE IF YOU CAN GUESS THE NAME OF THIS FIRST-
century Jewish teacher. He spoke about the
divine Word, which he compared to a stream. He
urged the spiritual seeker, whom he compared to a
runner, to drink from the stream[1] and he promised
that whoever did so would gain "eternal life."[2]
And he spoke of the "Logos," or "Word," as a mediator between God and man.[3]

Does it sound like Paul? John? Jesus?

Guess again. It's Philo of Alexandria.

He wrote during Jesus' lifetime and taught reincarnation. Passages of the New Testament seem to
echo his writings. His "Word" sounds like John's
"Word" that was "in the beginning with God."[4]
And his stream of water brings to mind the "living

water" Jesus describes in the Book of John as "gushing up to eternal life."[5]

Philo (20 B.C.–A.D. 50) played an important part in the unique commingling of Greek and Jewish thought that followed Alexander the Great's conquest of Egypt and Palestine. His writings can help us to better understand the parallels between first-century Judaism and Christianity.

Alexandria, Philo's home, was the Egyptian city that Alexander founded in 332 B.C. near the delta where the Nile empties into the Mediterranean. By the first century B.C., Alexandria was probably the largest city in the Mediterranean. Ruled by the heirs of Ptolemy, one of Alexander's generals, it attracted immigrants from Italy, Greece and the Middle East, including a large number of Jews. It became a center of finance and commerce.

The Jews of Alexandria became prominent in the trade of grain, papyrus, linen and glass, which made the city the largest marketplace in the world. They were respected by the Ptolemaic kings (first to fourth centuries B.C.) and given special protections by the Romans. Wealthy Alexandrian Jews supported the Jerusalem Temple.

By the time of Christ, more Jews lived in Alexandria than in all of Judea. The largest of Alexandria's synagogues, described in the Talmud, was said to hold twice as many people as those who left Egypt with Moses. It had seventy golden thrones "adorned with precious stones and pearls" and was so large that "flags had to be used to signal [people when to say] the Amen."[6]

Within two generations of Alexandria's founding, Greek had become the dominant written language of the Alexandrian Jews. In the third century B.C., they translated the Pentateuch (the first five books of the Bible) into Greek. And when early Christians wrote down the New Testament, they too used Greek.

GREEK MYSTICISM AMONG THE JEWS

During the first few centuries before Christ, Greek ideas transformed Judaism. In fact, some scholars even go so far as to call the Judaism of this time a Hellenistic religion, in other words, a religion under the influence of Greek culture as it developed after Alexander.

It may seem incongruous today to think of anyone trying to reconcile Judaism, with its jealous God and fiery prophets, with the many gods and philosophical musings of Greece. But that is just what many Jews did. In fact, scholars believe that neither rabbinic Judaism nor Christianity could have developed without the philosophical admixing that began with Alexander and accelerated with the Romans. As we will see, Church Fathers themselves built on the ideas of Philo and other Hellenized Jews.

Although the broad avenues of Alexandria were lined with statues of Greek gods, few educated people worshiped them. Both Jews and Greeks were looking for new religious approaches. They sought allegory in scripture—the Greeks in Homer and the Jews in the Torah.

Some Jews made public heretofore hidden aspects of Jewish mysticism and blended them with the Greek mysticism of Pythagoras and Plato. As time progressed, figuring out where one left off and the other began became as difficult as separating the eggs from the flour in a cake.

As early as the second century B.C., Aristobulus, Philo's intellectual ancestor, was claiming that the Greek philosophers taught in the tradition of Moses. Aristobulus was a Jew, a member of a family of anointed priests in Alexandria and tutor to one of the Ptolemaic kings, who were Cleopatra's forebears. He said that Pythagoras, Socrates and Plato had copied Moses, especially in their ideas about "the arrangement of the universe." Aristobulus was also familiar with Orphic beliefs, asserting that Orpheus, too, "imitates Moses."[7]

Saint philo?

Philo, contemporary of Jesus, mentor of the Church Fathers and Jewish mystic extraordinaire, was well respected in the Jewish community. So his ideas cannot have been too far out of the mainstream. His family was one of the wealthiest Jewish families in Alexandria and he was a highly visible figure, taking on important civic duties.

When anti-Semitic feeling in Alexandria erupted into a campaign of violence against Jews in A.D. 39 to 40, Philo was selected to lead a delegation of Jews to Rome to request help from the emperor Caligula.

The reason his writings have survived to this day is that they became popular with Christians. The Church Fathers, especially Clement of Alexandria, Origen and Ambrose, studied him and grafted some of his ideas onto a budding Christianity in the second through fifth centuries. Some Christians later tried to claim that Philo had converted to Christianity, and Saint Jerome said that Philo had met with the apostle Peter on a visit to Rome.[8]

Church historian Eusebius (c. 260–c. 340) tells us that "Philo became widely known as one of the greatest scholars."[9] Byzantine manuscripts often call him "the Bishop"[10] and some manuscripts even depict him in saintly robes embroidered with crosses.

Philo was a mystic. He believed that the goal of life is direct communion with God followed by divine union. He and others of his school interpreted the scriptures as the record of a spiritual journey that describes how the soul can free herself from the prison of the body and return to the higher spiritual world, her native home.

Philo wrote in the allegorical tradition, assigning a hidden or symbolic meaning to the people and events of the Old Testament. He saw the story of the Garden of Eden as a reflection

Philo of Alexandria was a Jewish teacher and contemporary of Jesus. Christians of later centuries revered him and preserved his writings. This illustration comes from a ninth-century Christian manuscript, which portrayed him as a Christian (note the crosses on his robe). Philo taught both reincarnation and the soul's opportunity to become one with God.

of the spiritual quest, with Adam and Eve symbolizing aspects of every human being. Adam represents the mind and Eve represents sense perception. Philo realized, writes scholar Samuel Sandmel, that "we cannot possibly have any interest in some journey some man made a long time ago, unless it is a spiritual journey that we too can make."[11]

In Philo's view, even the obscure dietary restrictions of Jewish law become symbols of our soul's journey. Leviticus forbids eating "winged insects" that creep but permits the Israelites to eat "those that have legs above their feet so that they can leap over the ground."[12]

The two kinds of insects, according to Philo, symbolize two kinds of souls. The insects that cannot leap are the souls that are attracted to earth. The leaping insects represent souls who "soar on high" and take "the heaven in exchange for the earth, and immortality in exchange for destruction."[13] In other words, the leaping insects are preferred because they represent souls who can escape from the prison of mortal bodies.

This kind of allegorical interpretation may seem unusual to us today, but it was common in the first century. The apostle Paul, for instance, uses allegory in Galatians when he compares Abraham's wife, Sarah, and her servant Hagar to the two covenants God had made with his people.[14]

PHILO ON REINCARNATION

Reincarnation was a part of Philo's world view and he discusses it in detail. He writes, "Those [souls] which are influenced by a desire for mortal life...again return to it."[15]

Philo seems to have adopted Plato's images for describing the history of the soul. He tells us that life is like a stream that entraps souls. The angels are souls who never enter the stream but act as "ministers and helpers" of the Father. Other souls are caught by the stream and swallowed up "in the swirl of its rushing torrent." However, they may be able to rise to the surface, free themselves of the torrent and soar "upwards back to the place from whence they came."[16]

Here we can see the Orphic-Platonic influence on Philo's thought, for he tells us that the souls that are freed from bodies are "those who have been taught some kind of sublime philosophy, meditating, from beginning to end, on dying as to the life of the body, in order to obtain an inheritance of the incorporeal and imperishable life."[17]

The souls that remain in the stream—returning to mortal bodies after death—are those who disregard wisdom and remain attached to things related to "the dead corpse connected with us, that is to the body, or to things which are even more lifeless than that, such as glory, and money, and offices, and honours."[18] What draws souls back to mortal life, Philo writes, is both familiarity with and desire for the things of the flesh.

What about those who are progressing toward immortality but die before attaining it—those who are neither good enough for heaven nor bad enough for hell? Philo implies that they will be allowed to experience further lifetimes to prepare themselves to escape mortality.[19]

If Philo taught reincarnation, perhaps other mystics of his day did too. Philo probably did not work alone. Rather, he was part of a mystical tradition. Sandmel believes that Philo's allegorical interpretations were "so thoroughly developed" that they had evolved over "a fairly long period of time" and reflected "not a single mind, but a sequence of them."[20]

Philo was not the only Jewish mystic we know of to teach reincarnation. The Kabbalists did too. And scholars have commented on the similarities between Philo's teaching and Kabbalism. Erwin R. Goodenough, one of the foremost Philo scholars, suggests that "the Kabbalah has its resemblances to Philo not from being a teaching worked out of Philo's writings by later generations, but from having its basis in a great tradition" that began when Jewish and Greek thought first blended.[21] This suggests that the Kabbalists' teachings on reincarnation may indeed have been based on early Jewish mysticism.

DID PHILO INFLUENCE JESUS?

We know that Philo affected the development of Christianity through his impact on the Church Fathers. But could he also have influenced the religion's founders?

Most scholars today reject the idea that Jesus or Paul had read Philo. They acknowledge, however, that some New Testament authors must have been familiar with the same topics as Philo. These authors probably include Paul and the authors of the Book of John and of Hebrews (who was probably not Paul). Philo and the author of Hebrews, scholar Ronald Nash writes, "share the common heritage of the Hellenistic Judaism of Alexandria."[22]

But Jesus was not in Alexandria; he was in Palestine. And some scholars think he never left Palestine. Were Philo's beliefs confined to Alexandria and other centers of dispersed Jews or did they reach the Jews of Palestine?

We know that Philo had ties to Palestine. His father had lived there before moving to Alexandria, and Philo himself made at least one pilgrimage to Jerusalem. There were also solid connections between the Alexandrian and Palestinian Jewish communities. Philo's brother Alexander, who supervised customs taxes in Alexandria, contributed the gold and silver that overlaid nine gates of the Temple in Jerusalem. He also bailed the Jewish king Herod Agrippa I (ruled A.D. 37–44) out of bankruptcy.

Scholars differ on the question of how much the Jews in Alexandria and Palestine influenced each other. The more recent scholars would agree with Martin Hengel, who wrote of the "many possibilities for mutual influence" in the "close connections between Alexandria and Jerusalem in the first and second centuries B.C."[23] The two cities were 315 miles apart as the crow flies, and it is difficult to believe that the Jews of the two cities would not have compared notes on doctrine.

At the very least, we can see Philo's writings as further proof that reincarnation was a part of early Judaism and as one possible route by which reincarnation may have entered Christianity. If we are looking for reincarnation beliefs specific to Palestine, we can look at the evidence we have already reviewed (chapter 5) that indicates reincarnation beliefs were held by the Pharisees and the Essenes. Both were Palestinian Jewish sects. And Philo also wrote about a branch of the Essenes called the Therapeutae and shared their beliefs.

Jesus could have come to believe in reincarnation through mystical Judaism like Philo's. He could also have gotten the belief (or confirmed it) from another source: the East.

CHAPTER 8

❦

Routes into Palestine

*The Brachmans [Brahmins], putting off
the body, like fishes jumping out of water
into the pure air, behold the sun.*
                                    Hippolytus
                                    Third century

C HRISTIANITY IS A WESTERN RELIGION AND
Buddhism is an Eastern religion—or so we've
been taught. But in the first century, there was not
such a high wall between East and West as we
generally think. If Jesus taught reincarnation, it
may have come from the Greeks or the Jews, as we
have seen, but it may have also come from India.

There was ample contact between India and
the West in the centuries before Christ. Alexander
the Great had opened the way when he invaded the
Indian subcontinent in 327 B.C., his Greeks fighting elephants for the first time.

His conquest had extended through present-
day Pakistan and into India, and he set up Greek
kingdoms in Bactria (a region of Afghanistan) and

Gandhara, near Kashmir. Greeks ruled and colonized these kingdoms and settled in other parts of India, retaining their culture
and language for several centuries.

SILK, SPICE AND BUDDHISM

About seventy years after Alexander retreated, India was sending emissaries west for a different kind of conquest. This spiritual conquest began during the reign of Asoka (c. 268–239
B.C.), the ruler of an empire that included most of modern
India. After a particularly bloody battle, Asoka had been over-
whelmed by feelings of remorse for the slaughter and carnage.
He converted to Buddhism and spent his life spreading the faith.

Asoka sent Buddhist missionaries across India and to Syria,
Egypt and Greece. As part of his religious conquest, he left
edicts explaining Buddhism carved in stone all over his empire.
Over thirty edicts have survived, etched in pillars, rock faces
and caves. Rock Edict XIII tells us that missionaries were sent
specifically to Alexandria, to King Ptolemy Philadelphus, son
of Alexander's general.[1] Another edict, written in Greek and Aramaic, was found at Kandahar in Afghanistan.[2] The target of the
proselytizing there would have been Alexander's Greek colonists.

Although the West retained no record of the Buddhist
monks' visits, we know that contact between the Greek and
Indian worlds continued, primarily for the purpose of trade.
The Ptolemaic kings of Egypt established a sea route from
Alexandria to India and exchanged ambassadors with Asoka's
heirs. Alexandrians may have also traded with Greek converts
to Buddhism.[3]

In the second century B.C., Alexander's Greek colonists had
invaded the Punjab (present-day Pakistan and northwestern
India). Although their Greco-Bactrian culture left a lasting
imprint on Indian art and architecture, the conquered also

influenced the conquerors, with a number of Greeks converting to Buddhism.

Menander, the Greek king who ruled the area from Afghanistan to central India during the second century B.C., was a convert. The Indians called him Milinda, and his purported discussion with the Buddhist sage Nagasena forms an important Buddhist text, *Milinda's Questions.* In the first century B.C., the Greek governor Theodoros built a Buddhist stupa in Pakistan.[4]

This cross-cultural pollination may have spread back to the Greco-Roman world, perhaps when the Greek rulers became part of the Alexandrian trade, sending cargoes of spices and jewels from western India to Egypt's Red Sea ports. The trade brought Indian merchants to Alexandria. Historians tell us that around 270 B.C. Alexandrians could view a procession of "Indian women, Indian dogs and. . . pure-white Indian cattle."[5]

Along with trade, the merchants must have brought at least some of their philosophy, which they may have discussed with the Jewish merchants who were also prominent traders. "It is not hard to imagine Buddhist and Jewish merchants, sitting around a table in cosmopolitan first-century Alexandria, at the time of Philo," writes Rodger Kamenetz in *The Jew in the Lotus,* "exchanging [not only] merchandise, but also ideas and religious concepts, such as rebirth."[6]

The Romans also established diplomatic contacts with India. During Augustus' reign (27 B.C.–A.D. 14), ambassadors from India came to Antioch accompanied by a "gymnosophist," or yogi.[7]

About this time, the Romans developed a tremendous demand for silk, a substance so precious that only rulers like Cleopatra could afford entire silken garments. For the wealthy it became a status symbol that they displayed in small squares or circles sewn into cotton robes.

The trade ran along the Silk Road, a caravan route that

stretched from Antioch, on the northeastern corner of the Mediterranean, through Iraq, Iran and Afghanistan and on into China, where silk was produced. Other roads, connected with the spice trade, branched off at Kashmir and went south into India.

The Romans also developed a demand for Indian spices, which traveled primarily by sea. By 24 B.C., as many as 120 ships a year were making the trip from Alexandria to India. The Roman Empire was soon spending an estimated hundred million sesterces a year on Oriental luxuries.

Along with silk and spices came Indian ideas. In the first century in Alexandria, both Philo[8] and Josephus[9] describe Indian ideas about the immortality of the soul. Hippolytus, a Christian theologian, gives a detailed description of the habits and

Alexander the Great set up a kingdom in Gandhara (in present-day northwest Pakistan) in the fourth century B.C. His Greek colonists retained their culture for several centuries, transmitting Greek culture and ideas to the Indians. This stone head of Buddha (third or fourth century A.D.) was carved in India in the style the Greek colonists introduced beginning in the first century B.C. Those Greeks may well have absorbed ideas like karma and rebirth from the Buddhists.

beliefs of Hindu yogis and Brahmins.[10] Church Father Clement of Alexandria (second century) describes "Gymnosophists in India" as philosophers, saying their ascetic practices were similar to those of the Encratites, an ascetic Christian sect. He also mentions those among the Indians who "follow the precepts of Buddha."[11]

Clement later tells us that the Brahmins believe in reincarnation and gives the first-century-B.C. Roman historian Alexander Polyhistor as his source.[12] If Polyhistor and others of his day were writing about Indian reincarnation beliefs, this information may well have been available in Jesus' time.

So there are any number of routes by which Indian ideas about reincarnation could have entered the Roman Empire and hence Palestine. But there is another way Jesus could have come in contact with Indian ideas: by going to India.

THE LOST YEARS OF JESUS

The Bible does not tell us what Jesus was doing between the ages of twelve and thirty. But in India, Kashmir and Tibet, there is a long-standing tradition that Jesus was in India during his teens and twenties. An ancient Tibetan manuscript tells the story.

It says that Jesus went with a caravan of merchants along the Silk Road to India, where he studied Hinduism and Buddhism, came into conflict with Hindu and Zoroastrian priests and was revered by the people as Saint Issa. In my book *The Lost Years of Jesus,* I have published three independent translations of this manuscript, which was discovered in a Buddhist monastery in Ladakh, a tiny province of India, just west of Tibet.

This idea of Jesus' going to India is not as implausible as it might sound. Merchants regularly made the journey in those times. And a biography of the first-century Greek sage and miracle worker Apollonius of Tyana tells us that he went to India to study with the Brahmins. The biography records a lengthy discussion between Apollonius and a Hindu sage about transmigration.[13]

If Jesus did visit India, he would have been exposed to ideas about reincarnation. In fact, a passage in one version of the manuscript implies that Jesus taught reincarnation.

The text was discovered in 1887 by a Russian writer named Nicolas Notovitch. Later, two other men made the same discovery—Swami Abhedananda, a Hindu teacher, in 1922, and Nicholas Roerich, a Russian anthropologist, in 1925. Each of the men brought back an independent translation of the text.

Notovitch found the manuscript in Himis, the largest and best-known monastery in Ladakh. The chief lama read to him in Tibetan from "two large bound volumes with leaves yellowed by time."[14] The lama said that his copy of the text was written in Tibetan but had been translated from Pali, the language in which Buddhist scriptures were composed, starting in the fifth century B.C. He told Notovitch that the Pali manuscript had come from India by way of Nepal and that it was in Lhasa, the capital of Tibet.

This account fits in with what we know about Buddhist history. After Gautama Buddha died in the fifth century B.C., his teachings spread north into Nepal, Tibet, China and Japan, where original Buddhist texts were preserved. When the Muslims invaded India in the twelfth century, they destroyed many ancient Buddhist manuscripts. But Tibet has saved many of the teachings that were lost to the rest of the Buddhist world. The Tibetan manuscript at Himis, therefore, could be a legitimate Buddhist text, preserved in Tibet while forgotten in its native country.

Notovitch copied portions of the books as the lama read them aloud and the interpreter translated. Notovitch says the text had been written by "Buddhistic historians."[15] The text itself claims to be partially based on accounts of "merchants from Israel."[16]

Although the three independent translations suggest that the Tibetan manuscript existed at one time, scholars are reluctant to analyze the text without seeing the manuscript. But so far, no one has been able to produce it.

Over a year after his discovery, Notovitch visited Rome, where he showed his manuscript to an unnamed cardinal. The cardinal told him that the text was "no novelty to the Roman Church" and that the Vatican Library possessed "sixty-three complete or incomplete" documents brought back by Christian missionaries concerning Jesus' activities in the East. These came "from India, China, Egypt, and Arabia," he said.[17]

Since the publication of my book in 1984, several scholars and interested persons have tried to get copies of the manuscript, even asking for help from the Dalai Lama at his headquarters-in-exile at Dharmsala, India. So far, no other Westerners have reported seeing the manuscript. If copies were at Lhasa, they may have been destroyed when the Chinese invaded in 1950 and suppressed Buddhism. Whether or not we find the manuscript, the translations do suggest another route by which reincarnation could have entered Christianity. Let us take a closer look at what it says Jesus did and what he learned.

JESUS IN INDIA

Here is a chronology of Jesus' travels, according to the Himis manuscript. At the age of thirteen, he set out toward Sind (a region in present-day southeast Pakistan in the lower Indus River valley) with "the object of perfecting himself in the Divine Word and of studying the laws of the great Buddhas."[18]

His spiritual power was already apparent, for his "fame spread" throughout northern Sind. He went to Juggernaut, where "the white priests of Brahma made him a joyous welcome."[19]

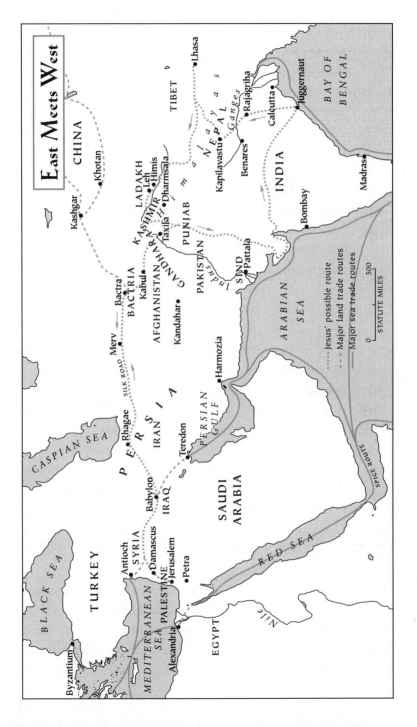

From these Hindu priests he learned "to read and understand the Vedas," the ancient scriptures of the East, and to teach them to the people. He also learned to work miracles: "to cure by aid of prayer... and to drive out evil spirits from the bodies of men."[20] Jesus spent six years between the ages of fourteen and twenty traveling to Juggernaut, Rajagriha, Benares and other holy cities, the text tells us.

Not unexpectedly, Jesus became embroiled in controversy. When he insisted on teaching the scriptures to the lower castes —the Vaisyas (farmers and merchants) and Sudras (peasants and laborers)—the priests decided to kill him. Jesus was warned and he fled into the foothills of the Himalayas to the birthplace of Gautama Buddha, who had founded Buddhism more than five hundred years earlier.

Jesus spent the next six years in Nepal, according to the text. He mastered the Pali language and became "a perfect expositor of the sacred writings" of Buddhism.[21] Sometime between the ages of twenty-seven and twenty-nine, he left the Himalayas and journeyed west, preaching along the way. The text says that Jesus returned to Palestine at the age of twenty-nine and gives a brief description of his three-year ministry.

Unlike the four Gospels, however, the manuscript blames the Romans rather than the Jews for Jesus' crucifixion. Scholars today think that this is a more accurate version of events and that the Romans were almost certainly the ones who made the decision to execute Jesus. This suggests that the writers of the Himis manuscript may have had access to a tradition about Jesus' life that was independent of the Gospels.

But who were these writers? Were the authors really Buddhist historians who interviewed eyewitnesses to the crucifixion? It is difficult to say. The text seems to have been written from a Buddhist standpoint, especially since it criticizes Hinduism in several places.

It could have been written by Buddhists. Or it could have been edited by them after it was written down by someone else—perhaps early Christian missionaries or merchants returning from Alexandria. Regardless of who wrote it, the text does add information to our study of reincarnation and Christianity.

Issa and reincarnation

The manuscript tells us that Jesus spent twelve years studying both Hinduism and Buddhism and suggests that he learned to perform miracles at the feet of Hindu sages. If this is so, he would undoubtedly have been familiar with reincarnation, which is at the heart of both religions.

The Himis manuscript itself does not say anything about reincarnation. But Nicholas Roerich, the Russian anthropologist who published a manuscript strikingly similar to the Himis manuscript, also quotes from another manuscript. One passage in it tells us that Jesus taught reincarnation.

It treats reincarnation in relation to the question of why people are born different. The context is similar to the story in the Gospel of John about the man born blind. In John, the disciples ask what the man had done to deserve to be born blind. In Roerich's manuscript, Jesus asks why some people are born with talent as singers. Here is the passage as it appeared in Roerich's travel diary *Himalaya:*

> Said Jesus of skilled singers: "Whence is their talent and their power? For in one short life they could not possibly accumulate a quality of voice and the knowledge of harmony and of tone. Are these miracles? No, because all things take place as a result of natural laws. Many thousands of years ago these people already molded their harmonies and their qualities. And they come again to learn still more from varied manifestations."[22]

The text is unmistakably confirming reincarnation: "They come again." Even if the passage doesn't represent Jesus' authentic words, it represents the spirit of his teaching. And this spirit is what comes out in the Himis manuscript as well.

The picture that we get of Jesus from all these texts is of a man who is learning, receiving spiritual training and thereby progressing toward godhood. By portraying him as both student and teacher, these texts suggest that Jesus wanted us to follow in his footsteps and become Sons of God like him. (More on this in Part 4.)

JESUS AS STUDENT AND TEACHER

Perhaps the Vatican really does possess a copy of the Himis manuscript or other manuscripts that tell the same story. If so, why has it not released the material? The text may give us a hint. It tells us that Jesus was not born fully divine but that he was an extraordinary human being who worked to accumulate knowledge and progress spiritually, just as we do. If he went through a process of learning and growing, that leaves open the door for us to follow him. Now we can approach him and identify with him as our brother.

Accepting that Jesus needed to study and learn does not diminish his greatness. But it does enhance our understanding of a spiritual path that we can make our own. We can follow in Jesus' footsteps, not necessarily to the Himalayas but all the way to the heart of the Father as we too "perfect" ourselves "in the Divine Word."

Having a picture of what Jesus did in his youth can give us purpose and direction today. Whether you are in your teens or twenties, getting married and starting a family, changing careers or retiring, you can benefit from the idea that you can begin the process of progressing toward godhood just as Jesus did. You too can learn to work the works of him that sent you.[23]

This is the most important message we can derive from the traditions of Jesus in India. We find it reinforced in another passage from the manuscript quoted by Roerich. While it may not record Jesus' exact words, it was certainly inspired by him: "Jesus said to them, 'I came to show human possibilities. What has been created by me, all men can create. And that which I am, all men will be. These gifts belong to all nations and all lands—for this is the bread and the water of life.' "[24]

We can all take heart that we are the inheritors of the universal path to salvation that this passage reveals. When Jesus says, "That which I am, all men will be," he means, "You can be like me."

We will see this message repeated as we explore the writings of the Gnostics, who claimed to possess Jesus' secret teachings. But first, let us examine in detail what the New Testament says about karma and reincarnation and how they affect our understanding of Christianity and our own spiritual destiny.

❦

CHAPTER 9

Jesus' Teaching on Reincarnation

I can read reincarnation into the Bible—
and you can read it right out again!

Edgar Cayce

SOME NEW TESTAMENT PASSAGES IMPLY REIN-
carnation. Others seem to teach the opposite—
that we have only one life to live. To complicate
matters, many scholars think that the passages that
imply reincarnation represent the Gospel writers'
views rather than Jesus' teachings.

The primary focus of the debate over whether
the New Testament teaches reincarnation has been
the passages that say John the Baptist was the
prophet Elijah come again. Although three Gospels tell us this, the Church has resisted the reincarnation interpretation.

To set the stage: It was a popular belief among
the Jews of Jesus' day that Elijah would return as
the forerunner of the Messiah and the day of judgment. In the last book of the Old Testament, the
prophet Malachi had said that God would send a

messenger to "prepare the way." After he came, then God would "draw near to you for judgment." The closing verses of Malachi told of the "great and terrible day of the LORD." When God sent "the prophet Elijah," people would know that that day was coming.[1]

There were two views about how Elijah would return. The first was that he would reappear in a heavenly, or spiritual, body. (His earthly body had presumably been transformed when he was taken away in a chariot of fire nine hundred years before.) Jewish mysticism and folklore regularly described Elijah as appearing in a spiritual body, so people might naturally have expected that his prophesied return would also take place in a spiritual body.

But there were some who saw Elijah's return as taking place another way—through reincarnation. It is this view that is reflected in the Gospels. Matthew, Mark and Luke tell us that after Jesus began teaching, there was speculation that *Jesus* was the reincarnation of Elijah or Jeremiah or "one of the prophets."[2]

And the Gospels repeatedly tell us that people wondered whether or not John was Elijah. The issue arises three times. The first instance is when John is preaching in the wilderness and priests and Levites come to question him. Here he actually denies that he is Elijah. But he does identify himself as "the voice of one crying out in the wilderness, 'Make straight the way of the Lord.' "[3]

The Jews in Jesus' day generally believed that this "voice" was the Messiah's forerunner identified in Malachi as Elijah. If this conversation really took place, perhaps John was being evasive for a very good reason, denying he was Elijah to avoid repercussions from the spiritual and political authorities—who later beheaded him—but then giving a veiled confirmation to reassure his followers.

"ELIJAH HAS COME"

In the two other instances when the question of Elijah comes up, Jesus himself proclaims that John is Elijah come again. The first time is while John is in prison and Jesus delivers a public tribute to him. He says, "It was towards John that all the prophecies of the prophets and of the Law were leading; and he, if you will believe me, is the Elijah who was to return."[4]

The more important of the two revelations comes after John the Baptist's death, at the transfiguration. The scene is "a high mountain" where Jesus has taken Peter, James and John. As Jesus is transfigured, his face shines and his clothes

Did Jesus teach reincarnation when he said that John the Baptist was Elijah come again? According to the Old Testament, Elijah, who was taken to heaven in a chariot of fire about 900 B.C., was to return as the forerunner of the Messiah. Scholars and Christian theologians are reluctant to conclude from the John-as-Elijah statements that Jesus taught reincarnation. However, they at least confirm that the writers of the Gospels believed in reincarnation.

become "dazzlingly white, whiter than any earthly bleacher could make them."[5] Then Elijah and Moses appear and talk with Jesus. Suddenly they disappear, and the disciples can see no one but Jesus.

As they go down the mountain, the disciples ask Jesus, "Why do the scribes say that Elijah has to come first?"[6] In other words, "If Elijah was supposed to come first as the prophet to prepare the way for your coming, then why is he appearing to us out of heaven in his celestial body? What's he doing in heaven when we haven't yet seen him on earth?"

According to Mark, Jesus answers, "True, Elijah is to come first and to see that everything is as it should be....However, I tell you that Elijah has come and they have treated him as they pleased."[7] Matthew gives the same story but adds to his trans-figuration account: "The disciples understood then that he had been speaking of John the Baptist."[8]

What the Gospel authors are trying to show here is that John was indeed Elijah reincarnated and that he had performed the prophesied role of messenger of the LORD and preparer of the way. The disciples would have understood "they have treated him as they pleased" to refer to John's execution. King Herod Antipas had ordered John beheaded after he criticized the king for marrying his own brother's wife.

After these three confirmations, it would seem difficult to deny that Jesus taught reincarnation—at least in the case of Elijah. But there are two other views on the Elijah passages. The first, held primarily by Christian theologians, is that they represent Jesus' authentic words but that they don't imply a general doc-trine of reincarnation. The second view, held by most modern scholars, is that Jesus did not make the statements about Elijah that were attributed to him. Rather, they were inserted into the Gospels in order to prove that Jesus was the Messiah and there-fore they cannot be used to prove that Jesus taught reincarnation.

Let's take up the theologians' argument first. It holds that just because Jesus said John was Elijah "who was to return," he didn't mean to imply the prophet had reincarnated. Elijah was unique because he did not die in the normal way but was taken up in a chariot to heaven. Thus his body was different from that of any other person in history.

In his book *Reincarnation and Christianity,* Dr. Robert Morey supports the standard Christian contention: Since Elijah never died, when he appeared on the Mount of Transfiguration, he was showing himself to be "still alive and in his original body."[9] (He doesn't mention what body Moses came in!)

Morey is neglecting the other possibility—that Elijah came in a spiritual body. This would have been the conclusion drawn by someone familiar with Jewish mysticism. (The transfiguration event bears a number of similarities to the visions of the *Merkabah* mystics, as we will see in chapter 23.) These mystics, like the later Kabbalists, saw both Enoch (whose ascent was similar to Elijah's) and Moses as divinized beings. Their bodies had been transformed from corruptible, mortal bodies into spiritual bodies—the "celestial bodies"[10] that Paul describes.

Jews who believed in reincarnation could have easily accepted the idea that John had been the reincarnation of Elijah. Since John was now dead, his soul could appear at the transfiguration as Elijah wearing a spiritual body.

When Morey tries to convince us that Elijah was still wearing his nine-hundred-year-old physical body, he ignores the clear statement in the Gospels that "Elijah has come and they have treated him as they pleased." Obviously, reincarnation is what the authors mean here.

Many scholars think that Jesus didn't make the "John-as-Elijah" statements. Rather, they believe they were added in by the Gospel writers. Presenting a view common among scholars, twentieth-century Catholic theologian Hans Küng tells us that the Elijah passages are "popular traditions marginal to the gospel."[11] The Jesus Seminar, a group of over two hundred moderate and liberal scholars, sees the passages as inventions by those who wanted to prove that John the Baptist was the prophesied forerunner of Jesus, the Messiah.[12]

Whether or not the scholars are right, their argument does not disprove that the Christians who wrote the Gospels in the latter part of the first century believed in reincarnation. And we know that at least some early Christians tried to use these passages to prove reincarnation.[13]

If, in fact, belief in reincarnation was present in early Christianity, did it originate with Jesus himself? As we trace the belief back into Christian Gnosticism (chapters 12 and 13) and further link it with Jewish mysticism (chapters 22 and 23), the answer may become clear.

For additional proof of the presence of the belief in early Christianity, let's examine the story in the Gospel of John about the man born blind.

"WHO SINNED?"

Jesus walks by a man "blind from birth." His disciples ask him, "Rabbi, who sinned, this man or his parents, that he was born blind?" Jesus answers, "Neither this man nor his parents sinned; he was born blind so that God's works might be revealed in him." Jesus makes a mud paste from saliva and dirt, puts it on the man's eyes and tells him to "wash in the Pool of Siloam."[14] When the man returns, he can see.

The crucial sentence in this passage is the disciples' question: "Who sinned, this man or his parents, that he was born blind?" The disciples were presenting two possible explanations for why people are born different. The latter was commonly accepted in

Judaism: people suffer for their parents' transgressions. Didn't the LORD say when he gave the Ten Commandments to Moses that he punished children for the sins of their parents?[15]

But what about the first explanation presented by the disciples—that the man suffered for his *own* sins? By including this, the author of John is making it clear that he understood reincarnation as a legitimate explanation for why people are born different. He would not have entertained the question of whether the man's sins caused him to be *born* blind unless he believed the man had had a previous existence in which he could have sinned.

John portrays Jesus as not even making an issue of reincarnation, which he would have done if he had disagreed with it. Instead, Jesus goes beyond the mind-set of his listeners and brings them to a new level. "Neither this man nor his parents sinned; he was born blind so that God's works might be revealed in him." The author of this Gospel was demonstrating that the man had been born blind not because of his past deeds but because his soul had responded freely to a calling from God. He had agreed to endure blindness until he met the prophet who would restore his sight.

Before we leave the story of the man born blind, let us look at a controversial question it raises about reincarnation: Are people who are born with handicaps responsible for their own misfortunes? The answer is, in many cases, yes. Their actions in previous lives may dictate that they experience and learn from limitation in another life. Limitation can actually lead to the growth of the soul. The varying needs of the soul determine whether people are born either wealthy or poor, to kind parents or cruel parents.

But it is a mistake to look down on people for their misfortunes or handicaps. It is only too easy to say, "They must have done something to deserve it." Although knowing about reincarnation may help us to understand our own suffering and that of others, we should not pretend that it enables us to fathom the depths of each one's personal karmic history.

In fact, a handicap may not be karmic at all but may be a condition that a soul—such as the blind man—has agreed to endure for the purpose of teaching or encouraging others. The poor and unfortunate may be unheralded saints bearing the sins of the world.

The story of the man born blind demonstrates that belief in reincarnation was a part of first-century Christianity. But then what about the New Testament passages that appear to deny reincarnation?

"TODAY YOU WILL BE WITH ME IN PARADISE"

First there are the verses that imply we go straight to heaven or hell after death. "Man has but one life on earth in which to earn his eternal destiny," declares the *New Catholic Encyclopedia* and cites two incidents from the New Testament.[16]

The first, in Luke, takes place when Jesus is on the cross. Two criminals have been crucified with him. One jeers at him. The other defends him, saying, "This man has done nothing wrong." This second criminal then asks Jesus for a favor: "Remember me when you come into your kingdom." "Indeed, I promise you," Jesus answers, "today you will be with me in paradise."[17]

Another passage in Luke, the parable of the rich man and a man named Lazarus, gives a fairly vivid picture of heaven and hell. It tells of a rich man who used to "feast magnificently every day" and a poor man named Lazarus—so miserable that dogs licked his sores—who used to yearn for the scraps from the rich man's table. When the two men die, the poor man is "carried away by the angels to the bosom of Abraham," while the rich man is sent to "torment in Hades."[18]

When the rich man appeals to Abraham to send Lazarus to help him, Abraham responds that there is no crossing over between heaven and hell. He says, "Between us and you a great gulf has been fixed to stop anyone, if he wanted to, crossing from our side to yours, and to stop any crossing from your side to ours."[19]

While I have my doubts about whether Jesus actually spoke this parable, neither of these passages denies reincarnation. They merely state the existence of a good place, heaven, and a bad place, hell, to which souls may be sent after death.

After all, before Christianity, both heaven and hell were usually seen as transition points between incarnations on earth. They were Greek concepts. And Luke, like other Jews of Jesus' day, had absorbed Greek concepts about heaven, hell and judgment after death.

Thus I believe that Jesus' statement to the second criminal indicates only that he will be transported to the heaven-world. It doesn't deny the possibility of his future rebirth on earth. Gaining entrance to one of the heavenly spheres does not guarantee that the soul will stay there forever.

Before we leave these two passages, let me say that the Jesus Seminar questions whether Jesus told the Lazarus story and made the statement on the cross.[20] But whether or not these passages reflect Jesus' authentic words, it is enough for now to say that they neither prove that the New Testament denies reincarnation nor do they outweigh other passages that imply it.

"ONCE TO DIE"

The passage that is most often cited to prove the Bible's opposition to reincarnation is Hebrews 9:27, 28: "Since men only die once, and after that comes judgment, so Christ, too, offers himself only once to take the faults of many on himself, and when he appears a second time, it will not be to deal with sin but to reward with salvation those who are waiting for him" (Jerusalem Bible).*

The Catholic catechism cites this verse in its refutation of re- incarnation. "When 'the single course of our earthly life' is com- pleted, we shall not return to other earthly lives: 'It is appointed for men to die once.' There is no 'reincarnation' after death."[21]

The first thing to note in considering the "once-to-die" pas- sage is its context. The author of Hebrews is not trying to deny reincarnation. Rather, he is explaining that repetitive blood sac- rifices of animals were a part of the old covenant established by Moses but are not needed in the new covenant established by Jesus. Under the old covenant the priests of Israel were required to make many sacrifices, using the blood of animals. But under the new covenant, Jesus shed his own blood, a sacrifice that was needed only once.

What does the author mean by saying "since men only die once"? The easiest explanation is that he is referring to the fact that our mortal bodies die only once. The human body *is* a one- shot deal. No one has tried to argue otherwise except Chris- tians who believe in a bodily resurrection.

And "after that comes judgment"[22] can refer to life reviews such as those reported in near-death experiences. But a post- life judgment does not preclude the possibility of the soul's returning to earth in another mortal body. For the passage does not say, "It is appointed unto man *once to live.*"

Another possibility is that the author of Hebrews has in mind a mystical meaning when he uses the phrase "once to die." This option occurred to Christian reincarnationists at least as early as the seventeenth century.

---

*King James Version: "And as it is appointed unto men once to die, but after this the judgment: So Christ was once offered to bear the sins of many; and unto them that look for him shall he appear the second time without sin unto salvation."

In London in 1684, Franciscus Mercurius van Helmont published a book titled *Two Hundred Queries Moderately Propounded Concerning the Doctrine of the Revolution of Humane Souls, and Its Conformity to the Truths of Christianity.* If "once to die" were meant to be taken literally, as it is "generally understood," asks the author, then what about people that have been raised from the dead—like Lazarus and Jairus' daughter? Didn't they die again in the natural course of life, therefore dying twice? He then asks, "Must not these words then have another, a deeper and less obvious sense?"[23]

Here is one "less obvious sense": What dies once and only once is the "carnal mind," as Paul termed the human ego. He wrote in Romans, "For to be carnally minded is death; but to be spiritually minded is life and peace." The carnal mind is a mind that is set on "the things of the flesh."[24] It refers to the portion of us that must die in order for us to "put on" our "immortality."

Sometime, somewhere, in order to achieve eternal life, we must fully and finally slay the carnal mind. It doesn't happen all at once. Paul said, "I die daily."[25] The unreal self dies a slice each day until it is finally dead. And we put on our immortality a slice each day. The death of the ego is a process, just as achieving immortality is a process. Until we have accomplished this, we continue to embody and continue to experience a judgment (though not the final judgment) at the conclusion of each life.

But when we have put on our immortality, we come to the end of living and dying. As Paul wrote:

> When this corruptible shall have put on incorruption, and this mortal shall have put on immortality, then shall be brought to pass the saying that is written, "Death is swallowed up in victory.
>
> "O death, where is thy sting? O grave, where is thy victory?"[26]

As we will see in future chapters on the resurrection, it is the immortality of the soul and not the body that is at issue in this passage.

So where does our walk through the New Testament leave the question of reincarnation? I think it tends to confirm my belief that Jesus taught reincarnation. First, there is no record—either in the Gospels, the writings of the apostles, the Book of Revelation or the Gnostic texts—of Jesus denying reincarnation. Second, reincarnation is clearly mentioned in the New Testament and hence was a valid part of some forms of early Christianity. Third, it is implied in both the Old and New Testaments, as we will see in the next chapter.

CHAPTER 10

Karma Implies Reincarnation

I the LORD *your God am a jealous God,*
punishing children for the iniquity of parents,
to the third and fourth generation.

Deuteronomy 5:9

THE OLD TESTAMENT CONJURES UP IMAGES OF a Charlton Heston–like God raining arbitrary vengeance on his hapless worshipers.

When Moses returns from Mount Sinai, tablets of the law in hand, he sees the people worshiping a golden calf made for them by his brother, Aaron. In anger, he breaks the tablets of the law that he has received from God.

The LORD tells Moses, "I have seen this people and, behold, it is a stiffnecked people."[1] He says he will consume the Israelites as the penalty for breaking their covenant with him. But Moses prays for mercy and the nation is spared. However, God, through Moses, orders the Levites to take their swords and kill the idolators. Three thousand Israelites die that day.

There are plenty of Old Testament examples of God punishing people harshly for seemingly not-so-bad crimes. Without an understanding of reincarnation, these incidents seem unjust. But looking through the lens of past lives, we can see them as karma come due. We can interpret them as retribution for the karma not only of the day but of thousands of years.

When reincarnation—the missing link—is restored, the Old Testament begins to make sense. And that may be why it appealed to first-century Jews like Philo, as well as the second-century Gnostics and the medieval Kabbalists. Both the Kabbalists and the Gnostics interpreted the Old Testament God in light of reincarnation.

The Kabbalist text the *Bahir,* you will recall, takes the biblical term *generations* to mean "incarnations." Before the Kabbalists, the Christian Gnostic teacher Basilides, from Alexandria, also used this word substitution in the second century to explain God's threat to punish children for the sins of their parents to "the third and fourth generation." Basilides said that God didn't mean he was punishing innocent children but that people's own sins followed them for three and four incarnations.[2]

We know that both Gnostics and Kabbalists drew on pre-Christian Jewish mysticism. Therefore, this reincarnationist interpretation may have come from Judaism and thus may have been accessible to Jesus. It provided a way to defend God's justice while upholding the eye-for-an-eye Old Testament law.

"AN EYE FOR AN EYE"

In the Old Testament you will find as clear a statement of karma as you could ask for. In Genesis, God says, "Whoso sheddeth man's blood, by man shall his blood be shed."[3] In Exodus, God details the law-code for Israel, which includes the familiar command: "He that smiteth a man so that he die shall be surely put to death. . . . If any mischief follow, then thou shalt give life for life, eye for eye, tooth for tooth, hand for hand, foot for foot, burning for burning, wound for wound, stripe for stripe."[4]

The Book of Obadiah reaffirms the principle of karmic return: "As you have done, so will it be done to you: your deeds will recoil on your own head."[5] And in the New Testament, Jesus echoes this idea: "All they that take the sword shall perish with the sword."[6]

Karma is spelled out as clearly in the New Testament as it is in the Old. In his Sermon on the Mount, Jesus says, "Think not that I am come to destroy the law or the prophets: I am not come to destroy but to fulfill."[7] As I see it, when he speaks of the law, he is including the law of karma, which underpins all other laws of the Old Testament.

For Jesus said that not one "jot or one tittle" would pass from the law, i.e., not one letter or part of a letter, until "all be fulfilled."[8] This jot and tittle that we all must pay is our karma. The law of karma is the law of the causal relationship between a man's acts and the universe's re-action that returns to his doorstep. This return of positive and negative energy continues daily and hourly until his soul is perfected in Christ and he escapes the round of rebirth.

In the Sermon on the Mount, Jesus states with mathematical precision the law of karma: "With the judgment you make you will be judged, and the measure you give will be the measure you get." He goes on to give the Golden Rule: "In everything do to others as you would have them do to you; for this is the law and the prophets."[9] The entire sermon concerns the consequences of thoughts, feelings, words and deeds.

I interpret another passage in Matthew as implying that each person has accumulations of both good and bad karma. Jesus says, "A good man out of the good treasure of the heart bringeth forth good things [that is, good works, good karma], and an evil man out of the evil treasure bringeth forth evil things [bad works, bad karma]."[10] I understand this to mean that you will tend to act according to the patterns of behavior already etched in your being and you will receive good and bad things according to the store of good and bad deeds you have accumulated.

If Jesus taught that we must pay for our misdeeds, wouldn't he have also taught that we would have the opportunity to do so in our next lifetime if we couldn't do it in this one? If God is just and merciful, then karma implies reincarnation—an opportunity to make amends.

BEYOND "AN EYE FOR AN EYE"

At the same time that Jesus confirms the Old Testament law of karma, he tells people to go beyond it. He gives them advice that must have seemed outrageous at the time—don't fight back if you are struck; give away your possessions. He says:

> You have learned how it was said: "Eye for eye and tooth for tooth." But I say this to you: offer the wicked man no resistance. On the contrary, if anyone hits you on the right cheek, offer him the other as well; if a man takes you to law and would have your tunic, let him have your cloak as well. And if anyone orders you to go one mile, go two miles with him. Give to anyone who asks, and if anyone wants to borrow, do not turn away.[11]

Jesus is setting forth a higher path, a royal road to divine union in which the seeker must go beyond simply balancing karma. What must his audience have thought, steeped as they were in the debit-credit mentality of the Old Testament, when he gave the unheard-of command "Love your enemies"? He says: "You have learned how it was said: 'You must love your neighbor and hate your enemy.' But I say this to you: love your enemies and pray for those who persecute you."[12]

One can't help but see parallels between these statements

and the Eastern scriptures. The Dhammapada, a sacred Buddhist text, tells us: "Hate is not conquered by hate: hate is conquered by love. This is a law eternal."[13] Another Buddhist text sounds much like "Love your enemies and pray for those who persecute you." It tells people to pray: "May all who say bad things to me or cause me any other harm, and those who mock and insult me have the fortune to fully awaken."[14]

Buddha taught that right action should be our first concern but beyond that comes detachment from even those actions. Only by being completely unconcerned about our fate can we truly escape the round of rebirth.

In one of his readings, Edgar Cayce speaks of the path of doing good to those who persecute you as a way of escaping bondage to your negative karma. Since we must reap what we sow—both good and bad—Cayce advises that we follow Jesus' commandment to do good to our enemies, for "then ye overcome in thyself whatever ye may have done to thy fellow man!"[15]

When you go beyond the debit-credit way of looking at karma and go out of your way to do good, you are transcending the karmic state. Jesus not only affirms the law of karma as set forth by Moses; he goes far beyond it by establishing what I call the law of love as the standard for the perfecting of the soul. Jesus is saying: "The law of karma cannot be broken, but it can be fulfilled through Divine Love. Moreover, since you seek the crown of everlasting life, you must compensate more, not less, for every wrong you do to others."

And even when you have done no wrong at all, you must give and give again, for your life is not to be merely a story of balancing bad karma; it is to be the history of one who has gained his soul's self-mastery in love and union with Christ while bringing generous blessings to all people. It is to be a history of one who does not simply rack up good karma for the purpose of continued enjoyment but who seeks to transcend this life for one beyond pleasure and pain.

It is worth noting here that many liberal scholars do not believe that Jesus said everything that is attributed to him in the New Testament. As we will explore further in the next chapter, they believe that many of Jesus' statements were added by the Gospel writers. The Jesus Seminar sees Jesus as someone who was anti-establishment and who therefore would have argued against the Old Testament eye-for-an-eye mentality rather than confirming it. Thus they believe that he did tell us to love our enemies but that he did not say things like "all they that take the sword shall perish with the sword."

They think that it would have been inconsistent for him to have preached both messages. However, I see no contradiction between the two. Jesus did not intend to deny that we are responsible for our actions when he told us to love our enemies. For further proof, we have only to look at the earliest surviving Christian writings, the letters of Paul.

KARMA IN THE EPISTLES

Paul ratified Jesus' statements that what we send out comes back to us: "[God] will repay each one as his works deserve.... Pain and suffering will come to every human being who employs himself in evil.... Renown, honor and peace will come to everyone who does good.... God has no favorites."[16]

In his letter to the Galatians, Paul clearly states the law of karma: "Every man shall bear his own burden.... Be not deceived; God is not mocked: for whatsoever a man soweth, that shall he also reap. For he that soweth to his flesh shall of the flesh reap corruption; but he that soweth to the Spirit shall of the Spirit reap life everlasting."[17]

In his writings to the church at Corinth, Paul teaches of the trial by fire. He says, "Every man shall receive his own reward according to his own labor." A man's labor *is* his karma. Paul says, "The fire shall try every man's work of what sort it is," i.e., what kind of spirit and emotion has gone into its creation. If the work survives the fire, then the builder will "receive a reward." Otherwise, he will "suffer loss."[18]

Paul is telling us that if we create with love and positive energy, then our works will survive God's consuming fire and be made permanent. But if we create with anger, hatred or pride, then the works and the negative energy that went into them will be consumed by God's purifying fire. The fiery trial is an ongoing process that we experience from day to day. Our works are tried and we receive their fruits. But that return of both positive and negative karma is often reserved for future lifetimes.

Through the centuries, Christians have read these passages I have quoted and concluded that the payback takes place at some future final judgment, not through reincarnation. In fact, the Church cites the following passage from Paul about the "law court of Christ" to refute the idea that retribution occurs in some future lifetime.

The passage reads: "For all the truth about us will be brought out in the law court of Christ, and each of us will get what he deserves for the things he did in the body, good or bad."[19] The Catholic Church tells us that this payback can occur only in heaven, hell or purgatory, but Paul does not state where it occurs. And, as I will show in future chapters, there were early Christians who believed that it came in future lives on earth.

The doctrine of karma cannot be separated from the doctrine of reincarnation. Since we continue to make negative karma that we must then balance (until we learn to stop making it), we need an opportunity to balance it. Reincarnation becomes the opportunity that a merciful God would provide.

Three strikes and you're...born again?

What convinces me more than anything else that Jesus taught reincarnation is that he set forth requirements for salvation that most people would find impossible to fulfill in one lifetime.

Take, for instance, the "born again" passage in John 3. Nicodemus, a high-ranking Pharisee, comes at night to speak to Jesus. They have the following conversation:

Jesus: No one can see the kingdom of God without being born from above.

Nicodemus: How can anyone be born after having grown old? Can one enter a second time into the mother's womb and be born?

Jesus: No one can enter the kingdom of God without being born of water and Spirit. What is born of the flesh is flesh, and what is born of the Spirit is spirit.[20]

In the mystical interpretation, being born of water and Spirit would mean being transformed into the Divine Self. The central issue this passage raises is: If Jesus stipulated that a man cannot enter the kingdom of God unless he is transformed into the Divine Self, then wouldn't Jesus have allowed the possibility for the requirement to be fulfilled in a future life if it could not be fulfilled in this life?

As Christian theology would have it, you get only one lifetime to fulfill Jesus' requirement. If you fail to do it in this life, you have failed. Period. You won't make it into the kingdom of God *ever.*

Some Christians speak of other religions as having strange gods. Strange to me is a God who would set up a condition for his children and then make it impossible for them to meet it.

Why, for instance, would God cause people to be born in non-Christian countries where they never have a chance to become Christian and then say they cannot enter the kingdom because they did not become Christians? I am a stranger to a

God who, because I'm not a good baseball player, simply says, "Three strikes and you're out of my ball game."

What the passage really implies is the following: If someone is not born of water and of the Spirit in this life, he must be born again through another mother's womb—and so on—until he takes the opportunity to enter the kingdom of God, which I call the consciousness of God. (See chapter 24 for a further discussion of the kingdom.) The reincarnationist view provides an alternative to the all-or-nothing view of heaven or hell. If someone is not born again in this life, God lets him come back again to have another chance to seek rebirth by the Spirit.

In the Book of Revelation, the last book of the Bible, we find a final text that implies reincarnation—or, rather, an end to it. It suggests a time when one who has successfully passed through his series of lifetimes will achieve liberation from rebirth. Revelation 3:12 reads: "Him that overcometh will I make a pillar in the temple of my God, and he shall go no more out."[21]

"And he shall go no more out." He shall no longer enter into earthly bodies. There is an end to the "sorrowful weary Wheel." There is an "abode of Eternity," as the Hindu text the Bhagavad Gita tells us, and "those who reach that abode return no more."[22]

The Greeks and some Jews, especially Hellenized Jews such as Philo, believed in reincarnation. Paul, the Gospels and the Old Testament implied it. The idea pervaded Jesus' world like salt in seawater. Jesus would have to have grown up in a bubble not to have known about it. And if he had disagreed with reincarnation, his teaching would have reflected the disagreement. Barring any evidence to the contrary, we must conclude that Jesus taught reincarnation and that he meant it to help us reach the abode of Eternity.

PART 3

Early
Christians and
Reincarnation

❦

CHAPTER 11

Sifting the New Testament

In the New Testament there is internal
evidence that parts of it have proceeded
from an extraordinary man; and that other
parts are of the fabric of very inferior minds.
It is as easy to separate those parts, as it is
to pick out diamonds from dunghills.

Thomas Jefferson
Letter to John Adams, 1814

WHEN MATTHEW'S WISE MEN FOLLOW LUKE'S
shepherds onstage during the Christmas
pageant each year, few of us stop to think that they
come from different Gospels—or that the Gospels
reflect not one but several points of view about Jesus.

Matthew and Luke both tell us that Jesus was
born in Bethlehem, but Matthew's wise men show
up at a house days or weeks after the birth, while
Luke's shepherds arrive at the manger that very
night. Matthew says nothing about shepherds and
Luke doesn't mention wise men. Nevertheless, the
traditional Nativity scene shows both shepherds

and wise men adoring the newborn at the same time—a harmless collation.

But do Matthew's and Luke's stories about Jesus' birth represent what actually happened? Did Luke, for example, interview Mary? Or did Matthew and Luke each make up his own story about Jesus' birth, perhaps working from earlier written accounts?

The other Gospels, Mark and John, don't talk about Jesus' birth at all. They skip right over his early years and start with his baptism in the Jordan River. And they simply refer to him as Jesus of Nazareth, without a word about Bethlehem. Was he born in Bethlehem or Nazareth? Were there wise men or shepherds or both?

There are other discrepancies in the Bible. We have three versions of Jesus' last words. His statement in Matthew and Mark is a quotation from Psalms: "My God, my God, why have you forsaken me?"[1] Luke implies that Jesus draws on another verse from Psalms when he says, "Father, into your hands I commend my spirit."[2] And John has him simply say, "It is finished."[3] Which one is correct? Or did he say all three, as some Christians believe?

Questions like these led scholars to conclude that the Gospel writers allowed their views to obscure those of Jesus. As early as the eighteenth century, scholars began looking for the historical Jesus. Hermann Samuel Reimarus (1694–1768), a professor of Oriental languages in Hamburg, Germany, made the first attempt to separate the real Jesus from the layers of myth and tradition surrounding him. Thomas Jefferson embarked on a similar quest.

In this chapter we will trace the footsteps of these biblical sleuths. It would be too much to expect that their trail would lead us to a definitive portrait of the historical Jesus. There is simply not enough historical evidence to "prove" anyone's portrait of Jesus.

There are many conceptions of Jesus—reflected in the Bible, in other ancient sources as well as in the secret chamber of our hearts, where we commune with our Lord. Your communion with your own Higher Self will lead you to your own portrait of Jesus. It may or may not coincide with mine—that Jesus was a mystic who taught reincarnation and showed us how to become one with God.

As we sift through the New Testament we will discover how the Gospels came to be written and how the real face of Jesus may have been obscured over the centuries.

ARE THE GOSPELS HISTORY?

The quest starts with the surviving New Testament manuscripts. From the time the New Testament was written in the first and second centuries until the Gutenberg Bible was printed in 1455, the Bible was duplicated by hand. Monks and scribes painstakingly copied each manuscript.

Since the originals have not survived, we must rely primarily on these copies to find out what the original New Testament manuscripts said. We have some early fragments of the Gospels (one from the Gospel of John dating to A.D. 125), but the earliest substantially complete manuscript we possess goes back only to about A.D. 200.

People make mistakes when they copy things, and the scribes were no exception. Their mistakes, interjections and edits come to light when scholars compare all of the existing Bible manuscripts. Today there are over five thousand Greek manuscripts of the New Testament and they differ from each other in thousands of ways.

By analyzing the manuscripts, scholars have demonstrated that the Bible of today cannot be error-free since the manuscripts contradict each other frequently. While the scriptures may be divinely inspired, they are not infallible and thus cannot, as the First Vatican Council (1869–70) put it, "have God as their author."[4] Rather, they are the product of a tradition that developed over a period of time.

For example, what is the last sentence in the Lord's Prayer? The King James Version concludes with "For thine is the kingdom, and the power, and the glory, for ever. Amen."[5] But this sentence is missing from many of the early manuscripts. Thus modern translations such as the New Revised Standard Version (1989) and the Scholars Version (1992) leave out this final sentence.

In some cases, the varying manuscripts show us how and why the Gospels were edited. Codex Sinaiticus, copied down about A.D. 340, shows us how the story of Jesus cleansing a leper in the first chapter of Mark was changed to reflect evolving views. The codex is one of the oldest existing copies of the Bible, but it was not available to the translators of the King James and other familiar versions of the Bible.

In the story, a leper comes to Jesus and begs to be healed. Codex Sinaiticus tells us that Jesus, "angry, stretched out his hand and touched him, and said, 'I will; be clean.'"[6] By the time of the King James Version, "angry" had been changed to "moved with compassion."[7] This edit reflects the orthodox attempt to make Jesus less human by denying him human emotions. It reflects recurring controversy about the true nature of Christ—human or divine—particularly the Arian controversy, as we will see.

Using this kind of analysis, scholars concluded early in this century that the Gospel writers were not historians. They were not eyewitnesses to the events of Jesus' life, nor did they interview eyewitnesses. In fact, they wrote some forty to sixty years after Jesus' crucifixion.

The quest for the historical Jesus has led scholars in unexpected directions and, finally, to the complete unraveling of the stories about Jesus' birth. From evidence in the Gospels themselves as well as historical research, scholars have now concluded that Jesus was not born in Bethlehem, that he was conceived in the normal manner and that the miraculous stories about his Bethlehem birth were invented.

THE MISSING CENSUS

Why would anyone want to change the place of Jesus' birth? In the eighth century B.C., the prophet Micah had predicted that the Messiah would "come forth" from Bethlehem,[8] and some early Christians wanted to show that Jesus fulfilled that prophecy.

Here are just a few of the reasons for the scholars' conclusion. First, Luke makes a big error. He tells us that Jesus was born in Bethlehem because Joseph and Mary, who lived in Nazareth, went to Bethlehem after the Roman emperor Augustus instituted a census requiring everyone to return to his birthplace to register to pay taxes.

There are two problems with this story. First, which census was it? Luke tells us that Jesus was born during the reign of Herod the Great, a king who ruled Judea on behalf of the Romans. There was no worldwide Roman census during the reign of Herod the Great, and if there had been, it would not have affected the Jews because they were taxed by Herod, not Rome. There was a census in A.D. 6. But that was ten years after Herod died, and it would have affected residents only of Judea and not of Nazareth, which was under independent rulership, along with all of Galilee.

Furthermore, if Joseph had been included in a census at the time of Jesus' birth, he would not have been required to go to Bethlehem. He would have registered in his place of residence,

Nazareth. Roman censuses were based on property ownership, and Joseph clearly did not own any property in Bethlehem—he had to seek lodging at an inn.

Another reason scholars doubt Matthew's and Luke's Nativity stories is that the other New Testament authors don't mention Jesus being conceived in a special way. Neither Paul (who wrote between A.D. 48 and 64), Mark (around A.D. 70) nor John says anything about conception by the Holy Spirit or a virgin birth.

Matthew and Luke are the only sources for supernatural accounts of the conception, and scholars have now concluded that they were written after Mark, probably A.D. 80 and 90 respectively.[9] Luke sent the Holy Family to Bethlehem because he was trying to prove that Jesus was the Messiah, not because it really happened. Thus, as Marcus Borg explains it, scholars now see the birth stories as "symbolic narratives created by the early Christian movement."[10]

What does this new information mean for our Christmas pageant? Can we still set up the crèche scene, put on Nativity plays and sing "O Little Town of Bethlehem"? Of course. The larger truths that we affirm remain the same and there is no reason why we cannot celebrate them in the context of our culture.

We can get even more enjoyment out of watching our children reenact the drama each year when we consider that it represents Christ being born in each of our hearts. Thus the Christian pageantry that pervades our culture can become a celebration of our own spiritual transformation. It can be both enlightening and uplifting when we remember that it does not exclude us but celebrates our own nascent divinity.

If we can't necessarily trust the Gospels as history, where then do we go in our search for the historical Jesus? The search has driven scholars right back to the Gospels. But instead of looking at the narratives, they look at the words that are purported to have come from Jesus' lips. They search for the primitive structure that underlies the more elaborate edifice created by the Gospel writers. These authors—who probably were not named Matthew, Mark, Luke and John—left telltale signs when they created different contexts for Jesus' sayings.

Search for the Sayings of Jesus

Matthew and Luke often quote similar sayings of Jesus but put them in different settings—for example, the Sermon on the Mount. Or is it the "Sermon on the Plain"? Matthew and Luke each tell us that Jesus was giving a sermon early in his ministry. In Matthew, Jesus is seated on a mountain, surrounded by his disciples. In Luke, he is standing "on a level place," surrounded by a group of disciples and "a great multitude of people."[11]

In both Gospels, he gives parallel teachings but with slight variations. The Beatitudes—his "Blessed are. . ." statements—are similar but not identical. In Luke we read, "Blessed are you who are poor, for yours is the kingdom of God."[12] Matthew adds the words "in spirit"[13] after "poor."

"Blessed are you who are hungry now, for you will be filled,"[14] we read in Luke. In Matthew, the same Beatitude reads: "Blessed are those who hunger and thirst *for righteousness,* for they will be filled."[15] In both cases, Matthew gives an interpretation not found in Luke. Apparently, he is broadening the sayings to make them more meaningful to Christians who may be neither poor, hungry nor thirsty.

Matthew's sermon is 111 verses long; Luke's is only 34. But Luke includes many of the rest of Matthew's sayings elsewhere, sprinkling them throughout his Gospel in different contexts.

Analyzing the similarities and differences between the Gospels has led many scholars to conclude that the Gospel writers were using earlier written collections of Jesus' sayings. They built stories about Jesus around the sayings, sometimes giving them different contexts and interpretations.

The collections of sayings were based on oral tradition— Jesus' words as people remembered them and passed them on. The collections were probably written down at least twenty years after Jesus' crucifixion. These scholars have concluded

The Gospel writers present similar material in different contexts. Matthew, for example, tells us that Jesus gave the Beatitudes during his Sermon on the Mount. But Luke tells us he spoke them while standing "on a level place." Discrepancies like these have led scholars to discard much of the Gospels' narrative and to focus instead on the sayings of Jesus, which they believe circulated in now-lost documents that predated the Gospels.

that the Gospel writers, although they claimed to be Jesus' apostles or their students, were actually further removed. They wrote under the names of the apostles or their companions to give their works authenticity. This was a common practice in Jesus' world.[16]

Mark was the earliest Gospel. By comparing Matthew and Luke with Mark, scholars have concluded that Matthew and Luke copied from Mark and from an unidentified source gospel called "Q" after *Quelle*, German for "source." As early as 1838, they speculated that Q contained the material that was shared by Matthew and Luke but absent from Mark.

Q would have been one of a number of collections of sayings circulating in the early years after Jesus' death, each one focusing on a different aspect of his message. Scholars imagined that Q was a collection of sayings without narrative framework. There was only one problem. No such collection had ever been discovered.

Then, in 1945, an Egyptian farmer named Muhammed 'Ali went out with his brother to dig for fertilizer at the base of the cliffs along the Nile near the town of Nag Hammadi. As they dug near a large boulder, they uncovered an earthenware jar containing thirteen ancient books, or codices. Each was made up of papyrus leaves sewn into a leather cover.

This library in a jar contained over fifty works written in Coptic, which is a form of written Egyptian using the Greek alphabet. Coptic was used by Christian missionaries in Egypt. Most of the works were Christian but some were obviously based on Jewish and Greek wisdom writings. The texts reflected a Gnostic viewpoint, which was accepted in some early Christian circles but was later declared heretical.

From references on the covers, scholars concluded that the books had been copied in the fourth century at one of the oldest Christian monasteries, which was nearby. Most scholars

*The base of the cliffs near the Nile River at Nag Hammadi, Egypt. Here,
in 1945, thirteen books were discovered, buried in an earthenware jar.
They contain fifty-two ancient scriptures, mostly Christian Gnostic works,
that give us new insights into early Christianity. Scholars think that some
of the scriptures may have been written at the same time as or even before
the four Gospels.*

believe the original language of the texts was Greek. Although
the manuscripts were produced in the fourth century, the
Christian manuscripts from which they were copied were probably composed as far back as the second century and even the
first.

Some scholars have surmised that monks at the monastery
buried these manuscripts in the fourth century when the archbishop Athanasius decreed that all books reflecting heretical
ideas be purged. Other scholars believe that the collection

belonged to a heretical Gnostic group who lived in that area of Egypt.

In the second volume, sandwiched between texts called the *Secret Book of John* and the *Gospel of Philip*, was the *Gospel of Thomas*, a collection of sayings without narrative, just as scholars had imagined Q might have been. It consisted of 114 sayings, most beginning simply, "Jesus said." Many of the sayings had parallels in Mark, Matthew and Luke, and five had parallels in John.

Here are the crucial questions: Was *Thomas* based on the four Gospels or was it written earlier? If it predated the Gospels, was it a new source of authentic sayings of Jesus?

After the Nag Hammadi find, scholars soon realized that they already possessed fragments of *Thomas*—in Greek! In the late nineteenth century, these first-century papyrus fragments of *Thomas* had been discovered in an ancient garbage dump near the ruins of the Egyptian town of Oxyrhynchus. From these fragments they were able to conclude that *Thomas* was composed in Greek as early as the first century.

Scholars also looked at the form of the *Thomas* sayings. Since they lacked interpretation and elaboration, they appeared to be more primitive than the same sayings published in the Gospels. This has led most American scholars to put the date of *Thomas* in the last three decades of the first century, i.e., before Matthew, Luke and John were written, and roughly at the same time as Mark. Some European scholars disagree and say that *Thomas* was written after the four Gospels.[17] But the American view seems more persuasive.

In some cases, comparing the four Gospels with the *Gospel of Thomas* suggests how the Gospel writers edited and interpreted Jesus' sayings. Here are some examples: *Thomas* has parallels to three of the Beatitudes that are in both Matthew's and Luke's sermons.

LUKE	MATTHEW	THOMAS
Blessed are you when people hate you, and when they exclude you, revile you, and defame you on account of the Son of Man. Rejoice in that day and leap for joy, for surely your reward is great in heaven.[18]	Blessed are you when people revile you and persecute you and utter all kinds of evil against you falsely on my account. Rejoice and be glad, for your reward is great in heaven.[19]	Blessed are you when you are hated and persecuted; and no place will be found, wherever you have been persecuted.[20]

Scholars have a difficult time translating and interpreting the second half of *Thomas'* saying. But, in any case, the Beatitude clearly does not carry the same meaning for *Thomas* as for Matthew and Luke, who use it to encourage Christians who were beginning to be persecuted. For scholars, this was further evidence that the Gospel writers had added their own interpretations to sayings of Jesus that were hard for them to understand.

Another example is the parable of the vineyard found in Matthew, Mark, Luke and *Thomas*. It concerns someone who plants a vineyard, leases it to tenant farmers and then goes away. He repeatedly sends servants to collect the rent, but the tenants beat them and refuse to pay. The fourth time, he sends his son, but the tenants kill him so that they can get his inheritance.

Thomas gives the parable without interpretation. But Matthew, Mark and Luke turn it into an allegory for what happens when the Jews reject the Son of God. In Mark, Jesus comments: "What will the owner of the vineyard do? He will come in person, and do away with those farmers, and give the vineyard to someone else."[21] Matthew and Luke put similar words in Jesus' mouth.

Most scholars think that the Gospel writers added these interpretations because they wanted to imply that the tenants were the Jews and that they had forfeited the covenant (the vineyard), which had now been given to others, the Christians. The Jesus Seminar, a group of scholars mentioned in previous chapters, concluded that *Thomas'* "simpler edition of the parable is undoubtedly closer to the original version."[22] Other *Thomas* experts also see *Thomas'* simplicity as proof that it predates the four Gospels.[23]

THE ORTHODOX VERSUS THE MYSTICAL JESUS

The *Gospel of Thomas* has created a ferment in the scholarly world. Some conservative scholars believe it was written after the four Gospels. Those who give it an earlier date believe it supports the idea that there were many competing views of Jesus that flourished in the centuries after his death. For these

This is a page from the second of the thirteen books found at Nag Hammadi. On this page, one can make out in Greek letters the words Peuaggelion Pkata Thomas—*"The Gospel according to Thomas." The language of the texts is actually Coptic, a form of written Egyptian using the Greek alphabet.* Thomas *tells us that some Christians saw Jesus not as an apocalyptic Saviour but as a wisdom teacher who wanted to show us how to become one with God.*

scholars, the orthodox view holds no more claim to legitimacy than the Gnostic view.

Based on *Thomas* and other early Gnostic texts, they have concluded that Jesus' original teachings were taken in different directions by different groups of followers. Thus they have come to speak of "Thomas Christianity"[24] and the "school"[25] that wrote John.

Matthew shows us that there was a group of Christians who interpreted Jesus' sayings in an apocalyptic and messianic manner. On the other hand, *Thomas* shows that there existed in the first century a group of Christians who interpreted Jesus' sayings in an esoteric and mystical manner. Therefore, the scholars conclude that no one kind of Christianity can claim to have the only true interpretation of Jesus' sayings. In their view, *Thomas* is not necessarily more authentic than Matthew, just different.

The Jesus Seminar, while certainly controversial, has done some important work in sifting the New Testament to determine which sayings go back to the historical Jesus and which were created to support the ideas of divergent schools of followers.[26]

I think their most important conclusion is that what has come down to us through the Church is not the only authentic interpretation of Jesus' message. Rather, it is probably just one among several interpretations that flourished in the early centuries of the Christian era.[27]

In their work *The Five Gospels,* the Jesus Seminar included the *Gospel of Thomas* alongside the four Gospels. In so doing, they showed that the views promoted by orthodoxy for the last two thousand years have no greater claim to legitimacy than the mystical, esoteric view of Jesus I will present in the next few chapters.

This is not to say that they think Jesus spoke every word in *Thomas.* Rather, they believe that *Thomas* was edited by someone who had mystical leanings.

Stephen Patterson, an expert on the *Gospel of Thomas,* believes that Jesus' enigmatic statements were interpreted in different ways by the different Christian communities. One example is a saying that is quoted by both Matthew and *Thomas:* "Do not let your left hand know what your right hand is doing."

Matthew uses it in a passage on charity where Jesus admonishes people not to flaunt their religion in public because then they won't get recognition from God. "When you give alms, *do not let your left hand know what your right hand is doing,* so that your alms may be done in secret; and your Father who sees in secret will reward you."[28]

Thomas, however, puts the saying in another context. *Thomas* 62 reads, "Jesus said, 'I disclose my mysteries to those who are worthy of my mysteries. *Do not let your left hand know what your right hand is doing.*'"[29] The author of *Thomas* thus gives the saying a radically different meaning than Matthew. He is telling us that Jesus has secret teachings that he does not reveal to everyone. He is an esoteric wisdom teacher.

Thomas presents a mystical, esoteric Christianity that, as we will see in future chapters, emphasizes the soul's identification with Christ. I believe it is more true to Jesus' original message than is the orthodox interpretation.

What we can learn from modern scholarship is that the image of Jesus as an esoteric wisdom teacher stands on an equal footing with the crucified Christ upon which orthodox Christianity was built. This image stands out vividly in the Gnostic gospels and will emerge like the sun from the clouds when we discover the keys to unlock the Gospel of John and the letters of Paul.

With this in mind, let us take a closer look at the Gnostics.

CHAPTER 12

❦

What Is Gnosticism?

Whoever discovers the interpretation of
these sayings will not taste death.
Gospel of Thomas

CALLING SOMEONE A SEXUAL PERVERT IS usually a good way to discredit his ideas. And that's just what the Church Fathers did to the Gnostics. By characterizing them as insane, depraved, life-hating freaks who held orgies, practiced free love and homosexuality, ate aborted fetuses and refused to bear children, early theologians were able to convince people that the Gnostics' teachings were absurd and misguided.[1]

Their portrait of the Gnostics held for sixteen hundred years—until the Nag Hammadi library was discovered in 1945. Before that we had only a few fragments of the Gnostics' writings. And so we were forced to look at the Gnostics through the eyes of the Church, which considered them its most dangerous enemy.

But the Nag Hammadi texts show little trace of

advocating bizarre behavior. As scholar Henry Chadwick writes, "The new discoveries from Nag Hammadi have taught us, among many things, that the gnostics were not such irrational and psychopathic nihilists as their ancient Christian and pagan opponents wanted us to believe."[2]

There were probably a wide range of practices among Gnostic groups. Some were licentious and some were ascetic. Some were celibate and some chose to bear children.[3] Gnostics disagreed with each other on a number of things, including whether Jesus was ever human or was a divine being who only appeared to be human. But they tended to agree on things like the meaning of the resurrection, the process of salvation and the existence of reincarnation.

It appears that the Church Fathers exaggerated or invented details about the Gnostics' religious practices to obscure the real areas of difference between their theology and Gnosticism. For the Gnostics had something that could undermine the entire fabric of the Church: a competing interpretation of scripture. They said that the interpretations of Church Fathers like Irenaeus (c. 130–c. 200) and Tertullian (c. 150–c. 225) were simplistic and incomplete since they were based on a partial understanding. The Gnostics claimed to possess the full interpretation—based on Jesus' secret teachings, handed down to them by the apostles.

Gnosticism was not a unified movement. In its heyday in the second and third centuries, there were a variety of Gnostic groups, some Christian and some not, who competed for adherents with Christians, Neoplatonists and mystery cults. Some Gnostics were even a part of the early Church and held prominent positions in Christian communities, especially at Alexandria.

The Gnostic teacher Valentinus (c. 100–175) was educated in Alexandria, where he encountered Greek philosophy as well as Gnosticism and began his career as a Christian teacher. He moved to Rome about 140, where he was active as a teacher and leader. At one time he even expected to be chosen bishop of Rome (a position that had not yet evolved into the papacy). However, Valentinus was passed over for the office and soon after left the Church, but he continued teaching on his own. The philosophical school he founded continued for centuries after his death and produced its own body of writings.

Valentinians and members of other Gnostic sects moved freely within the early Church. The Valentinian Florinus held the office of presbyter under Bishop Victor of Rome but was later removed from office at the insistence of Church Father Irenaeus. A Gnostic named Peter was also presbyter of a congregation in Palestine.

Other Gnostics held prominent positions—as evidenced by orthodox* writers' complaints that "heretics" occupied Church offices.[4] These Gnostics functioned almost as a secret society inside the Church, participating in its rituals and structure while imparting their secret knowledge and mystical interpretation to those they trusted.

Where did Gnosticism come from? For a time, scholars thought it had sprung out of Christianity. However, the Nag Hammadi library and the Dead Sea Scrolls changed all that. Scholars now believe that a Jewish Gnosticism existed before Christianity and probably continued to develop alongside Christian Gnosticism. It was probably linked to Jewish mysticism, as we will discover in future chapters.

By whose authority?

How seriously can we take the Gnostics' claim to possess Jesus' secret teachings? The Alexandrian Gnostic teacher Valentinus

---

*My use of the term orthodox here may be premature, considering that orthodox doctrine was not solidified until the fourth century. I have used it instead of the more cumbersome proto-orthodox to refer to the doctrine that later became orthodox.

said he learned them from Theudas, a student of Paul's. The teacher Basilides claimed to have gotten his teachings from the apostle Peter via a man named Glaukias.

It was common in the ancient world for teachers to give secret teachings orally to their students. As we have seen in chapter 5, there was a secret tradition in Judaism, which may have originated with the patriarchs (as the Kabbalists claimed) or may have been drawn from the Greeks.

The Jewish writer Aristobulus (second century B.C.) was familiar with secret traditions. He quotes an Orphic hymn that includes the words "I will sing for those for whom it is lawful, but you uninitiate, close your doors."[5] In other words, secrets were to be given only to those who had been initiated into the mysteries.

The rabbis who interpreted the Jewish scriptures taught that the texts had at least four levels of meaning. And *Merkabah* mystics claimed to have discovered the mystical, hidden meanings of the scriptures. Jesus, like the rabbis of his time, may very well have embedded multiple meanings in his sayings and passed down secret interpretations orally to his disciples.

We see signs of a secret tradition in the New Testament—in Mark, for example, when Jesus tells his disciples, "To you has been given the secret of the kingdom of God, but for those outside, everything comes in parables." Later in the chapter, Mark tells us that Jesus taught the multitudes in parables but "explained everything in private to his disciples."[6] Even if, as some argue, this tradition does not go back to the historical Jesus,[7] these passages do give further evidence that secret Christian teachings existed at an early stage.

A fragment of the *Secret Gospel of Mark* discovered in 1958 at Mar Saba, a Greek Orthodox monastery in the Judean desert, describes Jesus performing secret initiation rites. We do not know whether it was written by the author of the New

Testament Gospel of Mark. Our only knowledge of it comes from a letter written by Church Father Clement of Alexandria (c. 150–c. 211), which quotes this secret gospel and refers to it as "a more spiritual Gospel for the use of those who were being perfected." He said, "It even yet is most carefully guarded [by the church at Alexandria], being read only to those who are being initiated into the great mysteries."[8]

Clement insists elsewhere that Jesus revealed a secret teaching to those who were "capable of receiving it and being moulded by it."[9] Clement indicates that he possessed the secret tradition, which was handed down through the apostles.

Even if a secret tradition existed, how can we know whether the Gnostics possessed it? Scholars have concluded that the *Gospel of Thomas* (composed c. 70) contains some of Jesus' original sayings. But most of the other Gnostic gospels were composed after *Thomas* and primarily reflect the Gnostics' view of how Jesus' sayings should be interpreted. We can look at most of these texts as having been developed by the Gnostics to communicate their ideas.

But what about the core beliefs of the Christian Gnostics? Do they date back to Jesus? They very well could have been based on Jesus' original secret teachings distilled from Jewish mysticism. Or they could have been inspired revelations from the risen Christ. Or both. Whenever and wherever they arose, I believe they represent the inner meaning of Jesus' message.

How are we saved?

The Gnostics created elaborate stories to explain their ideas about the origin and destiny of the soul. The following story about the quest for a pearl gives the Gnostic answer to the perennial questions: Who am I? Why am I here? Where am I going?

Imagine you are a prince. One day your parents, the King and Queen, send you on a mission to Egypt. You must find a pearl guarded by a hungry dragon.

You take off your royal robe and leave the kingdom of your parents. You journey to Egypt, putting on dirty clothing and disguising yourself as an Egyptian.

Somehow the Egyptians discover that you are a foreigner. They give you food that makes you forget your royal birth and makes you believe that you are one of them. You sink into a deep sleep.

Your parents see your plight and send you a letter that tells you to awaken. It reminds you of your quest to recover the pearl. You remember who you are, a child of kings. You quickly subdue the dragon, recover the pearl and depart, leaving the dirty clothing behind.

When you return to your native land, you see your royal robe, which reminds you of the splendor you lived in before. The garment speaks to you, telling you that it belongs to the one who is stronger than all human beings. You put on your royal robe once more and return to your father's palace.[10]

The King and Queen symbolize the Creator and a feminine being the Gnostics called the holy mother Sophia (Wisdom). Their kingdom is a realm of light, a place totally outside of matter as we know it. It is spoken of as the *pleroma,* or "fullness." Your royal robe represents your True Self, your divine image. The dirty clothing represents your earthly body, which you put on when you entered Egypt, the material world.

When you descended into mortality, you left behind your divine image and became a fractured person. You "fell asleep" when you forgot your true origin. The message sent by your parents represents the Saviour. He will awaken you and remind you what you must do to achieve salvation. You must recover the pearl (the fallen aspects of your soul), find your way back to the realm of light and clothe yourself once more in your royal robe—in other words, reintegrate with your divine image. By recovering your soul and reintegrating with your divine image, you will have achieved gnosis, or salvation.

Gnosis was a common Greek word, meaning "knowledge" or "acquaintance." For the Gnostics, achieving gnosis meant to know the self as God. But "to know" meant not merely to understand your divine origin but to achieve the classic goal of the mystic: union with God.

Putting on a royal garment and recovering the pearl were just some of the images the Gnostics used to describe achieving gnosis. They also used the Hindu and Orphic image of integrating with the divine seed. The Gnostics too believed that God is transcendent—infinite, perfect, ultimate, unfathomable, an invisible Spirit—and that each person has a seed, or spark, of the Divine within him.

Gnostics believed that people are composed of three parts— the body, the soul and the divine spark, or Spirit. The divine spark, the God within, acts almost as a pilot light—sustaining the divine potential of the soul and body until the soul is ready to be awakened, or ignited. The awakened soul pursues union with the God within, and this union is salvation.

In the *Book of Thomas the Contender,* probably written in the second century, the Saviour tells Thomas, "He who has not known himself has known nothing, but he who has known himself has at the same time already achieved knowledge about the depth of the all."[11] In other words, when you become one with (know) the God within, you will have become one with all that is.

Until you do this, you will continue to "taste death"—to partake of mortal life, to die and live and die again. The only way to escape the round of rebirth is to enter eternal life by achieving gnosis. This is the way to avoid tasting death.

"BECOME LIKE ME"

The Gnostics had a different view of Jesus than the Church Fathers had. They saw him as a wayshower and believed that their souls came from the same source as his. They even sought to become like him. In the *Gospel of Thomas,* Jesus says, "Whoever drinks from my mouth will become like me; I myself shall become that person, and the hidden things will be revealed to that person."[12]

The Church Fathers considered these teachings blasphemous, particularly the idea that our souls came from the same source as Jesus' soul. Writing in the second century, Irenaeus said the Gnostics believe that "their souls derive from the same surroundings [as Jesus'], and therefore... are counted worthy of the same power, and return again to the same place." "Some say they are like Jesus," he fumed. "Some actually affirm that they are even stronger."[13] These arguments are echoed in the Arian controversy of the fourth century (see chapter 17).

The Gnostics found support for their beliefs in such scriptures as Galatians 2:20, where Paul says, "It is no longer I who live, but it is Christ who lives in me." The Nag Hammadi scripture the *Teachings of Silvanus* tells us that a "wise man" is one who "exists on earth" but "makes himself like God."[14]

The *Gospel of Philip* expresses elegantly the Gnostic goal of merging, or union, with the Ultimate. For the Gnostics, knowledge and wisdom lead to eternal life, while ignorance is equivalent to a state of bondage to death. *Philip* tells the seeker, "The word said, 'If you know the truth, the truth will make you free' [John 8:32]. Ignorance is a slave. Knowledge is freedom. If we know the truth, we shall find the fruits of the truth within us. If we are joined to it, it will bring our fulfillment."[15]

What emerges, then, in Gnosticism is a personal path of salvation, one that doesn't require membership in a particular church or participation in a group. It was this very personal element and lack of structure that became the undoing of the Gnostic sects. They were so diverse and loosely organized that they could not compete with the orthodox Church, which stressed an established organization based on a lineage traced back to the apostle Peter.

In the next chapter, we will look at how reincarnation helped tie the Gnostic belief system together.

CHAPTER 13

Seeking the "Things That Exist"

Watch and pray that you may not be
born in the flesh, but that you may leave
the bitter bondage of this life.
                              Book of Thomas

REINCARNATION WAS AN IMPORTANT PART OF Gnostic theology. The Gnostics claimed that Jesus had taught it both explicitly (in his private teachings to his disciples) and implicitly (in his sayings and parables).

They saw the passage about the accuser in the Sermon on the Mount as implying reincarnation. Jesus says: "Come to terms quickly with your accuser while you are on the way to court with him, or your accuser may hand you over to the judge, and the judge to the guard, and you will be thrown into prison. Truly I tell you, you will never get out until you have paid the last penny."[1]

To understand the Gnostic interpretation of this passage, we must look at the Gnostic view of creation. Some Gnostic groups, in order to explain the imperfection and evil that exist in the world, conceived of the creator of the material world not as the absolute God but as a lesser, imperfect being, who was sometimes described as ignorant or evil.

The Gnostics saw the accuser as this imperfect creator, and the judge and the guard as the archons, angels that serve the creator. The Gnostics believed that Jesus was saying that people must come to terms with this creator while they are alive. In Eastern terminology, this means that people must pay their karmic debts during life. If they don't pay these debts, the Gnostics said, then after death the creator will hand them over to the archons, who will throw them into prison—into new bodies. Gnostics and Platonists alike called the body a prison. So the Gnostics believed that Jesus was alluding to both karma and reincarnation in the Sermon on the Mount, a cornerstone of Christianity!

This interpretation comes to us from a second-century source,[2] so we know that reincarnation was present in Gnosticism then. We have no solid proof that reincarnation was a part of first-century Gnosticism. However, there is some indication that it was.

The *Gospel of Thomas,* the earliest known Christian Gnostic scripture (c. 70), does not mention reincarnation. However, it does imply the preexistence of the soul when it discusses "images." Saying 84 reads: "When you see your likeness[es], you are happy. But when you see your images that came into being before you and that neither die nor become visible, how much you will bear!"[3]

Gnosticism absorbed concepts from Platonism. And for some Platonists, images were not simple reflections, as in a mirror, but forms of people and things that are more real and true than the pale copies that exist in the visible world.

I interpret this passage to mean that the image that "came

into being before you" is your True Self (which existed before your body), the royal robe that you took off before you descended into the material world. The Gnostics taught that we are destined to merge with that Self. Therefore I believe *Thomas* is saying that when you "see" your immortal image, i.e., unite with your True Self, you will be able to "bear," or "tolerate," a state of immortal bliss.

This is as close to the idea of reincarnation as the *Gospel of Thomas* gets. But the concept appears in a later book produced by the same school, the *Book of Thomas the Contender,* probably written toward the end of the second century. In it the Saviour tells his disciple Thomas that after death those who were once believers but have remained attached to things of "transitory beauty" will be consumed "in their concern about life" and "will be *brought back to the visible realm.*" Scholar Marvin Meyer reads this as an obvious reference to reincarnation.[4]

At the end of the *Book of Thomas,* Jesus says: "Watch and pray that you may not be *born in the flesh,* but that you may leave the bitter bondage of this life."[5] In other words, pray that you are not reborn on earth but that you return to higher realms.

These references show that reincarnation was an element of second-century Gnosticism. But do they reflect an earlier tradition? The *Secret Book of John* places reincarnation at the heart of its discussion of the salvation of souls. The book was written by A.D. 185 at the latest but contains many elements of Jewish Gnosticism that are actually *older* than Christianity.

Here is *Secret John's* perspective on reincarnation: All people have drunk the water of forgetfulness and exist in a state of ignorance. Some are able to overcome ignorance through the Spirit of life that descends upon them. These souls "will be saved and will become perfect,"[6] that is, escape the round of rebirth.

John asks the Saviour what will happen to those who do not attain salvation. They are hurled down "into forgetfulness" and thrown into "prison," the code word for new bodies.[7]

The only way for these souls to escape, says the Saviour, is to emerge from forgetfulness and acquire knowledge. A soul in this situation can do so by finding a teacher or saviour who has the strength to lead her home. "This soul needs to follow another soul in whom the Spirit of Life dwells, because she is saved through the Spirit. Then she will never be thrust into flesh again."[8]

This passage from *Secret John* shows the importance of reincarnation in Gnostic theology. If the passages on reincarnation stem from Jewish Gnosticism, this could show that reincarnation was a part of early Jewish mysticism. As a Jewish mystic, Jesus would have been familiar with it and may have incorporated it into his secret teaching.

HELL ON EARTH

The Gnostics used the concept of reincarnation to explain pain, suffering and the inequities of life. The Christian philosopher Basilides, who taught in the early second century and probably before, said that reincarnation explains why seemingly innocent people suffer martyrdom.

Basilides believed that martyrs "must have committed sins other than what they realize, and so have been brought to this good end."[9] (Although today martyrdom may not seem a good end, early Christians saw it as an honor.) Basilides taught that the soul of a martyr was undergoing punishment for sins committed in a previous life.[10]

Another Gnostic text, *Pistis Sophia,* outlines an elaborate system of reward and punishment that includes reincarnation. The text explains differences in fate as the effects of past-life actions. A "man who curses" is given a body that will be continually "troubled in heart." A "man who slanders" receives a body that will be "oppressed." A thief receives a "lame, crooked and blind body." A "proud" and "scornful" man receives "a lame and ugly body" that "everyone continually despises."[11] (While these punishments may seem overly harsh to us, they probably appeared reasonable to readers in the ancient world.) Thus earth, as well as hell, becomes the place of punishment.

According to *Pistis Sophia,* some souls do experience hell as a shadowy place of torture where they go after death. But after passing through this hell, the souls return for further experiences on earth. Only a few extremely wicked souls are not allowed to reincarnate. These are cast into "outer darkness" until the time when they are destined to be "destroyed and dissolved."[12]

But Gnosticism does not emphasize the idea of eternal punishment as much as Christianity does. Although the Gnostics believed some souls can be lost, the goal is always progress. The series of reincarnations is meant to be consummated by a final lifetime in which union with God is achieved.

THE PROGRESS TOWARD GOD

Several Gnostic texts combine the ideas of reincarnation and union with God. The *Apocalypse of Paul,* a second-century text, describes the *Merkabah*-style ascent of the apostle Paul as well as the reincarnation of a soul who was not ready for such an ascent. It shows how both reincarnation and ascents fit into Gnostic theology.

As Paul passes through the fourth heaven, he sees a soul being punished for murder. This soul is being whipped by angels who have brought her "out of the land of the dead" (earth). The soul calls three witnesses, who charge her with murder. The soul then looks down "in sorrow" and is "cast down" into a body that has been prepared for her.[13] The text goes on to describe

Paul's further journey through the heavens, a practice run for divine union.

Pistis Sophia combines the ideas of reincarnation and divine union in a passage that begins with the question: What happens to "a man who hath committed no sin, but done good persistently, but hath not found the mysteries"?[14] This sounds like the question we asked at the beginning of this book: "What happens to someone who dies neither good enough for heaven nor bad enough for hell?"

The Gnostics believed that the souls of sinners are given a "cup of forgetfulness" before they are reborn so that they do not remember either their divine origin or their past lives. But *Pistis Sophia* tells us that the soul of the good man who has not found the mysteries will receive "a cup filled with thoughts and wisdom." This will allow the soul to remember her divine origin and so to pursue the "mysteries of the Light" until she finds them and is able to "inherit the Light for ever."[15] To "inherit the Light forever" is a code for union with God.

Another Gnostic text, *Zostrianos*, gives us further clues about the process of inheriting the Light and escaping the round of rebirth. It divides souls into two categories—those who are attracted to "mortal things" and those who seek the "things that exist." What are "things that exist"? They are spiritual things—"the immortal intellect and the immortal soul,"[16] says *Zostrianos*.

Like Philo, then, the Gnostics are telling us that in order to escape the round of rebirth we must change our values and seek spiritual things. *Zostrianos* tells us that the soul who finds the things that exist is the soul who "experiences within itself a discovery of truth."[17] Thus, seeking the things that exist means contacting the God within.

This change of values could be called a spiritual awakening. It happens as the soul realizes her divine origin and, says

Zostrianos, begins "once more to dwell within." It is only then that she is able to realize that she possesses "immortal eternal power." When the soul lives in oneness with the God within, she is always conscious of the things which truly exist. Thus she gravitates toward the realm of Spirit when next she exits the body. The text refers to this person as one who "becomes god and has withdrawn into god."[18]

Seeking the "things that exist" will become a theme as we take a closer look at the goals of the Gnostics. We will realize that the spiritual awakening to the divine origin is the first step to becoming God. And we will ask how this awakening compares with the Christian beliefs in resurrection, eternal life and the kingdom of God.

❧

CHAPTER 14

Does Resurrection Rule Out Reincarnation?

*People who say they will first die
and then arise are mistaken. If they
do not first receive resurrection while
they are alive, once they have died
they will receive nothing.*

Gospel of Philip

IT WAS A STRANGE DAY AT THE BILLIKAN BITSIES cereal manufacturing plant. Although Archangel Gabriel had blown the Last Trump at 7:01 a.m., announcing the end of the world, Horatio J. Billikan came in to work as usual. "It gives me a chance to straighten out my personal correspondence without interruptions," he said. Things were proceeding smoothly until his father, looking just as he did when he died, but healthier, walked in the door, demanding to know why the factory was shut down.

Father and son argued about who was in charge until Grandfather Billikan walked in the door, fresh from the twenty-mile walk from the graveyard, and demanded to take over as manager. The discussion came to a halt when they realized that none of them had any appetite and that in the hereafter no one would be interested in eating Billikan Bitsies.

This scene comes from "The Last Trump," Isaac Asimov's acid caricature of bodily resurrection. In his story, babies come back from the dead—babies who will never eat and never grow. Thousands of people rise up naked from their tombs and begin wandering home. Cars and televisions no longer work and animals disappear. Clothing and houses begin to disintegrate, the ground turns gray and the sky a cloudy white. As life settles down to a boring monochrome, people begin to realize that eternity is pretty depressing.

Richard Levine, a history professor, gloomily watches naked women walk down the street, lamenting that his earthly passions are gone. With no eating, drinking, travel, commerce or sex, all that remains is "ourselves and thought," observes Levine. "We have been judged, and condemned, too," he concludes, "and this is not Heaven, but hell."[1]

Asimov manages to point up some of the key difficulties in the concept of a resurrection of the body. Would we really *want* to see all of our relatives again, picking up conflicts where we left off? Would any of us be happy living forever with our current character defects? Without eating, drinking or sex, why would we want to return to physical life? And is there any point to an eternal life in which we neither grow nor change?

Of course, Christ is missing from Asimov's story. In the conventional Christian view of resurrection, Christ reigns in glory and dissolves all of the negative aspects of our humanness, making us happy. But would we really want to be changed, even in a positive direction, by a powerful outside force? Is this what eternal life means? Or is there a deeper meaning?

"FLESH AND BLOOD. . ."

Since the first century, Christians have debated the meaning of the resurrection, along with the scriptural promises of eternal life and the coming kingdom of God.

The New Testament presents conflicting views of the resurrection. It in turn reflects the variety of Jewish resurrection concepts. Some Jews believed that only righteous Israelites would resurrect. Others thought that all Israelites would resurrect but only the unrighteous would be judged. Some thought the resurrection would be on earth, others in paradise. Some thought the resurrected would have physical bodies, others that their bodies would be transformed into spiritual bodies.

Which of these views did Jesus espouse? Or did he have a different vision?

The conventional Christian view of the resurrection as a single event at the end of time derives in part from Revelation, which tells us that the dead will "stand before God" and be judged.[2] But where does this place the resurrection of the martyrs described earlier in Revelation and the resurrection of the saints described by Matthew?[3]

If the resurrection is a single event at the end of time, why were these saints and martyrs raised ahead of time? And were they in physical or spiritual bodies? Clearly, the Bible reflects several ideas about resurrection that were current in the authors' day.

I believe the general resurrection described in Revelation is meant to be taken as a symbolic, not literal, description of future events. For many years, I have taught that Revelation describes our own personal path of struggle with aspects of our psychology and karma. We are all somewhere on the journey of Revelation, even experiencing different elements of it simultaneously.

I can understand how the literal interpretation of the resurrection could have arisen out of the passages in Revelation. But

When the last trump sounds, will everyone awaken from the sleep of death, bodies miraculously recomposed? The concept of a bodily resurrection, as illustrated in this detail from a medieval book of Psalms, was more popular in medieval times than today. A resurrection of the flesh would rule out reincarnation. But an alternate view, held by Gnostics and other mystical Christians, is that the resurrection is a present spiritual awakening of the soul.

I think that it does not fit with what we know of Jesus' message nor with the spiritual interpretation of the resurrection, which we will review in the next chapter. This spiritual view was held by some Jewish mystics and Gnostics. They saw the resurrection as a spiritual awakening that occurs during life on earth. But this view is also present in the Bible—if you know where and how to look.

The Church has chosen to adopt the literal interpretation of the resurrection. It has concluded that resurrection means that all people will rise up from the dead at some point in the future. Only then can they live in the kingdom and experience eternal life. After death, souls will wait for this event either in heaven, hell or purgatory. But the fate of the souls after resurrection will have already been ordained by their conduct on earth. The

souls of the righteous will reunite with their bodies to live forever in the kingdom, while the souls of the wicked will also be
reunited with their bodies to feel eternal pain in hell.

By definition, a bodily resurrection rules out reincarnation.
But the spiritual view of the resurrection does not conflict with
reincarnation. The Jewish mystics and some Christians, including the Gnostics, believed that the resurrection, eternal life and
the kingdom were not only future events but could also be
experienced while on earth. People who were able to tap into
the stream of eternal life by experiencing the resurrection *now*
would escape from mortal life *after* death.

Early Christian theologian Origen of Alexandria suggested
a modified version of this idea. He believed that there will be
two resurrections, one at the end of time and another of the
"spirit, will and faith" that can happen during life.[4] Origen also
thought that the resurrection body will be a spiritual one, unrelated to the mortal body.[5]

Before we further examine this spiritual view of the resurrection, I will review four major difficulties with the Christian
doctrine of a bodily resurrection and show why I believe it is
inconsistent with Jesus' message.

First, many people find the idea of a bodily resurrection at
the end of time absurd and difficult to accept.

Second, it robs us of a personal path of salvation. If, as
many Christians believe, all we have to do is accept Jesus Christ
as our Lord and Saviour and be baptized in order to achieve
salvation after our bodily resurrection, then where do personal
striving and responsibility for our actions come in?

Third, it reinforces Christianity's one-shot theology: either
you achieve eternal life through the resurrection or you don't
achieve it. If you don't, you are on the outside forever, eternally
damned.

Fourth, the resurrection may be on shaky ground historically.

The Church tells us that Jesus' bodily resurrection is the precursor to the resurrection of all people. But many scholars today believe that the accounts of Jesus physically rising from the dead do not go back to the historical Jesus.

Let's take up these problems one by one.

"THE FACT IS CERTAIN, BECAUSE IT IS IMPOSSIBLE"

The resurrection of the flesh was not a foregone conclusion in the early days of Christianity. But it remains, in a modified form, a fundamental tenet of both Protestant and Catholic Christianity today. Both accept the Apostles' Creed, which states: "I believe in... the resurrection of the body." No matter how difficult it is to accept a bodily resurrection, you can't get away from it without exiting orthodox Western Christianity altogether.

Even though Paul had explained that the resurrection body was a "spiritual body" and that "flesh and blood" could not "inherit the kingdom of God,"[6] most early Fathers insisted that the resurrection was of the flesh. Church Father Jerome declared that the resurrection body would include flesh, blood, bones and genital organs.[7]

Tertullian defended the idea that Jesus had resurrected in the body by saying, "The fact is certain, because it is impossible."[8] Presumably this would also have been his explanation for how bodies that had decayed or turned to dust or even the bodies of those who had been tortured or mutilated would be reassembled: "The fact is certain, because it is impossible."

The orthodox used the text "With God all things are possible"[9] to explain away the illogicalities of a bodily resurrection. But Origen traced the belief to "poverty of intellect" or "a lack of instruction." Calling it an "exceedingly low and mean idea,"[10] he said that speculations about it contradicted Paul, who says that the risen body is spiritual. Origen thought that the doctrine of a bodily resurrection was for the "simple-minded" and the "common crowd who are led on to live better lives by their belief."[11]

Nevertheless, the idea of the resurrection of the flesh continues today. Christian writer Grant R. Jeffrey offers a modern version: "We can safely trust that the God of creation knows the location of every atom of our bodies and He will resurrect and transform them at the last day."[12] (Given the increasing frequency of organ transplants and skin grafts, this could get quite complicated.)

The idea of resurrection of the flesh has given rise to elaborate visions of the afterlife that sound more like life on earth than in heaven. Some fundamentalist Christians tell us that in our resurrection bodies we will be able to eat or drink whatever we want. They use as proof Luke and John's account of how after his resurrection, Jesus ate fish and honeycomb and invited the disciples to touch him, demonstrating that his body was corporeal.[13]

But when Jesus promised the kingdom of God, didn't he have in mind something more than an in club where the lifetime membership reward is the chance to eat turkey and gravy again with our friends and relatives? (The idea of eating in heaven made Origen ask whether we would need to eliminate there as well.[14])

The bodily resurrection *is* a difficult concept to explain, which is probably why the Catholic Church tells those who ask how it occurs that the answer "exceeds our imagination and understanding; it is accessible only to faith."[15]

The Church's explanation raises more questions than it answers. Interpreting the Apostles' Creed in the 1994 catechism, the Church says the meaning of the "resurrection of the body" is "not only that the immortal soul will live on after death, but that even our 'mortal body' will come to life again."[16] The Church insists it is our *mortal* body that rises, calling it a "truth revealed by God... that all men will arise with the same bodies they now have."[17] However, the Church also says this mortal body will be changed into a "spiritual body," as Paul promised.

Most Protestant denominations have settled on a resurrected body somewhere between physical and spiritual. This body will be like Christ's resurrection body. Within Protestantism, the more liberal view is that the resurrection body will be spiritual, identical with the earthly body only in the sense that it is recognizable as the deceased person. But conservatives still call the resurrection body one of flesh, guaranteed to us by Jesus' resurrection in the flesh, as described in Luke.

However, many people today are troubled by this interpretation and can no longer accept it. In the next chapter, we will examine the alternate early Christian view of the resurrection as a spiritual awakening unrelated to the flesh or to the end of time.

A MAGICAL TRANSFORMATION?

Besides being absurd, a bodily resurrection implies that the baptized, whether they are ready for heaven or not, are magically transformed after death. All of their human flaws are removed involuntarily. This means that we would see Asimov's Horatio Billikan, his father and grandfather instantly become as mild as lambs. The three would live in peace, giving up their attempts to control each other.

One passage from Paul has fueled the idea of a miraculous transformation and led to the popular idea of the Rapture. He writes: "We will not all die, but we will all be changed, in a moment, in the twinkling of an eye, at the last trumpet. For... the dead will be raised imperishable, and we will be changed. For this perishable body must put on imperishability, and this mortal body must put on immortality."[18]

For centuries, Christians have interpreted this passage as simply describing the resurrection. A current interpretation, however, is that it describes the Rapture—a moment when all Christians will be transported to heaven without having to die. Many people believe it will happen soon and that they will experience it.

But when Paul says that we will not all die, he doesn't necessarily mean physical death. And when he says we will be changed in the twinkling of an eye, he does not necessarily mean that God will solve all of our problems and instantly make us immortal. Paul has a different view of the resurrection, as we will see in the next chapter.

Still, both Catholic and Protestant theologians insist that the resurrection includes a miraculous transformation. In heaven, says Catholic scholar John Hardon, all sadness, regret, envy and the spirit of competition will be eradicated. In addition, babies who died will have a second chance to grow up—maturing in heaven. God will endow their minds "with what is wanting," writes Hardon.[19]

In Grant Jeffrey's post-resurrection world, described in his book *Heaven...the Last Frontier,* we will retain our earthly character but with all the flaws removed.[20] He tells us that marriage relationships will continue, asexually, in heaven. Thus whatever marital problems existed—spousal abuse, infidelity, et cetera—will be resolved instantaneously once the threshold of death has been crossed. (Jeffrey doesn't take up the issue of multiple marriages.)

If God solves everything in heaven, when do we reap what we have sown on earth? If we advance to the kingdom without passing first grade down here, does personal striving make any sense? Reincarnation seems more equitable than the resurrection for people who die before they are ready for heaven.

Leslie Weatherhead, pastor of City Temple in London from 1936 until 1960, reaches a similar conclusion. He writes: "Can we really skip the tests of life in the flesh on earth and pass on to the higher forms [grades] in God's school for the soul?"[21] Weatherhead believes that reincarnation is a part of God's plan and that souls who don't pass their earthly tests cannot be admitted to higher levels of existence until they reincarnate to "take some of the exams again."[22]

We might ultimately come to resent a God who removed every vestige of our humanness and made us "perfect" without any effort on our part. This vision of the afterlife does not fit in with all of the biblical statements that imply free will, as we will see when we look more deeply into the ideas of Origen of Alexandria.

AN EXCLUSIVE CLUB

The third difficulty with the Christian resurrection belief is that it tells us that we have only one shot at life. If we blow it—let's say we hear the Christian message but fail to accept it—then we can never be saved. This idea occasioned much glee among some early Christians. Tertullian looked forward to the "joy" of watching the suffering of the damned.[23]

The Church has relaxed its stance on unbelievers somewhat. It now tells us that God's plan for salvation extends to all, even Jews and Muslims. Yet it contradictorily affirms that those who know about the Church but do not enter through baptism cannot be saved.[24]

Evangelical churches are even less merciful about what happens after resurrection. In the words of Robert Lightner, professor of systematic theology at Dallas Theological Seminary, "Those who reject the Lord Jesus Christ as their personal Savior will go to a place of eternal torment that the Bible calls the 'lake of fire.'"[25]

Today, many liberal denominations have backed away from

the traditional heaven-hell-judgment resurrection scenario. But the more conservative, exclusivist view of the afterlife (Christians only; everyone else goes to the basement) has driven many people away from Christianity.

It reminds me of the story about the Eskimo hunter and the missionary priest. The Eskimo asks the priest, "If I did not know about God and sin, would I go to hell?"

"No," says the priest, "not if you didn't know."

"Then why," asks the Eskimo earnestly, "did you tell me?"

Despite the difficulties the doctrine creates, the Church still considers the bodily resurrection a fundamental tenet of the faith. Why? Perhaps because it cements the Church's authority as the gatekeeper to eternal life or eternal damnation. According to their definition, you cannot enjoy eternal life unless you first live and die a good Christian.

Beginning in the fourth century, the Church sought to solidify its position by developing the doctrine that God creates body and soul together as a unit. This doctrine supports the idea of a bodily resurrection and rules out reincarnation by asserting that the soul is inextricably tied to one and only one body. But, as we will see in chapter 17, this was not an original part of the Christian faith.

"CHRIST AROSE..."

The last problem with the Church's doctrine of the resurrection is the growing skepticism about Christ's own resurrection. Christian ideas about the resurrection are tightly linked with the belief that Jesus rose bodily from the grave. His experience is said to be proof that we, too, will live again. It is the precursor of what will happen to the whole world at the end of time.

But what if Jesus didn't actually rise from the dead in his physical body? Does that negate the whole of Christianity?

Today, many scholars believe that the scriptural passages about Jesus rising bodily from the dead are not based on eyewitness accounts.[26] Paul, who wrote the earliest testimony of Christ's resurrection, does not mention Jesus being in a body but rather says he "appeared" to the apostles, presumably in a spiritual body.[27]

The scholars believe that the stories about Jesus acting in the material world—eating fish and honeycomb and inviting the disciples to touch him—did not occur. They may have been added later to bolster faith in a bodily resurrection. Mark, the earliest Gospel, simply tells us that Jesus "appeared" to the disciples and Mary Magdalene after his resurrection.[28] He doesn't mention Jesus doing anything that would have required a physical body.

I will not draw any conclusions here about the issue. If Jesus did not resurrect physically, he may have appeared to his disciples in his spiritual body after his crucifixion. Or, as some have suggested, he may have appeared physically, not having died on the cross at all.[29]

But even if these scholars are correct, their conclusions do not undermine our faith. Christianity doesn't have to rest on whether or not Jesus rose bodily from the grave. The faith can still go on without a flesh-and-blood resurrection.

As we will see when we look more closely at the scriptures, a resurrection of the flesh at the end of time is probably the opposite of what Jesus really taught. To discover the heart of his message we have to look at the full range of Jesus' statements about death, eternal life and the kingdom.

Our quest will lead us to new hope, not just the hope of being reincarnated after death, but hope for a spiritual resurrection, an entirely new state of existence that we can experience while we are alive on earth.

CHAPTER 15

A Spiritual Resurrection

> *Neither are the good good, nor the evil evil,*
> *nor is life life, nor death death.... Thus one*
> *who hears the word 'God' does not perceive*
> *what is correct.... So also with... 'life'*
> *and 'light' and 'resurrection'.*
>
> Gospel of Philip

FROM COMPUTER NERDS TO SURFERS, EVERY group has a lingo. If you understand it, you know what they mean. If you don't, you might think they're talking about riding a wave when they're really looking for information.

The Gnostic Christians had their own lingo—a kind of insider talk they said Paul and even Jesus had used. For them, the resurrection was not a one-time physical occurrence. In fact, they referred to the idea that God would all at once reanimate the corpses of believers as the "faith of fools."[1]

For the Gnostics, resurrection was a spiritual event—simply the awakening of the soul. They believed that people who experience the resurrection can experience eternal life, or union with God, while on earth and then after death, escape rebirth. People who don't experience the resurrection and union with God on earth will reincarnate.

The Gnostics had their own interpretations for the passages in Paul that seemed to imply a bodily resurrection. Paul taught on two levels, they claimed—one for the *psychics,* those who existed at the level of material things, and another for the *pneumatics,* those who were "spirit-endowed" and thus able to comprehend the wisdom of God.

The Gnostics considered themselves to be pneumatics and the larger body of Christians to be psychics. They believed that only pneumatics could understand the higher level of Paul's teaching. But this did not forever exclude the psychics. By undergoing a spiritual awakening, they could become pneumatics and thus understand the mysteries.[2]

Looking for hidden levels of meaning in scripture was common in the Greco-Roman world. The rabbis interpreted the Torah on four levels, Philo of Alexandria saw allegory in the Old Testament stories, and Origen of Alexandria said the scriptures "have two senses," a literal meaning and a hidden meaning.[3]

THE MEANING OF LIFE AND DEATH

What did Jesus, Paul and the authors of the Epistles[4] really mean when they talked about the dead being raised "imperishable" and the righteous being granted "eternal life"? The simple answer may not be the correct answer. For in the Bible, there is more than one meaning of both *life* and *death.*

This is apparent in the Old Testament, as Philo pointed out. There are two meanings of death in the story of the Garden of Eden. God tells Adam and Eve not to eat a particular fruit. For "in the day that you eat of it [the fruit], you shall die."[5] Adam and Eve eat the fruit but do not die immediately. They go on living and even bear children.

Philo explains that there are two forms of death, one of the body and the other of the soul. He concludes that it was soul death that Adam and Eve experienced after they ate the apple. This death occurs, says Philo, when the soul is "made subject" to the body and lives in the body "as if in a tomb."[6] This is not a final death but rather a state of soul bondage.

The Epistle to the Colossians also uses the term *dead* in the sense of soul bondage when it tells believers "you were dead in trespasses" until God "made you alive."[7] This concept of death may shed light on Jesus' promise to Martha: "I am the resurrection and the life. Those who believe in me, even though they die, will live, and everyone who lives and believes in me will never die."[8] Many Christians interpret this passage to mean that people who believe in Jesus will live forever in their physical bodies after a bodily resurrection. But isn't it obvious that this passage refers to something more than the reanimation of corpses?

All bodies die. So when Jesus said that those who live and believe in him "will *never* die," was he simply saying that their bodies will never die? I think he meant that their souls will never return to the state of bondage.

The Gnostics argued that those who believe in the Christ (the Word, or Logos) will be awakened to a spiritual state that transcends life on earth, a higher level of being that makes the transition between physical life and death insignificant.

PAUL THE GNOSTIC

Paul is known as the apostle of the resurrection because he makes it the crux of his faith. Many Christians see Paul as the opponent of the Gnostics.[9] But the Gnostics actually looked to him for support of their views on the resurrection. They found in his letters evidence that he, too, saw the resurrection as a state of spiritual awakening.

Paul's letters have been a conundrum to commentators in every century, but the Gnostics may have had the key to interpreting them. After all, they were the earliest Christian theologians to comment on Paul. The orthodox left his letters alone until they realized that they disliked the Gnostics' conclusions. And so the earliest orthodox interpretations of Paul actually arose in criticism of the Gnostics.

The Gnostics claimed that their terminology was sprinkled throughout the Epistles. For example, the author of Ephesians uses the words *awake, sleep* and *dead* in a Gnostic sense: "Awake, thou that sleepest, and arise from the dead, and Christ shall give thee light."[10] The Gnostics believed that the psychics (unawakened souls) were asleep and needed to be awakened to their divine nature. By equating the concept of awakening from sleep with rising from the dead, Ephesians bolsters the Gnostic contention that resurrection is a spiritual and not a physical rebirth.

The idea that resurrection has something to do with awakening is certainly plausible. Some of the Greek words in the New Testament translated as "resurrection" also mean to "rise" or "awake." Therefore, argued the Gnostics, when Paul says people can be part of the resurrection, he is really saying that their souls can be awakened to their divine nature.

Resurrection—Now

We know that in some passages Paul writes about the resurrection as a present rather than a future event. In Romans, Paul says that all Christians who have been baptized have been "buried with him [Christ]." Thus baptism is a symbolic death.

Paul then promises that Christians will be raised through a "resurrection like his [Christ's]." But Paul does not put this resurrection in the future. He tells Christians that they are *already* "alive," i.e., resurrected: "So you also must consider yourselves dead to sin and alive to God in Christ Jesus."[11]

The literal interpretation of this passage is that baptism ensures that Christ will restore the believers to physical life after their physical death. But the Gnostics rejected that idea. Instead, as Elaine Pagels explains in her book *The Gnostic Paul*, "They claim that... Paul is not speaking here literally of a future bodily resurrection: instead he is speaking symbolically of the process of receiving gnosis."[12]

Colossians also seems to describe the resurrection as a present-day event. The author says, "If ye then be risen with Christ, seek those things which are above.... Lie not one to another, seeing that ye *have put off* the old man with his deeds; and *have put on* the new man, which is renewed in knowledge."[13] In this passage, putting off the old man and putting on the new is a code for the resurrection, which, again, is described as a present-life event.

But is there a contradiction in the Epistles? Although these passages seem to tell us the resurrection is a spiritual awakening that can happen in one's lifetime, other passages seem to point to a future resurrection that is patterned after Jesus' resurrection. For example, 1 Corinthians says:

> Now if Christ is proclaimed as raised from the dead, how can some of you say there is no resurrection of the dead? If there is no resurrection of the dead, then Christ has not been raised; and if Christ has not been raised, then our proclamation has been in vain and your faith has been in vain.... For if the dead are not raised, then Christ has not been raised.... But in fact Christ has been raised from the dead, the first fruits of those who have died. ...For as all die in Adam, so all will be made alive in Christ. But

each in his own order: Christ the first fruits, then at his coming those who belong to Christ.[14]

This passage has stood as the cornerstone of Christian belief in bodily resurrection. To the orthodox, it simply means that the resurrection of the dead is the foundational belief for Christians and that Christ's resurrection is the precursor of our own. But if Paul really was writing in a sort of Gnostic code, it could take on an entirely different meaning.

For the Gnostics, of course, the "dead" were the psychics, and the "resurrection of the dead" meant the awakening of the psychics to their divine origin. From a Gnostic perspective, the passage could be paraphrased as:

"Now, if Christ, who was in a mortal form, is proclaimed as awakened to his divine origin, how can some of you say there is no awakening of men to their divine origin? If psychics, or unawakened souls, can't be awakened, then Christ, who was in a mortal form, couldn't have been raised, or awakened, either—in which case your faith has been in vain. But, in fact, Christ has been raised into a higher, spiritual level of existence. For as all die to the Spirit when they identify with the body (as Adam did), so all will be made alive in Christ and return to God when they remember their divine origin."

Seen through Gnostic glasses, this passage can be said to support the view of resurrection within this life. Further on in Corinthians we find another verse that lends credence to the Gnostic interpretation. Referring again to the question of whether or not there is resurrection from the dead, Paul asks why people are baptized "in behalf of the dead"[15] if the dead do not rise.

Commentators have struggled with the passage, assuming it implies that people were being baptized on behalf of departed loved ones. To the Valentinian Gnostics, however, it was simple. They actually practiced baptism on behalf of the psychics

(unawakened souls). Pagels explains that the Valentinians believed that Paul was asking "what purpose there could be in
performing such baptism for 'the dead' unless the psychics indeed *can* be 'raised from the dead.'"[16]

Another passage from Romans may seem, on the surface, to
support bodily resurrection: "If the Spirit of him who raised
Jesus from the dead dwells in you, he who raised Christ from
the dead will give life to your mortal bodies also through his
Spirit that dwells in you."[17]

But the Gnostics didn't see this as a reference to bodily resurrection. They argued that the phrase "mortal bodies" refers to
those who are spiritually dead, the psychics. To the Gnostics,
the passage meant that the psychics would be raised to the life
of the Spirit. A Gnostic rephrasing of the passage might read:
"If the same Spirit that made Jesus spiritually alive lives in your
body, it will change you from the condition of being spiritually
'dead' to being spiritually 'alive.'" Paul was not talking about
the reassembling of corpses.

The "transition into newness"

One reason the Epistles can be confusing is that they do not set
forth one clear doctrine from beginning to end. As letters to the
Christian communities of the day, they focus on the questions
at hand, dealing with doctrine in a peripheral manner. Therefore Christians through the centuries have had a hard time figuring out just what is Paul's doctrine of the resurrection.

The Gnostics, on the other hand, left several texts that spell
out their views systematically. While there is no way to prove
whether their views are the original teachings of Paul and Jesus,
they certainly make more sense of Paul than orthodoxy does.

The Gnostic manuscripts present a clear, simple and strong
vision of the resurrection. First, the *Gospel of Thomas* disabuses

people of the notion that the resurrection is a future event. Saying 51 tells us:

"His followers said to him, 'When will the rest for the dead take place, and when will the new world come?'

"He said to them, 'What you look for has come, but you do not know it.' "[18]

Thomas is saying that the resurrection and the kingdom are already here. We simply do not realize it—or, in the Gnostic sense, we simply have not integrated with them.

Another Nag Hammadi text, the *Dialogue of the Saviour*, takes up the question of what kind of bodies people will have after death. Instead of concluding, like the orthodox, that our physical bodies will return to life, it tells us that our mortal bodies are impermanent and will not last. "Not with these transitory garments are you to clothe yourselves."[19]

The idea of being "clothed" and of changing clothing is a Gnostic metaphor that will help us to understand the Gnostic idea of the resurrection. Gnostic texts explain that we must go through a process of undressing, or stripping, in order to participate in the resurrection and then we must clothe ourselves in a spiritual garment—our divine identity, our royal robe. The *Dialogue of the Saviour* says, "You will become blessed when you strip yourselves!"[20] To undress or strip means to cease to identify with the mortal form. It means to disassociate, or detach, ourselves from all of the outer trappings that we use to establish our identities. This is how we achieve true life, resurrected life.

This stripping does not mean that you lose your personality or creativity, only that you stop thinking of yourself as a body with skin, eyes, teeth, hair and X number of possessions. You understand that the undying part of you is all that is really important.

The *Gospel of Philip* elaborates on the concept of stripping when it addresses the question of people who are afraid of life without a body: "They do not know that it is those who wear the flesh who are naked. It is those who. . . unclothe themselves who are not naked."[21] The text is saying that you can be clothed in your divine identity only when you cease identifying with what is mortal.

The Gnostic *Treatise on Resurrection* tells us that we must identify with the part of us that is God. In a Buddhist vein, it reminds us that mortal life is changeable, illusory and affirms that only God, the "fullness," is real.

> Everything is prone to change. The world is an illusion! . . .
>
> But the resurrection does not have this aforesaid character, for it is the truth which stands firm. It is the revelation of what is, and the transformation of things, and a transition into newness. For imperishability descends upon the perishable; the light flows down upon the darkness, swallowing it up.[22]

By saying that in the resurrection "imperishability" will descend "upon the perishable," the author is echoing Paul's statement: "For this perishable body must put on imperishability, and this mortal body must put on immortality."[23] From that same verse in Corinthians, the orthodox developed the absurd belief that at some distant point in the future the mortal body would be reassembled and returned to life.

But to the Gnostics, the concept of putting on imperishability meant that those who were able to experience the resurrection would enter a different state of existence, one characterized by light rather than darkness. The resurrection is "the revelation of what is, and the transformation of things, and a transition into newness."

What a beautiful concept!

In my understanding, the resurrection is a spiritual awakening that begins the process of union with God. It is an infiring and an impelling. It is when the flame in your heart has been fanned to such an extent that you are no longer comfortable identifying with impermanent things. It happens when your soul decides that her goal is divine union and places that goal before any other. When you have experienced the resurrection, you have both the vision of what is attainable and the commitment to achieve it.

The resurrection is not the final goal but an important step on the way to immortality. The next step is to pursue divine union—described in both Gnosticism and Jewish mysticism as a process of putting on a spiritual garment or of ascending to heaven. We will explore both concepts further in Part 5 as we delve more deeply into Jewish mysticism.

The Gnostics believed that the ascent to heaven was meant to follow the resurrection. The *Treatise on Resurrection* tells us, as Paul does, that we are meant to die and rise with Christ. But it adds the idea that we are also meant to ascend with the Saviour: "So then, as the apostle said of him, we have suffered with him, and arisen with him, *and ascended with him.*"[24]

In other words, once we have "risen"—i.e., experienced the resurrection—we can begin the process of ascent to divine union. This is not a physical journey into the clouds but rather an identification with the Christ, or Logos, the part of God that mediates between the Absolute and the world of form. We will talk more about this later as we further explore Jesus' secret teachings.

❦

CHAPTER 16

The Different Fates of Twins

His work is perfect,
for all his ways are Equity.
A God faithful, without unfairness,
Uprightness itself and Justice.

Deuteronomy 32:4

TWINS. GOD LOVED ONE AND HATED THE OTHER. Why?

The twins were Jacob and Esau, grandsons of Abraham. The question of why God treated them differently preoccupied the apostle Paul, Church Father Origen of Alexandria, rabbis who wrote commentaries on Genesis and, later, Saint Augustine.

This question is similar to one that has arisen in the minds of Christians for twenty centuries: Why are people born different?

This question has always been at the heart of the reincarnation debate—in the second century as well as today. The question led some early Christians to the belief in reincarnation. In effect, the Church sidestepped the issue when it said we live only once. But the question won't go away. It is as vital today as when it was first asked.

According to Genesis, Jacob and Esau (sons of Isaac and Rebekah) had different destinies from birth. While the boys were still in her womb, God told Rebekah that "the one shall be stronger than the other, the elder shall serve the younger."[1]

In the well-known story, the twins' animosity predated their birth—they were struggling in the womb. Esau, red and hairy, was born first, and Jacob followed, gripping Esau's heel.

It certainly seemed that God loved Jacob more. Jacob got both Esau's birthright and his paternal blessing, although he resorted to trickery for both. By putting on goatskins to make his hands feel hairy like Esau's, Jacob convinced the nearly blind Isaac that he was Esau and so got his brother's blessing.[2] Jacob was favored with twelve sons, who fathered the twelve tribes of Israel. But Esau, the Bible tells us, was the ancestor of the hated Edomites, who were later conquered by David.

"I loved Jacob, and I hated Esau,"[3] said God, according to the prophet Malachi (c. fifth century B.C.). Whether or not God actually hated Esau, Jacob was clearly the favored son. This story led people to ask: Was God unjust? Did he arbitrarily decide to love Jacob and hate Esau? Or had Jacob and Esau committed acts that made God choose one over the other?

Early rabbis came to an unusual conclusion. Since scripture said the twins' destinies were different from birth and since God was clearly just, they thought the only possible answer was that Esau had sinned in the womb. Strange as it sounds, that is just the speculation we find in a commentary on Genesis written around A.D. 400. The rabbis conjectured that as Rebekah walked past "houses of idolatry," Esau indicated his preference by kicking, but "when she went by synagogues and study-houses, Jacob would kick, trying to get out."[4] For these actions, the rabbis reasoned, God preferred Jacob and his seed over Esau and his seed for generation after generation.

This explanation seems far-fetched at best. Does it imply that all differences in people's lots should be attributed to their actions in the womb? But short of Esau's sinning in the womb, there are only two possible explanations for the story: (1) God is unjust or (2) the boys earned their fates in previous existences.

In Romans, Paul toys with the question and discards the first option. He begins by noting that when God said that the elder should serve the younger, Jacob and Esau had not even been born or "done anything good or bad." Paul asks: "Is there injustice on God's part?" and then answers himself: "By no means!"[5] But Paul does not go on to affirm preexistence. Rather, he skips the issue and discourses on God's mercy, attempting to clear God of the charge of injustice.

However, Church Father Origen of Alexandria, writing a century and a half later, took the argument to its logical conclusion. In so doing, he sowed the seeds of the Christian debate over reincarnation that lasted for the next three centuries.

He believed that the only answer to the question was that Jacob and Esau had previous existences in which to earn God's "love" and "hatred." We can believe God is just, he wrote, only if we believe that Jacob was given preference in the womb as a result of his "merits in some previous life."[6] Origen next made a theological leap that the Gnostics would have easily accepted. He said that the question surrounding Jacob and Esau could be applied to everybody.

To the age-old question of why people are different—why one person is born with good health and genius and talent and another is born deaf or dumb or blind—Origen would offer the same answer he gave about Jacob and Esau: their fates resulted from their "merits in some previous life."[7]

Origen's ideas were the linchpin of the controversy over reincarnation that lasted through the sixth century. Origen defended God's justice with the argument that our past-life actions—and not God's caprice—are the cause of our present condition. But when the Church rejected his arguments on pre-existence, it was forced to refashion its concept of God.

Since Christians could no longer say that their own past-life actions caused their different fates, they seemed to have no other choice than to blame an unjust God when they faced misfortune. But some chose to conclude that God was powerless rather than unjust. (In chapter 20 we will see how the Church tried to resolve this dilemma by defending both God's omnipotence and his justice, thereby painting itself into a corner, where it remains to this day.)

The portrait of God that evolved within the Church resembled an earthly ruler—a Roman emperor, for example—more than the Greek God, the transcendent and all-pervasive Spirit

Before Jacob and Esau were born, God told their mother, according to Genesis, that the older twin would serve the younger. Theologians have struggled with this story, trying to explain how a just God could prefer one innocent child over the other before either had committed any actions. Christian theologian Origen of Alexandria believed that God's preference was based on the twins' actions in a previous life.

residing in all creation. As the image of God changed within the Church, so did the image of man. No longer did the Church see man as made in the image of God the transcendent Spirit. Rather, man became a cringing subject of the whimsical God-emperor.

Origen's writings had touched off a debate that ultimately changed the face of God and man in the eyes of Christianity for centuries to come.

ALEXANDRIAN BEGINNINGS

Origen exerted enormous influence on the early Church. Dictating to a staff of stenographers, copyists and calligraphers provided by a wealthy patron, Origen wrote almost two thousand books. He ranks as the greatest Christian thinker of his age. One modern Christian theologian compares him to "an oak on the prairie" of the third-century Church.[8]

Despite his prominent place in the early Church, Origen fell into disfavor in the fourth and fifth centuries, in large part for his teachings on the origin and fate of the soul. Yet the Church had difficulty constructing its theology without him. Church Fathers like Jerome and Gregory of Nyssa publicly criticized Origen's radical ideas while carefully cribbing his homilies.

Origen (c. 185–c. 254) lived in Alexandria and became famous as the head of the Church's catechetical school there. He was responsible for teaching the young men and women who came to Christianity with their minds full of questions.

These students would have been intelligent people searching for sophisticated answers. After all, they lived in the cultural and scientific center of the Roman Empire, a city with the cosmopolitan air of a New York or a Paris.

On moonlit nights, the city's vast quantities of white marble created a floodlit atmosphere, turning night into day. Its broad avenues were often filled with processions from any one of ten religions. It boasted the empire's best singers and dancers, the biggest theaters, the longest racetrack and a lighthouse that was one of the Seven Wonders of the World.

Its jaded citizens were proud of their city and its luxuries. The wealthy dined on delicacies—kids of Melos, turbots of Attica and oysters of Abydos—and pampered themselves with chamber pots of silver or crystal. Its women used all the artifices of civilization—rouge, eyebrow pencil, anklets, bracelets and earrings, strategic padding to enhance their figures and platform shoes to add height.[9]

If Alexandria had the cultural sophistication of a modern city, it also had the intellectual atmosphere. Near the famous library was the Mouseion, perhaps the world's first research center, where great minds from around the Mediterranean gathered to use the library and teach small groups of students.

The stimulating atmosphere produced new discoveries in geography, mathematics, medicine and astronomy. Here Euclid wrote down his principles of geometry, Aristarchus of Samos observed that the earth traveled around the sun, and Herophilus proved that the brain and not the heart is the seat of intelligence.

Alexandria had replaced Athens as the center of philosophy. Neoplatonism, Neo-Pythagoreanism and Stoicism vied for attention. Mystery cults were prominent, with pursuit of personal immortality the foremost goal. It was in this setting that Alexandrian Christianity developed.[10] If it was to compete with pagan religion and philosophy, it had to provide some good answers to the questions of life. Origen answered them and gave Christianity a coherent voice.

He began writing in an attempt to explain the Christian faith to educated Alexandrians. One of his early converts to Christianity was Ambrosius, a wealthy Gnostic who became his patron. Ambrosius had originally rejected Christianity because, as Origen wrote, it seemed to be "an irrational and ignorant faith."[11] But Origen made sense of it.

In contrast with many of the early Church Fathers, Origen insisted on a philosophical approach to the Bible. He came to many of the same conclusions modern man has reached. It is common today to view the Creation story as allegory.

Origen also took it figuratively. He tells us that the first chapters of Genesis do not describe actual events but indicate "certain mysteries." He also tells us we can't take everything in the Gospels literally, concluding that "episodes which did not occur are inserted among those which are literally recorded."[12]

In contrast, Saints Irenaeus and Epiphanius tell us that paradise was a real place on earth with real trees and rivers.[13] And Augustine argues that the world has existed for only six thousand years.[14] Their ideas monopolized religion for more than fifteen hundred years.

Today we have restored the kind of intellectual freedom that existed in Greco-Roman times, and so we need to reexamine our theology. We may find that there is more sense in Origen than in the orthodox Fathers.

PREEXISTENCE OR REINCARNATION OR BOTH?

Since many of Origen's writings were destroyed and the rest heavily edited, scholars debate whether he actually taught reincarnation. Some say he merely taught preexistence, that the soul existed before the body. But in Origen's day, preexistence and reincarnation were inseparable.

At times Origen seems to confirm reincarnation, at other times he skirts the issue and in one case he denies it. But in order to discover what Origen really believed, we must take his single denial in the context of his other writings, the times in which he lived and his deliberate practice of secrecy. When we have examined all of these elements, it will become clear that he did secretly teach reincarnation. For Origen, reincarnation was part of the whole scheme of salvation—salvation based on individual effort, the soul's relationship to the God within, leading ultimately to union with God.

In the second and third centuries, many educated people accepted reincarnation. We know that Origen was exposed to at least five sources of reincarnation beliefs:

1. Christian and Jewish scriptures—Origen was familiar with Jewish traditions about reincarnation and divinization and at times seems to echo Philo (who taught reincarnation). Origen believed that the Jews taught reincarnation.[15]

2. The Greek classics—Plato and Pythagoras were part of Origen's education.

3. Gnosticism—Origen absorbed it from a teacher named Paul the Antiochene.

4. Neoplatonism—Origen studied under its founder, Ammonius Saccas.

5. Clement of Alexandria, a Christian teacher who headed the catechetical school before Origen—He is said to have taught reincarnation.[16]

There is a sixth possible source for Origen's belief in reincarnation. He may have accepted it because he was convinced—through studying Gnosticism, the writings of Clement or other scriptures that have since been lost—that reincarnation was part of Jesus' secret teachings.

If Origen had rejected reincarnation, he would have had to argue that position coherently for his educated audience because many of them, being Neoplatonists and Gnostics, held the belief. But there is no record of his doing this. Instead, he persistently asks whether actions in previous existences are the cause of people's present troubles.

Origen's *On First Principles* explains that souls are assigned to their "place or region or condition" based on their actions "before the present life." God has "arranged the universe on the principle of a most impartial retribution," he tells us.[17] God didn't create "from any favouritism" but gave souls bodies "according to the sin of each." Origen asks, "If souls did not preexist, why is it that we find some blind from their birth, having done no sin, while others are born having nothing wrong with them?"[18] He answers his own question: "It is clear that certain sins existed [i.e., were committed] before the souls [came into bodies], and as a result of these sins each soul receives a recompense in proportion to its deserts."[19] In other words, people's fates are based on their past actions.

These passages demonstrate that Origen taught preexistence. And they certainly imply reincarnation. As the thirteenth-century Church theologian Thomas Aquinas observed, everyone who has affirmed the preexistence of the soul has also implicitly affirmed reincarnation.[20]

By saying that our fates are the result of our previous actions, Origen is telling us that we have had some form of existence prior to our present bodies. For Origen, the obvious implication is that this previous existence was also in human form.

A STORMY SEA

The primary reason we cannot find reincarnation stated explicitly in Origen's writings is that he kept his beliefs secret for fear of reprisals from his superiors, who were already developing a theology that excluded it. When he wrote *On First Principles*, he intended to reserve it for his advanced students. But copies leaked out and embroiled him in controversy. He later compared his troubles over his doctrines to a stormy sea and became more careful with his writings.

Origen's bishop, Demetrius, was jealous of his growing prestige and nervous about his philosophical speculations. By

215, Origen had headed the catechetical school for over ten years, but Demetrius refused to let him preach in church because he was not an ordained priest. He was, however, in great demand elsewhere. On a visit to Caesarea (in Palestine), he preached at the local bishop's request. Demetrius angrily summoned him back to Alexandria. Yet his fame continued to spread across the empire, even to the imperial court. Julia Mammaea, the mother of Emperor Alexander Severus and the power behind the throne, sent for Origen and commanded him to explain Christianity to her.

Sometime around 231 Origen left Alexandria and again went to Caesarea, where the bishop ordained him without Demetrius' approval. Demetrius began a campaign against Origen on the grounds of his unauthorized ordination and questionable views. He accused Origen of having said the Devil would be saved. Demetrius gained the support of the rest of the bishops of Egypt, who rescinded Origen's ordination and excommunicated him.

Origen defended himself, pointing out that he had said only that the Devil *could* be saved. As we will see, this question about the Devil is pivotal to Origen's doctrines of free will and God's justice, which include preexistence.

After Demetrius died, Origen gained a respite. He settled in Caesarea, which had become the most prominent city in Palestine after the destruction of Jerusalem in A.D. 70. Under the protection of the Palestinian bishops, Origen finally got the respect he deserved.

The conflict between Origen and his bishop, Demetrius, represents in miniature the later conflicts between the Church and "heretics." Origen, studying Greek philosophy as well as Jewish and Christian scriptures, came in the tradition of Greek and Jewish sages—solitary, inspired teachers who took truth where they found it. The Church, as it attempted to establish a structure and consolidate its authority, could not allow such teachers to remain autonomous. Over the next centuries, as we will see, the Church severely curtailed their freedom as it codified doctrine and defined scripture, substituting order for illumination.

The attacks of Demetrius and other bishops had a chilling effect on Origen's later writings. As a refugee from Alexandria, he knew that his position in Caesarea was tenuous. In his *Commentary on John,* Origen took up the question of reincarnation but did not provide an answer, saying, "The subject of the soul is a wide one, and hard to be unravelled.... It requires, therefore, separate treatment."[21]

Although Origen did argue against reincarnation in his *Commentary on Matthew,* which he wrote when he was over sixty years old (c. 246–48), the context leads us to ask if he might have been denying it in an attempt to mislead his enemies.[22] For Origen, like the Gnostics and the Greek mystery initiates, practiced secrecy.

ORIGEN'S SECRET TEACHING

Clement, Origen's predecessor at the catechetical school in Alexandria, claimed to possess a secret tradition handed down from Peter, James, John and Paul, which was meant to be reserved for the select few who could understand it. Clement said that the hidden mysteries that Christ revealed to the apostles were different from the teaching given to ordinary Christians.

Origen also had a secret teaching. Unlike Clement, he did not claim that it had been passed down from the apostles but said that it was embedded in the scriptures. He claimed to have the inspiration, knowledge and grace to uncover it.

But that doesn't mean he revealed it to everyone. Origen tells us that the man who finds the hidden meaning of the scriptures

Origen of Alexandria was a third-century Church Father who taught both reincarnation and the soul's opportunity to become one with God through mystical contemplation. Origen was a respected Christian teacher during his life and was tortured by the pagan Romans for his faith. But his works fell into disfavor with the Church in the fifth and sixth centuries. Although several Church councils condemned Origen's writings, Christians have continued reading them to the present day.

conceals it: "A man who comes to the field... finds the hidden treasure of wisdom.... And, having found it, he hides it, thinking that it is not without danger to reveal to everybody the secret meanings of the Scriptures, or the treasures of wisdom and knowledge in Christ."[23]

What was the content of this secret teaching? In *First Principles,* Origen gives us a hint. In a list of the most important doctrines necessary to learn, he includes the "question of the differences between souls and how these differences arose."[24] Scholar R. P. C. Hanson concludes that this list of doctrines clearly represents "the articles of Origen's secret teaching."[25] If Origen's secret teaching dealt with why souls are different at birth, it would be logical that it included preexistence and reincarnation.

If any doubt remains as to whether Origen taught reincarnation, we can rely on the fourth-century Church Father Jerome, who accused him of it. Jerome had access to Origen's unedited writings in Greek and said that one passage from *First Principles* "convicts" Origen "of believing in the transmigration of souls."[26]

DEFENDING GOD'S JUSTICE

If Origen did teach reincarnation, why did he think it was important? It is closely linked with two of his favorite themes: God is just, and human beings have free will. God's justice can be defended, Origen argued, only if each person "contains within himself the reasons why he has been placed in this or in that rank of life."[27] Thus, we can believe God is just only if we believe that our actions in some previous existence are the cause of our present fate. If we are unfortunate, we can either blame God or see our misfortune as the result of our own past actions —and then do something to change it.

The idea that we are responsible for our fate leads directly to the other key concept in Origen's thought: free will. It was for this idea, as much as any other, that his writings came under fire. The concept of free will made the orthodox uncomfortable because it implied that someone who had been saved could someday fall again and that a beggar or a prostitute could rise to the level of the angels.

Origen believed that God had created earth as a place for human beings to exercise free will. For Origen, there wasn't much point to a religion in which God predestined everyone, even for salvation. He wrote:

God...for the salvation of all his creatures...thus ordered all these things in such a way that no spirit or soul...might be forced against the freedom of their own wills in any direction other than that in which the motion of their own minds might lead them, and thus the faculty of freewill be taken away from them (which would indeed change the quality of their very nature).[28]

Church Father Jerome didn't like what Origen was implying. It turned the ladder of heaven topsy-turvy. Where was job security when angels could become devils and the devil an archangel? Jerome fretted that according to Origen, "We may have to fear that we who are now men may afterwards be born women, and one who is now a virgin may chance then to be a prostitute."[29]

Even though Origen's world view doesn't provide absolute security, it is actually more loving than Jerome's. Yes, it tells us that we can fall down the ladder of soul evolution, but it also tells us that we can climb back up again. As scholar G. W. Butterworth puts it, Origen placed no limit on "the power of God's love, when once the human soul had responded to its healing and uplifting influence."[30]

Reincarnation goes along with the idea that the soul, with God's help, is responsible for achieving salvation. It provides the repeated opportunity, lifetime after lifetime, for the soul to "work out" her own salvation.[31]

The conflict between a budding orthodoxy on the one side and the Neoplatonists, mystery adherents, Gnostics and Origenists on the other is the perennial conflict between those who want a lockstep, guaranteed path to salvation and those who see religion as an individualized, unpredictable path.

Origen believed that free will is implied throughout scripture and that free will in turn implies reincarnation. He saw any passage affirming moral responsibility as also affirming free will. As historian Joseph W. Trigg writes, "Since [such passages] affirm moral responsibility they presume that we have within ourselves the power to do the good and to shun evil."[32]

In *First Principles,* Origen cites twelve texts to prove that people have free will. Deuteronomy 30:15, 19 says: "See, I have set before you today life and...death....Choose life so that you and your descendants may live."

If God encourages us to choose good, Origen reasoned, then we must have the freedom to choose either good or evil. If God has given us that freedom, then we advance or decline on our own merits. If we advance or decline on our own merits but are destined to return to God, then, logically, we must have more than one chance to do it.

For Origen, freedom equals opportunity. If there is only one opportunity—and that often cut short—then there is no freedom. And he believed that freedom is a part of God's plan. Hadn't Paul written, "Where the Spirit of the Lord is, there is liberty"?[33]

Origen's interpretation of the Fall in the Garden implies both free will and reincarnation. He taught that the story represents the experience of every soul. Each of us once existed in a primordial state of divine union. Then came the Fall, after which our souls were imprisoned in matter, bound to return to earth again and again, each time acting and experiencing the corresponding reaction. Thus the differences in our circumstances are not based on God's whim but on our own actions. God's creation was equal and just—in the beginning.

Origen may have been the first person to articulate the belief enshrined in the Declaration of Independence that "all men are created equal." He wrote that God "created all those whom he did create equal and alike."[34] In other words, God gave all of us the same opportunities and potential. But our own actions have caused our differences.

From his safe harbor in Caesarea, Origen preached for nearly twenty years. His popular sermons and commentaries—which highlighted the idea of the soul's union with God—were widely disseminated. Rather than rejecting him, the congregations welcomed and revered him. He became so closely associated with the Church that at about the age of sixty-eight he was arrested by the Romans at the order of Emperor Decius.

Origen dreamed of martyrdom, but he was not to receive it. Although Decius fed other Christians to the lions, he only tortured Origen. The torture must have been intense, however, for Origen died soon after his release—a martyr in spirit if not by strict definition. Little did he know that his writings would cause centuries of controversy in the Church he had given his life for —and that the Church would ultimately declare his writings heretical, curse and burn them.

In the next chapters, we will examine how Christianity changed after Origen's day and how the Church Fathers replaced his explanation for the inequities of life with one that remains entirely mystifying.

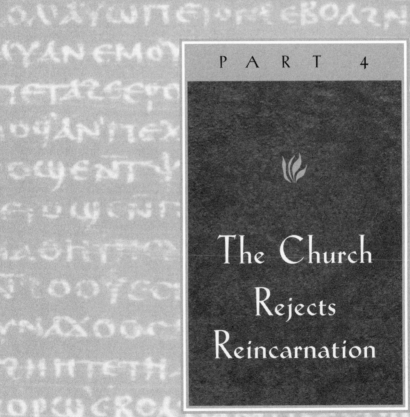

PART 4

The Church
Rejects
Reincarnation

❦

CHAPTER 17

The Mystery of God in Man

The accursed ones [the Arians] say,
"Certainly we also are able to become
sons of God, just like that one [Christ]."
> Bishop Alexander of Alexandria
> Fourth century

ONE DAY EARLY IN THE FOURTH CENTURY, while Bishop Alexander of Alexandria was expounding on the Trinity to his flock, a theological tsunami was born.

A tall, thin Libyan priest named Arius, whose long gray hair fell to his shoulders, stood up and posed the following simple question: "If the Father begat [sired] the Son, he that was begotten had a beginning of existence." In other words, if the Father is the parent of the Son, then didn't the Son have a beginning? Or, as Arius said it, "There was a time when the Son was not."[1]

Apparently, no one had put it this way before. For many bishops, Arius spoke heresy when he said that the Son had a beginning. A debate erupted, led by Arius on the one side and by Alexander and his deacon Athanasius on the other. Athanasius became the Church's lead fighter in a struggle that lasted his entire life. With his dwarflike stature and red beard, Athanasius was an almost comic counterpoint to the severe Arius, who was nearly old enough to be his grandfather.

In 320, Alexander held a council at Alexandria to condemn the errors of Arius. But this did not stop the controversy. Arius took the matter to the common people, summarizing the issues in catchy songs. His verbal tidal wave swept across the empire as the songs echoed in the streets from Alexandria to Constantinople (modern Istanbul). "There was a time when the Son was not" had a lyric quality in Greek. And soon every shopkeeper became a theologian. From money changers to bath attendants, entire cities were discussing whether the Son had a beginning.

The Church had nearly split over the issue when the controversy reached the ears of the Roman emperor Constantine. He decided to resolve it himself in a move that permanently changed the course of Christianity.

But what was the controversy all about? What did it matter if the Son had a beginning or not?

The orthodox accused the Arians of attempting to lower the Son by saying he had a beginning. But, in fact, the Arians gave him an exalted position, honoring him as "first among creatures."[2] Arius described the Son as one who became "perfect God, only begotten and unchangeable," but also argued that he had an origin. "We are persecuted," he wrote, "because we say that the Son has a beginning."[3]

If, then, the Arians were not out to attack the status of the Son, what were they after? The Arian controversy was really about the nature of man and how we are saved. It involved two pictures of Jesus Christ: Either he was a God who had always been God or he was a man who became God's Son.

If he was a man who became God's Son, then that implied that other men could also become Sons of God. This idea was unacceptable to the orthodox, hence their insistence that Jesus had always been God and was entirely different from all created beings. As we shall see, the Church's theological position was, in part, dictated by its political needs. The Arian position had the potential to erode the authority of the Church since it implied that the soul did not need the Church to achieve salvation.

BODY AND SOUL

The outcome of the Arian controversy was crucial to the Church's position on both reincarnation and the soul's opportunity to become one with God. To understand the Arian controversy, we must go back to the time when, as we learned in chapter 4, the Church decided that the human soul is not now and never has been a part of God. Instead it belongs to the material world and is separated from God by a great chasm.

Origen and his predecessor, Clement of Alexandria, lived in a Platonist world. For them it was a given that there is an invisible spiritual world which is permanent and a visible material world that is changeable. The soul belongs to the spiritual world, while the body belongs to the material world.

In the Platonists' view, the world and everything in it is not created but emanates from God, the One. Souls come from the Divine Mind, and even when they are encased in bodily form, they retain their link to the Source.

Clement tells us that man is "of celestial birth, being a plant of heavenly origin."[4] Origen taught that man, having been made after the "image and likeness of God," has "a kind of blood-relationship with God."[5]

While Clement and Origen were teaching in Alexandria,

another group of Fathers was developing a countertheology. They rejected the Greek concept of the soul in favor of a new and unheard-of idea: The soul is not a part of the spiritual world at all; but, like the body, it is part of the mutable material world.

They based their theology on the changeability of the soul. How could the soul be divine and immortal, they asked, if it is capable of changing, falling and sinning? Because it is capable of change, they reasoned, it cannot be like God, who is unchangeable.

Origen took up the problem of the soul's changeability but came up with a different solution. He suggested that the soul was created immortal and that even though it fell (for which he suggests various reasons), it still has the power to restore itself to its original state.

For him the soul is poised between Spirit and matter and can choose union with either: "The will of this soul is something intermediate between the flesh and the spirit, undoubtedly serving and obeying one of the two, whichever it has chosen to obey."[6] If the soul chooses to join with spirit, Origen wrote, "the spirit will become one with it."[7]

My definition of the soul is similar to Origen's. I describe her as the living potential of God. She is endowed with free will and can embrace the path of mortality or immortality—the low road or the high road. But whichever she chooses, the soul is definitely divine in her origin. Therefore she can choose to attain union with God on a disciplined path that leads to soul perfection.

Although the soul fell away from God through her use of free will, she can achieve immortality and freedom from the round of rebirth by reuniting with the divine spark, the essence of God within.

If God did not allow us this choice, we would be mere robots. Without free will, we could not choose to strive for union with God or celebrate when we achieve that goal.

The second-century theologian Tatian believed, with the Greeks, that the soul has the potential to become immortal. But he turned centuries of Greek thought upside down when he said that the soul and the Spirit come from different places—the soul from "beneath" and the Spirit from "above."[8] Therefore, the soul is more a part of the material world than the spiritual. And, as orthodox theologians later concluded, man cannot cross into the spiritual world without the aid of the Church.

This theology, which linked the soul with the body, led to the ruling out of preexistence. If the soul is material and not spiritual, then it cannot have existed before the body. As Gregory of Nyssa wrote: "Neither does the soul exist before the body, nor the body apart from the soul, but... there is only a single origin for both of them."[9]

When is the soul created then? The Fathers came up with an improbable answer: at the same time as the body—at conception. "God is daily making souls," wrote Church Father Jerome.[10] If souls and bodies are created at the same time, both preexistence and reincarnation are out of the question since they imply that souls exist before bodies and can be attached to different bodies in succession.

The Catholic Church still teaches that the soul is created at the same time as the body and therefore that the soul and the body are a unit.

This kind of thinking led straight to the Arian controversy. Now that the Church had denied that the soul preexists the body and that it belongs to the spiritual world, it also denied that souls, bodies and the created world emanated from God.

THE ABYSS

Rejecting the idea that the soul is immortal and spiritual, which was a part of Christian thought at the time of Clement and

Origen, the Fathers developed the concept of *creatio ex nihilo,* creation out of nothing.[11] If the soul were not a part of God, the orthodox theologians reasoned, it could not have been created out of his essence.

Therefore, they concluded, God must have created souls— along with bodies and the rest of the matter universe—out of nothing at all. As Church Father Tertullian described it, God "fashioned this whole fabric with all its equipment of elements, bodies, spirits... out of nothing, to the glory of His majesty."[12] The soul, thus constituted, has no part of God inside of her.

The doctrine persists to this day. Claude Tresmontant, a modern Catholic theologian, tells us: "According to orthodox Christian thought, the human soul is created, and is not of the divine substance."[13] The soul is therefore weak, that is, she has never had the strength to exist on her own. She is entirely de-pendent on and different from God. As the *New Catholic Ency-clopedia* tells us:

> Between Creator and creature there is the most profound dis-tinction possible. God is not part of the world. He is not just the peak of reality. *Between God and the world there is an abyss....*
>
> To be created is to be not of itself but from another. It is to be non-self-sufficient. This means that deep within itself it [the soul] is in a condition of radical need, of total dependence.... It means to accept the fact that the world has no reality except what the Creator thinks and wills.[14]

In other words, there is not, as the Platonists believed, a great chain of being linking the creation to the Creator and enabling the creation to return to the Creator. There is no divine spark inside each heart. Instead, there is an abyss between Creator and creation.

This new vision of our relationship to God is not a hopeful one. It tells us that we human beings are crouched in misery at the edge of the great abyss. We peer down into nothingness and strain to see the opposite side, where God and his Son reign eternally. Stretching across the chasm is a single arch, the Church, its approach securely gated. Some of us are admitted at the gate and are escorted to the other side. Those who try to cross on their own plunge helplessly into the chasm.

When they said that man was created out of nothing, how far orthodox theologians had strayed from the days of Clement! Clement had dignified man with the description "A noble hymn of God is man, immortal, founded upon righteousness, the oracles of truth engraved upon him."[15]

By denying man's divine origin and potential, the doctrine of creation out of nothing rules out both preexistence and reincarnation. Once the Church adopted the doctrine, it was only a matter of time before it rejected both Origenism and Arianism. In fact, the Arian controversy was only one salvo in the battle to eradicate the mystical tradition Origen represented.

THE ARIAN CONTROVERSY

Arius was born around the time of Origen's death. And he came in the same tradition of the solitary, inspired teacher, echoing Origen's ideas as well as his style. However, he could not espouse all of Origen's ideas since he was constrained to operate within the parameters of existing theology, including the doctrine of creation out of nothing.

When Arius asked whether the Son had a beginning, he was, in effect, pointing out a fundamental flaw in that doctrine. The doctrine did not clarify the nature of Christ. So he was asking: If there is an abyss between Creator and creation, where does Christ belong? Was he created out of nothing like the rest of the creatures? Or was he part of God? If so, then how and why did he take on human form?

The Church tells us that the Arian controversy was a struggle against blasphemers who said Christ was not God. But the crucial issue in the debate was: How is man saved—through emulating Jesus or through worshiping him?

The Arians claimed that Jesus *became* God's Son and thereby demonstrated a universal principle that all created beings can follow. But the orthodox said that he had *always been* God's Son, was of the same essence as God (and therefore was God) and could not be imitated by mere creatures, who lack God's essence. Salvation could come only by accessing God's grace via the Church.

The Arians believed that Jesus had been adopted as God's Son at his resurrection and that human beings could also be adopted as Sons of God by imitating Christ. They taught, as scholars Robert C. Gregg and Dennis E. Groh write in *Early Arianism,* that "Christ gains and holds his sonship in the same way as other creatures."[16] For the Arians, the incarnation of Christ was designed to show us that we can follow Jesus and become, as Paul said, "joint heirs with Christ."[17]

Origen would have agreed with the Arians' idea that the goal of the Son was to help other creatures achieve divinity. He wrote that the work of the Son was to help the creatures "to become Gods." He said that Jesus came to give people "the means by which they may be made divine."[18]

The orthodox Church, by creating a gulf between Jesus and the rest of us, denied that we could become Sons in the same way he did. Athanasius criticized the Arians, saying: "Hearing that men are called sons, they hold themselves equal to the true and natural Son....They are so arrogant as to suppose that as the Son is in the Father, and the Father in the Son, so will they be."[19] Furthermore, Athanasius saw the virgin birth as proof that Jesus was different from the rest of us. He was God's only natural Son, conceived not by a human father but by the Holy Spirit.

"This is my body..."

The reason why Athanasius had such a hard time seeing Jesus' humanity was that he could not understand how anyone could be human and divine at the same time. He saw it as an either-or equation. Either Jesus was human (and therefore changeable) or he was divine (and therefore unchangeable).

The orthodox vision of Jesus as God is based in part on a misunderstanding of the Gospel of John. John tells us: "In the beginning was the Word, and the Word was with God, and the Word was God.... All things were made by him; and without him was not any thing made that was made." Later John tells us that "the Word was made flesh and dwelt among us."[20] The orthodox concluded from these passages that Jesus Christ is God, the Word, made flesh.

What they didn't understand was that when John called Jesus "the Word," he was referring to the Greek tradition of the Logos. When John tells us that the Word created everything, he uses the Greek term for *Word—Logos*. In Greek thought, Logos describes the part of God that acts in the world. Philo called the Logos "God's Likeness, by whom the whole *kosmos* was fashioned."[21] Origen called it the soul that holds the universe together.

Philo believed that great human beings like Moses could personify the Logos. Thus, when John writes that Jesus is the Logos, he does not mean that the man Jesus has *always been* God the Logos. What John is telling us is that Jesus the man *became* the Logos.

Some early theologians believed that everyone has that opportunity. Clement tells us that each man has the "image of the Word [Logos]" within him and that it is for this reason that Genesis says that man is made "in the image and likeness of God."[22] The Logos, then, is the spark of divinity, the seed of Christ, that is within our hearts. Apparently the orthodox either rejected or ignored this tradition.

We should understand that Jesus became the Logos just as he became the Christ. But that didn't mean he was the only one who could ever do it. Jesus explained this mystery when he broke the bread at the Last Supper. He took a single loaf, symbolizing the one Logos, the one Christ, and broke it and said, "This is my body, which is broken for you."[23]

He was teaching the disciples that there is one absolute God and one Universal Christ, or Logos, but that the body of that Universal Christ can be broken and each piece will still retain all the qualities of the whole. He was telling them that the seed of Christ was within them, that he had come to quicken it and that the Christ was not diminished no matter how many times his body was broken. The smallest fragment of God, Logos, or Christ, contains the entire nature of Christ's divinity—which, to this day, he would make our own.

The orthodox misunderstood Jesus' teaching because they

"Jesus took a loaf of bread, . . . broke it, gave it to the disciples, and said, 'Take, eat; this is my body.'" What did he mean? The bread may have symbolized the body of God, the Word (or Logos), which the mystics believed was inside of each person. As a mystic, was Jesus telling his disciples to assimilate, to become one with, that particle of divinity within themselves?

were unable to accept the reality that each human being has both a human and a divine nature and the potential to become wholly divine. They didn't understand the human and the divine in Jesus and therefore they could not understand the human and the divine within themselves. Having seen the weakness of human nature, they thought they had to deny the divine nature that occasionally flashes forth even in the lowliest of human beings.

THE DIVINIZATION PROCESS

The Church did not understand (or could not admit) that Jesus came to demonstrate the process by which the human nature is transformed into the divine. But Origen had found it easy to explain.

He believed that the human and divine natures can be woven together day by day. He tells us that in Jesus "the divine and human nature began to interpenetrate in such a way that the human nature, by its communion with the divine, would itself become divine." Origen tells us that the option for the transformation of humanity into divinity is available not just for Jesus but for "all who take up in faith the life which Jesus taught."[24]

Origen did not hesitate to describe the relationship of human beings to the Son. He believed that we contain the same essence as the Father and the Son: "We, therefore, having been made according to the image, have the Son, the original, as the truth of the noble qualities that are within us. And what we are to the Son, such is the Son to the Father, who is the truth."[25] Since we have the noble qualities of the Son within us, we can undergo the process of divinization.

The Himis manuscript, which records the traditions of Jesus in India (see chapter 8), also makes this point. It tells us that Jesus came to show us "the means of self-identification with Divinity" and to "demonstrate by example how man may attain... the degree of perfection necessary to enter into the kingdom of heaven."[26] We are meant to follow in the Son's footsteps as we identify with the Father.

Origen used Jesus' statement "I and my Father are one"[27] to describe the relationship between Jesus and the Father.[28] Jesus, a human being, can tell us that he is one with the Father while in a fallible human body because he knows that there is an eternal part of himself that is always one with the Father.

His life's purpose was to teach us how each day a portion of the soul can *become* imperishable by entering into union with God. I believe that we too can say, "I and my Father are one," and reinforce this union through our works day by day. As Jesus said, "My Father worketh hitherto, and I work."[29]

To the Arians, the divinization process was essential to salvation; to the orthodox, it was heresy. In 324, the Roman emperor Constantine, who had embraced Christianity twelve years earlier, entered the Arian controversy. He wrote a letter to Arius and Bishop Alexander urging them to reconcile their differences, and he sent Bishop Hosius of Cordova to Alexandria to deliver it. But his letter could not calm the storm that raged over the nature of God—and man. Constantine realized that he would have to do more if he wanted to resolve the impasse.

CHAPTER 18

God in Man's Image

It was wrong in the first instance
to propose such questions as these,
or to reply to them when propounded.

Constantine
Letter to Alexander and Arius, c. 325

THE RULER OF THE WORLD STOOD NAKED AND dying before a Christian bishop. Constantine was emperor over some eighty million people when he took off his purple robes and prepared to receive baptism. Although he had won a major victory under the sign of the cross nearly twenty-five years earlier, he had waited until his final illness to formally join the Church.

Why the reluctance? Constantine believed that baptism granted a once-in-a-lifetime opportunity to be absolved of all sin. And he didn't want to waste it in case he sinned again before he died. As historian Michael Grant puts it: "He delayed his baptism through fear of God. Believing, as he did, in divine anger, he... was terrified about the future of his soul, which would be imperilled if, after baptism, he did anything wrong."[1]

Constantine's reluctance to be baptized reveals his theology. For him, being a Christian was more about escaping punishment for sins than about achieving union with God. This outlook may explain, in part, his position on the Arian controversy.

After baptism, feeling confident that he would now receive eternal life, Constantine put on white robes, went to a villa nearby, lay down on a couch and died. Church historian Eusebius tells us that when close to death Constantine said, "Now I feel assured that I am accounted worthy of immortality."[2]

Even though Constantine did not formally join the Church until just before his death, he exercised enormous influence over it. After winning control over the western half of the empire in 312, he embraced Christianity and refashioned it.

Christians had suffered horribly under Diocletian, the previous emperor. He had hunted them down, burned them alive and destroyed or confiscated their churches. Constantine ended the persecution of Christians and gave them back their lands. He exempted the churches from taxation and subsidized them with public money. His allowances to the clergy were so large that a succeeding emperor cut them by two-thirds.

Under Constantine, the faces of the gods were replaced by the faces of Christ and the apostles. In government, the emperor gave Christians precedence over pagans.[3] He built the Lateran Basilica in Rome as well as the original Basilica of Saint Peter. In Constantinople, his capital, he constructed several major churches, one as his mausoleum.

Constantine ruled with the iron hand of a Roman emperor, but when he touched Christianity he wore velvet gloves. Although he appointed and dominated the bishops, he treated them with respect and even thought of himself as one of them.

But did he believe in what Christianity taught? Or, as some

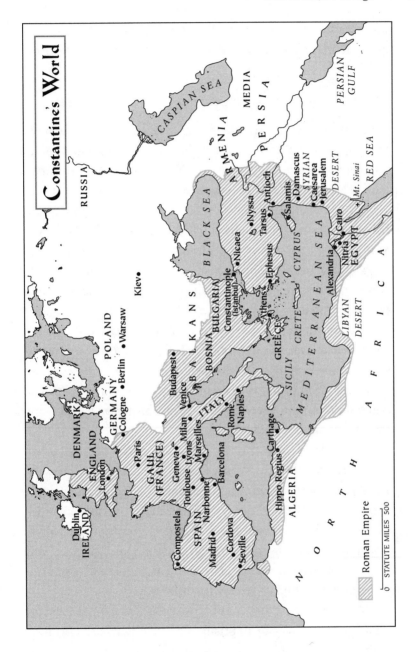

historians have concluded, did he see it simply as an instrument of political unity? The answer probably lies somewhere in between.

THE THIRTEENTH APOSTLE

Constantine saw Christianity first as a tool he could use to unify the empire he had fought for eighteen years to control. With pagan religion fragmented, it was said that there were only two unified forces in the empire—the army and the Christian Church.

But Constantine also believed in Christianity, although his belief may have been simplistic. He thought that God had given him a special mission in the Church. He took an active role, giving public sermons and ordering official celebrations of Easter. Although his sermons occasionally lacked clarity, they were the product of many hours' labor and delivered with sincerity.

Yet Constantine was far from adopting Christian standards of respect for life. Ten years after his conversion, he was still condemning criminals to be crucified. He was a ruthless ruler in the tradition of many Roman emperors, not above intrigue and murder. Grant describes him as "an absolute autocrat" who "believed that he could kill anyone."[4]

He ordered the execution of his oldest son, Crispus, over an unsubstantiated accusation of conspiracy. His second wife, Fausta, the mother of his three remaining sons, also came under suspicion, and he had her suffocated in an overheated steam room. He also executed the philosopher Sopater, one of his principal friends and advisers, on trumped-up charges. These deaths must have weighed on his mind as he took off his purple robes and prepared to receive the holy waters.

Non-Christians laughed at Christians like Constantine for inflating the power of baptism. The Neoplatonist Porphyry (c. 232–c. 303), who wrote extensively against Christianity, criticized the Christian belief that a single baptism could wash

This gigantic head once topped a statue of Constantine, the first Christian emperor of Rome. Even though the Romans deified him upon his death, as they did other Roman emperors, the Church remembers Constantine for making Christianity the Roman Empire's official religion. His influence, particularly in convening the Council of Nicaea, changed the course of Christianity.

away all prior sin. He argued that this belief only encouraged people to do wicked deeds, holding their baptism in abeyance like some kind of trump card.[5]

Constantine's behavior demonstrated Porphyry's point. The emperor committed all kinds of injustices yet waited until just before death to undergo the baptism that would absolve him of his sins. Under Constantine's kind of Christianity, people believed that they could do almost anything as long as they were reconciled with the Church afterward.

Constantine wasn't about to let his sins get in the way of his status in the Church. After he died, his body was placed in a golden coffin covered with purple and was entombed in the gold-encrusted Church of the Holy Apostles, which he had constructed as his mausoleum. Beneath the central dome of the church stood two rows of tombs, six on each side, as memorials to the apostles. To affirm his status as the thirteenth apostle, Constantine had ordered that his sarcophagus be placed in the center. Had he not done as much for the Church as they had?

Although he saw himself as an apostle, he was still made a

Roman god after death, in the tradition of Roman emperors since Augustus. Constantine's deification, like Alexander's, was based on earthly power rather than on spiritual transformation. It seems that Constantine conceived of God as being like a Roman emperor. When he changed Christian theology, he stamped it with the portrait of God in man's image.

AN "INSIGNIFICANT" CONTROVERSY

If Constantine's Christianity was as simple as it seems, it is no wonder that he completely missed the point of the Arian question. In his letter to Arius and Alexander, delivered by Bishop Hosius, Constantine betrays his childish understanding of the Christian faith. He says that after having "made a careful enquiry" into the controversy, he found the cause to be "of a truly insignificant character."

To Constantine, all the fuss was little more than hairsplitting. In his opinion, there ought to have been no argument at all. He tells Arius and Alexander, "You are in truth of one and the same judgment: you may therefore well join in communion and fellowship" and thereby rectify the "general course of affairs."

He chides them for arguing over an "unprofitable question" and says that Arius' contention "ought never to have been conceived at all, or if conceived, should have been buried in profound silence." Perhaps the disputants have too much time on their hands, he suggests. Their "contentious spirit" is "fostered by misused leisure."[6]

The letter did no good. Eusebius tells us that "in every city bishops were engaged in obstinate conflict with bishops, and people rising against people; and . . . coming into violent collision with each other." Some, writes the horrified Eusebius, were so "reckless" and "outrageous" as to "insult the statues of the emperor."[7]

Constantine had been sole ruler of the empire for barely a

few months when he took decisive action to promote unity in the Christian Church. He called a general council of the Church, inviting bishops from all over his domain and even providing transportation.

The site was Nicaea, a lakeshore town southeast of Constantinople. The council could hardly be called ecumenical. Out of eighteen hundred Christian bishops, scarcely three hundred attended, with only six from the Latin-speaking West. The bishop of Rome sent representatives since he was too old to travel the distance.

Nicaea set an important precedent. For the first time, a secular ruler was in a position to influence Christian doctrine. And the bishops had good reason to want to please their imperial patron. Some of them still bore marks of torture from Diocletian's persecution.

Nicaea

It is June 325 and the council is ready to open. The bishops are gathered expectantly, seated on benches. The emperor is preceded by three of his family members, his guards remaining outside the hall. At last he enters, the man who is referred to as sacred and divine. The bishops cannot help but be awed. He dresses like an Oriental ruler—his hair is long; his purple robe glitters with gold and precious stones. He takes his seat on a low, gold-covered chair and begins his speech.

Constantine's chief aim is clear—to see the bishops "united in a common harmony of sentiment." He calls the schism "far more evil and dangerous than any kind of war or conflict." He commands the bishops not to delay and to "begin... to discard the causes of that disunion" existing among them.[8]

Constantine then sits back and acts as moderator. The storm breaks. Both sides try to state their cases at once. Although we don't have the exact words of the debate, the following is my reconstruction of the arguments based on the records of later controversy.

We know that the central issue was whether Jesus was a creature and therefore whether he was capable of change, as we are. As we saw in the last chapter, if Jesus is considered to be part of God's creation, as the Arians argued, salvation can be achieved through becoming like him. But if he is uncreated, or equal to God, as the orthodox argued, he is totally unlike the creation. Therefore man, the creature, can only find salvation through absolute subservience to the Church and its law.

The orthodox, in order to avoid any idea of similarity between Jesus and the creation, put him far above man. This forced them to deny his humanity. But they had to stretch the scriptures to accommodate their new theology. They denied or ignored the passages that suggested Jesus had human limitations.

The Arians brought these passages to their attention. For example, they referred to the place in Mark 13 where Jesus says he doesn't know when the Second Coming of Christ will be: "About that day or hour no one knows, neither the angels in heaven, nor the Son, but only the Father."[9] Isn't it obvious from this statement, the Arians asked, that the Son is less than the Father? Athanasius and Alexander argued that Jesus did know the day and the hour; he just didn't want to tell anyone.[10]

Jesus wanted us to become like him, the Arians argued, pointing to Jesus' prayer to the Father on behalf of his disciples as recorded in John: "Holy Father, protect them in your name... so that they may be one, as we are one."[11] Jesus seems to have been implying that he wanted his disciples to become united with the Father in the same way that he and the Father "are one."

But Athanasius argued that Jesus wasn't asking God to give his disciples the same relationship he enjoyed as the Son. Rather, he was asking his Father to help his disciples to get along with

The dramatis personae of the Council of Nicaea, a watershed in Christian theology. Convened by Constantine and attended by some three hundred bishops, the council produced a confession of faith called the Nicene Creed, which says humans are separated from God by a vast gulf. In this Renaissance painting, Arius, the creed's chief opponent, stands before the pulpit while a deacon (possibly Athanasius) reads it aloud. Bishop Hosius of Cordova presides at the rear center, while Constantine observes in the foreground.

each other—to become "one" in harmony.[12] The sonship of Jesus was completely different from the sonship offered to other men, argued Alexander: "It must be seen that the sonship of our savior has no community with the sonship of the rest [of men]. ... There are no other natural sons besides himself."[13]

Athanasius went so far as to argue that just because Jesus called God "our Father," he didn't mean that God was *our* father in the same way he was Jesus' Father. "It is not necessary," he wrote, "on account of this, to equate ourselves with the Son according to nature."[14] Athanasius closed the door on our own personal Christhood when he wrote: "Neither we shall ever be as he, nor is the Word as we are."[15]

In vain, Arius and his supporters attempted to show that

Jesus was a created being like the rest of us. The Arians quoted a passage from Proverbs that they believed referred to the Son: "God *created me* in the beginning of His way."[16]

The council met for two months, with Constantine attending. He both listened to and joined in the debate, always pressing for unity. Old Hosius, bishop of Cordova, suggested that one way of resolving the difficulty might be to agree upon a creed.

The bishops modified an existing creed to fit their purposes. The creed, with some changes made at a later fourth-century council, is still given today in many churches. The Nicene Creed, as it came to be called, takes elaborate care by several redundancies to identify the Son with the Father rather than with the creation:

> We believe in one God, the Father Almighty, maker of all things visible and invisible; and in one Lord Jesus Christ, the Son of God, the only-begotten of his Father, of the substance of the Father, God of God, Light of Light, very God of very God, begotten, not made, being of one substance with the Father. By whom all things were made. . . . Who. . . was incarnate and was made man. . . . [17]

Only two bishops, along with Arius, refused to sign the creed. Constantine banished them from the empire, while the other bishops went on to celebrate their unity in a great feast at the imperial palace.

A TRULY DIVINE INJUNCTION

The creed is much more than an affirmation of Jesus' divinity. It is also an affirmation of our separation from God and Christ. It takes great pains to describe Jesus Christ as God in order to deny that he is part of God's creation. He is "begotten, not made," therefore totally separate from us, the created beings. As scholar George Leonard Prestige writes, the Nicene Creed's description of Jesus tells us "that the Son of God bears no resemblance to the...creatures."[18]

The description of Jesus as the only Son of God is carried forward in the Apostles' Creed, which is used in many Protestant churches today. It reads: "I believe in God, the Father almighty. ...I believe in Jesus Christ, his only Son, our Lord."[19] But even that language—calling Jesus God's *only* Son—denies that we can ever attain the sonship that Jesus did.

Christians may be interested to know that many scholars analyzing the Bible now believe that Jesus never claimed to be the only Son of God.[20] This was a later development based, I believe, on a misinterpretation of the Gospel of John.

As we will see in Part 5, there is further evidence to suggest that Jesus believed all people could achieve the goal of becoming Sons of God. But the churches, by retaining these creeds, remain in bondage to Constantine and his three hundred bishops.

After the council, as the bishops entered the palace for Constantine's feast, they walked between drawn swords held by cordons of the emperor's bodyguard. They lay on soft couches, feasting on tender meats and fruits. As they accepted gifts of gratitude from the emperor, did they realize that these imperial favors, together with the earthly churches Constantine would build, would stand between them and their opportunity to journey through the heavenly palaces of the indwelling God?

Some of the bishops who attended the council were uncomfortable with the council's definition of the Son and thought they might have gone too far. But the emperor, in a letter sent to the bishops who were not in attendance at Nicaea, required that they accept "this truly Divine injunction." Constantine said that since the council's decision had been "determined in the holy assemblies of the bishops," the Church officials must regard it as "indicative of the Divine will."[21]

The Roman god Constantine had spoken. Clearly, he had

concluded that the orthodox position was more conducive to a strong and unified Church than the Arian position and that it therefore must be upheld.

Constantine also took the opportunity to inaugurate the first systematic government persecution of dissident Christians. He issued an edict against "heretics," calling them "haters and enemies of truth and life, in league with destruction."

Even though he had begun his reign with an edict of religious toleration, he now forbade the heretics (mostly Arians) to assemble in any public or private place, including private homes, and ordered that they be deprived of "every gathering point for [their] superstitious meetings," including "all the houses of prayer."[22] These were to be given to the orthodox Church.

The heretical teachers were forced to flee, and many of their students were coerced back into the orthodox fold. The emperor also ordered a search for their books, which were to be confiscated and destroyed. Hiding the works of Arius carried a severe penalty—the death sentence.

Constantine knew how to get things done. As an autocratic ruler, he was thorough in his demand for unity. But he could also bend when it suited his fancy. Two or three years after this show of strength, he reinstated Arius, now nearly eighty, and allowed him to preach until his death eight years later.

Nicaea, nevertheless, marked the beginning of the end for the concepts of both preexistence and salvation through union with God in Christian doctrine. As we will see in the next chapter, it took another two hundred years for the ideas to be expunged.

But Constantine had given the Church the tools with which to do it when he molded Christianity in his own image and made Jesus the only Son of God. From now on, the Church would become representative of a capricious and autocratic God—a God who, as we will see, was not unlike Constantine and other Roman emperors.

CHAPTER 19

The Stream Goes Underground

*If anyone asserts the fabulous pre-existence
of souls, and shall assert the monstrous
restoration which follows from it:
let him be anathema.*
                                    Anathema attached to the
                        Decrees of the Fifth General Council

THE THREE HUNDRED MONKS WATCHED WITH resignation as the imperial troops tossed torches into their cells. Their only possessions of value, their books, already lay smouldering in a pile before them.

The year was 400 and the place was Egypt, which once again took center stage in the battle of ideas. Theophilus, bishop of Alexandria, had turned against the Origenist monks of the desert and stormed into their community at Nitria, south of Alexandria, backed by imperial muscle.

The leaders of the colony had already been expelled. Now the troops burned the library and the monks' cells and sent the remaining three hundred monks into exile. They were forbidden to reestablish their colony elsewhere and were forced to scatter in different directions.[1] It was time for another round in the battle against Origen and his ideas.

As we will see, the Church would condemn Origenism repeatedly between the fifth and sixth centuries. But Origen's ideas would continue to resurface until the emperor Justinian weighed in against them.

After Constantine and Nicaea, Origen's writings had continued to be popular among those seeking clarification about the nature of Christ, the destiny of the soul and the manner of the resurrection. Some of the more educated monks had taken Origen's ideas and were using them in mystical practices with the aim of becoming one with God. The Church hierarchy had tolerated these practices, and even Bishop Theophilus had sympathized with them.

But toward the end of the fourth century, orthodox theologians again began to attack Origen. Their chief areas of difficulty with Origen's thought were his teachings on the nature of God and the Christ, the resurrection and the preexistence of the soul.

Their criticisms, which were often based on ignorance and an inadequate understanding, found an audience in high places and led to the Church's rejection of Origenism and reincarnation. As we will see, the Church's need to appeal to the uneducated masses prevailed over Origen's coolheaded logic.

The confrontation in the Nitrian desert had been touched off by Epiphanius (c. 315–403), bishop of Salamis, in Cyprus. He was the chief opponent of Origenism, which he saw as the foundation of Arianism. His attack on the Origenist "heresy" was both inaccurate and inflammatory. (He also wrote some of the most virulent and inaccurate attacks that had yet been made on the Gnostics.)

In his assault on Origen, he reserved his strongest venom

for a polemic claiming that Origen denied the resurrection of the flesh. However, as scholar Jon Dechow has demonstrated, Epiphanius neither understood nor dealt with Origen's ideas. Nevertheless, he was able to convince the Church that Origen's ideas were incompatible with the emerging literalist theology. On the basis of Epiphanius' writings, Origenism would be finally condemned a century and a half later.[2]

Epiphanius was the stirring stick for a debate that extended from Palestine to Egypt to Constantinople. Jerome, a contemporary of Epiphanius, articulated many of the arguments. Jerome occasionally appeared less than saintly, calling one of his opponents Grunnius Corocotta Porcellius (Porky the Grunter).[3]

As in Origen's day, the lines were drawn between those who took scripture literally and those who saw it as allegory. Epiphanius and Jerome were literalists, like Church Fathers Irenaeus and Tertullian. Epiphanius insisted that the Creation story really happened and that Eden had a geographical location.[4] Methodius of Olympus, another anti-Origenist, believed that Eden was located near the source of the Tigris and Euphrates Rivers.[5]

Jerome believed that resurrection bodies would be flesh and blood, complete with genitals—which, however, would not be used in the hereafter. But Origenists believed the resurrection bodies would be spiritual. Origenist women confronted Jerome, tapping their breasts, bellies and thighs, and asking, "Is this poor, weak body to rise? If we are to be like the angels, we will have the nature of angels!"[6]

The Origenist controversy spread to monasteries in the Egyptian desert, especially at Nitria, home to about five thousand monks. There were two kinds of monks in Egypt—the simple and uneducated, who composed the majority, and the Origenists, an educated minority.

The controversy solidified around the question of whether God had a body that could be seen and touched. The simple monks believed that he did. But the Origenists thought that God was invisible and transcendent. The simple monks could not fathom Origen's mystical speculations on the nature of God.

In 399, Bishop Theophilus wrote a letter defending the Origenist position. At this, the simple monks flocked to Alexandria, rioting in the streets and even threatening to kill Theophilus.

The bishop quickly reversed himself, telling the monks that he could now see that God did indeed have a body: "In seeing you, I behold the face of God."[7] Theophilus' sudden switch was the catalyst for a series of events that led to the condemnation of Origen and the burning of the Nitrian monastery.

Early in 400, Theophilus called a council in Alexandria that condemned Origen's writings. In Rome the pope passed a similar condemnation and encouraged other bishops to follow his lead. Theophilus then was able to enlist the aid of imperial troops to burn the Origenists' cells and force them into exile. Seemingly, the debate over Origenism had closed, with Epiphanius, Jerome and the simple monks the victors.

However, in the fifth century Origenism continued a secret life among the monasteries of Upper Egypt. Even Theophilus kept reading Origen's works, claiming that he was capable of separating the flowers from the thorns.[8]

"Do unto others. . ."

In turning against the Origenists, Theophilus was empowered by the policies of Emperor Theodosius I. Theodosius (ruled 379–95) had been the first emperor since Constantine to vigorously enforce the decisions of the Nicene Council. He issued edicts against Arianism and other heresies.

Under Theodosius, Christians, who had been persecuted for so many years, now became the persecutors. God made in man's image proved to be an intolerant one. The orthodox Christians practiced sanctions and violence against all heretics (including Gnostics and Origenists), pagans and Jews. In this climate, it became dangerous to profess the ideas of innate divinity and the pursuit of union with God.

It may have been during the reign of Theodosius that the Nag Hammadi manuscripts were buried—perhaps by Origenist monks. For while the Origenist monks were not openly Gnostic, they would have been sympathetic to the Gnostic viewpoint and may have hidden the books after they became too hot to handle.[9]

Theodosius also issued edicts against polytheism, and Christians took this as license to attack pagans, including the adherents of mystery religions. Bishop Theophilus was now able to provoke mobs to destroy the great symbol of paganism in Alexandria, the mystery temple of the god Serapis. They hacked apart the huge statue of Serapis, which had inspired worshipers for six hundred years. The mob destroyed at least one of Alexandria's great libraries. And violence spread around the Mediterranean, where Christians destroyed pagan temples, demolishing statues and frescoes.

Bishop Theophilus was succeeded by his nephew, Bishop Cyril, patriarch of Alexandria (412–444). Cyril instigated the death of the philosopher Hypatia, a notable mathematician who headed the Neoplatonic school in Alexandria. Hypatia taught a form of mystical contemplation and pursuit of divine union derived from Plotinus. She told her students, as Plotinus had said, to "raise up the divine within you to the first-born divine."[10]

Although Hypatia was not opposed to Christianity and even included Christians among her students, she seems to have offended Bishop Cyril and so sealed her fate. He spread rumors that she was a witch who practiced black magic and cast spells upon the city's residents.[11] Incited by these rumors, a mob led by a Christian lector accosted her and dragged her to the street, where they killed her, scraped the flesh from her bones with pottery shards, then burned what was left.

Cyril also incited a Christian mob to plunder the Jewish quarter in Alexandria, bringing to an end a community that had enriched the city and its culture throughout its seven-hundred-year history.

BYZANTINE POWER PLAYS

The Origenist monks of the desert did not accept Bishop Theophilus' condemnations. They continued to practice their beliefs in Palestine into the sixth century until a series of events drove Origenism underground for good.

The renewed conflict over Origen's ideas began at Mar Saba, a monastery in the Judean desert where the *Secret Gospel of Mark* was later discovered (see chapter 12). Here the more learned monks practiced a mystical form of Origenism. Like the Origenist monks a century and a half earlier, these monks sought the rapture of divine union.

But the monk Sabas, leader of the monks of Palestine (and founder of the monastery), was a strong supporter of orthodoxy and probably didn't understand the complexities of Origenism. A group of Origenist monks, dissatisfied with Sabas, left his monastery and formed their own around 507.

When the anti-Origenists took control of the new monastery as well, several of the Origenist monks went to Constantinople, where they gained access to the emperor Justinian. For the next decade or so, Origenist and anti-Origenist factions battled for the emperor's ear.

Justinian (ruled 527–65) was the most able emperor since Constantine—and the most active in meddling with Christian theology. Justinian issued edicts that he expected the Church to rubber-stamp, appointed bishops and even imprisoned the pope.

His wife, a former courtesan named Theodora, manipulated Church affairs from behind the scenes.

After the collapse of the Roman Empire at the end of the fifth century, Constantinople remained the capital of the Eastern, or Byzantine, Empire. The story of how Origenism ultimately came to be rejected involves the kind of labyrinthine power plays that the imperial court became famous for.

Around 543, Justinian seems to have taken the side of the anti-Origenists since he issued an edict condemning ten principles of Origenism, including preexistence. It declared "anathema to Origen. . . and to whomsoever there is who thinks thus."[12] In other words, Origen and anyone who believes in these propositions would be eternally damned. A local council at Constantinople ratified the edict, which all bishops were required to sign.

Justinian was diverted for a time from enforcing the anathemas by a controversy that took up an inordinate amount of time, the matter of the Three Chapters.

But in 551, the anti-Origenist monks again succeeded in focusing Justinian's attention on their cause. The emperor wrote a letter to the bishops denouncing the Origenist monks of Palestine and attached fifteen anathemas specifically against Origen.[13]

In 553, Justinian convoked the Fifth General Council of the Church to discuss the controversy over the Three Chapters. These were writings of three theologians whose views bordered on the heretical. Justinian wanted the writings to be condemned and he expected the council to oblige him.

He had been trying to coerce the pope into agreeing with him since 545. He had essentially arrested the pope in Rome and brought him to Constantinople, where he held him for four years. When the pope escaped and later refused to attend the council, Justinian went ahead and convened it without him.

The council, which first met in May of 553, was held in the

huge Hagia Sophia, a church dedicated to Holy Wisdom. Its dome seemed to defy gravity as it floated above the incense-filled interior. Although Justinian didn't attend, he had packed the council with bishops who would vote his way.

This council produced fourteen new anathemas against the authors of the Three Chapters and other Christian theologians. The eleventh anathema included Origen's name in a list of heretics.

A list of fifteen anathemas against Origenist propositions—bearing a strong resemblance to those in Justinian's 551 letter—was later attached to the decrees of the council. These fifteen anathemas echoed Epiphanius' earlier criticism of Origen. Several of these anathemas form the foundation for the Church's rejection of reincarnation today.

The first anathema reads: "If anyone asserts the fabulous pre-existence of souls, and shall assert the monstrous restoration which follows from it: let him be anathema."[14] ("Restoration" means the return of the soul to union with God. Origenists believed that this took place through a path of reincarnation.)[15] It would seem that the death blow had been struck against Origenism and reincarnation in Christianity.

After the council, the Origenist monks were expelled from their Palestinian monastery, some bishops were deposed and once again Origen's writings were destroyed. The anti-Origenist monks had won. The emperor had come down firmly on their side.

A CRACK IN THE DOOR

Questions still remain as to whether the condemnation of the Fifth General Council was legitimate. Although the pope later approved the acts of the council, the anathemas against Origen do not appear in those acts. Thus it seems questionable whether the bishops formally accepted the anathemas. They may have been a later addition to the council's decrees.

The Catholic Encyclopedia admits that the Origen question remains open: "Were Origen and Origenism anathematized? Many learned writers believe so; an equal number deny that they were condemned; most modern authorities are either undecided or reply with reservations."[16] But this crack in the door is not wide enough to admit preexistence and reincarnation as an acceptable belief for Catholics.

The Protestant churches also reject preexistence and reincarnation, primarily on the basis of Justinian's anathemas. Martin Luther did not accept Origen, in part because he disliked Origen's practice of looking for allegory in scripture. He wrote: "In all of Origen there is not one word about Christ."[17]

In theory, it would seem that the missing papal approval of the anathemas leaves a doctrinal loophole for the belief in reincarnation among all Christians today. But since the Church accepted the anathemas in practice, the result of the council was to end belief in reincarnation in orthodox Christianity.

In any case, the argument is moot. Sooner or later the Church probably would have forbade the beliefs. When the Church codified its denial of the divine origin of the soul (at Nicaea in 325), it started a chain reaction that led directly to the curse on Origen.

Church councils notwithstanding, mystics in the Church continued to practice divinization. They followed Origen's ideas, still seeking union with God. It makes me think of a new twist on the old saw: Old heretics never die; they just keep reincarnating as heretics!

But the Christian mystics were continually dogged by charges of heresy. At the same time as the Church was rejecting reincarnation, it was accepting original sin, a doctrine that made it even more difficult for mystics to practice.

CHAPTER 20

A New Explanation for Human Misery

> "If Jesus suffered the children to come
> why does the church send them all to hell
> if they die unbaptized?.... Because the church
> is cruel like all old sinners," Temple said.
> "Are you quite orthodox on that point,
> Temple?" Dixon said suavely.
> "Saint Augustine says that about unbaptized
> children going to hell," Temple answered,
> "because he was a cruel old sinner too."
>
> James Joyce
> *A Portrait of the Artist as a Young Man*

IS THERE ANYONE HERE WHO HASN'T BEEN BAP-
tized?" asked the vicar. Twelve-year-old Nigel
raised his hand. "You have to be baptized today,"
the priest said. "Otherwise, if you leave this church
and go outside and get hit by a car, you'll go straight
to hell." On this sobering note, Nigel decided to be
baptized immediately.

This incident happened to him in 1962 in the Church of England. Although most priests and ministers today might not make such a strong statement, the idea that unbaptized children and infants go to hell persists to this day. It originated in the fifth-century debates over original sin.

After the Church had begun to reject Origenism and preexistence, it had to come up with another explanation for why bad things happen to good people. Without past actions to explain differences in fate, the Church turned to the doctrine of original sin. This doctrine, which has left such a deep scar upon the soul of Western civilization, is a direct outcome of the denial of preexistence and reincarnation. Original sin is also the Church's ultimate denial of the Christian's right to contact the God within.

Picking up the Apple

In the early fifth century, the debate over human suffering centered around newborn babies, who obviously had not committed any sins. If they hadn't sinned before, why were some born with handicaps or low intelligence while others were born normal? The Church had ruled out Origen's answer: their fates resulted from previous actions. So it had to come up with a new answer for the question of why innocent babies (and good people in general) suffer and die.

Early theologians had toyed with the idea that man's wretched state of affairs is somehow related to the Fall of Adam and Eve in the Garden. But it was Saint Augustine (A.D. 354–430) who picked the dusty apple off the ground, polished it on his bishop's robe and fashioned it into what remains a cornerstone of Christian theology—original sin.

Bad things happen to good people because all people are bad by nature, Augustine argued, and the only chance for them to overcome this natural wickedness is to access God's grace through the Church. As Augustine wrote, "No one will be good who was not first of all wicked."[1]

Although the Church has since rejected some of Augustine's arguments, the Catholic catechism still tells us: "We cannot tamper with the revelation of original sin without undermining the mystery of Christ."[2] Original sin is linked so closely with Christ, the Church argues, because it is Christ who liberates us from original sin.

Adam and Eve, Augustine believed, lived in a state of physical immortality. They would neither have died nor grown old if they had not tasted the forbidden fruit and thus lost the privilege of God's grace. After their Fall, people began to experience suffering, old age and death.

According to Augustine, when Christ came he offered people the chance to be restored to the state of grace. He would act as mediator between the Father and a disobedient creation. Although Christ's intercession would not save them from physical death, it would allow them to return to the state of physical immortality through the bodily resurrection. Grace wouldn't stop bad things from happening to them on earth, but it would guarantee their immortality after death.

The most important implication of original sin is that because we are descended from Adam, we bear his permanently flawed nature. "Man... does not have it in his power to be good," writes Augustine.[3] He believed that we are no more capable of doing good than a monkey is of speaking. We can do good through grace alone. (Augustine's ideas, taken to their extreme, probably *lead* people to sin. "I can't help it" is a pretty good excuse.)

Augustine's take on sex has also left a deep mark on our civilization. He, more than anyone else, was responsible for the idea that sex is inherently evil. He called it the most visible

When Adam and Eve bit into the apple, they permanently changed the nature of their descendants, according to Saint Augustine's doctrine of original sin. This early nineteenth-century Pennsylvania Dutch illustration (left) shows the apple as the symbol of man's Fall. After the Fall, people became incapable of doing good, Augustine argued, and Christ brought grace to deliver us from original sin, symbolized (right) by Christ lifting the apple. The doctrine of original sin replaced reincarnation as an explanation for why the innocent suffer.

indication of man's fallen state. As scholar Elaine Pagels puts it, he saw sexual desire as the "proof" of and "penalty" for original sin.[4]

Through the centuries, many groups such as the Stoics, Pythagoreans and Neoplatonists had taught that control of the sexual impulse helped the soul to break the chains of bondage to the body. But Augustine took the extreme view that sex, even in marriage, is evil. (See note for further explanation.)[5]

Original sin was also a politically useful doctrine, which may be why it gained favor. As we will see, it solidified the portrait of God in man's image—as an absolute ruler to be obeyed without question. In this way, Saint Augustine provided the justification for absolute submission to the rule of both king and bishop.

Augustine arrived at the idea of original sin by a circuitous route. He was born in North Africa twenty-nine years after the council of Nicaea and was raised by a Christian mother and a pagan father. As a student, he took up Manichaeism and for nine years followed the teachings of the Persian prophet Mani, who combined Christian, Gnostic and Buddhist ideas.[6] He then went to Italy and became a Neoplatonist, adopting the idea of a transcendent, indwelling God. However, he later broke with this view and developed his own portrait of God.[7]

Becoming Christian was, for him, an agonizing process. Although he was attracted to Christianity, he believed that for him it entailed celibacy—and he wasn't ready for that. After much struggle, at age thirty-two he underwent a conversion and was able to send away his concubine, break off his engagement to an aristocratic maiden and accept baptism.

He formulated his famous doctrine not long after Bishop Theophilus' Alexandrian council condemned Origen's writings.

SHOW ME IN THE BIBLE

Many people react to the idea of original sin with disbelief. It isn't anywhere in the Bible, they say. When I first learned about it as a child, I could not understand how the sins of someone who lived five thousand or more years ago could make me a sinner.

Augustine found the chief scriptural support for his doctrine in Romans 5:12. In the modern New Revised Standard translation, the verse reads: "Sin came into the world through one man, and death came through sin, and so death spread to all *because* all have sinned."

But Augustine's version of this verse contained a mistranslation. Augustine didn't read Greek, the original language of the New Testament, so he used a Latin translation now called the Vulgate. It renders the last half of the verse as "and so death spread to all men, through one man, *in whom* all men sinned."[8] He concluded that "in whom" referred to Adam and that somehow all people had sinned when Adam sinned.

He made Adam a kind of corporate personality who contained the nature of all future men, which he transmitted through his semen. Augustine wrote: "We all were in that one man." Even though we didn't yet have physical form, "already the seminal nature was there from which we were to be propagated."[9]

Thus all of Adam's descendants are both corrupt and condemned because they were present inside of him (as semen) when he sinned. Augustine described the sin as something that is "contracted"[10] and passed through the human race like a venereal disease. Jesus was exempt from original sin since, according to the orthodox, he was conceived without semen.

Augustine concluded that as a result of Adam's sin, the entire human race is a "train of evil" headed for the "destruction of the second death."[11] Except, of course, those who manage to access God's grace through the Church.

THE BABY CONTROVERSY

Augustine's doctrine of original sin led to the debate over infant baptism. The central question was: What happens to babies who die without being baptized? Do they go to heaven or to hell?

It seemed hard to believe that God would send them to hell, since they had committed no sins. But if they went to heaven, why did they need to be baptized at all? In fact, why did anyone need to be baptized? Clearly, the controversy had grave implications for the authority of the Church.

In Augustine's day, many Christians postponed their baptisms well into adulthood for the same reason that Constantine had postponed his less than a century earlier. They didn't want to waste the chance to wipe out all their sins. Furthermore, they didn't relish the thought of performing public penance, which the Church required for sins committed after baptism.

But Augustine was able to convince Christendom that all infants needed to be baptized because all had been tainted by original sin. Since the babies hadn't committed any sins on their own, he wrote, "original sin only is left" to explain why they suffer. Unless babies are baptized, "they are manifestly in danger of damnation"—going to hell—he warned.[12]

Even within Augustine's lifetime, this doctrine evolved into a terrifying curse for parents, as we can see from the following story, which Augustine related to his congregation: A mother was in despair because her son had died unbaptized. She took her child's body to the shrine of Saint Stephen. The child was miraculously brought back to life, baptized, and died again.[13] The mother presumably took this second loss much better than the first, for now she could be certain her son would avoid the eternal pain of hell.

The fear of infant damnation reverberates today. A few days before June 6, 1996, thousands of Colombian women crowded churches in Bogotá, clamoring to have their children baptized. They were afraid that if their children were not protected by baptism, they would be vulnerable to the Antichrist, whose coming was rumored to be at hand. The rumor stemmed from a prediction made by a fundamentalist Christian sect.

The Catholic priests did everything they could to allay the fears of the parents, telling them the children had done nothing wrong. But the fears stemmed, in part, from Augustine's legacy. Although the Church has retreated from the doctrine of infant damnation, it still retains the basic framework of original sin that Augustine established.

SELLING THE APPLE

Getting the Church to swallow the bitter pill of original sin was not an easy task. But Augustine devoted twenty years to it. After his conversion to Christianity, he returned to Africa from Italy and became bishop of the North African seaport of Hippo Regius (in modern Algeria). He began composing letters and treatises which he sent with the ships that carried corn to the disintegrating Roman Empire. Safely ensconced among olive groves and fertile vineyards, he battled bishops and influenced both popes and Church councils.

He effectively combated the ideas of John Chrysostom (c. 347–407), patriarch of Constantinople, who argued that we should not be blamed for Adam's sin. Chrysostom said that when bad things happen to us, they are punishment not for Adam's sins but for our own.[14] Although Chrysostom's argument was logical, it did not explain the inequities of life—including why innocent babies suffer.

Augustine's explanation for original sin was at least logically consistent. And it fit in nicely with the image of God as emperor that Constantine had drawn. Augustine wrote: "God, the highest Ruler of the universe, justly decreed that we, who are descended from that first union, should be born into ignorance and difficulty, and be subject to death, because they [Adam and Eve] sinned and were hurled headlong into the midst of error, difficulty and death."[15]

Augustine's chief opponent was a British theologian named Pelagius (c. 354–c. 418), who thought original sin was absurd. He couldn't understand a belief that said men are wicked by nature and incapable of self-improvement. Pelagius, like Arius, believed that we have a higher destiny. He wrote: "There is no more pressing admonition than this, that we should be called *sons* of God."[16]

But Augustine was able to convince the pope and Honorius,

Saint Augustine, shown here in a medieval portrait by Simone Martini, crafted the doctrine of original sin. One of its most important ramifications was that infants who died before being baptized went to hell. The Church has since modified the doctrine and now says that unbaptized infants go to limbo, a place of "perfect natural happiness" but of permanent separation from God. Augustine was the bishop of Hippo Regius, in modern Algeria.

emperor of the western half of the empire, to excommunicate Pelagius (who lived in Rome) and send him into exile, along with his followers. Pelagius died soon after. One of his followers, Julian, the young Italian bishop of Eclanum, took up the fight from exile in Asia Minor. Julian and Augustine hurled parchment missiles at each other across the Mediterranean from 418 until Augustine's death in 430. But Augustine had already won.

Julian lost the battle because he could not defend God's justice in allowing babies to suffer. Scholar Elizabeth Clark sees their battle as a continuation of the Origenist controversy because the issues were the same—defending God's justice and explaining human differences.[17]

Augustine argued that if God is just and people are good, how could he let babies suffer? Specifically, why would God allow the souls of infants to be "tormented in this very life by afflictions of the flesh"?[18]

He told Julian, "You must answer why such great innocence is sometimes born blind; sometimes, deaf" or "feebleminded." The only solution, he believed, was that original sin had been "contracted" from the child's parents.[19]

Julian countered by asking how a just God could condemn an infant to suffer for "another's sins" (Adam's) that he had contracted "without knowledge or will."[20]

Augustine fired back: "If there were no such [original] sin, then infants... would suffer nothing evil in body or in soul under the great power of the just God." If one exempts infants from original sin, one accuses God of injustice. "We both perceive the punishment," Augustine wrote to Julian, "but you who say that nothing deserving of punishment is contracted from parents, while we both confess God is just, must prove, if you can, that there is in infants guilt deserving such punishment."[21]

Short of resorting to reincarnation, Julian could not prove that infants had done anything deserving of the "punishments" they suffered. And that is why the Church ultimately rejected Julian's arguments.

Augustine was quite familiar with the idea of reincarnation. In his nine years as a Manichaean he probably accepted it, since it is a fundamental tenet of the faith. And we know that at least some of his opponents in the original sin debate did suggest reincarnation as an alternative explanation for human suffering.

But Augustine—and ultimately the Church—rejected it out of hand. He called it a "revolting opinion" that souls be required to "return again to that burden of corrupt flesh to pay the penalty of torment."[22] Apparently, Augustine found the torment of hell and the second death preferable to the "torment" of "corrupt flesh."

The controversy over original sin was settled in A.D. 529 when the Council of Orange accepted Augustine's doctrine of original sin. The council decreed that Adam's sin corrupted the body and soul of the whole human race and that sin and death are a result of Adam's disobedience.

JACOB AND ESAU REVISITED

Like Origen, Augustine took up the question of why God treated the twins Jacob and Esau differently. The question led Origen to preexistence. It led Augustine to predestination, the illogical but necessary underpinning of his thought and the one on which it founders today. Although the Catholic Church no longer accepts Augustine's ideas about predestination, it has yet to find a sensible replacement for them.

If Constantine had begun to etch a portrait of God in man's image, Augustine completed it. In his eyes, God is like a great emperor who moves people about as if they were pawns.

The fundamental tenet of Augustine's thought is that God is both all-powerful and perfectly good. Since he is all-powerful, he must know and determine every event before it happens. This reasoning led Augustine to the idea that God decides before souls are born which will go to heaven and which to hell and that salvation results from the unmerited grace of God.

Thus, Augustine explains the divergent fates of Jacob and Esau by telling us that God is free to save or damn whomever he pleases. He concludes that both boys deserved damnation before birth because they were already tainted by original sin. Nevertheless, he tells us, God arbitrarily decided to forgive Jacob but to leave Esau to his fate. God "aids whom he will" and "leaves whom he will," Augustine writes.[23]

Augustine further illustrates his principle of predestination with a ghastly story. Imagine, he tells us, that there are two men. One is good and kind but born in a place where he cannot hear the Gospel. Another is a criminal and "addicted to lust," yet he hears the message of salvation and becomes a believing

Christian. At the final judgment, the good and kind man is sentenced to the second death because he is not a Christian. The criminal is saved.[24]

Augustine cannot sustain the image of God as both all-powerful and perfectly good. When discussing Jacob and Esau, he tries to preserve God's goodness by telling us that God's seemingly arbitrary actions toward the two boys are justified by some "hidden equity that cannot be searched out by any human standard of measurement."[25] But when forced to pick between the two attributes, he chooses to preserve God's power rather than his goodness.

Augustine tells us that the entire "clay of sin"[26] (everyone) is damned from the moment of creation and incapable of loving God unless God chooses to impart the ability to love him. As scholar T. Kermit Scott points out, this leads to the conclusion that God damns people for failing to love him when he hasn't given them the power to do so in the first place. "And that is surely unjust," Scott concludes.[27] With a Christian God as Augustine describes him, no wonder some people hate him!

Augustine never admitted what Scott calls the "ultimate incoherence in his thought."[28] His portrait of God is blurred by his inability to conceive of an all-powerful and just God who would give his creation the free will to act lifetime after lifetime.

It is time to erase Augustine's flawed portrait of God. Each of us can replace it with our own original sculpture, chipping away at the marble to discover the divine image within.

Dirty Bathwater

Today, Christianity has backed away from some of Augustine's more difficult conclusions. For example, the Catholic Church tells us that unbaptized infants do not go to hell but go to a place of "perfect natural happiness."[29] Here they are excluded from the heavenly vision of God but otherwise experience no pain.

However, most denominations have retained the framework of Augustine's thought. The Protestant Reformation absorbed much of Augustine through its leaders. Martin Luther, who began as an Augustinian monk, kept the worst of Augustine. So did John Calvin, who preserved the idea of absolute predestination. Both theologians reaffirmed the Catholic doctrine that original sin is tied to sexuality and lust.

Calvin's beliefs led to the kind of Puritanism described in Nathaniel Hawthorne's *The Scarlet Letter*. In this novel, a woman who bears a child as the result of an adulterous affair is ostracized and condemned to wear a red A on her chest. Her sexual indiscretion was seen as a glaring reminder of man's original wickedness.

Modern Christian positions on original sin differ widely. Today Protestants and liberal Catholics do not ask us to believe that sin is transmitted sexually or that everyone sinned in Adam. Nevertheless, they say, since people still suffer, it is clear that original sin exists.

Popular Catholic theologian Andrew Greeley defines original sin as a "badly flawed" genetic nature or a "root predisposition" that leads to sin. He tells us that we suffer not so much for the sins of Adam as for those of the whole human race. Children are conditioned to sin by "parental behavior and the cultural influences of the society in which children are born." The human race itself is "critically defective," he argues.[30] But his explanation fails to account for children who suffer before they have even been conditioned to sin.

Protestant theologians John Dillenberger and Claude Welch tell us that sin is "a distortion and perversion which exists at the center of the self. . . . Sin is the opposite of faith, . . . the placing of ultimate trust in anything less than God."[31] Their explanation, too, fails to explain why innocent children suffer.

Some Lutherans believe we are inherently sinful and that (except through Christ) we cannot escape from sin, which is with us from the moment we are conceived. And other Protestants believe that sin stems from "lack of fear and trust and love of God"[32] or standing "in opposition to God."[33]

The official Catholic position harks back to Augustine's ideas about the Fall. "The whole of human history is marked by the original fault freely committed by our first parents," the latest Catholic catechism tells us. The Church still says that human "misery" and "inclination toward evil" are transmitted to us as a result of "Adam's sin."[34]

But unlike Augustine, the Church admits that we are capable of doing good after baptism. It tells us that while our post-baptism nature is still "weakened" and "inclined to evil," grace gives us the power to battle against it. Yet the Church continues to link sin with sex, as the catechism puts it, with an "inclination to evil that is called 'concupiscence'" (sexual desire or lust).[35] Therefore we should still feel guilty for the natural urges that lead to procreation.

In effect, the Church hierarchy has not thrown out the dirty bathwater of Augustine's theology. However mildly they put it, they are still saying that every baby born is already mired in original sin, unable to move without divine grace and cursed by a twisted nature to suffer at the capricious hand of fate.

The Church has not gotten out of the tangled knot of original sin because there is nowhere to go but preexistence. And if it were to admit that, it would have to deny fifteen hundred years of doctrine. But Origen had already cut the knot before it was tied.

The true meaning of the fall

The main reason Augustine's scheme seems so far-fetched is that it hinges on the idea that sin was transmitted from one couple, Adam and Eve, to billions of innocent descendants. But in Origen's world view, *you* are Adam and Eve. Each one of us once existed in higher states of being, enjoying divine union, Origen says, and each of us made the choice at some moment to leave that state and to "fall" into bodies.

Origen calls the Fall a "decline from unity."[36] He speculates that souls may have fallen for various reasons—some because they became satiated with the divine, others because they lost their ardor for God, others out of simple curiosity.

Not everyone fell equally. Souls fell for different reasons and to different levels. Once they fell, they were "tossed about" by their desires and attracted to different sorts of bodies by attachments and wants. So their fates differ because of "different tendencies."[37] Origen doesn't assign guilt for the Fall. The souls' states in life are simply the result of their freewill choices.

I describe the Fall in terms similar to Origen's. Tens of thousands of years ago, when we chose to leave the "paradise" of heaven that was a higher state of consciousness, we lost our connection with God. We then became subject to the laws of karma and mortality. The only way to free ourselves from this condition is to return to that state of divine union.

The Fall is imprinted on our soul memory. Many people tell me that they *know* within themselves that their souls existed before the formation of their bodies. Not only do they remember other lives, but they also remember being one with God. And they long to return to his presence.

We all have a sense of having lost the best part of ourselves, the part of ourselves that is immortal. We long for the blissful state of union with God and a paradise waiting for us somewhere—and, yes, a fulfillment that no mortal can ever provide.

The message of this book is that you can return to that state starting right now, today. Having been scrubbed clean of the doctrine of original sin by the liberating logic of reincarnation, you no longer have to think of yourself as a miserable sinner. You can make your decision to return to your source and begin the process of your soul's reunion with God.

A POLITICALLY USEFUL DOCTRINE

Before we go on to explore how to accomplish that reunion, let us examine why the Church chose to accept Augustine's theology and how it affected future generations of Christians.

Augustine's musings might have remained so much wasted ink if he hadn't been able to convince the Church hierarchy that they were useful. In the fight against Pelagius, Augustine wrote a letter to Pope Innocent I, warning that the Pelagian view of human nature must be condemned if Church authority were to prevail. Pelagius had argued that salvation is achieved by personal striving and not by simple adherence to Church rules.

Augustine pointed out to the pope that if the Pelagian view prevailed, then people would no longer turn to the Church for the administration of grace or the guarantee of salvation. Even the prayers offered by the clergy would appear to be but "idle words,"[38] he complained, urging that Pelagius' views on free will be anathematized.

Put in those terms, the controversy became a matter of survival for the Church. If it wanted to retain its authority, the Church would have to accept Augustine's solution.[39]

Original sin was also attractive to secular rulers. Since the doctrine held that man was naturally wicked, he was obviously incapable of self-government. Therefore he should obey his rulers even if they were wicked and unjust. Although Augustine may not have had this in mind, it was the de facto result of his theology.

This portrait of God as an imperial ruler proved useful to the authoritarian state. As Scott writes: "One [reason for the success of Augustinian Christianity] is certainly that it was an ideology uniquely suited to serve the needs of the dominant classes of Roman society. It provided a cosmic justification for the existing hierarchical order as rooted in human sinfulness and divine justice, and it encouraged every person to accept her or his place in that order."[40]

Augustine was also partly responsible for the Church's later attitude toward persecuting heretics. He taught that coercion was an acceptable means of achieving Church unity. And it was better, he argued, to coerce a heretic into belief than to allow his soul to perish in the fires of hell after death.[41]

Contrast this with the ideas of John Chrysostom, who argued the opposite: "Christians, more than all [other] people, are not allowed to correct by force the faults of those who sin."[42] Chrysostom's views against coercion fell by the wayside, while Augustine became the most influential theologian in the Church. After Augustine, absolute and unquestioning obedience became the only offering good Christians could make to the Church.

In the next chapter, we will see how the Church's interpretation of Augustine's ideas about coercion led to one of the most brutal repressions in history.

CHAPTER 21

Smoke Rises from Montségur

God does not create new souls for
little children. He would have a lot to do.
The soul of a dead person goes from body
to body until it comes into the hands
of the good men [Cathar perfects].

Toulousian woman
Inquisition records, 1273

RAYMOND D'ALFAR SLAMMED HIS MACE INTO
William Arnaud's head, crushing his skull.
Arnaud didn't have a chance. D'Alfar and his co-
conspirators hacked Arnaud to death, along with
his fellow inquisitor and their nine companions.

Arnaud and his party were guests in the castle
in the small town of Avignonet in southern France.
They had arrived on a spring day in 1242 and
d'Alfar, the count's bailiff, had received them and
housed them in his master's castle hall.

Arnaud was a Dominican inquisitor. He and his
party knew they were not popular in southern

France. Perhaps that is why they barricaded the door of the hall before settling down for some quiet drinking and, later, sleep. In the morning they planned to open their tribunal and begin to hunt out Cathar heretics from among the town's inhabitants.[1]

As soon as he thought they were asleep, d'Alfar, wearing a white surcoat and carrying a torch, opened the small postern gate of the castle and admitted a party of men armed with axes. Some were townspeople and some had come from the Cathar fortress of Montségur. D'Alfar led them to the hall where the inquisitors were sleeping. Together they broke down the door and rushed in.

"Va be, esta be!" shouted d'Alfar, "This is it!" and jubilantly began the slaughter.[2] Afterwards the men took booty—clothing, books and horses—and returned to the forest where the rest of their party was waiting.

Pierre Roger de Mirepoix, garrison commander of Montségur, was anxious for the news. He asked one of the assassins, Acermat, "Where is [Arnaud's] cup?"—in other words, his skull.

"It is broken," Acermat said.

"Why did you not bring me the pieces? I would have bound them together with a circlet of gold, and drunk wine from this cup all the days of my life."[3]

Why did de Mirepoix hate the inquisitors so much? It wasn't just because they persecuted the Cathars. It was also because they represented the Church that had brought an army to lay waste his country and had given his ancestral lands to a northerner.

The raid at Avignonet was successful but ill-fated. It was part of a rebellion against northern French rule, which had been imposed on Languedoc, a region of southern France, for thirteen years. The massacre of the inquisitors was to be the signal for a general revolt. But when the revolt failed, the murders brought down the wrath of both the Church and the French Crown on the Cathars and led to their final extermination.

The Cathar priests, known as "perfects," were peace-loving and committed to nonviolence. Although none of the perfects took part in this raid, some of the assassins were probably Cathar believers. What could have led them to so rash an act as the cold-blooded murder of two inquisitors and their retinue?

FERTILE SOIL

In order to understand why the Cathars participated in this bloody raid, we must review the history of the preceding thirty years, starting with an examination of the fertile soil of Languedoc, in which Catharism took root.

At the close of the twelfth century, Languedoc was one of the most prosperous parts of Europe. Its merchants grew rich from trade between the lands to the north and the Mediterranean. It had its own architectural style (Romanesque) and culture, including a poetry and literature that gave birth to the troubadours. Languedoc was culturally diverse. Its strong merchant class developed ties to the Muslim world. Unlike much of Europe, Languedoc offered citizens' rights to Jews and permitted them to teach their ideas openly.

The French Crown did not control the region. It was ruled independently by the count of Toulouse and other barons. Cities operated as independent republics where citizens were protected by common law.

Jewish mystics felt comfortable enough to write down and teach the Kabbalah in these cities.[4] And the region's tolerance and sophistication made it an ideal spot for Catharism to flourish.

Catharism was a heretical Christian sect that claimed to be the true Christian church. The Cathars taught reincarnation and union with God in a Christian context. Their faith took hold in Languedoc in the mid-twelfth century. By the 1140s the Cathars had established an organized church with a hierarchy of bishops,

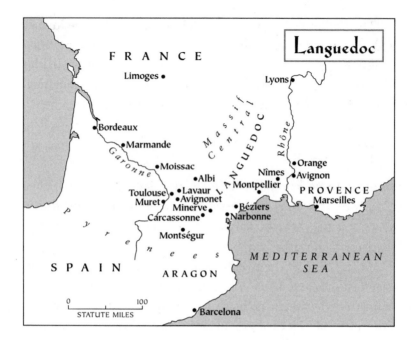

a liturgy and a system of doctrine. Their strength around the town of Albi earned them the alternate name Albigenses.

Unlike some heretical movements that were popular only among the common people, Catharism appealed to nobles as well. Its first converts were among the educated and the nobility, who spread it among the poor. This broad base of support made it difficult for the Church to combat.

Catharism highlighted the sorry state of the orthodox Church. In twelfth- and thirteenth-century Languedoc, the Catholic bishops set the tone for the rest of the clergy when they neglected Mass while selling Church offices and sacraments. They charged fees for everything from appointing people to clerical posts to breaking wills and approving illegal marriages. Bishops lived like nobility, devoting themselves to hunting, gambling and merrymaking.

People ridiculed the priests as idle parasites who, like the bishops, absented themselves from services while living off tithes and keeping mistresses. Even Pope Innocent III criticized his clergy. "Throughout this region the prelates are the laughing-stock of the laity," he wrote, lamenting that God and the Church were held in contempt by both gentry and the common people.[5]

Bernard de Clairvaux (later Saint Bernard) came to Langue-doc to preach in 1145. He reported that "the churches are without congregations, congregations are without priests, priests are without proper reverence, and, finally, Christians are without Christ."[6]

A FIRMLY ROOTED FAITH

The Cathars were divided into two classes—the perfects and the believers. The perfects, Cathar clergy, lived an ascetic lifestyle and were set apart from the believers by a ceremony of initiation, or spiritual baptism, the *consolamentum*.

They devoted themselves to contemplation and were expected to maintain the highest moral standards. Strict ascetics, they tended to be pale and gaunt from their regimen of fasting and sparse diet, which excluded meat, eggs and dairy but included fish.

They traveled on foot from town to town wearing coarse black robes, conducting services in private homes, nurturing the living and preparing the dying for eternal life. Although they lived in austerity, they were not so otherworldly that they neglected material things. They gave alms to the poor and often practiced medicine.

The Cathars gave women a prominent role. They could become perfects, although not bishops. Male believers venerated female perfects just as they would male perfects and listened to them preach. Cathar noblewomen often became perfects after their children were grown. They established communal homes for other Cathar women, where they practiced rituals, taught their faith and healed the sick.[7]

Although the perfects adhered to strict standards, the rank-and-file Cathar believers probably did not live all that differently from their Catholic neighbors. Cathar believers could be found in every level of society. They dominated the weaving craft and appeared among both merchants and farmers.

The Cathar faith was so firmly rooted among the nobility that separating out the Cathars from the orthodox Christians would have torn apart the entire fabric of the country. As one knight told the bishop of Toulouse when he asked the knight why the nobility did not drive out the heretics: "We cannot do it. We were all brought up together. Many of them are related to us. Besides, we can see for ourselves that they live decent, honourable lives."[8]

The Cathars did not have churches but held their simple services in private homes. Their burgeoning congregations no doubt provided a disagreeable contrast to the sparsely populated cathedral naves.

By the mid-twelfth century, the Church had realized the threat from this fast-growing heresy and was taking steps to combat it. The campaign against Catharism in Languedoc began with persuasion. Cadres of priests were dispatched to travel the country and exhort the people to return to the fold. But their preaching campaigns met with little success. Even when the Catholic preachers reduced their lifestyles to match those of the Cathar perfects, they did not make many converts.

Dominic de Guzman (later Saint Dominic) was even more ascetic than the perfects, but his arguments apparently were not as persuasive. One debate—Dominic and his companion against two Cathar perfects—lasted for eight days without Dominic gaining a single convert.

Saint Dominic spearheaded the Church's preaching campaign against Catharism. Although he made few converts, miracles are said to have accompanied him. This painting (c. 1490) by Pedro Berruguete depicts one such miracle in which dissertations summarizing Catholic and Cathar positions were thrown into a fire. The Cathars' writings burned briskly while Dominic's reportedly rose into the air unsinged.

Saint Bernard had written the pope that "faith is a work of persuasion, and cannot be imposed by force."[9] But Dominic came to a different conclusion. By the end of his four-year exercise in futility, he reportedly made the exasperated comment, "As the common saying goes in Spain, Where a blessing fails, a good thick stick will succeed." He told the unresponsive heretics, "Now we shall rouse princes and prelates against you. ... Thus force will prevail where gentle persuasion has failed to do so."[10]

By 1208, Pope Innocent III was ready to use force. The immediate catalyst was the murder of the pope's representative, Pierre de Castelnau, allegedly on the orders of the count of

Toulouse, Raymond VI, a suspected Cathar.

Innocent sent out a call for a Crusade to be launched against Languedoc. Until now, the term "Crusade" had been reserved for wars against the Muslims. This was the first time a Crusade had been launched against a Christian people. But the pope declared the Cathars to be worthy of a Crusade, labeling them "worse than the very Saracens [Muslims]."[11]

He promised the crusaders the same rewards as were given to those who fought in Palestine—a reprieve from debts for the period of the Crusade and the forgiveness of all sins, which guaranteed entrée into heaven. All this for a forty-day commitment. The pope also promised booty and land from the rich towns of Languedoc. The combination of earthly and heavenly rewards lured a large army of knights and peasants, primarily from northern France, to serve under the banner of the cross.

By June 1209 the army was ready to advance. The wealthy burghers and noblemen of Languedoc made only minor preparations to defend their towns. They had little understanding of the fury that the "army of God" was about to unleash upon their land, where Catholic and Cathar lived side by side in peace.

A HORSE FINDS HIS OWN LOST SHOE

What did the Cathars believe and why did the Church consider them to be so dangerous? It is hard to decipher the Cathar beliefs since the Church obscured them in the same way it did those of the Gnostics—sketching a hideous caricature and attempting to make it stick by destroying any evidence to the contrary.

Church chronicles portray Catharism as an insane faith, focusing on the Cathars' rejection of the Eucharist, the bodily resurrection and the worship of the cross. They accused the Cathars of such life-hating practices as voluntary suicide and the refusal to bear children. If the Cathars had, in fact, practiced these things, they could have been accused of being a danger to humanity.

However, history shows that Cathar believers did marry and bear children, and it was only the perfects who remained celibate. Many noble families remained in the faith for generations, raising children and grandchildren as believers.

The Church accused some perfects of practicing a fast to the death, called the *endura,* and of sometimes swallowing poison to speed the process.[12] If anyone did undergo this fast, it appears to have been a late development and not a general practice among Cathars.[13]

The Cathars doubtless had some beliefs that would seem strange to us today. But the core of their religion was none other than a fresh upsurge of Gnostic-Origenist-Arian ideas that the Church thought it had eradicated six hundred years before!

Reincarnation appears to have been an integral part of their faith from its inception. The Cathars believed that the purpose of reincarnation was to give souls the opportunity to incarnate in the body of a perfect and so obtain reunion with God.

"The spirits go from tunic to tunic until they arrive in a 'good tunic,' that is to say the body of a man or a woman who has understood the 'good,'" says one source.[14] The source uses "understood the good" in the Gnostic sense to mean that the spirit has become one with the good, or God. This, as we will see, was precisely the goal of the Cathars.

Cathars had differing ideas as to how many lives were allowed to each person. Some thought the number of incarnations was limited and that if the soul did not find salvation, she would be lost. Others thought that the opportunity for salvation was extended to all souls for as long as required. Believers elaborated on the concept and may have told their own past-life stories.

The Cathar concept of reincarnation included the belief that souls could migrate into the bodies of animals. The Inquisition squeezed the following humorous anecdote out of one accused Cathar woman, highlighting the concept of transmigration into animals:

> A man's soul after having left his body, entered into the body of a horse. He was owned by a feudal lord for a while. One night this lord was chasing his enemies on this particular horse and riding through rocks and stones. The horse caught his foot in between two rocks. He had a hard time getting his foot loose and left his shoe behind. Then when he died, his soul passed into a human body and this man became a "good Christian" [Cathar perfect].
>
> One day he and another heretic [Cathar] passed by the place where he as a horse had lost his shoe. He told his companion that when he was a horse he had lost his shoe in this spot and the two looked for the shoe between the rocks and found it.[15]

The woman told the inquisitors that when she originally recounted this story, her audience laughed loudly. One can imagine a scene, perhaps a medieval inn, in which she regaled both Catholic and Cathar alike with this past-life tale.

THE REINCARNATION OF A HERESY

We can trace the Cathar beliefs from fourth- and fifth-century Gnostics, Origenists and Arians. After Constantine and other Roman emperors began persecuting Christian "heretics," they fled east into Armenia and then west into Bulgaria. The Balkans became a melting pot for heresies of every sort.

Sometime before the year 950, a Bulgarian priest called Bogomil (loved of God) is said to have founded Bogomilism, a faith pieced together from elements of heretical early Christian mysticism. By the eleventh century it had spread across Asia Minor.

Sometime during the twelfth century, the Bogomils fled Bulgaria and went to Bosnia, where they were permitted to practice openly. The Bogomils sent missionaries across the Christian world. They influenced noble families in Constantinople, including the patriarch, as well as Byzantine colonies in Italy. Around the same time, French crusaders in the Holy Land learned about Bogomilism and, upon their return to southern France, probably joined with Bogomil missionaries to found the Cathar faith.[16]

If we look more closely at the beliefs of the Cathars, we will see further parallels with Gnosticism, Origenism and Arianism. The Cathars, like the Gnostics, did not worship the cross,[17] and they were accused of having adopted Origen's heretical ideas, including the belief that the resurrection was not of the flesh.[18]

Like the Protestants in the sixteenth century, the Cathars focused on personal illumination and reading the scriptures in their own language.[19] (The perfects traveled with a translation of the Gospel of John hung from their belts.)

But unlike the Protestants, the Cathars did not accept the Old Testament or the Nicene Creed. Instead, they seem to have preserved a pre-Nicene form of Christianity. Like the Arians, they said that we share in Jesus' nature and that we are meant to become like him. This affected their view of salvation. They believed that their destiny was to attain a spiritual marriage in which their soul would unite with the Spirit it left in heaven.[20]

THE GARMENT OF CHRIST

The most sacred of the Bogomil and Cathar ceremonies was the *consolamentum*, the receiving of the Holy Spirit, celebrated by the perfect's placing his hands on the head of the believer. This ceremony was generally performed only once in a believer's life. Afterwards the believer had to live as a perfect. Cathars believed that during this ceremony, the fallen soul was restored to its holy Spirit and a state of divine union.[21] They thought that if they received this *consolamentum* before death, they would not reincarnate but instead would remain with that Spirit.

Souls who had achieved this union were destined, after death, to put on the garment of Christ and take their place with the angels.[22] This is clearly a description of divinization, or union with God. As we have seen, this thread of divinization connected Gnosticism, Origenism and Arianism. The Cathar faith, then, picked up this thread when it reconnected divinization and reincarnation with Christianity.

The Bogomils and Cathars even preserved an early second-century Jewish-Christian scripture called the *Vision of Isaiah.* The text describes the journey of Isaiah through heavenly realms and his eventual transformation into an angel. Not only does the manuscript describe Isaiah's ascent into the heavens, but it also encourages the reader to follow him.[23]

Isaiah reports that the angel tells him that when he returns to heaven after death, he will be clothed in a spiritual garment, a heavenly robe. And then he will be "equal to the angels who (are) in the seventh heaven." Isaiah makes it clear that others can enjoy his destiny. He rejoices that "those who love the Most High and his Beloved [Son] will at their end go up there [to the seventh heaven] through the angel of the Holy Spirit."[24] There they will receive robes, thrones and crowns of glory. In Jewish mysticism, being robed, crowned or enthroned symbolizes union with God.

The presence of this text among the Cathar scriptures indicates that the Cathars (like the Gnostics) preserved teachings on soul journeys that led to divinization. And, as we will see in Part 5, such soul journeys were a part of early Christianity as well.

According to historians, the Cathars also seem to have preserved remnants of early Christian ceremonies. This gives further indication that they had access to a primitive form of Christianity. We can see the Cathars, then, as the recipients of

Jesus' original teachings and perhaps his secret teachings.

But for the Cathars in southern France, the opportunity to practice these teachings was short-lived. While the Cathar perfects sought a heavenly crown of glory, the Catholic prelates were more concerned about preserving their earthly kingdom.

"KILL THEM ALL"

The army of more than fifteen thousand crusaders and mercenaries was led not by a general but by the pope's personally appointed representative, Arnaud Amaury. Its first target of siege was the wealthy, fortified town of Béziers.

The Catholic bishop of Béziers tried to avoid siege by negotiating a deal with the crusaders. He offered to give up 222 heretics if the army would bypass the town. But when he presented the plan to the Catholic citizens, they refused the deal. They saw it as an infringement on their sovereignty and a betrayal of their Cathar friends.

The Catholics said they "would rather be drowned in the salt sea's brine" than accept the terms.[25] They would trust to their city's high walls, gates and encircling moats to protect them from the army. So the bishop abandoned the city, leaving both Catholic and Cathar citizens behind, along with a number of his priests.

Béziers seemed to have good chance of surviving a long siege. But the very next day at dawn, July 22, 1209, a group of its citizens left the protective walls of the city and made an ill-conceived attack on a group of mercenaries. Aroused, these seasoned fighters stormed the gates and took the walls. They surged through the streets, followed by the entire crusading army, and slaughtered the unprepared citizens.

Many of the panicked people took refuge in the churches. The crusaders forced open the doors and massacred everyone inside —men, women, children, invalids and priests. The crusaders tried to take booty from the looting mercenaries. Angered, the mercenaries set fire to the town, which burned fiercely. The fire destroyed even the stone cathedral, which cracked and "collapsed in two halves."[26]

Four days later, the army left the smouldering ruins and the piles of mangled corpses—Catholic and Cathar together—and moved on, banners streaming in the wind.

The crusaders had been unsure how to tell the heretics from the Catholics, according to a Cistercian monk who chronicled the Crusade. They did not want to kill good Catholics, but neither did they want the "wicked" to escape by pretending to be "good."

According to popular lore, Arnaud Amaury, the pope's representative, provided a simple solution: "Kill them all; God will recognize his own."[27] Whether or not he actually used those words, it became the policy for the Crusade. Striking terror into the region wherever towns resisted, the crusaders executed Catholics as if they had been heretics.

It was this policy that polarized Languedoc against the Church and led to the kind of vicious slaughter unleashed when Raymond d'Alfar's mace crushed the skull of the Dominican inquisitor. In the long and bloody years of Crusade that followed, both sides committed atrocities. But the residents of Languedoc paid the heaviest price.

SCORCHED EARTH

The Crusade lasted for twenty years. Although the nobles of Languedoc gained brief periods of respite for their land, they could not withstand the continued battering by fresh contingents of crusaders supported by the combined force of the French Crown and the Church.

Since the Catholics refused to give up their independence or turn against their Cathar neighbors, they all suffered together in one of the most brutal wars of medieval times. Not trusting to battles alone, the northern armies also sought to starve the people into submission by systematically destroying crops, uprooting vineyards and killing cattle.

Some towns were spared the fate of Béziers when they gave their perfects the choice of either recanting or execution at the stake. But others witnessed unspeakable horrors. The French crusaders mutilated prisoners, gouging out eyes and cutting off lips, and slaughtered women and children. They stoned to death the charitable Cathar noblewoman Guiraude, chatelaine of Lavaur.

The crusaders created such a bloodbath at the riverside town of Marmande that brains, limbs and mashed livers and hearts littered the streets, which ran with blood. No one—from knight to infant—was spared.

The pope and his bishops were aware of the atrocities. But, as historian Zoé Oldenbourg points out, "not one Conciliar decision stigmatized the atrocities committed by the Soldiers of Christ, or proscribed such conduct for the future."[28]

The Crusade galvanized the population—Catholic and Cathar, noble and commoner—to fight side by side. In defense of Toulouse, a capital of the region, wealthy burghers armed themselves with picks and shovels and fought beside humble laborers. From maidservants to noble chatelaines, the women fought beside their husbands, fathers and children.

By 1229 the region was weary and hungry, barely recognizable as the major center of industry, commerce and culture it had been twenty years before. Although the population of Languedoc was willing to fight to the last, neither the Church nor the French Crown would rest until the region had succumbed. The pope summoned a council of bishops who declared the king of France to be the rightful sovereign of Languedoc.

After Saint Dominic's preaching campaign against Catharism failed, he supported using force to stamp out heresy. In this illustration, Saint Dominic Presiding over an Auto da Fé, *two heretics are being executed in the foreground. (Thousands of Cathars—male and female—were executed and burned alive during the Crusade and Inquisition.) Dominic died before the Inquisition began, but members of the Dominican order he founded became the first and most zealous inquisitors.*

Raymond VII, count of Toulouse, agreed to sign a brutal peace treaty, perhaps hoping to gain a respite. Instead, he lost his country. Languedoc was never able to resist again after the treaty, which called for Raymond to forfeit two-thirds of his land, dismantle many of his fortresses and for the remainder of the region to pass to the Crown after his death if his daughter and her husband were childless.

But all the bloodshed and ruin had not accomplished its aim— the extermination of heresy. The crusaders had burned hundreds of perfects at the stake, yet Cathar bishops and perfects continued to hold services in secret throughout the Crusade.

The people still held the Church in contempt and, if anything, clung more firmly to the Cathar faith.[29] It had come to represent the national identity they struggled to retain.

Seeds of suspicion

By 1233 the Church had a new strategy to combat the Cathar heretics—persistent questioning by monks who were backed by the authority of French soldiers. The pope had inaugurated the Inquisition, which would terrorize Europeans for at least six hundred years. Where the blunt force of invasion had failed, the Church would employ a more elegant weapon, one designed to ferret out heretics by turning neighbor against neighbor.

The Church had a simple routine. The monks would arrive in a town, set up a tribunal and begin by promising amnesty to those heretics who confessed voluntarily. The monks elicited lists of names from these voluntary confessors, gave them penances and began following up on the leads. Since testimony was given in secret, without lawyers, people often took the opportunity to secretly indict their enemies, whether or not they were Cathars.

The inquisitors arrested people and held them until they confessed and generated still more names. They arrested even those who professed orthodoxy in order to seek out, in the words of historian Henry Lea, their "secret misbelief."[30]

The Church created new laws that required the secular authorities to obey the monks in the arresting and punishing of heretics. Prison conditions were unspeakable. The accused were often kept in the dark or in cells so small they could neither lie down nor stand up. King Louis had to construct new jails to accommodate the flood of accused heretics. The accusations snowballed and even the dead were not safe.

If a dead person was accused of heresy, his body would be exhumed and burned. And, more importantly, his estate could be confiscated and turned over to the French Crown. Heretics who refused to recant were jailed or burned. Those who renounced their faith were given stiff penances and released. The penances ranged from lengthy pilgrimages to the confiscation of homes and possessions. Pilgrimages led to a worsening of poverty and starvation as pilgrims left their fields untended and families unfed while they made their way to Rome or to Compostela in Spain.

The Inquisition was succeeding where twenty years of Crusade had failed. Its tactics created an atmosphere of suspicion and fear in which one's closest friends could be informers and the slightest gesture of support for Cathars could lead to the ruin of an entire family.

The Dominican order, founded by Saint Dominic, was on the front lines of the struggle. And William Arnaud, who came to his bloody end at Avignonet, was among the first Dominicans chosen as an inquisitor. He toured the province, setting up tribunals and condemning heretics.

At a town called Moissac, he seems to have struck a rich vein of heresy; he and his fellow inquisitor condemned 210 people to be burned at the stake. No wonder his mere arrival at Avignonet could strike terror in the population and inspire the conspiracy that led to his death.

One of Arnaud's assassins, William de Mas-Saintes-Puelles, was a bailiff who had participated unwillingly in the arrest and burning of heretics. Perhaps by murdering Arnaud he sought to stop the anguish and distrust the inquisitors spread as they tried to undermine the loyalty the citizens of Languedoc felt for each other.

But the inquisitors' efforts eventually bore fruit. Slowly, painstakingly, they taught the people that neighborly intercourse between Catholic and Cathar was unacceptable. Cathars were to be shunned and exposed.

The records of the Inquisition reveal the kind of casual contact that was now frowned upon. A priest was removed from his parish for speaking to heretics, reading their books and eating pears with them. Others were punished for seeking medical treatment from heretics or eating with them. Giving them provisions such as food, wine, wool or cloth was a crime.

THE LAST PYRE

The Inquisition succeeded in driving the Cathar faith underground. But it managed to survive for decades, with perfects taking refuge in forest huts and hideouts in the Pyrenees. The most famous of these, the mountain fortress of Montségur, was where about two hundred perfects chose to make their last stand.

The knights who rode down from Montségur to lead the attack on the inquisitors at Avignonet that fateful night in 1242 were part of the garrison that defended Montségur. They may have participated against the advice of the perfects. In any case, their foolish act aroused church and state against the last group of Cathar leaders.

The small fortress, shaped like an uneven pentagon, was perched on a peak that rose a thousand feet from its base. The mountain plunged dramatically on three sides. On the fourth side a steep switchback road led up to the fortress gates.

When the Inquisition began tightening its noose, Montségur became a popular destination for refugees as well as pilgrims who simply wanted the chance to practice their faith openly once again. It soon became the headquarters of the Cathar church in Languedoc.

Eventually, the fortress became the home of four hundred to five hundred people—about two hundred perfects together with fifty to one hundred soldiers, their wives, camp followers and servants.[31] The perfects included Bishop Raymond Aiguil-her, who had spent a lifetime in passive resistance and had debated Saint Dominic forty years earlier.

The Avignonet murders convinced the Church that it was time for a final blow to be struck against the Cathars. In May 1243, an army of several thousand soldiers besieged Montségur. But the army had a difficult time pressing the siege. It could not cut off supplies to the fortress, which were delivered along narrow mountain paths. These supplies allowed the Cathars to hold out for nearly a year. From May to October, they used catapults, called stone-guns, to keep the French army from approaching.

But the French hired a group of Basques who helped them scale the east face and set up their own stone-gun to target the eastern defenses. By Christmas, the French had rushed the eastern tower, aided by local mountaineers who betrayed the Cathars.

The defenders must have then realized that it was only a matter of time before the fortress would fall. Perhaps they held out on the slight hope that the count of Toulouse would come to their aid. But his power had been so eviscerated by the French Crown and the pope that he could do nothing.

It is difficult to imagine the conditions the defenders endured —several hundred people, with limited food and fuel, trapped on a mountaintop in winter. Since only a small part of the fortress had a proper roof, the stone projectiles were a constant hazard. Most of the people lived in fragile huts huddled against the walls. The stones splintered the roofs, demolishing the huts. Some defenders had already been wounded in the fighting and the remainder were struggling against exhaustion, cold and exposure.

On the last day of February, a horn echoed off the frosty peaks surrounding Montségur. Raymond de Péreille, seigneur of the fortress, and Pierre Roger de Mirepoix, commander of the garrison, were ready to sue for peace. The French allowed

Only treachery could take the castle of Montségur, a nearly impregnable fortress in the Pyrenees. Here, two hundred Cathar perfects and their garrison chose to make their last stand. They endured ten months of siege and a winter of bitter cold but could not hold out after local mountaineers guided the besieging Crusaders along an almost invisible track and helped attack the eastern tower.

de Mirepoix and his soldiers to go free, pardoning even their participation in the Avignonet massacre, provided they surrendered the heretics who refused to recant.

Seventeen members of the garrison post—six women and eleven men—chose to join the ranks of the nearly two hundred perfects to be executed. Among them was Corba de Péreille, wife of the seigneur of Montségur. His daughter Esclarmonde, an invalid, was also a perfect and so must be given up to the French. Raymond and Pierre Roger gained a two-week grace period during which the defenders held their last ceremonies and said their final good-byes.

On March 16, 1244, French soldiers chained the unresisting

perfects and dragged them from the fortress. The soldiers roughly herded the perfects into an enclosure of stakes that was already heaped with piles of brush. The perfects did not try to escape the flames that soon turned them into human torches. The smoke from the great pyre spiraled upward along with the aspirations of a dying faith. Today the field is known as the Prat dels Crematz, "Field of the Burned."

Perfects tended to go to their deaths with great serenity, which has sometimes been taken as proof of their hatred of life. But the perfects' attitude, taken as a whole, was that of seeking to preserve life rather than to lose it unnecessarily. Why else would they hide out in forests and mountains, braving the elements and living on scraps of food for years on end?

When captured, they faced death with grace rather than falsely deny their faith. They believed that lying was a sin that could cause them to lose their chance of salvation.

Although some may have sought death to hasten their entry into heaven, they can only have been a minority. For, like the Gnostics and Origenists, the Cathars believed that divine union was a state that could be experienced before death. Perhaps the Cathars were serene in the face of death not because they wanted to die but because they had already attained this state of divine bliss. They had reached the point in which the transition between life and death is insignificant.

It was 1310 before the Inquisition had hunted down and burned the last Cathar teacher in France. But the pyre that blazed up on the slopes of Montségur marked the formal end of this particular strand of the faith that combined the ideas of reincarnation and union with God.

PART 5

Jesus' Secret
Teachings on the
God Within

❦

CHAPTER 22

Your Divine Image

Beloved, now are we the sons of God,
and it doth not yet appear what we shall be:
but we know that, when he shall appear,
we shall be like him; for we shall see him
as he is.

I John 3:2

THE ARIANS RISKED IMPERIAL WRATH WHEN they taught people to become Sons of God. The Origenists were expelled from their monasteries for practicing union with God. The Cathars were burned alive for believing that they could be transformed into angels.

But now, some scholars are concluding that ideas like these could have been an original part of Christianity. In this chapter, I will review the evidence that the apostle Paul taught union with God and that he used images from Jewish mysticism.

As we saw in chapter 5, medieval Jewish mystics sought union with God. Although scholars used to think that these ideas did not date back to the time of Jesus, today they are rethinking that chronology. They believe that the same mystical ideas about union with God that are a part of medieval Kabbalah also influenced Paul and possibly Jesus. Where did these ideas originate?

The world in which Christianity was born nurtured a variety of ideas about divine union. In Jewish mysticism, as well as in Greek, Roman and Egyptian mystery religions, people sought personal identification with God. They tried to accomplish this in several ways, one of which was the practice of a spiritual journey known as an ascent.[1]

The mystics sometimes described the ascent not as a journey upward into heaven but rather inward, into the sacred spaces of the heart. Usually the ascent culminated in either a vision of a divine being or in the experience of being transformed into a divine being. Being seated on a throne or being clothed in new garments often symbolized the transformation.

The mystics saw these soul journeys as practice runs for a final journey in which the transformation would actually take place. Some believed this transformation took place after death. Others sought it during life. In any case, the ascent is linked with transformation into God. Where we see a description of an ascent, we can postulate that people believed they could be transformed into God.

These ideas are clearly present in early Judaism and, as we will see, in Christianity as well. Let us review the evidence for these ascents in Judaism before we trace them to Jesus' essential message.

HEAVENLY JOURNEYS

Jewish mystics believed that extraordinary figures of the past like Enoch and Moses had been transformed into angels or divine beings. A second-century-B.C. text about Moses describes him as being enthroned as a ruler or god in heaven.[2]

There is an unmistakable tradition (dating to the first century and earlier) that some mystics tried to imitate Enoch and Moses. Philo, a first-century Jewish mystic and contemporary of Jesus, believed that human beings could also become divine beings like Moses.

Philo calls Moses not only a "sort of God" but also *"a model for all those who were inclined to imitate him."*[3] Moses, Philo tells us, was not created divine; he gradually became divine. Philo presents Moses' divinity as a goal for everyone: "Happy are they who have been able to take, or have even diligently laboured to take, a faithful copy of this excellence in their own souls."[4] Philo probably didn't reach this conclusion on his own but based his writings on an even earlier tradition.

First Enoch (around the first to third century B.C.) also describes a transformation of ordinary believers into a divine likeness. In one passage, Enoch sees the Messiah born as a snow-white cow. Believers are then also transformed into snow-white cows, symbolizing divine beings.[5] "The believers symbolically share the being of the messiah. The messiah not only saves but serves as the model for transformation of believers," writes Alan Segal, professor of religion at Barnard College.[6]

The Jewish mystical text *2 Baruch* (written sometime between A.D. 70 and 130 but relying on earlier sources) also describes the transformation of the righteous. The righteous are "those who possessed intelligence in their life, and those who planted the root of wisdom in their heart." God tells them that they will be "like the angels and be equal to the stars," and their "excellence" will be "greater than that of the angels."[7]

There is some evidence in the Gospels that Jesus may have been influenced by the tradition of ascents, but there is even more evidence in Paul's letters. In fact, the Epistles have convinced many scholars that Jewish mysticism impacted Christianity.

In 2 Corinthians, Paul describes a journey to the "third heaven," where he received "visions and revelations of the Lord." It bears the earmarks of ascent mysticism:

> I know a man in Christ who fourteen years ago was caught up to the third heaven—whether in the body or out of the body, I do not know, God knows. And I know that this man was caught up into Paradise—whether in the body or out of the body, I do not know, God knows—and he heard things that cannot be told, which man may not utter.[8]

Segal believes that this passage demonstrates both that ascent mysticism was practiced in the first century and that Paul was a Jewish mystic. He suggests we view Paul "as a Jewish mystic, with a special Christian cast."[9]

Christopher Morray-Jones, associate professor of religion at the University of California, Berkeley, believes that Paul is "describing an ascent to the heavenly temple and a *Merkabah* vision of the enthroned and 'glorified' Christ." He concludes that *Merkabah* mysticism is "a central feature of Paul's experience and self-understanding."[10]

CLOTHES OF GLORY

Other passages in Paul's letters provide further evidence that he was a Jewish mystic. In them, he teaches Christians to identify with Christ in the same way Jewish mystics identified with the enthroned divine being.

In 2 Corinthians, Paul describes a process of glorification that parallels one recorded in 2 Enoch. Enoch is brought before "the LORD," a divine being seated on a throne. In the vision, the Archangel Michael "extracts" Enoch from his "earthly clothing," anoints him with oil and puts him into "clothes of glory." After this, Enoch tells us that he looked at himself and he had become "like one of the glorious ones, and there was no observable difference."[11]

In Corinthians, Paul uses the same metaphor for transformation as Enoch does—exchanging earthly clothing for heavenly clothing. He contrasts living in an "earthly tent" (presumably the mortal body) with living in an eternal, heavenly dwelling. He compares the two modes of existence with clothing: "For in this tent we groan, longing *to be clothed with our heavenly dwelling*... because *we wish not to be unclothed but to be further clothed* [in the heavenly dwelling], so that what is mortal may be swallowed up by life."[12]

Both passages use the process of changing clothes to describe entering an altered state. For Enoch that state is being transformed into a "glorious one," and for Paul, it is mortality being "swallowed up by life." Paul has simply replaced the divine being of Jewish mysticism with Christ. Thus we can conclude that when Paul taught people to be clothed in a heavenly dwelling, he meant that they should seek oneness with the divine being—with the Christ, the universal Logos.

BEING IN CHRIST

The passages in which Paul describes being "in Christ" give further support to the argument that Paul was exhorting us to seek union with Christ. The traditional interpretation is that being in Christ means being a Christian, one with the body of Christians on earth. But I give it a deeper meaning; I believe it refers to the state of being identified with Christ through a mystical experience.

My interpretation fits Paul's usage of the term. For example, he calls himself a man "in Christ." He tells us that "as all die in Adam, so all will be made alive in Christ." He describes those who are in Christ as "one body," "members one of another," and says that someone who is in Christ is part of "a new creation."[13] The definition that best fits Paul's descriptions is that being in Christ means being identified with Christ.

Through analyzing Paul's use of the term *in Christ,* Segal concludes that Paul is indeed referring to the process of identification, or union, with a divine being. "Being in Christ in fact appears to mean being united with Christ's heavenly image."[14] Transformation into Christ, therefore, is an integral part of Paul's theology. The Christ has taken on the role of the enthroned divine being of Jewish mysticism.

In Judaism, this enthroned divine being came to symbolize the "ideal and immortal man,"[15] the prototype from which all have descended and to which all are destined to return. In other words, the divine being represents the higher part of ourselves that did not take part in the fall into mortal bodies. I call this being the Divine Self.

Three Epistles describe the Christian's transformation from a state of soul bondage to reunion with the Divine Self. Ephesians: "God, . . . even when we were dead through our trespasses, made us alive together with Christ. . . and raised us up with him and seated us with him in the heavenly places in Christ Jesus."[16] Second Corinthians: "For while we live, we are always being given up to death for Jesus' sake, so that the life of Jesus may be made visible in our mortal flesh."[17] Galatians: "It is no longer I who live, but it is Christ who lives in me."[18]

When the Pauline Epistles tell us we are being seated in "heavenly places in Christ" and that Jesus' life is "made visible in our mortal flesh," they are describing the process by which we too can be transformed into the Christ. Remember, the Christ is not simply the man Jesus who lived on earth. The Christ is the Logos, the divine Word that he became, the Divine Self of all of us.

The most important message that we can get from Paul's

letters is that Jesus was the prototype for every Christian. As Paul says in Romans, "They are the ones [God] chose specially long ago and intended to become true images of his Son, so that his Son might be the eldest of many brothers."[19] Here Paul is saying that it is the destiny of every Christian to be transformed into a divine being, a sibling of Jesus, who is the firstborn.

FROM GLORY UNTO GLORY

In the above passage from Romans, Paul uses the word *image:* "conformed to the *image* of his Son." This word had a special meaning in *Merkabah* mysticism. As Segal tells us, the image of God, or *eikon,* was "an especially glorious and splendid form that humanity lost when Adam sinned."[20]

We can now understand the grand scope of Paul's theology when he says that "all of us, with unveiled faces, seeing the glory of the Lord as though reflected in a mirror, *are being transformed into the same image* from one degree of glory to another"[21]—from glory unto glory. This verse, often quoted by Mark Prophet, is the blueprint of your own spiritual journey. You are destined to be transformed into your own lost divine image, becoming more like him every day.

Paul's use of the term *image* is key to interpreting his famous passage from 1 Corinthians, chapter 15. In it, Paul tells us that we are meant to bear the image of Christ. He compares Adam ("the first man") with Christ ("the last Adam"). "Just as we have borne the image of the man of dust [Adam]," he tells us, "we will also bear the image of the man of heaven [Christ]."[22]

The Gnostics, who emerged out of Jewish mysticism, also saw the image as our Divine Self, the Higher Self with which we were once united. The Gnostics believed that the Divine Self, our true divine identity, is something already inside of us.

In the *Gospel of Thomas,* replacing the human image with

the divine image is the prerequisite for entering the kingdom: "When you make the two into one, when you make the inner like the outer...when you make...an image in place of an image, then you will enter the kingdom."[23]

My interpretation of this quote is as follows: When you transform the human image into the divine image, when you make the outer man conform to the inner man, and when you replace the mortal image with the immortal image, then you will enter the kingdom; for you will have transcended duality.

Thus, the goal of spiritual development is transformation into a divine being. Paul, the Jewish mystics and the Gnostics agree on this concept. If you think I am reading too much into Paul, go back and read his letters with the mystical interpretation in mind and see if they don't become clearer in this new light. "For now we see through a glass, darkly. But then face to face."[24]

PAUL'S SOURCES

Did Paul's mysticism express Jesus' original theology or was it some wild fantasy he introduced on his own? He said he got his message directly "through a revelation of Jesus Christ."[25] And the Bible gives us every indication that the Christians of Paul's day accepted him. Paul himself tells us that the other apostles did not contest his interpretations.

Seventeen years after Paul received the Gospel, he visited James and Peter and John at Jerusalem, where they gave him "the right hand of fellowship"[26] and agreed that he should preach the Gospel to the Gentiles. Would they have done so if his Gospel differed greatly from the one they had heard Jesus preach?

It would have been difficult for Paul to have inserted mysticism into Christianity unless it had already been a part of Jesus' teaching. As Segal observes: "Ultimately, someone Jewish must have brought [the heavenly visions of Jewish mysticism] into Christianity, and there is not much time between the end of Jesus' ministry and the beginning of Paul's."[27]

If it wasn't Paul who introduced mysticism, it almost has to have been Jesus.

CHAPTER 23

The Original Christian Mystic

*Jesus took with him Peter and James
and John, and led them up a high mountain
apart, by themselves. . . . And there appeared
to them Elijah with Moses, who were
talking with Jesus.*

Mark 9:2, 4

IF THE DEAD SEA SCROLLS HAD BEEN DISCOVERED
in the early fourth century, the Arian controversy
might have turned out differently. The scrolls, along
with other Jewish and Gnostic texts, demonstrate
that in Jesus' day some believed that people could
become Sons of God.

While the scrolls are yielding other important
insights into Judaism and Christianity, I think this
is one of the most rewarding.* It supports my thesis

---

*The scrolls do not mention reincarnation, although they do im-
ply preexistence. But, as I have shown, preexistence is just one
step removed from reincarnation. In addition, we have Josephus' testimony that the Essenes, who are believed to have lived
at Qumran, believed in reincarnation. If he was accurate, the
Qumran tradition could be another link in the daisy chain that
entwines the ideas of reincarnation and divine union.

that Jesus was a mystic who came to teach others how to become Sons of God and achieve divine union.

Our discussion will focus first on interpreting the concept of the Son of God. Today many scholars doubt that Jesus said he was the "only Son of God,"[1] the Second Person of the Trinity, or the Messiah. They believe that these ideas were introduced after his death, reinforced by the fiction that he was born of a virgin who had been inseminated by the Holy Spirit and that he was therefore literally descended from God. (Neither the Dead Sea Scrolls nor other Jewish texts say anything about God impregnating a human female that she might bear his Son.)

John alone among the Gospel writers uses the term "only" to describe the Son. But he does not specifically tell us that it is Jesus who is this "only Son." However, in several places he describes the only Son in terms that some have interpreted as applying to Jesus.

The most famous passage about the only Son is: "For God so loved the world that he gave his only Son, so that everyone who believes in him may not perish but may have eternal life."[2] The early Church identified the "only Son" with Jesus. But since John does not specifically refer to Jesus when talking about the only Son, it could be that he had another interpretation.

John could easily have been referring to the Logos (Word) when he spoke of the only Son. (The Logos, you will remember, is the part of God that acts in the world and that can be outpictured in human form—see chapter 17.)

As we have seen, divine union is union with the Logos, that is, the Christ. It would follow, then, that to become one with the Logos is to become a Son. John seems to describe this union when he says: "As many as received him, to them gave he power to become the sons of God, even to them that believe on his name."[3]

The other Gospels, rather than calling Jesus the only Son, often identify him simply as "Son of God" or "Son of man."

Some scholars argue that Jesus did not call himself God's Son. But others argue that he did—without making exclusive claims to be God's *only* Son.[4]

"SONS OF GOD" IN JUDAISM

In identifying himself as a Son of God, Jesus would have been drawing on a long tradition in Jewish mysticism attested to in several texts. These include one of the Dead Sea Scrolls, published in full for the first time in 1992. A fragment (discovered in Qumran Cave IV and dated to the first century B.C.) tells us that an unidentified human being will be called "Son of God" and will reign over an "everlasting kingdom" and possess "everlasting sovereignty."[5]

This fragment indicates that the tradition that human beings can be adopted as Sons predates Jesus. (In the next chapter, we will examine the concept of sovereignty, or possessing a kingdom, which provides further links between Jesus and the Jewish mystics.)

Other Jewish texts support the tradition that people can be adopted as God's Sons. Here are three examples from the first and second centuries B.C. In Sirach, a Jewish text dating from about 180 B.C., someone who possesses wisdom is told he will be like a "son of the Most High."[6] In another work, God calls Moses his Son, and the *Testament of Levi* tells us that Levi is destined to become God's Son.[7]

As scholar James Charlesworth points out, these references do not imply that human beings have actually descended from God but that during their tenure on earth they earned the right to be called the Sons of God. One text even tells us that a heavenly voice proclaimed that the first-century Jewish mystic Hanina ben Dosa was God's Son.[8]

What this evidence suggests is that Jesus didn't think of

himself as God's exclusive Son—he wanted to show us how we, too, could become God's Sons. Psalm 2:7 reflects the tradition: "I will tell of the decree of the LORD: He said to me, 'You are my son; today I have begotten you.'"

Paul was familiar with this tradition of acquired sonship. He tells us that Jesus came "to redeem the subjects of the Law and to enable us to be adopted as sons."[9] How are Sons adopted? The explanation that comes most readily to mind is by transformation into, or mystical identification with, Christ, the "firstborn."[10]

As we saw in the last chapter, this mystical identification is an important part of Paul's theology. Now that we have seen that Jewish mystics taught that people could be transformed into Sons of God, let us examine the evidence that Jesus was part of this tradition.

THE RABBI MYSTICS

As we have seen, the scholars who are sifting the New Testament in search of Jesus' original message have discarded much of what the Christian world considers central—the bodily resurrection, the virgin birth and the belief that Jesus proclaimed himself the only begotten Son of God.[11] These scholars also question whether Jesus said most of the words attributed to him in the Gospels.[12] As they sort through the sayings that they consider authentic, they are competing for the right to chalk in the definitive new profile of the elusive Nazarene.

Out of the variety of portraits that are emerging, two are worth mentioning here. One sees Jesus as a Cynic-style preacher —a critic of the establishment and a teacher of subversive wisdom. Another portrays him as a wisdom teacher, healer and mystic.

Cynics were adherents of an ancient Greek school of philosophers who encouraged people to live a life of self-sufficiency, suppression of desires and the rejection of wealth, pleasure and family responsibilities. There is some evidence to support the Jesus-as-Cynic theory. Jesus appears to have commented on Cynicism. But I believe the majority of the evidence supports the image of Jesus as mystic. (See note for discussion.)[13]

Some members of the Jesus Seminar support the view that Jesus was a Jewish mystic. Marcus Borg, a professor of philosophy at Oregon State University and a member of the Seminar, writes, "The more we realize that there was a form of Jewish mysticism in first-century Palestine, the more likely it seems that Jesus stood in that experiential tradition."[14] As a mystic, Jesus would have been familiar with the scriptures and been able to expound on them. (Some scholars today reject the Jesus-as-mystic theory because they have concluded that he was illiterate. See note.)[15]

Jewish mystics at the time of Jesus would have taught in the tradition of Jewish rabbi-sages that goes back to the sixth century B.C. The sages were among those who began returning from captivity in Babylon in 538 B.C. and started rebuilding the Temple at Jerusalem, which had been destroyed by the Babylonian armies. They were at the heart of a reinvigorated Judaism, interpreting the scriptures and giving them meaning in changing times. We know that they also secretly passed down traditions on the Creation and the chariot, which became the backbone of Jewish mysticism.

The first-century sages bear several similarities to the Jesus of the Gospels. These sages taught in parables and short, pithy sayings. In Jerusalem, they imitated Greek philosophers, teaching groups of students at the city gates, under trees and in private homes. This fits in well with some of the Gospel images of Jesus.

Jesus bears other similarities to early Jewish mystics. We know that some mystics were widely regarded as miracle workers. Honi ha-Meaggel (Honi the Circle-Drawer) was known for his success in praying for rain. Hanina ben Dosa was renowned for his healings.

One can almost imagine Jesus, called "Rabbi" in John, traveling the country, healing, commenting on current ideas like Cynicism and secretly initiating his disciples into the mystery of divine ascents.

One of the most famous of the sages was Hillel, a founder of rabbinic Judaism and a leader of the Sanhedrin for forty years (30 B.C.–A.D. 10). Some have speculated that Jesus was familiar with Hillel's teachings. Hillel's "Do not unto others that which you would not have them do unto you"[16] is similar to the Golden Rule of the Gospels.

Hillel even taught a version of karma. He said to a skull floating on the water, "Because you drowned someone, you have been drowned by others; and in the end those who drowned you shall themselves be drowned."[17] Did he have in mind that this drama would play itself out through reincarnation?

One of Hillel's pupils, Yohanan ben Zakkai, is regarded as an important father of *Merkabah* mysticism. Remember, *Merkabah* mysticism focused on union with a divine being. Finding *Merkabah* mysticism in the lineage of Hillel, a contemporary of Jesus, is an important clue. It shows that Jesus could have also been exposed to these ideas.

The apostle Paul, a Pharisee, may have also studied Hillel's teachings. Acts tells us that Paul was educated "at the feet of Gamaliel,"[18] who was a son or grandson of Hillel. And we know that Paul practiced ascents and taught people to become one with Christ.

JESUS PRACTICES ASCENTS

If Jesus was a Jewish mystic, we would expect him to have taught both mystical ascents and identification with a divine being. We can find both in the Gospels if we know where to look.

The transfiguration provides strong evidence that Jesus practiced these ascents and suggests that he taught his disciples to practice them. In the story, which appears in Matthew, Mark and Luke, Jesus takes Peter, James and John up a "high mountain."[19] Jesus is transfigured—his face and clothing begin to shine. The disciples are "terrified."[20] Moses and Elijah appear to them and talk with Jesus. A voice out of a cloud says, "This is my beloved Son: hear him."[21]

This story contains the essential elements of ascent mysticism. Going up on a high mountain sounds like a metaphor for a soul journey or ascent. The disciples are afraid, a common experience of *Merkabah* mystics. The light that shines from Jesus' face and clothing suggests the brilliant light often seen during ascents. Moses and Elijah are both prominent figures in ascent mysticism. And the voice out of heaven is an important element also found in other Jewish mystical experiences. Here it echoes the idea from Jewish mysticism that people can be adopted as God's Sons—"This is my beloved Son: hear him."[22]

Scholars debate whether the transfiguration account reflects the disciples' experience with Jesus while he was alive or their own mystical experiences following his crucifixion and resurrection. Either way, the transfiguration story further indicates that mystical elements entered Christianity at an early stage.

The ascension itself is another piece of evidence that Jesus practiced ascents. The idea that Jesus ascended to heaven after his resurrection is based on a passage in Acts that describes Jesus being "lifted up, and a cloud took him out of their sight."[23] Could this incident have roots in a *Merkabah* ascent that Jesus undertook in the presence of his disciples?

The Book of Revelation describes the heavenly ascent of its author. According to Morton Smith, a prominent scholar, this and other stories indicate that early Christians approved of mystical ascents and that this approval went back to Jesus. He finds it unlikely that the apostles themselves, including John the Revelator and Paul, initiated the tradition of mystical ascents.

Awestruck, Peter, James and John shield their eyes from the blinding light of the transfigured Christ. Moses and Elijah appear and converse with Jesus. Fra Angelico, who painted this version around 1440, has added the figures of the Virgin Mary and Saint Dominic to the scene. Some scholars speculate that the transfiguration was actually a mystical soul journey taken by Jesus and the apostles.

"We anticipate some distortion and innovation [by his disciples], but the proposition that a man's devoted followers radically misrepresented his teachings is *a priori* improbable," he writes.[24]

Although Smith does not see the ascents as genuine spiritual experiences (he calls them "hallucinations" induced by Jesus, a skilled magician), he believes they were an important part of early Christianity. The best explanation for the presence of ascents in Christianity, writes Smith, "is that Jesus, in his lifetime, believed he had ascended into the heavens, [and] told his most intimate disciples of his experiences."[25] This would account for the disciples being willing to accept Paul's visionary revelations and for the Church having adopted the Book of Revelation.

Smith demonstrates that Jesus was believed to have made heavenly ascents during his lifetime. As Jesus says to Nicodemus, "No one has ascended into heaven except the one who descended from heaven, the Son of Man."[26] Smith concludes that ascent to the heavens was the fundamental goal of early Christianity. "In sum, early Christianity... was constantly oriented towards ascent to the heavens," he writes.[27]

If Jesus practiced heavenly ascents, did he also experience identification with a divine being? Passages from the Bible suggest that he did.

Jesus called himself the Son of man,[28] apparently identifying himself with the Son of man described in the Book of Daniel. There, the Son of man is brought before the "Ancient of days" and given an everlasting kingdom.[29] Thus, by calling himself the Son of man, Jesus may have been indicating that he, too, had experienced such an empowerment or transformation into a king.

Christians later interpreted this passage to mean that Jesus would return at the end of the world for the final judgment. But Daniel's prophecy or vision of the empowerment of the Son of man could instead be describing mystical union in which the Son of man becomes like God.

A passage in the Gospel of John also affirms Jesus' identification with God. Jesus says, "I and my Father are one."[30] What's more, John implies that the disciples were taught to identify with Jesus in the same way that Jesus identified with the Father or that mystics identified with the figure on the divine throne. In John 14:4, Jesus tells his disciples, "And you know the way to the place where I am going." Smith interpreted this sentence as implying, "You can follow whenever you want to."[31]

To me this means "You have been there because I have already taken you there in the mystical ascents we have practiced together. You can reach the level of consciousness that I have reached."

Jesus then declares, "I am the way, the truth, and the life: no man cometh unto the Father, but by me."[32] Smith believes that this indicates that the disciples had already experienced psychological identification with Jesus through mystical ascents.

So when Jesus says, "No man cometh unto the Father, but by me," does he mean that no man can achieve divine union except by identifying with the Christ, which he had become? Identification equals transformation equals mystical union. I am convinced that this was Jesus' secret teaching, confirmed in Paul's mysticism: The purpose of Christianity is to experience union with the divine.

I believe that each of us can experience this mystical union— beginning with each fleeting glimpse of ultimate reality and culminating in our permanent union with God. This union is what I call the ascension. It is your destiny as a child of God evolving on earth. It is the prize you can win as you begin to experience God in your heart each moment of each hour of each day.

CHAPTER 24

Where Is the Kingdom?

*And our Lord opened my inner eye and
showed me my soul in the middle of my heart.
The soul was as large as an infinite world
and like a blessed kingdom.*

Julian of Norwich
Revelations of Divine Love

JESUS SPOKE OFTEN OF THE KINGDOM. BUT WHAT is it? How does one enter its gates?

As we will see in this chapter, attaining the kingdom is the same as achieving divine union. The kingdom is not a *where* as much as it is an *everywhere*—a state of being that you can access when you achieve oneness with God. Examining Jesus' sayings on the kingdom of God will help us to better understand how to find that state.

In Jesus' time, many people thought about and looked for a coming kingdom. "What will it be like?" they wondered.

Some thought of it as a future everlasting rule of God and his representative, the Messiah. If so, would it take place on earth or in the heavens? There was support for both views.

Supporting the earthly theory, the author of the *Psalms of Solomon* (first century B.C.) asks God to raise up a king, "the son of David," who would rule Israel at an undesignated future time.[1] But the *Testament of Moses,* a book written close to the time of Jesus, tells the righteous they will be taken to a heavenly kingdom: "God will raise you [Israel] to the heights. Yea, he will fix you firmly in the heaven of the stars."[2]

Even though there may have been a difference of opinion about whether the kingdom was in heaven or on earth, both of these passages describe the kingdom as a place and its coming as a future event. The Catholic Church adopted this view and affirms today that we must wait until "the end of time" after the last judgment for the kingdom of God to "come in its fullness." When the kingdom comes, the entire "visible universe" will be "transformed."[3]

But there is another concept of kingship that refers to an internal state of being—the ability, or power, to rule. The term *kingdom* in the New Testament comes from the Greek *basileia,* which means the *act* of ruling (rather than a place or event). It signifies the power to rule.

How does one attain this power? Jewish and Christian texts tell us that the power of rulership, or dominion, is granted to the wise—and that wisdom leads to personal immortality. The Wisdom of Solomon, written in Alexandria in the first century, says: "The beginning of wisdom is the most sincere desire for instruction... and giving heed to her laws is assurance of immortality, and immortality brings one near to God; so the desire for wisdom leads to a kingdom."[4]

WISDOM LEADS TO THE KINGDOM

We can learn more about the kingdom by looking at texts from the Jewish and Christian wisdom tradition. The Book of Proverbs refers to Wisdom as a divine feminine being created "before the beginning of the earth."[5] The concept of Wisdom (or Sophia) as a divine being comes from Jewish as well as Gnostic traditions. The pursuit of wisdom came to be equated with the pursuit of personal immortality and with *basileia,* rulership.

The Wisdom of Solomon promises immortality to the righteous, saying that they will "govern nations and rule over peoples."[6] In other words, they will have rulership. In Christianity, the role of Wisdom is transferred to Jesus. He becomes a human-divine mediator who, like Wisdom, can grant both immortality and rulership.

The Dead Sea Scrolls also link attaining wisdom with ruling a kingdom. The *Aramaic Testament of Levi* (third century B.C.), discovered at Qumran, tells us that "every man who teaches wisdom" will be seated "upon a throne of glory." Another passage tells those who seek wisdom that they will become kings, rulers in an eternal kingdom.[7]

Philo also tells us that the wise are the ones who participate in the kingdom. They are given the power to rule: "The Sage who possesses [virtues] is a king.... The Sage alone is a ruler and king, and virtue a rule and a kingship whose authority is final."[8]

Philo makes it clear that he is not describing an earthly kingdom when he speaks of the kingdom of the Sage: "Other kingdoms are established among men with wars and campaigns and numberless ills.... But the kingdom of the Sage comes by the gift of God, and the virtuous man who receives it brings no harm to anyone."[9]

THE WAY TO TRUE FREEDOM

Jews and Greeks both speculated about what the kingdom was and how to achieve it. Philo and the Greek Cynics tell us that possessing the kingdom is the only way to achieve true freedom. And this freedom comes only to those who find wisdom. The wise person becomes a king under the great King, God, says Philo. As such, he is considered free, his own master, even if he is ruled over by ten thousand men.[10] In other words, even if he is technically a slave, the wise man is more free than his master.

The Stoic-Cynic philosopher Epictetus compared himself to a king, even though he was as poor as a beggar: "I sleep on the ground; I have no wife, no children, no praetorium [official power], but only the earth and the heavens, and one poor cloak. And what do I want? Am I not without sorrow? Am I not without fear? Am I not free?...Who, when he sees me, does not think that he sees his king and master?"[11] Epictetus is poorer than any king, but he is freer because he is not controlled by his fears and desires.

Philo advises those who would achieve the state of freedom and rulership to reduce their wants and control their desires. Freedom doesn't depend on whether someone is a slave or a freeman but on whether he is controlled by his emotions and passions, he wrote, sounding like a Buddhist. A soul who is "driven to and fro" by appetite, pleasure, fear or grief "then makes itself a slave...of ten thousand masters." Souls who free themselves of these chains receive "power and authority"—rulership over self.[12]

Diogenes, founder of Cynicism, was an example of a free man, and therefore royal, Philo tells us in his work *Every Good Man Is Free*. Diogenes, even though taken prisoner by robbers and put up for sale as a slave, didn't let it dampen his spirits. Instead, he joked with his fellow slaves and ridiculed prospective buyers.[13] Philo is showing us that equanimity and nonattachment are qualities of a "king."

The *Sentences of Sextus,* one of the Nag Hammadi texts, speaks of freedom in the same way as Philo: "After God, no one is as free as the wise man. Everything God possesses the wise man has also. The wise man shares in the kingdom of God."[14]

"THY KINGDOM COME"

These speculations about the kingdom, widespread in the first century, would no doubt have been familiar to Jesus when he began to teach. He took them into account and built upon them.

Jesus' kingdom sayings withstood the analysis of the Jesus Seminar, who concluded they were an authentic part of his preaching. But the scholars don't believe he saw the kingdom as an apocalyptic future event. They believe that Jesus, like Philo and the Cynics, saw the kingdom as a state of being, something we don't have to wait until the end of the world to experience. We can enjoy it today—if we have the keys.

Let us look at some of the sayings that scholars believe represent the bare bones of Jesus' message on the kingdom. Two sayings that appear in both Luke and the *Gospel of Thomas* are pivotal:

> He said, "What is the kingdom of God like? To what should I compare it? It is like a grain of mustard which a man took and sowed in his garden. It grew and became a tree, and the birds of the air made nests in its branches."
>
> He also said, "The kingdom of God is like yeast which a woman took and hid in three measures of flour until it leavened the whole mass."[15]

What do yeast and a mustard seed have in common? Both have an effect out of proportion to their size. The tiny mustard seed becomes a tree so big that birds can nest in its branches.

"Then one of the seven angels.... carried me away [in spirit] to a great, high mountain and showed me the holy city Jerusalem coming down out of heaven from God." This painting by Gustave Doré shows the new Jerusalem. Many people believe that the new Jerusalem is the future kingdom of God. However, others take it as an allegory for the transformation of the soul.

The yeast, although small in proportion to the flour, leavens the entire lump of dough.

The kingdom of God is therefore both tiny and huge at the same time. As we saw in chapter 4, there is something else that has both of these properties—the divine spark, the Atman. Hidden inside of each person, it is so little that it can't be seen. Yet it also contains the allness of God; it is so vast it can't be comprehended.

When Jesus tells us that the kingdom is like yeast and a mustard seed, he is telling us that the kingdom is realized through the divine spark. As the tiny mustard seed becomes a large plant, so the divine spark can allow us to fully become the great tree of our divinity. As the yeast causes the entire batch of dough to rise, so the divine spark has the power to transform our entire being into God. When we realize the kingdom through the divine spark, we will have achieved divinity.

Jesus' other statements about the kingdom bring to mind another quality of God—his all-pervasiveness, inhabiting every part of life, ensouling the universe. Jesus tells us that the kingdom is present everywhere but not accessed by everyone.

In *Thomas* 113, the disciples ask Jesus, "When will the kingdom come?" He answers, "It will not come by watching for it. It will not be said, 'Behold, here' or 'Behold, there.' Rather, the kingdom of the Father is spread out upon the earth, and people do not see it."[16]

This sounds like Jesus' description of the kingdom in Luke 17:20–21. Jesus tells the Pharisees: "You won't be able to observe the coming of [the kingdom of God]. People are not going to be able to say, 'Look, here it is!' or 'Over there!' On the contrary, [the kingdom of God] is right there in your presence."[17]

For further confirmation that the kingdom is a personal condition and can be experienced in the present, we can look to the Book of Hebrews: "Since we *are receiving* a kingdom that cannot be shaken, let us give thanks."[18] The author of Hebrews gives us another insight into the nature of the kingdom. He describes it as made up of "what cannot be shaken" in contrast to "created things," which can be "shaken."[19] This shows that the kingdom is composed of spiritual, immortal things.

THE KEYS TO THE KINGDOM

Let's tally up what we know about the kingdom. In the Dead Sea Scrolls and the wisdom tradition, it is a state of being—the power to rule—that is granted to the wise and the righteous, and it leads to immortality. Philo tells us we can achieve it by detaching ourselves from the material world. Luke and *Thomas* tell us that it is available to us here on earth but that not everyone is able to access it. From Hebrews we learn that it is made up of spiritual things and not created things. Jesus tells us that it is both very small and very big and has a transformative power, thus suggesting a connection with the mystical idea that we can become one with God.

The *Gospel of Thomas* and the other Nag Hammadi texts also point in this direction. *Thomas* saying 3 tells us that the kingdom is both inside of us (very small) and outside of us (very big). The author of *Thomas* expands and builds upon the concepts of Philo and Hellenistic Judaism when he tells us that the kingdom is achieved through self-knowledge:

> Jesus said, "If your leaders say to you, 'Behold, the kingdom is in heaven,' then the birds of heaven will precede you. If they say to you, 'It is in the sea,' then the fish will precede you. Rather, the kingdom is within you and it is outside you.
>
> "When you know yourselves, then you will be known, and you will understand that you are children of the living Father."[20]

To "know" ourselves and to become "known" are Gnostic terms for the process of assimilating and being assimilated by the God within. Thus *Thomas* is telling us that in order to enter the kingdom, we must become one with the God within.

The *Book of Thomas* seems to echo Philo when it tells us that the key to becoming a "king" is to overcome the dominion of both pleasure and pain: "When you leave bodily pains and passions, you will receive rest from the Good One, and you will reign with the King."

The text then tells us that achieving kingship is the same as divine union. When you reign, you will be "united with the King and the King united with you, now and for ever and ever."[21]

The Gnostic text *Pistis Sophia* repeats this idea. Here, Jesus promises kingship and divine union to those who receive his mysteries. He says, "All men who will receive the mystery of the Ineffable will become fellow-rulers (kings) with me in my kingdom. And I am they and they are I."[22] In other words, when you become one with the Christ, exemplified by Jesus (the prototype of your immortal divine image), you will have attained the kingdom.

Other sayings in the *Gospel of Thomas* confirm that "finding the kingdom" is a code phrase for "divine union." First, Jesus compares himself to the kingdom: "Whoever is near me is near the fire, and whoever is far from me is far from the kingdom."[23] If the kingdom is like Jesus, then people wanting to attain the kingdom need to become more like Jesus, as implied in saying 108: "Jesus said, 'Whoever drinks from my mouth will become like me; I myself shall become that person, and the hidden things will be revealed to that one.'"[24]

"RETURNING TO THE BEGINNING"

In *Thomas*, another synonym for becoming divine is "returning to the beginning," the primordial state of perfection before souls ever descended into mortal form. Scholar Stevan Davies concludes that in the *Gospel of Thomas* "the beginning, the kingdom of God, Jesus, and the light are equivalent terms."[25]

When Jesus' disciples ask him about the "end," he tells them that the way to achieve eternal life is to return to the beginning. "Jesus said, 'Have you found the beginning that you search for the end? In the place where the beginning is, there the end will be. Blessed is he who will stand at the beginning, and he will know the end and he will not taste death.' "[26]

In saying 24, Jesus tells us more about how to attain the "beginning" (or perfected) state, which he has already achieved. His disciples say, "Show us the place where you are, for we must seek it." Jesus replies, "There is light within a person of light, and it shines on the whole world. If it does not shine, it is dark."[27]

Thus, when you discover how to make your light shine, when you become one with the light that is God in your heart, you will stand at the beginning—you will have discovered the kingdom.

BEING EVERYWHERE

What is it like to stand at the beginning? To actualize, or realize, the light? To be one with God?

Mystics have described the state of union as being "everywhere" at once. In *Thomas* 77, Jesus says: "I am the light which is above all things, I am all things; all things came forth from me and all things reached me. Split wood, I am there; lift the stone up, you will find me there."[28]

"Split wood, I am there." In other words, now that I have achieved divine union, I am present with God in every atom and molecule of the universe.

The *Gospel of Philip* elaborates on this form of existence— the state of being a part of all life. It calls this state "the real realm" and says that when we become one with God, we unite with the real, spiritual essence of things rather than with the unreality of the material world:

People cannot see anything in the real realm unless they become it. In the realm of truth, it is not as human beings in the world, who see the sun without being the sun, and see the sky and the earth and so forth without being them. Rather, if you have seen any things there, you have become those things: if you have seen the spirit, you have become the spirit; if you have seen the anointed [Christ], you have become the anointed [Christ]; if you have seen the father, you will become the father. Thus here [in the world], you see everything and do not see your own self. But there you see yourself; for you shall become what you see.[29]

In other words, in the kingdom, you become everything. When you achieve the kingdom, you will be present beneath every stone, just as Jesus is. You will both see and be the sun, the sky and the earth. The heart of Jesus' message is that we can find this state of mystical union, which truly is the kingdom and eternal life. As our elder brother, the "firstborn within a large family,"[30] Jesus did not desire to be a king exalted over all others; he wanted to show us the way to our own kingdom.

When we find it, we will have found a way out of the human dilemma—pain and suffering, the wheel of rebirth—and into a state of enlightenment as yet incomprehensible. This state of divine union is out of this world—out of the world of time, space and matter.

WHERE THERE IS NO TIME AND SPACE

Quantum physicists have recently made some discoveries that resonate with the experiences of the mystics. Before we conclude our discussion of the kingdom, let us take a trip through the subatomic world. Here we will find some amazing correspondences with the Gnostics' description of the kingdom. Their concept of a state of being in which everything is interconnected may not be so far-fetched after all.

Every student of high school physics learns that nothing can travel faster than the speed of light. But a new series of

experiments has given us two seemingly impossible alternatives: Either information can travel faster than the speed of light
(which would undermine much of modern physics) *or* matter
as we know it is not separate and apart as it appears to be but
is interconnected on some hidden level.

Physicists have long known that time and space are not absolute realities. At speeds close to the speed of light, time may
seem to run more slowly and space may shrink. Albert Einstein
spoke of time and space as a continuum. He also showed that
matter and energy are not separate from each other. Matter can
become energy and energy can become matter.

Another of the strange discoveries of quantum physics is
that some subatomic particles have a "nonlocal" quality. They
are interconnected with other particles and seem to be able to
communicate with each other instantaneously even when separated by large distances. For example, one particle could be in
New York and another in Los Angeles but, conceivably, they
could exchange information instantaneously.

The principle of nonlocality was demonstrated in a series of
quantum physics experiments during the 1980s. The experiments showed that pairs of photons—packets of light energy—
can influence each other instantaneously, even when shooting
off in divergent directions.[31] Since Einstein showed that it is
impossible for any signal to travel faster than the speed of light,
the best explanation for this is that the photons have a nonlocal
quality. This means that they can instantaneously influence
each other across large distances.

Nonlocal interaction stretches the imagination. We can see
an example of how nonlocal interaction might work in our
world if we imagine an experiment in which two pilots, Orville
and Wilbur, head off in opposite directions from Topeka,
Kansas. One heads for the East Coast, the other for the West
Coast. Each pilot knows that he has the option to choose a

northern or southern route but he cannot communicate with the other plane. Near Denver, Wilbur turns south. At exactly the same moment, without any communication between the craft, Orville turns south too.

Although the odds of this occurring by chance in real life are astronomical, this kind of correlation is what scientists tell us is happening in the subatomic world.

And we do see examples of seemingly correlated actions every day, although we can't prove that nonlocal action is what causes them—for instance, when people are suddenly aware that a loved one has been hurt. These "coincidences," call them synchronicities, may be examples of people briefly experiencing the interconnectedness that is the kingdom of God.

Nonlocal interaction is a condition beyond time and space in which terms like *distance, separation* and *particle* have no meaning. It indicates that subatomic particles are not really particles at all but the visible manifestations of an invisible whole. It means that the particles can be interconnected even though they are traveling away from each other at light speed.

Some thinkers believe that what is true for subatomic particles is also true for the entire universe. One of these, physicist David Bohm, suggests that there is a hidden order in the universe, a deeper level of reality that he dubs the "implicate order."

In the visible world, called the "explicate order," things appear to be separate and distinct. But if you were able to get beyond appearances, you would discover that there is an implicate order enfolded in all things that connects everything.[32] Everything is a part of everything else—just as the mystics have been telling us. While physics has not yet proved that there is such an implicate order, the theory does explain the nonlocal phenomenon.

We can better understand how the implicate order could be hidden within our world if we think of it as a drop of ink that was once a clearly visible whole on a tangled clump of string but has become barely visible as the string has been extended. As F. David Peat, a physicist and one of Bohm's collaborators, explains it: "When the string is unwound, the ink dots become very far apart. Measured along the string itself, the distance between the dots is several feet, but across the tangle they were only a few millimeters apart. The... points are both close together [as the drop] and far apart [on the extended string]."[33]

We can think of the visible world as the extended string and the implicate order as the hidden drop. It would be possible to reconstruct the drop by reproducing the tangle. And it may be possible to access the implicate order by identifying with the hidden reality (the drop) rather than with the visible world (the string).

The implicate order seems remarkably similar to the state of being described by the mystics in which the seeker, while alive, becomes one with his Higher Self and thus with the universe. Time does not exist for him. He can know things instantaneously because he is actually a part of them. Remember this saying from the *Gospel of Thomas:* "When you make the two into one, and when you make the inner like the outer... when you make... an image in place of an image, then you will enter the kingdom."

Today's mystic, using the language of modern physics, might say: "When you understand that the explicate order is only the visible manifestation of the implicate order and when you, the part, realize that you are also the whole, you will enter the kingdom."

❦

CHAPTER 25

Breaking the Chain of Rebirth

Rather monotonous, isn't it, the idea
that you have to be reborn, put into diapers
and pinned up and have oatmeal dribbling
down your chin. Some people have told me
that they don't want to go through it again.
I don't either.

Mark L. Prophet

R EMEMBER HOUDINI'S FAMOUS TRICK WHERE he had himself shackled, then locked inside of a weighted box that was roped on the outside and dropped into an ice-cold river?

Being imprisoned in matter, chained to the wheel of rebirth, is like being inside that box. You can't see the invisible, spiritual world outside the box—the "nonlocal" world, the world in which you are "everywhere." But you know it exists somewhere outside the box.

How do you find your way out of the box? Houdini didn't reveal his secret. But mystics have been pressing the boundaries of matter for thousands of years, and they have left a road map for us to follow.

The mystics tell us that liberation is a gradual process that comes in stages. First you contact the state of divine union for a single instant. It would be as if one second you were imprisoned in the box and the next second you were as free as a rainbow trout leaping over the sparkling surface of a stream.

The mystics tell us we do not have to wait for physical death to access the state of divine union. As you concentrate on finding eternity, you gradually begin to spend more time out of the box and in the nonlocal state—even as your human form is busy about its daily tasks. You may alternate between the free air and the watery tomb. And one day you may find that a part of you is living in freedom all the time.

In this chapter we will explore techniques you can use to contact the nonlocal state and how you can tell when you have found it.

THE LANGUAGE OF FIRE

Heraclitus, a sixth-century-B.C. Greek philosopher, believed that fire was the primordial substance, the substructure of the universe. Fire is a common thread that runs through mystical writings. Mystics associate the state of union with God with being filled with heavenly fire. This fire, unlike the earthly flames that consumed the bodies of heretics, transforms the mystic into God.

We can trace this heavenly fire through the history of mysticism. For example, in the fifth century, a disciple witnessed a famous desert monk, Abba Arsenius, glowing "like fire from head to feet." Another monk, Abba Joseph, told his pupil, with his fingers shining "like ten candles": "If you will, you could become a living flame."[1] Father Seraphim, a Russian Orthodox saint, once appeared so bright that his disciple commented that he could not look at him. Lightning flashed from his eyes and his face was brighter than the sun.[2]

Lightning also flashes in 3 Enoch, a Jewish mystical text that describes the author's transformation into a divine being. He says, "At once my flesh turned to flame, my sinews to blazing fire, my bones to juniper coals, my eyelashes to lightning flashes, my eyeballs to fiery torches, the hairs of my head to hot flames, all my limbs to wings of burning fire, and the substance of my body to blazing fire."[3] This sounds excruciating. But as a spiritual experience, it conveyed not pain but ecstasy.

In the fourteenth century, Catherine of Siena told of her discovery that her nature and God's were the same, "a fire of love."[4] The Dominican friar and mystic Henry Suso described a vision of the sun's radiance flooding forth from his own chest.[5] In the sixteenth century, Saint John of the Cross wrote of his pursuit of the living flame of love.

Perhaps the language of fire reappears throughout mystical writings because it is the closest thing in our experience to the condition of being one with the universe. Fire, sunlight and lightning all can appear to be everywhere at once. Fire can fill a room in an instant, sunbeams fill the air and lightning "comes from the east and flashes as far as the west."[6]

Fire also blazes up in the experiences of mystics in more recent times. Blaise Pascal (1623–62), the French mathematician, physicist and mystic, spent the last years of his life in a convent. Although he was a scientist (his experiments had led to the invention of the hydraulic press), he was convinced that mysticism held the key to the secrets of the universe.

After he died, a scrap of paper was discovered, sewn into his clothing, that described a mystical experience:

> From about half past ten in the evening [to] about
> half [an hour after] midnight.
> Fire.

> God of Abraham, God of Isaac, God of Jacob.
> not [the God] of philosophers and scholars:
> Certainty, joy, certainty, emotion, sight, joy. . . .
> Oblivious to the world and to everything except GOD. . . .
> This is life eternal.[7]

Pascal associated eternal life with an experience of fire.

The American philosopher William James (1842–1910) also had a mystical experience of fire. It happened while he was driving home through city streets late at night after an evening with friends. It lasted only a few seconds, but it stayed with him for the rest of his life. He wrote:

> All at once, without warning of any kind, I found myself wrapped in a flame-coloured cloud. For an instant I thought of fire, an immense conflagration somewhere close by in that great city; the next instant I knew that that fire was in myself.
>
> Directly afterwards there came upon me a sense of exultation, of immense joyousness, accompanied or immediately followed by an intellectual illumination quite impossible to describe. Among other things, I did not merely come to believe, I saw that the universe is not composed of dead matter, but is, on the contrary, a living Presence; I became conscious in myself of eternal life. It was not a conviction that I would have eternal life, but a consciousness that I possessed eternal life then.[8]

What the mystics seem to be telling us, then, is that a spiritual or physical vision of fire is a signal that one has entered the nonlocal state.

These mystics had discovered a way out of the box. For a few moments or even several hours, they had experienced oneness with God—a foretaste of what they would know when they were able to break the chain of rebirth. How did they do it?

Their experiences were the convergence of God's grace and their desire to become one with him. Both are necessary ingredients on the path to divine union.

The way to eternal life is different for each of us. In order to find the way that is right for you, you must first get in touch with the God spark inside of you, which will lead you unerringly to the quickest route home.

A true path to God generally contains at least four basic elements. It will show you how to:

1. Fulfill your karmic obligations to all of life by making up for your past negative actions.

2. Learn to identify with your spiritual self rather than your material self.

3. Access divine grace, which awakens you to your divine nature and enables you to find your way out of the bonds of karma.

4. Focus all of your mind on the purpose of reunion with God. This is often facilitated by various mystical techniques such as prayer, contemplation and visualization.

(The first three steps will prepare you for the fourth step, which actually provides the mechanism of divine union.)

Let us review these four elements of the path through the story of Marvin Baker, a mystic from Indiana.

YOUR NUMBER ONE PRIORITY: BALANCING KARMA

The first step on Marvin's path to God was to begin fulfilling his karmic obligations by making up for his past negative actions. Marvin, you will recall from the preface, was serving a sixty-year sentence for murder when he discovered my books.

Being in prison—the state penitentiary in Michigan City, Indiana, to be exact—is a sobering situation. Marvin complained of the "crueltys" as well as "lack of fresh air and sunshine." He compared being incarcerated to being in a prisoner-of-war camp and told me how other prisoners turned to drugs. But he chose instead to pursue union with God.

I told him: "The first thing you must know is that it does not matter where you are in physical location. You can attain union with God. Union with God is not conditioned by circumstance or karma or past crimes."

I told him his first steps were to recognize the wrong he had done and to be willing to pay the price. He had committed the murder during a drunken argument and he saw it as "one big mistake." Although the murder was not premeditated, he knew he had done wrong. "There is no excuse and I'm not offering any," he said. He knew that in order to pursue his ultimate union with God, his ascension, he needed to make up for his wrong actions—both the murder and any other harmful acts he had committed in his life.

Rather than succumb to despair at his seemingly hopeless situation, Marvin decided to try to balance that karma. He realized that he was paying off some of his karma simply by being in prison. But he wanted to accelerate the process. He pursued good works (encouraging and ministering to his fellow prisoners), appealed to "God's Amazing Grace" and began practicing a mystical technique called the invocation of the violet flame.

The violet flame is able to dissolve the effects of negative karma and propel the soul into the higher frequencies of energy that lead to divine union.[9] Combined with service to life, invoking the violet flame can form the foundation of your acceleration into God consciousness.

Even though most of us do not live in a situation as confining as Marvin's, we are all, in a sense, prisoners of mortality, of the boundaries of human existence, of time and space. And we, too, can make the decision Marvin made. We, too, can decide to pursue the ascension.

If you decide that your goal in life is reunion with God, the next thing to do is to figure out the best way to balance your karma. Ask your Higher Self to lead you into activities that will help you overcome past wrongs. There are people you need to help and serve. They may already be among your family and acquaintances. Or you may be required to conceive and bear them as children. Or you may find them through helping others in your community and the world.

You do not have to balance all of your karma in order to find the nonlocal state, the kingdom of God. But you do have to balance more than half of it in order to remain permanently in that state and not reincarnate. If you leave your work undone, it will pull you right back into the grayness of human existence after you leave this life.

You can imagine your material body as a birdcage filled with thousands of birds—and one special bird, your soul. Your soul cannot leave the cage (your material body) until all the other birds (karmic obligations) are gone. Each time you perform a good act or think a positive thought, you set one bird free. And one day, before you know it, you will have let loose all the birds and the last bird, your soul, will be free to leave the cage and soar sunward into permanent union with God.

IDENTIFYING WITH THE "THINGS THAT EXIST"

Tibetan lamas spend days making intricate patterns of sand only to brush them away. They say that the message we should take from their actions is that everything is impermanent. The most brilliant autumn leaves will fade, the widest sea will dry up and the brightest stars will die. Even Helen of Troy grew old. But God and the things of the Spirit are permanent.

The second step on the path to God is learning to identify with your spiritual self rather than your material self. The mystics would call this seeking the "things that exist." As we discussed in chapter 13, the "things that exist" are permanent, spiritual things.

How do we seek permanent things? The mystics have left us plenty of advice. Many have sought God by denying the body and the things of this world. They have practiced vegetarianism, celibacy, solitude and silence; they have endured extremes of heat and cold. They used these techniques to separate the human nature from the divine.

In Christian dogma, this renunciation was often associated with the guilt of original sin. Today, many people are questioning the doctrine of original sin and discarding it from their belief systems. But in discarding original sin, we should not necessarily reject the ancient tradition of renunciation, which, as a part of the mystery religions, predated Christianity.

The ascetic mystics were trying to demonstrate that the more attracted we are to the material world, where things are impermanent, the more distracted we will be from the spiritual world, where things are permanent. If we have decided that what is permanent is most important to us, then we should become less attached to the impermanent, material things.

While we should not adopt the extreme view that the world and our bodies are evil, we should realize that they are not the ultimate habitat of the soul. Rather than hating the world and our bodies, we should see them as the Greeks did—as impermanent copies of spiritual things.

Plotinus, the great Neoplatonist mystic and teacher of the third century, taught that we should see the body as a necessary part of life. We should care for and preserve the body as a musician would care for a fine musical instrument, keeping it in good repair for as long as we may need it.[10]

We can take our inspiration from the beauties of nature and of the human form as long as we do not attach ourselves to them. All of the beautiful things we see around us are simply copies and shadows of the permanent things in the infinite mind of God.

While perhaps too strict for some mystics today, the ascetic path has produced some remarkable examples of human potential. The desert monks who had the experiences of fire were strict ascetics. For long periods of time, they would limit themselves to only one meal a day and a few hours' sleep a night.

But what does asceticism mean for those of us who live in Western civilization? Do we need to be celibate? Starve ourselves? Withdraw from the world?

It depends. You could sit on top of a mountain praying for hours a day and still not make it if you had no love in your heart. You could spend your life feeding the poor and still not make it because your karma required you to bear and nurture children. The path home to God is different for every person. Only communion with your Higher Self will reveal your path to you.

Being perfect

Renunciation is not a goal in itself but a means to an end—the goal of transformation and divinization. There is no right way for everyone. Some may be attracted to the celibate path; others may prefer marriage. Marriage can be the foundation for a spiritual life if both partners are committed to each other's soul growth. Some may be drawn by their karma to live and work in cities and towns; others may prefer a life of isolation and contemplation.

Vegetarianism is not a requirement of the spiritual path, but reducing or eliminating your consumption of meat can help your mind maintain its focus on the God within. Sugar, alcohol, drugs and nicotine are impediments to the path. They only serve to nail us to the cross of the material world.

But if you're not ready to live an ascetic life, like the desert monks, you shouldn't let that stop you from becoming a mystic.

It's a common misconception today that you have to be "perfect" in order to be spiritual. Being perfect is a daunting task. It can make you feel like giving up before you start.

"How can I be on a spiritual path," some people ask, "when I can't even go one day without getting angry? Or when I don't even have time to meditate or pray?"

When the scriptures tell us to "be perfect," they use the Greek word *teleios,* which meant "initiate" in the terminology of the mystery religions.[11] If Jesus and Paul were mystics, then when they told us to be perfect, they were telling us to be initiates— that is, to present ourselves ready to participate in the *process* of divinization.

As we have seen, attaining union with God does not necessarily happen instantaneously, but over time. Some mystery cults practiced a ritual of spiritual rebirth each year. Each birth was seen as another rung on the ladder to heaven, bringing the initiate one step closer to divine union. Origen of Alexandria described being "born a son of God in Christ Jesus" as a continual process that happens with each good deed.[12]

Origen had his own answer to the inevitability of old age and death. As the body is getting old, the soul should be entering eternal youth. "It is possible, then," he wrote, "to pass over from old age and wrinkles to youth; and what is wondrous in this is that while the body progresses from youth to old age, the soul, if it comes to perfection, changes from old age to youth."[13] In other words, the older we get, the more of God we should have embodied. Progress is not necessarily made through physical perfection, but through soul perfection.

This doesn't mean that those who are "perfect," the initiates, don't have to be concerned about the consequences of their actions. Initiates, like everyone else, are governed by the law of karma and must make up for every flash of negative energy they send out. But you can continue to be on the path of soul perfection even if you occasionally stumble and fall because of human imperfection. For humans can never be perfect anyway.

It reminds me of the story from Dostoyevsky's *The Brothers Karamazov,* in which Father Zosima dies. He was a saintly man and his followers had expected that his body would preserve itself after he died, as had the bodies of some saints. But when his body begins to putrefy and stink like any other dead body, some of them are disillusioned, thinking it somehow negates his saintliness.

His pupil Alyosha is at first upset by the decay of the body. Then he has a mystical experience in which he sees Father Zosima inviting him to join a heavenly wedding feast. Alyosha realizes that true saintliness is of the soul and not the body.[14]

Although the bodies of some Catholic saints have, through grace, been preserved after death, just because a body decays does not mean that the saint is not saintly. We must remember that we are perfecting the soul, one particle at a time. This leads us back to the life—and death—of Marvin Baker.

After a yearlong battle with throat and lung cancer and numerous operations, Marvin Baker died in April 1996. Before his death, he had achieved a state of serenity and equanimity through his mystical practices. In his last letter to me, written in February, he joked about the surgery that had removed part of the cancer but also his tongue and voice box: "The cat got my tongue. Ha! Yes, . . . in spite of it all, I still have my sense of humor."

This is the kind of equanimity that we often see in saints. How wonderful to find it in the penitentiary as well! Through his devotion, Marvin was able to contact the state of eternal life. I believe that although his karma requires him to return to earth for further lessons, his soul achieved great gains through his spiritual practices.

SETTING YOUR SAILS

Marvin sought divine grace to help him out of the blindness of his karma. Grace is the third essential ingredient of the path. It brings you to the point of seeking God and enables you to make it home.

Grace is a connection with the divine. It is the intercession of the angels, of beings of light and of Jesus Christ, our Saviour. It is a spiritual awakening that propels us out of the rut of thousands of years of sowing and reaping. It is both prayer and the answer to prayer. We need grace because our karma blinds us and locks us into certain karma-making habits and behavioral patterns—stumbling-stones that we have tripped over time and again for thousands of years.

Ephesians tells us, "By grace you have been saved through faith, and this is not your own doing; it is the gift of God—not the result of works, so that no one may boast."[15] But, in fact, faith, grace and works are a tripod—each one is indispensable.

What exactly is grace? The Church, relying on an imbalanced interpretation of the Epistles, has given it the inflated power of a miracle pill. According to some denominations, grace alone accomplishes our salvation. I believe that although grace is an important factor in breaking the chain of rebirth, it is not a panacea. Grace is God meeting us halfway, not God picking us up and carrying us from here to eternity.

Christians who believe that Jesus as Saviour does it all for us base their interpretation on passages such as Hebrews 10, which tells us that Jesus gave his body to sanctify us "once for all." And "by a single offering he has perfected for all time those who are sanctified."[16] The author is telling us that Jesus gained for us the sanctification that allows us to become perfect—that is, initiates.

But the author of Hebrews did not mean to imply that Jesus' single sacrifice canceled out the requirement for us to balance our karma or, as Paul said, to "work out" our own salvation.[17]

Jesus is our Saviour in the sense that he awakens us to our divine reality and demonstrates the path that we can follow. Without this awakening, we would not have the option of pursuing union with God.

Orthodox Christianity inflated the power of grace to astronomical proportions. But the Gnostics and the Arians had a more balanced view. The Arians saw grace as opportunity—the opportunity to become Sons of God. The Gnostics saw grace as a boost, a leg up, rather than an elevator ride to the top. For them, the Saviour was a deliverer who came to show them the way to liberation from earthly existence. The Saviour had come to wake them from the sleep that was the death of the soul.

For the Gnostics, grace was the kindling of the spark within their hearts. Just as a person can blow on the ashes of a seemingly dead fire and rekindle a flame, so the Saviour had rekindled the divine spark in their hearts. But this grace did not do it all for them. Once the spark was kindled, it was up to them to expand the spark until it filled their whole being.

Grace may come to us as a reward for our past good actions. But we can also seek it by focusing our attention on God through prayer and good works. The Hindu saint Ramakrishna said, "The breeze of divine grace is blowing upon all. But one needs to set the sail to feel this breeze of grace."[18]

We set our sails by putting ourselves on a route home to God. And grace helps us to stay on course—and to reach the goal. It is the x factor on the voyage home. Unpredictable, it comes when we least expect it. When we have devoted every part of our being to achieving oneness with God, grace intervenes.

Balancing our karma takes us along the road to eternal life, but it alone isn't enough to get us there. If you have decided that it is your goal to find union with God, you can be sure that it was grace that awakened you to the goal and it is grace that will lead you home. As the hymn goes:

Through many dangers, toils, and snares
I have already come;
'Tis grace hath brought me safe thus far
And grace will lead me home.[19]

Focusing the Mind on God

The fourth essential element of divine union is to focus the mind on God. When we can do this, we will have a "place in both spheres,"[20] as Plotinus wrote, alternating between a life below and a life above—a life in the box and a life of freedom. Divine union comes when the mind is so focused on God that it thinks of him continually. When this state is achieved, the fiery experience of union with God is usually not far behind.

The German Christian mystic Meister Eckhart writes that we can achieve this union with God by raising the intellect up to God. (The intellect is not the brain but rather the highest part of the soul.) The Holy Spirit, by grace, then transports this part of the soul into God's image and unites the two.[21] In this way, Eckhart tells us, man can fulfill Paul's goal of being formed in God's image *"from one degree of glory to another."* If we want to achieve this goal, then we must start by raising our minds and souls into unity with the mind of God.

Huston Smith, in his book *The World's Religions,* offers the images of a ping-pong ball and a lump of dough to show the difference between an undisciplined mind and one that is fixed on God. The "ping-pong-ball" mind continually jumps from one thought to another. The "lump-of-dough" mind hits the wall and sticks to it.[22]

The goal of the mystics is to concentrate on God to such an extent that a portion of the mind is fixed on him even while the rest of the mind is engaged in everyday activities. A mind concentrated on God is not "zombified"; it does not lose its capacity for reason. Rather, its capacity and awareness are expanded through contact with the infinite mind of God.

The mystics tell us that one of the best ways to focus our attention on God is to use meditation, repetitive prayer and mantras. Some of us are born meditators, but others find themselves easily distracted. These people will benefit from repetitive prayer.

In the West, we are not accustomed to the idea of repeating a prayer. People have asked me, "Why should I have to ask God for something more than once?"

Repeating a prayer does two things. It helps the easily distracted ping-pong mind to focus. And it frees the soul in increments. Just as it has taken you hundreds of years and millions of acts to forge the fetters that bind the soul to the body, so it takes repeated prayer and constant effort to unloose those fetters. With each good act, with each devotional song you sing or mantra or chant you repeat, you are freeing more and more of your being to reside permanently in that state of divine union.

PRAY YOURSELF INTO A NONLOCAL STATE

Repetitive prayer is more prominent in Eastern religion than in Christianity, but it is still an important part of religious life in the West. Protestants sing hymns and offer lengthy prayers, depending on the denomination. Catholics repeat the Our Father and the Hail Mary, celebrate the Mass, sing hymns and experience peace in the sounds of ancient Gregorian chants. (The Cathars used to repeat the Lord's Prayer as many as forty times a day.) The Eastern Orthodox Church has also preserved a tradition of repetitive prayer.

For hundreds of years, Greek Orthodox monks have reported extraordinary mystical experiences that stemmed from their repetition of a simple prayer: "Lord Jesus Christ, Son of

God, have mercy upon me."[23] Their story demonstrates the immense power of the spoken word.

They repeated the prayer over and over again, while sitting with their chins resting on their chests to focus their attention on the heart. They believed the prayer facilitated divine union by attracting the mind to the heart, which they saw as the seat of divinity. As they said the prayer, the monks synchronized it with their breathing—a practice that is similar to Buddhist and Hindu techniques—breathing in with the first half of the sentence and out with the second.

The monks attempted to repeat the prayer continuously, pursuing Paul's directive to "Pray without ceasing."[24] One elder advised that they should even attempt to repeat the prayer while sleeping! He instructed them to meditate or repeat the prayer "without interruption, whether asleep or awake, eating, drinking, or in company."[25] (Hindu yogis also train their minds to repeat mantras during sleep.)

The monks claimed that after several weeks of repeating the prayer for hours a day, they would enter a transformed state of being. They said they could see a powerful light around them, as powerful as that witnessed by the disciples at Jesus' transfiguration.

One monk described the condition as a "most pleasant heat," a "joyful boiling." He claimed to live in a state that was beyond pleasure and pain, experiencing a "lightness and freshness, pleasantness of living, insensibility to sickness and sorrows."[26] This is a state in which "the flesh" is "kindled by the Spirit, so that the whole man becomes spiritual."[27]

The monks' description brings to mind the idea of nonlocal reality. Apparently, these monks had chanted and meditated themselves into a nonlocal state. The prayers had propelled them into a constant experience of heavenly fire.

Today, many of the modern-day mystics who are my students

have reported similar results. I teach a system of repetitive prayer called the science of the spoken word. It uses powerful prayers, called decrees, to facilitate union with God. Mark Prophet and I have been teaching people how to use these decrees since he founded The Summit Lighthouse in 1958. They are the most effective method available today for breaking free from the chain of rebirth.

Whatever your current spiritual practices, you can add decrees to them. For they are a step-up of the mystical traditions of all major religions.

One of the most powerful decrees for divine union that I know is the "Salutation to the Sun." It goes like this:

> O mighty Presence of God, I AM, in and behind the Sun:
> I welcome thy Light, which floods all the earth,
> > into my life, into my mind,
> > into my spirit, into my soul.
> Radiate and blaze forth thy Light!
> Break the bonds of darkness and superstition!
> Charge me with the great clearness
> > of thy white fire radiance!
> I AM thy child, and each day I shall become
> > more of thy manifestation!

If you repeat this and other prayers and decrees mentally and verbally as often as it is comfortable, you will build a momentum that can propel you into a state of divine union. You repeat each decree slowly at first, then more quickly as you get to know the words. Finally you will reach the state where your mind has become one with the prayer and goes on repeating it even when your lips have stopped and you are once more involved in daily cares. You will find that you do, indeed, each day become more of the manifestation of the God that is within you as you pass from glory unto glory.

Many years ago, after I had begun an intense use of daily

repetition of decrees, I began to experience an almost constant burning sensation in the center of my chest. I see this as the oneness with the flame of divine love in the heart of Jesus. I feel this oneness all the time, even while writing, counseling, lecturing, eating or putting my son to sleep.

Marvin Baker developed this burning sensation when he first began reading my books, including *The Science of the Spoken Word,* in which I teach the technique of decreeing. When he first noticed this burning, he wrote: "I changed T-shirts, thinking that there must be soap in this one." But the burning continued. He went on to describe his experience of fire:

> I began to worry that something was wrong with my heart. I thought this must be what they call heartburn (ha-ha), and I thought, "I'm just too young for all this." I actually thought of going to see a doctor to see why my heart and chest area felt hot.
>
> Then, after two weeks of this, it dawned on me that this is the flaming of the heart that they're talking about in these books. I literally sat down for one-half hour and thought on this. For something like this to happen in here, in this environment, made it hard to grasp. But I finally got used to it and now I can't live without it.

Marvin began to decree as many hours a day as possible. Even after his tongue and windpipe had been removed, he continued to repeat the decrees in his mind, determined to maintain that focused attention on God.

You, too, can experience this oneness through prayer, meditation and sending forth love to all of life. I invite you to try adding the practice of decrees to your life and to see how they can lead you back to your primordial state of oneness with God.[28]

Here is another decree you might like to try. It is called "I AM the Light of the Heart." You can intensify its action by seeing in your mind's eye a beautiful violet-colored flame surrounding you and all of those whom you love. See it dissolving the negative effects of your karma.

I AM the Light of the Heart
Shining in the darkness of being
And changing all
Into the golden treasury
Of the Mind of Christ.
I AM projecting my Love
Out into the world
To erase all errors
And to break down all barriers.
I AM the power of infinite Love,
Amplifying itself
Until it is victorious,
World without end!

THE ASCENSION, A JOURNEY WITHIN

Marvin Baker pursued his ascension night and day. He was determined to accomplish it in this life. I believe that although he will be required to return to earth to resolve his karma, he will be given circumstances where it will be easy for him to continue to pursue his resurrection and ascension.

You are meant to accomplish your own resurrection and ascension in this life. Your resurrection is your awakening to your identity as a Son of God. Your ascension is your final union with God. Each mystical experience is a preparation for that ultimate union, which can occur either before or after death when you have balanced a sufficient amount of your karma.

As you walk the homeward path, you can see yourself climbing a coil of white fire that represents the ascension. Each prayer, decree and mystical experience propels you higher on the coil. It expands the flame in your heart, a flame that is meant

In ancient times, mystics who sought reunion with God often imagined their return as a journey through seven heavenly spheres, each ruled by one of the planets. Dante describes such a journey in his Divine Comedy. *This fifteenth-century illustration shows Dante and Beatrice leaving the heaven of Venus and approaching the heaven of the sun. For the mystics, entering the heaven of the sun symbolized union with God.*

to grow until it consumes your entire form and you have become one with that flame.

Climbing this coil is not really going up or down or right or left. It is your soul's acceleration into the nucleus of the permanent atom that is God. It allows you to enter a state of eternal time, where there is no yesterday or tomorrow but only now. Jesus called this state "eternal life"—not in the sense that it goes on forever but that it is a state of existence in which time as we know it does not exist. This is a state outside of time and space. As Plotinus described it, "There all is one day; series has no place; no yesterday, no last year."[29]

Keep in mind, as you pray and meditate, that the God inside of you is more powerful than anything else in the world. The entire cosmos is imprinted on every atom of your being.

The experiences of the mystics confirm this. Some *Merkabah* mystics saw the journey through heavenly palaces as a journey through the chambers of the heart. They believed that all of the vastness of divinity was contained within. As the Jewish leader Hai Gaon (939–1038) wrote, the mystic "will gaze in the innermost recesses of his heart and it will seem as if he saw the seven halls [of the angels] with his own eyes."[30]

You can think of the universe as a set of wooden Russian *matryoshka* dolls, with each doll having a smaller one inside of it. The entire visible universe is the outermost doll, and nested inside it are galaxies, solar systems, stars, planets—right down to the smallest doll, which is you. But inside of you is an even smaller doll that somehow has the biggest doll inside of it. When you figure out this riddle, you will have discovered the key to your ascension!

The ascension is not an end—it is a beginning. When you transcend this narrow spectrum of human existence, you live forevermore, a Son of God, continually transcending planes of consciousness, exploring new dimensions, using free will, retaining your individuality and taking part in the grand evolutionary spiral of life throughout the cosmos.

The state that you enter when you achieve the ascension is the kingdom of God, eternal life—a timeless, spaceless state of eternal bliss. When you have found it, then you will know the unchanging unity that was the true prize Jesus promised. You will have entered a form of existence that offers ultimate freedom and ultimate possibility.

Chronological Guide to People, Events and Ideas

	JEWISH	GREEK	ROMAN	INDIAN
8TH CENTURY B.C.	**Assyrian captivity** Many Israelites deported.		**Rome founded** 753 B.C.	**Later Vedic period** c. 800–c. 500 B.C. Brahmanas, Upanishads and Mahabharata written before or during this time: teachings on reincarnation and union with Atman/Brahman.
7TH CENTURY B.C.		**Orphism** Ancient Greek mystery religion; earliest known source of Greek reincarnation belief.	**Etruscan culture** dominant in Italy c. 616–c. 510 B.C.	
	Jeremiah preaches c. 626–c. 586 B.C.	**Eleusinian Mysteries** c. 600 B.C.–c. A.D. 400 May have taught union with God.		
6TH CENTURY B.C.	**Babylonian captivity** c. 597–c. 538 B.C. Babylonians destroy Jerusalem; including Solomon's Temple; many Jews deported from Judah to Babylonia.	**Pythagoras** (c. 580–c. 500 B.C.) Greek philosopher, mathematician. Teaches both reincarnation and divinization.	**Roman republic** founded c. 500 B.C. Roman conquest of Italy c. 500–c. 275 B.C.	**Siddhartha Gautama** (c. 563–c. 483 B.C.) Founder of Buddhism. Teaches about karma, reincarnation and the indwelling God.
	Persians capture Babylon 538 B.C.	**Golden Age of Greece** c. 500–c. 320 B.C.		

	JEWISH	GREEK	ROMAN	INDIAN
6TH CENTURY B.C. *(continued)*	Jews return to Jerusalem c. 538 B.C. **Second Temple** built c. 517 B.C.			
5TH CENTURY B.C.		**Plato** (c. 427–c. 347 B.C.) Greek philosopher. Discusses reincarnation.		
4TH CENTURY B.C.		**Diogenes of Sinope** (c. 412–c. 323 B.C.) Prototype for the Cynics. **Cynics** 4th century B.C. into Christian times. Philosophical sect. **Alexander the Great** (356–323 B.C.) Macedonian ruler conquers Persia, Egypt and the lands extending to the Indus; conquest leads to cross-cultural exchange.		**First Indian (Mauryan) empire** established c. 325 B.C. First emperor, Candra Gupta Maurya, establishes friendly relations with Alexander's generals. Greek colonists in Gandhara, ancient India, c. 327 B.C.–c. 1st century A.D.
	Alexandria, Egypt City founded by Alexander the Great in 332 B.C.; trade and cultural center; here Jews absorbed Greek and possibly Eastern ideas about reincarnation.	**Stoicism** c. 300 B.C.–c. A.D. 200 Hellenistic school of philosophy.		

3RD CENTURY B.C.	**Earliest evidence of** *Merkabah* **mysticism,** a technique for divinization through ascents. **I Enoch** written c. 3rd–1st century B.C. Greek becomes dominant language of Alexandrian Jews. **Pentateuch** translated into Greek.	Alexandria establishes trade routes with India.	Carthage cedes Sicily to Rome 241 B.C.	**Asoka** reigns c. 265–c. 238 B.C. Emperor of Mauryan dynasty of India, patron of Buddhism; sends Indian merchants and ambassadors to Alexandria. The Indo-Greek kingdom of Bactria gains independence from the Seleucid king c. 250 B.C.
2ND CENTURY B.C.	**Aristobulus** Jewish philosopher. Teaches in Alexandria c. 170–c. 160 B.C. **Essenes at Qumran** through A.D. 68 Teach *Merkabah* mysticism: that humans can become Sons of God; possibly teach reincarnation. **Hasmonean Dynasty** c. 167–63 B.C. Jewish family rules an independent kingdom around Jerusalem.	Rome conquers Greece 146–63 B.C. Greek and Roman cultures are merging. Rome conquers and razes Carthage 146 B.C. Trade with East, silk and spice.		**Menander (Milinda)** Indo-Greek king rules an empire from Afghanistan to central India c. 160–c. 135 B.C. Patron of Buddhist religion. Greek influence on Gandharan art. Trade with Romans via the spice routes.

	JEWISH	GREEK	ROMAN	INDIAN
1ST CENTURY B.C.	*Songs of the Sabbath Sacrifice*, Jewish text, describes *Merkabah* mysticism. **Gnosticism** arises c. 1st century B.C. **Hillel** (c. 70 B.C.–c. A.D. 10) Rabbinic authority, Sanhedrin leader. Palestine conquered by Romans. **Herod the Great** King of Judea under the Romans 37–4 B.C. **Herod Antipas** Rules Galilee and part of Transjordan 4 B.C.–A.D. 39. Orders John the Baptist beheaded.		**Cicero** (106–43 B.C.) Roman statesman, author, lawyer, orator; writes about reincarnation. **Virgil** (70–19 B.C.) Roman poet and author of *Aeneid*; writes about reincarnation. Mystery religions become popular in Rome, practiced through 4th century. **Roman general Pompey** conquers Palestine 63 B.C. Republic ends 59–44 B.C. **Augustus** (Gaius Octavius) reigns 27 B.C.–A.D. 14. First Roman emperor. Defeats Antony and Cleopatra in 31 B.C. and gains control of Alexandria.	

1ST CENTURY	JEWISH	CHRISTIAN	GRECO-ROMAN
	Philo of Alexandria (c. 20 B.C.–c. A.D. 50) Jewish philosopher; teaches reincarnation and union with God.		**Caligula** (Gaius Caesar, 12–41) Emperor 37–41.
	John the Baptist 1st-century ascetic Jewish prophet; baptizes Jesus. **Jesus** (c. 4 B.C.–c. A.D. 30)		
	Herod Agrippa reigns c. 37–44.		
	Rebellion against Roman rule 66–70.		Romans destroy Qumran, 68, and Jerusalem, 70, in response to Jewish rebellion.
	Yohanan ben Zakkai, leader of rabbinic Judaism. Plays an important role in Jewish mysticism. Teaches at Academy of Yavneh, center of spiritual and intellectual life after destruction of Jerusalem.		
	Hanina ben Dosa, Jewish miracle worker.		
	Gamaliel, son or grandson of Hillel; Paul's teacher. **Paul** (c. 10–c. 65) may draw on mystical Greek and Jewish ideas about union with God or transformation into a divine being.		
	Flavius Josephus (c. 37–c. 100) Jewish historian; reports some Jews believe in reincarnation.	**Gospel of Thomas** c. 70 Talks about divine union as goal of life. Four Gospels written c. 70–c. 100.	

	JEWISH	CHRISTIAN	GRECO-ROMAN
2ND CENTURY	**Gnosticism** c. 1st century B.C.–3rd century A.D. Jewish-Christian religious movement teaches both reincarnation and union with God; flourishes in some Christian communities.		**Ammonius Saccas** (c. 175–c. 242) Founder of Neoplatonism, which teaches reincarnation and union with God.
	Bar Kokhba Revolt against Roman rule 132–135.	**Valentinus** teaches c. 135–c. 160. Christian Gnostic teacher in Alexandria and Rome.	Brutal suppression of Jewish rebellion. Many Jews leave Palestine.
		Basilides 2nd-century Christian Gnostic teacher.	
	Hekhalot and *Merkabah* texts written 2nd–c. 6th century.	**Clement of Alexandria** (c. 150–c. 211) Church Father, theologian and saint; said to have taught reincarnation.	
	Talmud written c. 200 B.C.–A.D. 500.	**Tatian** (c. 120–173) Church Father.	
		Irenaeus (c. 130–c. 200) Church Father.	
	Caesarea becomes center of rabbinic Judaism.		
3RD CENTURY		**Tertullian** (c. 150–c. 225) Church Father. Helps formulate doctrine of creation out of nothing.	**Neoplatonism** becomes popular. Greco-Roman school of philosophy teaches both reincarnation and union with God.

Origen (c. 185–c. 254)
Church Father. Teaches reincarnation and union with God.

Plotinus (c. 205–270)
Neoplatonist teacher.

Porphyry (c. 232–c. 303)
Neoplatonist, student of Plotinus.

Decius rules empire 249–251.

Diocletian (245–316) Emperor who divides the empire into East and West.

Constantine (c. 274–337)
Reunites the empire.

Battle of Milvian Bridge 312;
Constantine becomes ruler of western half of empire.
Constantine wins control of eastern half of empire 324.
Sole emperor 324–337.
Constantine declares Byzantium his capital, renames it Constantinople 330.

4TH CENTURY

Arius (c. 250–c. 336)
Libyan-born priest, originator of Arianism; teaches that men can be transformed into Sons of God.

Eusebius (c. 260–c. 340)
Church historian.

First Council of Nicaea 325
Formulates the Nicene Creed, which affirms Jesus' divinity as the only Son of God.

Athanasius (c. 298–373)
Theologian and defender of orthodoxy against Arianism.

Epiphanius (c. 315–403) Bishop of Salamis. Campaigns against Origen.

	JEWISH	CHRISTIAN	GRECO-ROMAN
4TH CENTURY *(continued)*		**Jerome** (c. 342–420) Church Father.	**Theodosius I** (347–395) Last ruler of united empire reigns 379–395; suppresses paganism and Arianism.
		John Chrysostom (c. 347–407) Church Father.	
		Arian heretics flee north and west c. 381–c. 400 +.	Mystery religions suppressed.
5TH CENTURY		Nag Hammadi texts buried c. 400.	
		Pelagius (c. 354–c. 418) British-born theologian and ascetic; debates Augustine and Jerome over original sin.	
		Augustine (354–430) Church Father.	
		Julian of Eclanum (c. 386–c. 454) Debates Augustine.	
		Theophilus (d. 412) Bishop of Alexandria; destroys Nitrian monastery, campaigns to destroy non-Christian shrines.	**Hypatia** (c. 375–415) Head of Neoplatonist school at Alexandria.
	Alexandrian Jewish Community destroyed 415; all Jews expelled.		

5TH CENTURY (*continued*)	Justinian persecutes Jews.	Arianism practiced by Goths and Visigoths c. 5th–7th century.	
6TH CENTURY		**Council of Orange** 529 Codifies Augustine's theology into Church doctrine. **Fifth General Council of the Church** 553; its anathemas form the foundation for the rejection of reincarnation.	**Justinian I** (483–565) Emperor from 527 suppresses heretics and pagans c. 529. Edict of c. 543: condemns 10 principles of Origenism. Letter of c. 551: 15 anathemas against Origenism. Calls Fifth General Council of the Church 553.
7TH–9TH CENTURIES		Members of Origenist and Arian sects flee to Armenia, later to Bulgaria 6th–10th century.	
10TH CENTURY		**Bogomils** Christian sect in the Balkans founded c. 950.	
11TH CENTURY	**Hai Gaon** (998–1038) Jewish mystic from Babylonia.		
12TH CENTURY	**Kabbalism**, Jewish mysticism, arises. Primary texts written in southern France; teaches both reincarnation and divinization.	**Catharism** takes root, southern France. Practiced c. 1150–1310; teaches both reincarnation and union with God.	

D A R K   A G E S   I N   E U R O P E

Notes

FOREWORD

1. 2 Cor. 3:18.

PART I | *What Reincarnation Means to Christians*

CHAPTER I **A Martyr for Infinite Worlds**

Opening quotation: William Boulting, *Giordano Bruno: His Life, Thought, and Martyrdom* (London: Kegan Paul, Trench, Trübner and Co., 1914), p. 163.

1. Giordano Bruno, *De l'infinito universi et mondi,* quoted in Boulting, *Giordano Bruno,* p. 139.

2. Bruno, *De gli eroici furori,* quoted in Frances A. Yates, *Giordano Bruno and the Hermetic Tradition* (Chicago: University of Chicago Press, 1964), p. 278.

3. Bruno, "Explanatory Epistle," in *The Expulsion of the Triumphant Beast,* trans. and ed. Arthur D. Imerti (New Brunswick, N.J.: Rutgers University Press, 1964), p. 72.

4. Bruno, *De l'infinito,* quoted in Dorothea Waley Singer, *Giordano Bruno: His Life and Thought* (New York: Henry Schuman, 1950), pp. 58–59.

5. Bruno, *De immenso,* quoted in Singer, *Giordano Bruno,* p. 75.

6. *The Catholic Encyclopedia,* 15 vols. (New York: Robert Appleton Co., 1907–14), s.v. "Bruno, Giordano."

7. See Zuane Mocenigo, Documents 1 and 3, quoted in I. Frith,

Life of Giordano Bruno, the Nolan, rev. ed. (London: Trübner and Co., 1887), pp. 262, 265; and Boulting, *Giordano Bruno,* pp. 265–66.

8. Gaspar Schopp to Conrad Rittershausen, Rome, 17 February 1600, quoted in Boulting, *Giordano Bruno,* p. 300, and Frith, *Life of Giordano Bruno,* p. 391.

9. Imerti, editor's introduction to *Expulsion of the Triumphant Beast,* p. 26.

10. Boulting, *Giordano Bruno,* pp. 164, 163.

11. See Singer, *Giordano Bruno,* p. 165; and Daniel G. Brinton and Thomas Davidson, *Giordano Bruno: Philosopher and Martyr* (Philadelphia: David McKay Publisher, 1890), pp. 52–54.

12. Vincenzo Spampanato, *Documenti della vita di Giordano Bruno* (Florence: Leo S. Olschki Editore, 1933), p. 96.

13. Eccles. 1:9. All Bible verses are from the New Revised Standard Version unless otherwise noted.

14. Pietro Redondi, *Galileo Heretic (Galileo eretico),* trans. Raymond Rosenthal (Princeton: Princeton University Press, 1987), p. 7.

15. Singer, *Giordano Bruno,* pp. 176, 177.

16. Ibid., p. 177.

17. Schopp to Rittershausen, quoted in Singer, *Giordano Bruno,* p. 179.

CHAPTER 2   **Unanswered Questions**

Opening quotation: Johnny Carson, quoted in Harry F. Waters, Lynda Wright and Jeanne Gordon, "Stranger in the Night," *Newsweek,* 25 May 1992, p. 98.

1. George Gallup, Jr., and Frank Newport, "Belief in Psychic and Paranormal Phenomena Widespread among Americans," *The Gallup Poll Monthly,* August 1990, p. 42.

2. George Gallup, Jr., with William Proctor, *Adventures in Immortality* (New York: McGraw-Hill Book Co., 1982), p. 193.

3. Hans TenDam, *Exploring Reincarnation,* trans. A. E. J. Wils (London: Penguin Group, Arkana, 1990), p. 3.

4. Gallup and Newport, "Belief in Psychic and Paranormal Phenomena," p. 42.

5. There were about 74 million Protestants and 50 million Catholics in America in 1980.

6. See "Stir in Danish Church over Reincarnation," *Christian Century*, 2 March 1994, p. 222.

7. W. Lutoslawski, *Pre-Existence and Reincarnation* (London: George Allen and Unwin, 1928), p. 29.

8. Brian Harley and Glenn Firebaugh, "Americans' Belief in an Afterlife: Trends over the Past Two Decades," *Journal for the Scientific Study of Religion* 32 (1993): 269.

9. Gallup and Proctor, *Adventures in Immortality*, p. 185.

10. "Man Kills Daughters, Wife, Self," *Washington Times*, 27 September 1994.

11. Joe Fisher, *The Case for Reincarnation* (New York: Carol Publishing Group, Citadel Press, 1992), p. 46.

12. W. B. Yeats, "Under Ben Bulben," st. 2.

13. Carl Van Doren, *Benjamin Franklin* (New York: Viking Press, 1938), p. 124.

14. William Q. Judge, *The Ocean of Theosophy* (Covina, Calif.: Theosophical University Press, 1948), p. 73.

15. Gina Cerminara, *Many Mansions* (New York: William Sloane Associates, 1950), p. 28.

16. Jess Stearn, *Edgar Cayce—The Sleeping Prophet* (Toronto: Bantam Books, 1968), p. 257.

17. For more detail and an in-depth presentation of these ideas, see John Davidson, *The Gospel of Jesus: In Search of His Original Teachings* (Shaftesbury, Dorset: Element Books, 1995).

CHAPTER 3   **Why They Believe**

Opening quotation: J. D. Salinger, *Nine Stories* (New York: Modern Library, 1953), p. 294.

1. Linda Tarazi, "An Unusual Case of Hypnotic Regression with Some Unexplained Contents," *Journal of the American Society for Psychical Research* 84 (October 1990): 309–44.

2. Ibid., p. 334.
3. Ian Stevenson, "A Case of the Psychotherapist's Fallacy: Hypnotic Regression to 'Previous Lives,'" *American Journal of Clinical Hypnosis* 36 (January 1994): 192.
4. Ian Stevenson and N. K. Chadha, "Can Children Be Stopped from Speaking about Previous Lives? Some Further Analyses of Features in Cases of the Reincarnation Type," *Journal of the Society for Psychical Research* 56 (January 1990): 82, 83–84.
5. Tom Buckley, "Intimations of a Former Life," *Quest*/78, September/October, p. 44.
6. All quotations from Jenny Cockell's story are from her book *Across Time and Death: A Mother's Search for Her Past Life Children* (New York: Simon and Schuster, Fireside Book, 1994), pp. 110, 56, 29, 54, 91, 118, 121, 125, 127, 148, 140.
7. Nicholas P. Spanos et al., "Secondary Identity Enactments during Hypnotic Past-Life Regression: A Sociocognitive Perspective," *Journal of Personality and Social Psychology* 61 (1991): 311.
8. Gallup with Proctor, *Adventures in Immortality*, p. 198.
9. Kenneth Ring, *Heading toward Omega: In Search of the Meaning of the Near-Death Experience* (New York: William Morrow and Co., 1984), p. 35.
10. Kenneth Ring, *Life at Death: A Scientific Investigation of the Near-Death Experience* (New York: Coward, McCann and Geoghegan, 1980), p. 186. Although many NDEers believe in reincarnation, one prominent NDEer has questioned it. In her 1992 best-seller, *Embraced by the Light*, Betty Eadie writes that in revelations during her NDE experience, she was given to understand that souls spend only one life on earth and that past-life memories are actually "memories contained in the cells." She calls earth a "temporary place for our schooling" and says that there are "many levels of development."

However, Eadie's experience does confirm preexistence. She observed a large group of souls waiting to put on bodies. And she reported that "all people as spirits in the pre-mortal world took part in the creation of the earth." *Embraced by the Light*

(Placerville, Calif.: Gold Leaf Press, 1992), pp. 93, 49, 83, 47.

In the past few years, Eadie herself seems to have experienced a belief shift. In her recent book, *The Awakening Heart,* she accepts a limited form of reincarnation. After restating her earlier position that souls have only one life on earth before going on "to further our development elsewhere," she says that some advanced souls can reincarnate on earth as teachers. She says she believes that she met one of these teachers, a little girl who was retarded, most likely with Down's syndrome. *The Awakening Heart: My Continuing Journey to Love* (New York: Pocket Books, 1996), p. 157.

If some can return as teachers, why not others as students—particularly when both their teachers and study partners may be here on earth?

11. See Amber D. Wells, "Reincarnation Beliefs among Near-Death Experiencers," *Journal of Near-Death Studies* 12 (Fall 1993): 17–31.

12. Ibid., p. 30.

CHAPTER 4 **Gods in Ruins**

Opening quotation: Swami Prabhavananda and Frederick Manchester, comps. and trans., *The Upanishads: Breath of the Eternal* (1948; reprint, New York: New American Library, Mentor Books, 1957), pp. 45, 46.

1. Mark L. Prophet, Christmas Eve sermon, 1971 (unpublished).

2. Gen. 1:26 King James Version, hereafter cited as KJV.

3. Ralph Waldo Emerson, *Nature,* in *Selected Essays, Lectures, and Poems,* ed. Robert D. Richardson, Jr. (New York: Bantam Books, 1990), p. 53.

4. Plotinus, *Ennead* 1.6, quoted in Andrew Louth, *The Origins of the Christian Mystical Tradition: From Plato to Denys* (1981; reprint, Oxford: Clarendon Press, 1983), p. 41.

5. Gal. 4:19.

6. Bruno, *De gli eroici furori,* quoted in Yates, *Giordano Bruno,* p. 283.

7. Bruno, *De gli eroici furori,* quoted in Frith, *Life of Giordano Bruno,* p. 123.

8. Mundaka Upanishad, in Prabhavananda and Manchester, *The Upanishads,* p. 45.

9. Julius Eggeling, trans., *The Satapatha-Brahmana,* 10.6.3 (1885; reprint, Delhi: Motilal Banarsidass, 1988), p. 400.

10. Satapatha Brahmana 10.6.3, quoted in R. C. Zaehner, *Hinduism,* 2d ed. (1962; reprint, Oxford: Oxford University Press, 1966), p. 50.

11. Ibid.

12. Bruno, *De magia,* quoted in Singer, *Giordano Bruno,* pp. 90, 91.

13. See chapter 24; also Kevin J. Sharpe, *David Bohm's World: New Physics and New Religion* (London: Associated University Presses, 1993); and F. David Peat, *Einstein's Moon: Bell's Theorem and the Curious Quest for Quantum Reality* (Chicago: Contemporary Books, 1990).

14. Svetasvatara Upanishad, in Prabhavananda and Manchester, *The Upanishads,* p. 118.

15. Mahabharata 13.6.6, in Christopher Chapple, *Karma and Creativity* (Albany: State University of New York Press, 1986), p. 96.

16. Some in the Eastern religious traditions believe that as a result of past misdeeds or cruelty, a human can reembody as an animal or can regress to an animal-like state. Others, like the Jains, do not see the animal state as a punishment but as a necessary experience in one's spiritual evolution.

17. Honoré de Balzac, *Seraphita,* 3d ed., rev. (Blauvelt, N.Y.: Garber Communications, Freedeeds Library, 1986), p. 159.

18. Kisari Mohan Ganguli, trans., *The Mahabharata of Krishna-Dwaipayana Vyasa,* 12 vols. (New Delhi: Munshiram Manoharlal, 1970), 9:296.

19. Svetasvatara Upanishad, in Prabhavananda and Manchester, *The Upanishads,* p. 118.

20. Since Buddha taught that there is no permanent self or soul, some have concluded that he did not teach reincarnation. "If

the self is not permanent, what is there to reincarnate?" they ask.

Buddha's intent in teaching this doctrine was not to deny reincarnation but to draw people's attention to the changing nature of the individual. He taught that when we see ourselves as permanent, we are bonding our souls to our egos. The concept of a permanent self, in the words of scholar Kenneth Ch'en, "breeds attachment, attachment breeds egoism, and egoism breeds craving for existence, pleasure, fame, and fortune, all of which keep one tied to the round of existence."

Reincarnation does exist in Buddhism but it differs by a philosophical hair from reincarnation in Hinduism. Buddhists believe that when one being dies, a new being comes into existence who, Ch'en says, "inherits the karma of the past." This being is "not the same as the one just passed away, but not different either." It is connected with the past life by a "life stream." *Buddhism in China: A Historical Survey* (Princeton: Princeton University Press, 1964), p. 8.

To illustrate this concept, the Buddhist sage Nagasena used the image of a river. It has the same banks and curves from day to day but has not one drop of water today that it had yesterday. So a reincarnated person, while of different substance than the former self, yet has the same tendencies and patterns of relating that the former self did.

Is a reincarnated person the same as the one who died? "Neither the same one nor another one!" said Nagasena. Why? Because, as Lama Anagarika Govinda, a German Buddhist monk explains it, "we ourselves are never exactly the same from one moment to the next." *Insights of a Himalayan Pilgrim* (Berkeley, Calif.: Dharma Publishing, 1991), p. 108.

So even if we cannot speak of a soul in Buddhism, we can speak of a self that reincarnates, changing from year to year as well as from lifetime to lifetime. Reincarnation has sometimes been called the transmigration of souls. Govinda suggested that rather than *transmigration,* the Buddhist teaching could be called the *"transformation"* of souls.

The confusion concerning the Buddhist concept of reincarnation may have come from a misinterpretation of the Hindu concept of Atman. Most Western scholars translate *Atman* as "soul." As the imperishable, undecaying core of man, *Atman* should be translated as "Spirit." Atman is identical with Brahman. Atman, therefore, cannot be the soul because the soul, by definition, has descended into the realm of matter and become enmeshed in karma, while Atman, by definition, belongs to the realm of pure Spirit.

The Hindu concept that most closely resembles the Western idea of soul is *jiva*. It is the self that inhabits the body, identifies with mind and personality, form and senses, and mingles with ignorance and evil. In one of his sermons, Buddha advised us to identify with the Atman rather than with the character traits associated with the jiva. The jiva contains the Atman but cannot become permanent unless it unites with Atman. The jiva, or soul, then, is the nonpermanent self that reincarnates. I think many Buddhists might agree with the definition of the soul as jiva.

Lama Govinda disagrees with those Buddhists who claim that it is impossible to speak of a soul in Buddhism: "It is just here that many Western Buddhists are in difficulties. They want to speak of 'rebirth without a soul.' But that is just as illogical as it would be to speak of 'psychology without a psyche.' Let us finally make an end of the prejudice of the early European Buddhists, who equated the 'soul' with the idea of a separate, unchanging ego or self, thereby robbing us of a word as beautiful as it is profound, and which, like the Greek *psyche,* denotes the totality and organic wholeness of all the spiritual powers that work and grow within us."

Govinda points out that karma and rebirth are logical necessities for Buddhism because they provide a continuity from life to life and a purpose to our actions. Without them, he writes, "the Buddhist teaching becomes senseless, because death would then automatically mean total obliteration and extinction, which would render all striving pointless." *A Living Buddhism for the West,* trans. Maurice Walshe (Boston: Shambhala, 1990), p. 48.

21. Juan Mascaró, trans., *The Dhammapada: The Path of Perfection* (New York: Penguin Books, 1973), p. 35.

22. Brahmacharini Usha, comp., *A Ramakrishna-Vedanta Wordbook* (Hollywood, Calif.: Vedanta Press, 1962), s.v. "karma."

23. *The Encyclopedia of Eastern Philosophy and Religion* (Boston: Shambhala Publications, 1989), s.v. "karma."

24. Mascaró, *The Dhammapada,* p. 67.

25. Claude Tresmontant, *The Origins of Christian Philosophy,* trans. Mark Pontifex, vol. 11 of the *Twentieth Century Encyclopedia of Catholicism* (New York: Hawthorn Books, 1963), pp. 64, 27.

PART 2 | *Reincarnation in Jesus' World*

CHAPTER 5 Reincarnation in Judaism

Opening quotation: S. Ansky, *The Dybbuk and Other Writings,* ed. David G. Roskies, trans. Golda Werman (New York: Schocken Books, 1992), p. 24.

1. *Tehillat Hashem* prayerbook, quoted in Yonassan Gershom, *Beyond the Ashes: Cases of Reincarnation from the Holocaust* (Virginia Beach, Va.: A.R.E. Press, 1992), p. 78.

2. "A Stone in the Wall," in Howard Schwartz, ed. and comp., *Gabriel's Palace: Jewish Mystical Tales* (New York: Oxford University Press, 1993), p. 97.

3. Ben Zion Bokser, *The Jewish Mystical Tradition* (Northvale, N.J.: Jason Aronson, 1993), p. 26.

4. Exod. 20:3 KJV.

5. We know that many of the rabbis who wrote the Talmud practiced ascent mysticism. See Aryeh Kaplan, *Meditation and Kabbalah* (York Beach, Maine: Samuel Weiser, 1982), pp. 21, 22. But they believed that the mystical experiences of the

Merkabah were so powerful that they had to be kept secret and revealed only to a few trusted students who were spiritually ready. Thus they passed down the tradition secretly and probably only by word of mouth. The rabbis wrote in the Mishnah: "It is not permitted to expound... the *merkabah* with an individual, unless he were wise and understands from his (own) knowledge." *Hagigah* 2.1, quoted in C. R. A. Morray-Jones, "Paradise Revisited (2 Cor. 12:1–12): The Jewish Mystical Background of Paul's Apostolate: Part 1: The Jewish Sources," *Harvard Theological Review* 86:2 (1993): 185.

The rabbis' commitment to secrecy was probably reinforced by heretical Gnostic Jews who revealed some of the mystical secrets, sharing them with the "profane." These Jews, called *"Minim,"* were considered a great threat by many rabbis. The Talmud itself tells us that these heretics should be hated with "perfect hatred," citing Psalm 139. See Birger A. Pearson, *Gnosticism, Judaism, and Egyptian Christianity* (Minneapolis: Fortress Press, 1990), p. 18.

There were two reasons why the rabbis disliked these Gnostic Jews. One was that they revealed publicly what the rabbis passed down in secret. Another was that some of them claimed the Old Testament God was evil. This sacrilege could not be tolerated. It made the rabbis even more secretive about mysticism, perhaps to the point of denying its very existence. Thus the Gnostics may have inadvertently caused the rabbis to hide the mystical teaching of Judaism. It did not reemerge publicly until the Middle Ages, when the Kabbalists wrote down their secret oral tradition.

6. See Simcha Paull Raphael, *Jewish Views of the Afterlife* (Northvale, N.J.: Jason Aronson, 1994), pp. 13, 25–26.

7. Some Kabbalists claimed that the *Bahir* had been written in the first century. But the language used in the text shows that it could not have been composed earlier than medieval times. Nevertheless, the text may contain ancient teachings passed down by oral tradition.

8. Gershom Scholem, *On the Mystical Shape of the Godhead: Basic Concepts in the Kabbalah,* trans. Joachim Neugroschel, ed. Jonathan Chipman (New York: Schocken Books, 1991), p. 201.

9. Aryeh Kaplan, trans., *The Bahir* (1979; reprint, York Beach, Maine: Samuel Weiser, 1989), pp. 77–78.

10. Gen. 17:7 KJV.

11. See Gershom, *Beyond the Ashes,* pp. 74–75, 76.

12. Jer. 1:5 JB.

13. Wisd. of Sol. 8:19–20 Anchor Bible.

14. *Testament of Naphtali* 2.2, 3, in James H. Charlesworth, ed., *The Old Testament Pseudepigrapha,* 2 vols. (Garden City, N.Y.: Doubleday and Co., 1983–85), 1:811.

15. *Testament of Naphtali* 2.4, in Charlesworth, *Old Testament Pseudepigrapha,* 1:811.

16. Josephus, *The Antiquities of the Jews* 15.10.4, and *The Wars of the Jews* 2.8.11, in *The Works of Josephus: New Updated Edition,* trans. William Whiston (Peabody, Mass.: Hendrickson, 1987), pp. 422, 607.

17. As we study the Pharisees, we cannot rely on the picture of them presented in the Gospels. To Christians, the Pharisees are the "hypocrites" and "blind guides" of the New Testament (Matt. 23). They have come to symbolize those who serve God with outward form and ritual but lack true spirituality.

   Today, scholars believe that the conflict between Jesus and the Pharisees that is recorded in the Gospels did not occur. Rather, they think this portrayal actually reflects a conflict that was going on between the Christians and the Pharisees at the time the Gospels were being written. Since the Pharisees refused to convert to Christianity, they were depicted negatively. As Bible scholar Anthony J. Saldarini writes, the Gospels' portrayal of Jewish leadership is generally neither "accurate" nor "consistent." Paul J. Achtemeier, ed., *Harper's Bible Dictionary* (San Francisco: Harper and Row, 1985), s.v. "Pharisees."

   The Pharisees were a large and varied sect to which both

Josephus and the apostle Paul claimed to belong. Although the Pharisees aimed at rigid observance of the Mosaic law, they were also open to innovation. In addition to perhaps believing in reincarnation, we know that they believed in angels, demons, the resurrection and a coming kingdom of God, concepts that were later adopted by Christianity.

18. Josephus, *The Wars of the Jews* 2.8.14, and *The Antiquities of the Jews* 18.1.3, Whiston, pp. 608, 477.

19. See Lawrence H. Schiffman, "New Light on the Pharisees," in Hershel Shanks, ed., *Understanding the Dead Sea Scrolls: A Reader from the* Biblical Archaeology Review (New York: Random House, 1992), pp. 217–24.

20. Ezek. 1:4, 5, 26.

21. Until just recently, Esther was the only book in the Hebrew Bible that had not been found among the Dead Sea Scrolls. However, with the new discovery of fragments of proto-Esther, the list now includes Esther. See Sidnie White Crawford, "Has Every Book of the Bible Been Found among the Dead Sea Scrolls?" *Bible Review* 12, no. 5 (October 1996): 28–33, 56.

22. Neil S. Fujita, *A Crack in the Jar: What Ancient Jewish Documents Tell Us about the New Testament* (New York: Paulist Press, 1986), p. 170. There is debate about whether *Merkabah* mysticism was actually practiced at Qumran. Some scholars interpret the *Merkabah* language in the Qumran texts as proof that the Qumran sect practiced heavenly ascents, possibly including divine union. But other scholars believe that the presence of *Merkabah* language does not necessarily mean that the members of the Qumran sect practiced divine ascents. Both groups of scholars agree, however, that the texts prove that *Merkabah* was rooted in earlier Judaism. See Lawrence H. Schiffman, *Reclaiming the Dead Sea Scrolls: The History of Judaism, the Background of Christianity, the Lost Library of Qumran* (Philadelphia: Jewish Publication Society, 1994), pp. 351–62; also Morton Smith, "Two Ascended to Heaven— Jesus and the Author of 4Q491," in James H. Charlesworth,

ed., *Jesus and the Dead Sea Scrolls* (New York: Doubleday, 1992), pp. 290–301.

23. Jude 14 KJV.

24. Gen. 5:24 KJV.

25. 1 Enoch 14:18, 20, in Charlesworth, *Old Testament Pseud-epigrapha*, 1:21.

26. Jer. 31:32, 33–34 JB.

CHAPTER 6   **Becoming God**

Opening quotation: Compagno tablet (a), in Jane Harrison, *Prolegomena to the Study of Greek Religion*, 3d ed. (1922; reprint, New York: Meridian Books, 1955), p. 585.

1. Eric M. Meyers, Ehud Netzer and Carol L. Meyers, *Sepphoris* (Winona Lake, Ind.: Eisenbrauns, 1992), pp. 3–5, 10–11.

2. See John J. Rousseau and Rami Arav, *Jesus and His World: An Archaeological and Cultural Dictionary* (Minneapolis: Fortress Press, 1995), p. 249.

3. See Carl Kerényi, *Eleusis: Archetypal Image of Mother and Daughter*, trans. Ralph Manheim, Bollingen Series 65 (1967; reprint, Princeton: Princeton University Press, 1991), pp. 144–47, 174; and Edward F. Edinger, *The Eternal Drama: The Inner Meaning of Greek Mythology*, ed. Deborah A. Wesley (Boston: Shambhala Publications, 1994), pp. 176–78.

4. See James D. Tabor, *Things Unutterable: Paul's Ascent to Paradise in Its Greco-Roman, Judaic, and Early Christian Contexts* (Lanham, Md.: University Press of America, 1986), pp. 77–79; Joscelyn Godwin, *Mystery Religions in the Ancient World* (London: Thames and Hudson, 1981), pp. 26–37; and S. Angus, *The Mystery-Religions: A Study in the Religious Background of Early Christianity* (1928; reprint, New York: Dover Publications, 1975), pp. 106–12.

5. *On Old Age* 22.78, in *De Senectute, De Amicitia, De Divinatione*, vol. 20 of *Cicero*, trans. William Armistead Falconer, Loeb Classical Library (Cambridge: Harvard University Press, 1923), p. 91.

6. Virgil, *Aeneid* 6, lines 750–51, quoted in Edinger, *The Eternal Drama,* p. 116.

7. For more on reincarnation in Plato, see *Meno* 81; *Phaedrus* 248–49; *Phaedo* 81–82, 113–14; *Gorgias* 523–27.

8. Plato, *Republic* 10.614–20, in *The Dialogues of Plato and The Seventh Letter,* trans. Benjamin Jowett and J. Harward (Chicago: Encyclopaedia Britannica, 1952), pp. 437–41.

9. Compagno tablets (a) and (b), in Harrison, *Prolegomena,* p. 585.

10. Xenophanes, quoted in J. V. Luce, *An Introduction to Greek Philosophy* (New York: Thames and Hudson, 1992), p. 34.

11. *Katharmoi* frag. 107, in *Empedocles: The Extant Fragments,* ed. M. R. Wright (New Haven, Conn.: Yale University Press, 1981), p. 270.

12. *Katharmoi* frags. 108, 132, in *Empedocles,* pp. 275, 291.

13. Kenneth Sylvan Guthrie, comp. and trans., *The Pythagorean Sourcebook and Library: An Anthology of Ancient Writings Which Relate to Pythagoras and Pythagorean Philosophy* (Grand Rapids, Mich.: Phanes Press, 1987), p. 91.

14. *Katharmoi* frag. 102, in *Empedocles,* p. 264.

15. J. A. Philip, *Pythagoras and Early Pythagoreanism,* supplementary volume 7 of *Phoenix: Journal of the Classical Association of Canada* (Toronto: University of Toronto Press, 1966), p. 158.

CHAPTER 7 Moses Meets Plato

Opening quotation: Aristobulus, frag. 4.4, in Charlesworth, *Old Testament Pseudepigrapha,* 2:840.

1. Philo, *On Flight and Finding* 97, in *The Works of Philo: New Updated Edition,* trans. C. D. Yonge (Peabody, Mass.: Hendrickson Publishers, 1993), p. 330.

2. Philo, *On Flight and Finding* 97, quoted in Abraham Terian, "Had the Works of Philo Been Newly Discovered," *Biblical Archaeologist* 57 (1994): 95.

3. Philo, *Who Is the Heir of Divine Things* 205, 206, Yonge, p. 293.

4. John 1:1, 2.

5. John 4:10, 14.

6. Joseph Mélèze Modrzejewski, *The Jews of Egypt: From Rameses II to Emperor Hadrian,* trans. Robert Cornman (Philadelphia: Jewish Publication Society, 1995), p. 91; and J. D. Douglas, ed., *New Bible Dictionary,* 2d ed. (Leicester, England: Inter-Varsity Press, 1982), s.v. "Alexandria."

7. Aristobulus, frag. 4.4, in Charlesworth, *Old Testament Pseudepigrapha,* 2:840.

8. See Jerome, *Lives of Illustrious Men* 11, in *A Select Library of Nicene and Post-Nicene Fathers of the Christian Church,* ed. Philip Schaff and Henry Wace (reprint, Grand Rapids, Mich.: Wm. B. Eerdmans Publishing, 1979), 2d ser., 3:365.

9. Eusebius, *The History of the Church from Christ to Constantine,* trans. G. A. Williamson (New York: Dorset Press, 1965), p. 77.

10. Bruce M. Metzger and Michael D. Coogan, eds. *The Oxford Companion to the Bible* (New York: Oxford University Press, 1993), s.v. "Philo."

11. Samuel Sandmel, *Philo of Alexandria: An Introduction* (New York: Oxford University Press, 1979), p. 25.

12. Lev. 11:20, 21 JB.

13. Philo, *Who Is the Heir of Divine Things* 239, Yonge, p. 296.

14. See Gal. 4:24–27.

15. Philo, *On Dreams* 1.139, Yonge, p. 377.

16. *On the Giants* 12, 13, in *Philo,* 10 vols., 2 suppl. vols., trans. F. H. Colson and G. H. Whitaker, Loeb Classical Library (Cambridge: Harvard University Press, 1929–62), 2:451.

17. Philo, *On the Giants* 14, Yonge, p. 153.

18. Philo, *On the Giants* 15, Yonge, p. 153.

19. See David Winston, *Logos and Mystical Theology in Philo of Alexandria* (Cincinnati: Hebrew Union College Press, 1985), p. 42.

20. Sandmel, *Philo of Alexandria,* p. 23.

21. Erwin R. Goodenough, *By Light, Light: The Mystic Gospel of*

Hellenistic Judaism (1935; reprint, Amsterdam: Philo Press, 1969), p. 367.

22. Ronald H. Nash, "The Notion of Mediator in Alexandrian Judaism and the Epistle to the Hebrews," *Westminster Theological Journal* 40 (1977): 92.

23. Martin Hengel, *Judaism and Hellenism: Studies in Their Encounter in Palestine during the Early Hellenistic Period,* 2 vols., trans. John Bowden (London: SCM Press, 1974), 1:171.

CHAPTER 8 Routes into Palestine

Opening quotation: Hippolytus, *The Refutation of All Heresies* 1.21, in *The Ante-Nicene Fathers: Translations of the Writings of the Fathers down to* A.D. *325,* 10 vols., ed. Alexander Roberts and James Donaldson (reprint, Grand Rapids, Mich.: Wm. B. Eerdmans Publishing, 1978–81), 5:22.

1. See N. A. Nikam and Richard McKeon, eds. and trans., *The Edicts of Asoka* (1959; reprint, Chicago: University of Chicago Press, Phoenix Books, 1966), p. 29.

2. Ibid., p. 20.

3. See Jean W. Sedlar, *India and the Greek World: A Study in the Transmission of Culture* (Totowa, N.J.: Rowman and Littlefield, 1980), p. 88.

4. See Hirakawa Akira, *A History of Indian Buddhism from Sakyamuni to Early Mahayana,* trans. and ed. Paul Groner, Asian Studies at Hawaii, no. 36 (Hawaii: University of Hawaii Press, 1990), p. 229.

5. Mostafa El-Abbadi, "Alexandria: Thousand-Year Capital of Egypt," in Gareth L. Steen, ed., *Alexandria: The Site and the History* (New York: New York University Press, 1993), p. 43.

6. Rodger Kamenetz, *The Jew in the Lotus: A Poet's Rediscovery of Jewish Identity in Buddhist India* (HarperSanFrancisco, 1994), pp. 273–74.

7. Francis Schmidt, "Between Jews and Greeks: The Indian Model," in Hananya Goodman, ed., *Between Jerusalem and Benares: Comparative Studies in Judaism and Hinduism*

(Albany: State University of New York Press, 1994), p. 42.

8. Philo, *Every Good Man Is Free* 93–96, Yonge, p. 691.

9. Josephus, *The War of the Jews* 7.8.7, Whiston, p. 767.

10. Hippolytus, *The Refutation of All Heresies* 1:21, in *The Ante-Nicene Fathers*, 5:21–22.

11. Clement of Alexandria, *Stromateis* 1.71, in *Stromateis: Books One to Three*, trans. John Ferguson, The Fathers of the Church, vol. 85 (Washington, D.C.: Catholic University of America Press, 1991), p. 76.

12. Clement of Alexandria, *Stromateis* 3.60, Ferguson, p. 293.

13. Philostratus, *The Life of Apollonius of Tyana* 3.19–24, 2 vols., trans. F. C. Conybeare, Loeb Classical Library (Cambridge: Harvard University Press, 1912), 1:269–83.

14. Nicolas Notovitch, *The Unknown Life of Jesus Christ*, in Elizabeth Clare Prophet, *The Lost Years of Jesus: Documentary Evidence of Jesus' Seventeen-Year Journey to the East* (1984; reprint, Livingston, Mont.: Summit University Press, 1987), p. 208.

15. Ibid., p. 117.

16. *The Life of Saint Issa* 1:5, in Prophet, *The Lost Years of Jesus*, p. 212.

17. Notovitch, *The Unknown Life of Jesus Christ*, p. 107.

18. *The Life of Saint Issa* 4:13.

19. *The Life of Saint Issa* 5:2, 3.

20. *The Life of Saint Issa* 5:4.

21. *The Life of Saint Issa* 6:4.

22. Nicholas Roerich, *Himalaya*, quoted in Prophet, *The Lost Years of Jesus*, p. 306.

23. John 9:4.

24. Roerich, *Himalaya*, quoted in Prophet, *The Lost Years of Jesus*, p. 305.

CHAPTER 9 Jesus' Teaching on Reincarnation

Opening quotation: Noel Langley, *Edgar Cayce on Reincarnation* (New York: Warner Books, 1967), p. 169.

1. Mal. 3:1, 5; 4:5.

2. Matt. 16:14; Mark 6:15; Luke 9:8.

3. John 1:23.

4. Matt. 11:13–14 JB.

5. Mark 9:2, 3 JB.

6. Mark 9:11 JB.

7. Mark 9:12, 13 JB.

8. Matt. 17:13 JB.

9. Robert A. Morey, *Reincarnation and Christianity* (Minneapolis: Bethany House Publishers, 1980), p. 34.

10. 1 Cor. 15:40 KJV.

11. Hans Küng et al., *Christianity and the World Religions: Paths of Dialogue with Islam, Hinduism, and Buddhism,* trans. Peter Heinegg (Garden City, N.Y.: Doubleday and Co., 1986), p. 235.

12. See Robert W. Funk, Roy W. Hoover, and the Jesus Seminar, *The Five Gospels: The Search for the Authentic Words of Jesus* (New York: Macmillan Publishing, Polebridge Press Book, 1993), pp. 81–82, 179, 210, 211.

13. See Church Father Tertullian's argument against the Carpocratians, a second-century sect of Christian Gnostics who believed that the Elijah-come-again passages supported reincarnation. See Tertullian, *Treatise on the Soul* 35, in *The Ante-Nicene Fathers,* 3:216–17.

14. John 9:1, 2, 3, 7.

15. Deut. 5:9.

16. *New Catholic Encyclopedia,* s.v. "Metempsychosis."

17. Luke 23:41, 42–43 JB.

18. Luke 16:19, 22, 23 JB.

19. Luke 16:26 JB.

20. Funk, Hoover, and the Jesus Seminar, *The Five Gospels,* pp. 361, 397.

21. *Catechism of the Catholic Church* 1013 (Liguori, Mo.: Liguori Publications, 1994), p. 264.

22. Some translations render this phrase "after that comes *the* judgment." But these are based on later and less accurate

manuscripts. The most authentic translations of this verse simply say "judgment." This is important because "*the* judgment" would seem to refer to the final, one-time event that many Christians have in mind.

23. Franciscus Mercurius van Helmont, *Two Hundred Queries Moderately Propounded Concerning the Doctrine of the Revolution of Humane Souls, and Its Conformity to the Truths of Christianity* (London, 1684), p. 82.

24. Rom. 8:7, 6, 5 KJV.

25. 1 Cor. 15:31 KJV.

26. 1 Cor. 15:54–55 KJV.

CHAPTER 10 Karma Implies Reincarnation

1. Exod. 32:9 KJV.

2. Basilides, cited in *Excerpta ex Theodoto* 1.28, in Werner Foerster, *Gnosis: A Selection of Gnostic Texts,* 2 vols., trans. R. McL. Wilson (Oxford: Clarendon Press, 1972), 1:226.

3. Gen. 9:6 KJV.

4. Exod. 21:12, 23–25 KJV.

5. Obad. 15 JB.

6. Matt. 26:52 KJV.

7. Matt. 5:17 KJV.

8. Matt. 5:18 KJV.

9. Matt. 7:2, 12.

10. Matt. 12:35 KJV.

11. Matt. 5:38–42 JB.

12. Matt. 5:43–44 JB.

13. Mascaró, *The Dhammapada,* p. 35.

14. Acharya Shantideva, *A Guide to the Bodhisattva's Way of Life,* trans. Stephen Batchelor (Dharamsala, India: Library of Tibetan Works and Archives, 1979), p. 25.

15. Langley, *Edgar Cayce on Reincarnation,* p. 75.

16. Rom. 2:6, 9, 10, 11 JB.

17. Gal. 6:5, 7–8 KJV.

18. 1 Cor. 3:8, 13, 14, 15 KJV.

19. 2 Cor. 5:10 JB. See also NRSV: "For all of us must appear before the judgment seat of Christ, so that each may receive recompense for what has been done in the body, whether good or evil."

20. John 3:3, 4, 5–6. The King James Version is the source of the familiar phrase "born again." Although most modern scholars do not trace this passage back to the historical Jesus, I see it as his inner, mystical teaching preserved by his trusted apostles.

21. Rev. 3:12 KJV.

22. Juan Mascaró, trans., *The Bhagavad Gita,* 15.5, 6 (New York: Penguin Books, 1962), p. 106.

PART 3 | *Early Christians and Reincarnation*

CHAPTER 11 Sifting the New Testament

Opening quotation: Thomas Jefferson to John Adams, 1814, quoted in Paul Scott, "The Riddle of Jesus," *The Fourth R* 6 (May/June 1993): 3.

1. Matt. 27:46; Mark 15:34; Ps. 22:1.

2. Luke 23:46; Ps. 31:5.

3. John 19:30.

4. First Vatican Council, quoted in Metzger and Coogan, *The Oxford Companion to the Bible,* s.v. "Inspiration and Inerrancy."

5. Matt. 6:13 KJV.

6. Codex Sinaiticus, quoted in James Bentley, *Secrets of Mount Sinai: The Story of the World's Oldest Bible—Codex Sinaiticus* (1985; reprint, Garden City, N.Y.: Doubleday and Co., 1986), pp. 132–33.

7. Mark 1:41 KJV.

8. Mic. 5:2.

9. In 1994, a challenge to the consensus on the dating of Matthew came from a German scholar, Carsten Thiede. Thiede claimed that a new method of script analysis could now assign three papyrus fragments of Matthew to the middle of the first

century, c. 65. Thus they would predate Mark. See Carsten Peter Thiede and Matthew d'Ancona, *Eyewitness to Jesus: Amazing New Manuscript Evidence about the Origin of the Gospels* (New York: Doubleday, 1996).

However, Thiede has received little support from the scholarly community. Graham Stanton, one of Britain's most eminent New Testament scholars, believes that his case is weak. Thiede rests his argument on similarities between these three Matthew fragments and other fragments that have been conclusively dated c. 66 or 79. However, the style of writing used in those dated fragments was popular for several hundred years and actually reached its peak in the fourth century. So the appearance of this style in the three fragments does not prove they were written in the middle of the first century. Stanton also points out that Thiede has largely ignored the differences between the way the letters are formed in his Matthew fragments and the way they are formed in the first-century fragments. These differences are significant, Stanton argues. He concludes that "there is no reason to abandon the view. . . that [these Matthew fragments] date from the end of the second century: there are no persuasive arguments in favour of a first-century dating." *Gospel Truth? New Light on Jesus and the Gospels* (Valley Forge, Penn.: Trinity Press International, 1995), p. 16. We might add that even if Thiede's date were to be adopted, it is thirty years after the crucifixion and would not prove that the author of Matthew was an eyewitness to Jesus' life.

10. Marcus J. Borg, *Meeting Jesus Again for the First Time: The Historical Jesus and the Heart of Contemporary Faith* (HarperSanFrancisco, 1994), p. 24.

11. Luke 6:17.

12. Luke 6:20.

13. Matt. 5:3.

14. Luke 6:21.

15. Matt. 5:6. (All italics within Bible quotations have been added for emphasis.)

16. See Burton L. Mack, *Who Wrote the New Testament? The Making of the Christian Myth* (HarperSanFrancisco, 1995), p. 153.

17. See the discussion in Stephen J. Patterson's introduction to *The Gospel of Thomas*, in *Q–Thomas Reader*, by John S. Kloppenborg et al. (Sonoma, Calif.: Polebridge Press, 1990), pp. 85–90.

18. Luke 6:22–23.

19. Matt. 5:11–12.

20. *Gospel of Thomas*, saying 68, in Kloppenborg et al., *Q–Thomas Reader*, p. 146.

21. Mark 12:9, in Robert J. Miller, ed., *The Complete Gospels: Annotated Scholars Version*, 3d ed. (1992; reprint, HarperSanFrancisco, Polebridge Press, 1994), p. 41.

22. Funk, Hoover, and the Jesus Seminar, *The Five Gospels*, p. 101.

23. See Helmut Koester, *Ancient Christian Gospels: Their History and Development* (Philadelphia: Trinity Press International, 1990), pp. 75–128.

24. See Stephen J. Patterson, *The Gospel of Thomas and Jesus* (Sonoma, Calif.: Polebridge Press, 1993), p. 4.

25. Funk, Hoover, and the Jesus Seminar, *The Five Gospels*, p. 20.

26. The aim of the Jesus Seminar is to present to the public in an easily understandable format a consensus of recent scholarship on the historical Jesus. The Seminar therefore formulated strict "rules of evidence" that grew out of the scholarship of this century. They then voted on each of the sayings attributed to Jesus, designating them on a scale from red ("Jesus undoubtedly said this or something very like it") to pink ("Jesus probably said something like this") to gray ("Jesus did not say this, but the ideas contained in it are close to his own") to black ("Jesus did not say this; it represents the perspective or content of a later or different tradition"). Funk, Hoover, and the Jesus Seminar, *The Five Gospels*, p. 36.

 While the idea of voting on the sayings of Jesus may seem irreverent, the Seminar's criteria developed from conclusions that they as individual scholars had reached during years of painstaking analysis. The scholars acknowledge that using these criteria may appear "heartless and irreverent," but they insist that their motive is to present "consistency and reliability." Robert M. Rock, "An Introduction to the Jesus Seminar," *The Fourth R* 5 (January 1992): 11. The Seminar gave only 18 percent of the sayings a red designation, concluding that Jesus did not say the other 82 percent of the words ascribed to him in the Gospels (including Thomas). However, a substantial number of sayings received a pink or gray designation, which indicates that the scholars think they represent Jesus' ideas.

Shocking as this outcome may seem, it may help us to sort out what Jesus really said from the conflicting views about him that were circulating in the early years after his crucifixion. The Seminar's primary goal is to determine what we can know about the historical Jesus and what were his authentic words. Although I disagree with some of their conclusions, I believe that in stripping away some of the accretions surrounding the life of Christ, the Jesus Seminar has done us a great service.

Most of these scholars are in secular universities rather than seminaries. Thus they are not bound by a theological viewpoint but are free to go wherever they are led by logic, textual analysis and archaeological evidence. Their liberation from theology has both helped and hindered them. Although they are no longer bound by orthodoxy, they may have gone to the other extreme and rejected the essential spirituality of Jesus' message. Nevertheless, I believe they have uncovered something valuable in their quest.

The Jesus Seminar has published some of their findings in *The Five Gospels*, which includes the *Gospel of Thomas* alongside Matthew, Mark, Luke and John.

27. Not all modern scholars support the conclusions of the Jesus Seminar, and some are quite strongly opposed to their findings. Among the latter, see Luke Timothy Johnson, *The Real Jesus: The Misguided Quest for the Historical Jesus and the Truth of the Traditional Gospels* (HarperSanFrancisco, 1996); and Ben

Witherington III, *The Jesus Quest: The Third Search for the Jew of Nazareth* (Downers Grove, Ill.: InterVarsity Press, 1995).

28. Matt. 6:3–4.

29. *Gospel of Thomas,* saying 62, in Kloppenborg et al., *Q–Thomas Reader,* p. 144. We have eliminated the scholarly use of brackets within Gnostic texts. Scholars use these brackets to indicate restored words.

CHAPTER 12 **What Is Gnosticism?**

Opening quotation: *Gospel of Thomas,* saying 1, in Marvin Meyer, trans., *The Gospel of Thomas: The Hidden Sayings of Jesus* (HarperSanFrancisco, 1992), p. 23.

1. The chief attacks on the Gnostics were authored by the Church Fathers Irenaeus, Tertullian and Epiphanius. But their work is seriously flawed and must be seen for what it is—a religious polemic rather than a history. Irenaeus, known as the first Church Father, devoted five volumes to a work, called *Adversus Haereses,* exposing the Gnostics. Scholars have criticized his work for lack of objectivity and muddled thinking.

   Tertullian composed numerous works against the Gnostics. He disliked the Gnostics' philosophical speculations, claiming that they were unnecessary. "Since Jesus Christ we have no need of any further investigation, nor of any research since the Gospel has been proclaimed," he wrote.

   The fourth-century bishop Epiphanius of Salamis entitled his work *Panarion,* or "medicine chest," because it was meant to ward off the influences of the Gnostic groups. He portrayed all heretics, including Gnostics, as "vain-glorious," "worthless" and "evilminded." See Tertullian and Epiphanius, quoted in Kurt Rudolph, *Gnosis: The Nature and History of Gnosticism* (San Francisco: Harper and Row, 1987), pp. 15, 19.

   Other Church Fathers portrayed the Gnostics as generally licentious, but Epiphanius was most graphic in his description. He said their practices included: having sex but forbidding the bearing of children, eating aborted fetuses, praying naked, "spending their time in lechery and drunkenness," practicing homosexuality and eating semen and menses. *The Panarion of St. Epiphanius, Bishop of Salamis: Selected Passages,* trans. Philip R. Amidon (New York: Oxford University Press, 1990), p. 77.

Modern scholars do not take Epiphanius seriously. His "blind zeal for orthodoxy," according to scholar Kurt Rudolph, led to an uncritical treatment of facts, "quite improbable reports" and "invention." "By this he brought the history of early Christian heresy into great confusion, and critical research has first laboriously had to separate the wheat from the chaff, a task which even today is still not complete," writes Rudolph. *Gnosis,* pp. 18, 19.

We have evidence that at least one Gnostic group attempted to distance itself from these charges. *Pistis Sophia,* a second- or third-century Gnostic text, promises the severest penalties after death for anyone who eats a lentil porridge to which semen and menses have been added. It quotes Jesus as saying, "This sin is more heinous than all sins and iniquities." He says that their souls will be cast into outer darkness, where they will be "destroyed and dissolved." G. R. S. Mead, trans., *Pistis Sophia,* 147 (Blauvelt, N.Y.: Garber Communications, Spiritual Science Library, 1984), p. 322. This shows that there may have been some sects who practiced the kinds of things Epiphanius claimed but that other Gnostic sects shunned such practices.

When we analyze some of the criticisms of Irenaeus, we will discover a contradiction that suggests the Gnostics may actually have leaned more toward asceticism than not. Irenaeus criticized a Gnostic sect called the Carpocratians for living "a dissipated life" and accused them of saying that "conduct is good and evil only in the opinion of men." They believed, he said, that they could not be liberated from rebirth until they had tried "every kind of life and every kind of deed." When Irenaeus accused the Gnostics of trying "every kind of deed," he presumably included acts that Christians were forbidden even to think about, such as prostitution, homosexuality and child molestation.

However, in an earlier passage, Irenaeus had already contradicted himself by accusing the Carpocratians of *attempting to rival Jesus and the apostles through asceticism.* Can both descriptions be correct?

We already know from other Gnostic texts that some sects believed that the way to avoid being born again was to deny bodily passions. Irenaeus tells us that the Carpocratians believed that Jesus was "like the rest of men" but was able to perceive his divine nature. Jesus had successfully "vanquished" his passions.

Irenaeus tells us that some Carpocratians had the audacity to attempt to be more ascetic than Jesus. He says, "But if anyone despise the things here more than he, he can be greater than he." The Carpocratians believed their souls had come from the same place as Jesus' soul and, to the extent they could emulate him, they were "counted worthy of the same power" and permitted to "return again to the same place." Irenaeus, *Adversus Haereses* 1.25.3, 4, 1, 2, in Foerster, *Gnosis*, pp. 37, 36.

How could the Carpocratians attempt to rival Jesus for purity on the one hand while trying "every kind of deed" on the other? It seems reasonable to ask whether Irenaeus' accusations about the Carpocratians are a garbled interpretation of the implications of reincarnation. Followed to its logical conclusion, the concept of reincarnation does tell us that someone could have been in any sort of life and still be saved. And this was one of the reasons the Church Fathers disliked it. Someone could be a thief or a prostitute in one life and progress to a merchant, nobleman or even a saint or martyr in the next. This undermined the Church's one-shot theology and thereby its authority.

Irenaeus may simply have been saying, if you believe in reincarnation, then you believe you have been guilty of every sort of wickedness throughout your many incarnations. In any case, the contradictions in his writings should give rise for suspicion about his accuracy. His description of the Carpocratians as ascetic is more in line with the Nag Hammadi revelations about Gnostic theology than his contradictory accusations of licentious behavior.

2. Henry Chadwick, "The Domestication of Gnosis," in Bentley Layton, ed., *The Rediscovery of Gnosticism* (Leiden: E. J. Brill, 1980), 1:3.

3. An analysis of some Gnostic texts may help to clarify the Gnostics' attitudes toward childbearing and sex. The Valentinian text the *Excerpta ex Theodoto* refutes the charge that the Gnostics refused to bear children. It tells us that childbearing is an important and necessary part of the scheme of salvation.

In one Gnostic text, the *Gospel of the Egyptians,* the Saviour says that "death reigns as long as women give birth." Some probably interpreted this as a rejection of childbirth. But the Valentinian author of the *Excerpta ex Theodoto* tells us that the Saviour's statement should not be interpreted as a criticism of childbearing. He says that it is "indispensable for the salvation of those who believe—for this child-bearing is essential until the previously reckoned seed is brought forth." Foerster, *Gnosis,* 1:230.

The "previously reckoned seed" refers to the divine sparks trapped in matter. Until these seeds have escaped from matter and returned to God, childbearing must go on.

This text indicates that the Gnostics differed in their attitudes toward procreation, and it probably reflects debates about childbearing that went on in Gnostic circles. Since Gnosticism was an individual path, it is possible that some groups expected people to choose for themselves whether to be married or celibate.

Scholar Elaine Pagels has developed a new interpretation of a passage in the *Gospel of Philip* that supports the view of individual choice. This Gospel contains an elaborate bridal-chamber image. Until now, most scholars have interpreted this imagery as either accepting or rejecting celibacy. But Pagels argues that the bridal-chamber image was meant to describe the union of the soul with the Spirit or Son of God. Gnostics did not advocate either celibacy or marriage, she says, but believed that what was important was a person's spiritual development.

Pagels notes that the Valentinian author of the *Gospel of Philip*, while saying that he prefers asceticism, "refrains from offering specific instructions and, in particular, refrains from exclusively advocating either celibacy or marriage. What matters, apparently, is not so much which practice one chooses but the quality of one's intention and the level of one's *gnosis*."

Pagels cites the following passage from the *Gospel of Philip* to prove her point: "Do not fear the flesh nor love it. If you fear it, it will gain mastery over you. If you love it, it will devour and paralyze you" (66.5–7). This passage advocates neither asceticism nor sensuality, but a middle way. See Pagels, "The 'Mystery of Marriage' in the *Gospel of Philip* Revisited," in Birger A. Pearson, ed., *The Future of Early Christianity: Essays in Honor of Helmut Koester* (Fortress Press, Minneapolis, 1991), pp. 453, 449.

(In espousing a personal path, however, these scriptures do not give the Gnostics license to commit evil. Rather, each believer becomes his own policeman. Gnostics have a special responsibility to balance knowledge with love and to consciously "dig down to the root of evil within" and "pull out the root from the heart," as the *Gospel of Philip* directs [83.18].)

And so we see that there was a wide variety of Christian beliefs and practices in the early centuries of Christianity, just as there is today. We know some Gnostics were ascetic; some may have been what the Church Fathers would call "morally licentious." But the point of Gnosticism was not the formation of a moral code—it was enlightenment.

4. See Bentley Layton, historical introduction to part 3: "The School of Valentinus," in *The Gnostic Scriptures* (Garden City, N.Y.: Doubleday and Co., 1987), pp. 270, 272.

5. Aristobulus, frag. 4.5, in Charlesworth, *Old Testament Pseud-epigrapha,* 2:840.

6. Mark 4:11, 34.

7. See Funk, Hoover, and the Jesus Seminar, *The Five Gospels,* pp. 55–56.

8. Clement of Alexandria, quoted in Morton Smith, *The Secret Gospel: The Discovery and Interpretation of the Secret Gospel According to Mark* (Clearlake, Calif.: Dawn Horse Press, 1982), p. 15.

9. Clement of Alexandria, *Stromateis* 1.1, quoted in R. P. C. Hanson, *Origen's Doctrine of Tradition* (London: SPCK, 1954), p. 54.

10. The story is based on *The Hymn of the Pearl.* See Layton, *The Gnostic Scriptures,* pp. 371–75.

11. *Book of Thomas the Contender* 138.16–18, in James M. Robinson, ed., *The Nag Hammadi Library in English,* 3d ed., rev. (San Francisco: Harper and Row, 1988), p. 201.

12. *Gospel of Thomas,* saying 108, Meyer, p. 63.

13. Irenaeus, *Adversus Haereses* 1.25.2, quoted in Foerster, *Gnosis,* 1:36.

14. *Teachings of Silvanus* 107.12, 108.25–27, in Robinson, *Nag Hammadi Library,* pp. 390, 391.

15. *Gospel of Philip* 84.7–13, in Robinson, *Nag Hammadi Library,* p. 159.

CHAPTER 13 Seeking the "Things That Exist"

Opening quotation: *Book of Thomas* 9:5, in Marvin W. Meyer, trans., *The Secret Teachings of Jesus: Four Gnostic Gospels* (1984; reprint, New York: Random House, Vintage Books, 1986), p. 50.

1. Matt. 5:25–26.

2. See Irenaeus, *Against Heresies* 1.25.4, in *The Ante-Nicene Fathers,* 1:351.

3. *Gospel of Thomas,* saying 84, in Meyer, *Gospel of Thomas,* p. 57.

4. *Book of Thomas* 4:7, 18, 17, in Meyer, *The Secret Teachings of Jesus,* pp. 44, 45 (emphasis added). The *Book of Thomas* is also known as the *Book of Thomas the Contender.* For Meyer's reference to reincarnation, see note to 4:17, p. 110.

5. *Book of Thomas* 9:5, in Meyer, *The Secret Teachings of Jesus,* p. 50 (emphasis added).

6. *Secret Book of John* 14:3, in Meyer, *The Secret Teachings of Jesus,* p. 81.

7. *Secret Book of John* 14:15, 17, in Meyer, *The Secret Teachings of Jesus,* p. 82.

8. *Secret Book of John* 14.20, in Meyer, *The Secret Teachings of Jesus,* p. 82.

9. Basilides, frag. G, *Commentaries* 23, quoted in Layton, *The Gnostic Scriptures,* p. 442.

10. Clement of Alexandria commenting on Basilides, in Layton, *The Gnostic Scriptures,* p. 443.

11. Violet MacDermot, trans., *Pistis Sophia,* 144, 146, Nag Hammadi Studies 9 (Leiden: E. J. Brill, 1978), pp. 749, 753, 757, 759.

12. *Pistis Sophia* 145, MacDermot, pp. 753, 755.

13. *Apocalypse of Paul* 20.9–10; 21.16–17, 18, in Robinson, *Nag Hammadi Library,* p. 258.

14. G. R. S. Mead, trans., *Pistis Sophia,* 147 (Blauvelt, N.Y.: Garber Communications, Spiritual Science Library, 1984), p. 322.

15. *Pistis Sophia* 147, Mead, p. 323.

16. *Zostrianos* 43, in Layton, *The Gnostic Scriptures,* pp. 132–33.

17. Ibid., p. 133.

18. *Zostrianos* 46, 44, in Layton, *The Gnostic Scriptures,* pp. 134, 133.

CHAPTER 14 Does Resurrection Rule Out Reincarnation?

Opening quotation: *Gospel of Philip* 73.1–4, in Layton, *The Gnostic Scriptures,* p. 345.

1. Isaac Asimov, "The Last Trump," in *The Complete Stories* (New York: Doubleday, Foundation Book, 1990), 1:108, 118.

2. Rev. 20:12 KJV.

3. Rev. 20:4–5; Matt. 27:52–53.

4. See Origen, *Commentary on Romans* 5.9, quoted in Hans Urs von Balthasar, *Origen, Spirit and Fire: A Thematic Anthology of His Writings,* trans. Robert J. Daly (Washington, D.C.: Catholic University of America Press, 1984), p. 322.

5. See *Origen: On First Principles,* 2.10.1–2, trans. G. W. Butterworth (1936; reprint, Gloucester, Mass.: Peter Smith, 1973), pp. 139–40.

6. 1 Cor. 15:44, 50.

7. See Jerome, *To Pammachius against John of Jerusalem* 31, 32, in *Nicene and Post-Nicene Fathers of the Christian Church,* 2d ser., 6:440.

8. Tertullian, *On the Flesh of Christ* 5, in *The Ante-Nicene Fathers,* 3:525.

9. Matt. 19:26; Mark 10:27 KJV.

10. Origen, *On First Principles* 2.10.3, Butterworth, p. 140.

11. Origen, *Against Celsus* 5.19, quoted in Jaroslav Pelikan, *The Emergence of the Catholic Tradition (100–600),* vol. 1 of *The Christian Tradition: A History of the Development of Doctrine* (Chicago: University of Chicago Press, 1971), p. 48.

12. Grant R. Jeffrey, *Heaven... the Last Frontier* (1990; reprint, New York: Bantam Books, 1991), p. 192.

13. Luke 24:42–43, 39 KJV; John 20:27.

14. See Origen, cited in Jerome, *To Pammachius against John of Jerusalem* 25, 26, in *Nicene and Post-Nicene Fathers,* 2d ser., 6:436, 437.

15. *Catechism of the Catholic Church* 1000, p. 261.

16. *Catechism of the Catholic Church* 990, p. 258.

17. *New Catholic Encyclopedia,* s.v. "Resurrection of the Dead."

18. 1 Cor. 15:51–53.

19. John A. Hardon, *The Catholic Catechism* (New York: Doubleday, 1981), p. 264.

20. Jeffrey, *Heaven... the Last Frontier,* pp. 47–52.

21. Leslie D. Weatherhead, *The Christian Agnostic* (Nashville:

Abingdon Press, 1965), p. 294.

22. Ibid., p. 332.

23. Tertullian, *De Spectaculis* 30, in *The Ante-Nicene Fathers,* 3:91.

24. *Catechism of the Catholic Church* 839–41, 847, 846, pp. 222–23, 224.

25. Robert P. Lightner, *The Last Days Handbook* (Nashville: Thomas Nelson Publishers, 1990), pp. 45–46.

26. See Funk, Hoover, and the Jesus Seminar, *Five Gospels,* pp. 397–98; also John Dominic Crossan, *Jesus: A Revolutionary Biography* (HarperSanFrancisco, 1994), pp. 160–66.

27. 1 Cor. 15:5–8.

28. Mark 16:9, 12, 14.

29. See Hugh J. Schonfield, *The Passover Plot: New Light on the History of Jesus* (1966; reprint, New York: Bantam Books, 1967).

CHAPTER 15   A Spiritual Resurrection

Opening quotation: *Gospel of Philip* 53.17–19, 27–28, 29, 31, in Robinson, *Nag Hammadi Library,* p. 142.

1. Elaine Pagels, *The Gnostic Paul: Gnostic Exegesis of the Pauline Letters* (Philadelphia: Trinity Press International, 1975), p. 81.

2. In addition to pneumatics and psychics, there was a third category of men, "the 'fleshly' (sarkic, from Greek *sarx* 'flesh, body') or 'earthly' (choic, from Greek *choikos* 'earthly'), also called 'hylic' (Greek *hylē,* 'matter')." Rudolph, *Gnosis,* pp. 91–92. Hylic man was not even interested in spiritual things.

    Valentinian Gnostics thought that every person had pneumatic, psychic and hylic elements and that the dominant element determined the class into which a person fell. Some Gnostics believed that the hylics could become psychics and then pneumatics and ultimately be saved, while others denied that the hylics could move to a higher class.

3. Origen, *On First Principles* 1, quoted in Matthew Black, ed., *Peake's Commentary on the Bible* (Surrey, England: Thomas Nelson and Sons, 1962), p. 5.

4. I speak of the "authors of the Epistles" because most modern scholars, including many Catholics and Protestants, believe that Paul did not write all of the letters traditionally assigned to him. The scholars base their opinion on an analysis of the vocabulary and world view of each Epistle. Seven Epistles are believed to be authentically Pauline: Romans, 1 and 2 Corinthians, Galatians, Philippians, 1 Thessalonians and Philemon. But many scholars attribute Ephesians and Colossians to Paul's disciples since they discuss issues that would not have concerned Christians in Paul's day or fail to include words that are distinctly Pauline. Most scholars do not believe Paul wrote 2 Thessalonians, 1 and 2 Timothy, Titus or Hebrews. However, the Gnostics considered all of the following to be Pauline: Romans, 1 and 2 Corinthians, Galatians, Ephesians, Philippians, Colossians, 1 Thessalonians and Hebrews. See Pagels, *The Gnostic Paul,* p. 5.

5. Gen. 2:17.

6. Philo, *Allegorical Interpretation* 1.106, 108, Yonge, p. 37.

7. Col. 2:13.

8. John 11:25–26.

9. The chief support for the idea that Paul opposed the Gnostics is said to be Paul's condemnation in 1 Corinthians of "the wise" and teachers of "wisdom." But the Gnostics thought that he was attacking not them but rather those who tried to interpret the scriptures literally, with worldly wisdom. In Corinthians, after condemning the "wise," Paul goes on to explain that he *does* teach wisdom but "not a wisdom of this age." Instead, it is "God's wisdom, secret and hidden" (1 Cor. 2:6, 7). The Gnostics believed that *they* were the inheritors of that secret wisdom and that they alone had the key to Paul's mysteries.

10. Eph. 5:14 KJV.

11. Rom. 6:4, 5, 11.

12. Pagels, *The Gnostic Paul,* p. 29.

13. Col. 3:1, 9–10 KJV.

14. 1 Cor. 15:12–14, 16, 20, 22–23. A crucial verse, 23, refers to the timing of the resurrection. The New Revised Standard Version (quoted in the text) tells us the resurrection occurs "each in his own order: Christ the first fruits, then at his coming those who belong to Christ." Pagels translates the verse as: "each in his own order, the first fruit, Christ, then those of Christ in his presence," avoiding any reference to Christ's "coming" or return. The resurrection of "those of Christ in his presence," then, can be thought of as occurring any time after the resurrection of Jesus and not at the future Second Coming.

But some people might say the Gnostic interpretation runs into a snag in the next section of the chapter. For in the very next sentence, Paul starts talking about the "end":

"Then comes the end, when he hands over the kingdom to God the Father, after he has destroyed every ruler and every authority and power. . . . When all things are subjected to him, then the Son himself will also be subjected to the one who put all things in subjection under him, so that God may be all in all" (1 Cor. 15:24–28).

Does this refer to the end of time, as Christians have interpreted it? Some scholars believe references to "the end" were not a part of Jesus' sayings but probably represent Paul's mistaken belief that Jesus would return soon. They have concluded that Jesus did not prophesy his imminent return.

The Gnostics, however, interpreted the "end" as the end of the age, of a cycle of time rather than the end of all time. However, the cycles were not meant to continue forever. Gnostics believed that the promise of God being "all in all" would be fulfilled when all souls were returned to the Fullness, i.e., the transcendent God. See Pagels, *The Gnostic Paul,* pp. 82–83. This belief was later rejected by the Church. See chapter 19.

15. 1 Cor. 15:29.

16. Pagels, *The Gnostic Paul,* p. 83.

17. Rom. 8:11.

18. *Gospel of Thomas,* saying 51, Meyer, p. 43.

19. *Dialogue of the Savior* 143.20, in Robinson, *Nag Hammadi Library,* p. 254.

20. *Dialogue of the Savior* 143.22–23, in Robinson, *Nag Hammadi Library,* p. 254. For more on the interpretation of this passage, see April D. De Conick, "The *Dialogue of the Savior* and the Mystical Sayings of Jesus," *Vigiliae Christianae* 50 (1996): 178–99.

21. *Gospel of Philip* 56.29–32, in Robinson, *Nag Hammadi Library,* p. 144.

22. *Treatise on Resurrection* 48.26–28, 30–49.4, in Robinson, *Nag Hammadi Library,* p. 56.

23. 1 Cor. 15:53.

24. *Treatise on Resurrection* 45, in Layton, *The Gnostic Scriptures,* p. 321 (emphasis added).

CHAPTER 16 The Different Fates of Twins

1. Gen. 25:23.

2. Gen. 27:15–29.

3. Mal. 1:2, 3 KJV. NRSV: "I have loved Jacob but I have hated Esau." JB: "I showed my love for Jacob and my hatred for Esau."

4. *Genesis Rabbah* 63.6.3, in Jacob Neusner, *Genesis Rabbah: The Judaic Commentary to the Book of Genesis,* 3 vols. (Atlanta: Scholars Press, 1985), 2:353.

5. Rom. 9:11, 14.

6. Origen, *On First Principles* 2.9.7, Butterworth, p. 135.

7. Ibid., p. 136. Origen discusses the question of God's justice in relation to preexistence, citing Paul to develop his argument.

   In Romans 9, after discussing Jacob and Esau, Paul does not confirm or deny preexistence but rather stresses that God, the Creator, does not need to explain his actions to his creation and that the creation should not question God's actions.

   In a passage that has often been interpreted to imply predestination, Paul writes: "He has mercy on whomever he chooses, and he hardens the heart of whomever he chooses.

You will say to me then, 'Why then does he still find fault? For who can resist his will?' But who indeed are you, a human being, to argue with God? Will what is molded say to the one who molds it, 'Why have you made me like this?' Has the potter no right over the clay, to make out of the same lump one object for special use and another for ordinary use?" (Rom. 9:18–21). Or, as Origen's translation reads, "To make one part a vessel unto honor, and another unto dishonor?"

In this passage, Paul seems to imply that our differences are the result of God's mysterious choices and that we have no right to ask God why he made us different from one another. But Origen doesn't see it this way. He tells us that there must be a reason why God chooses to make people different from each other—and that reason predates their entrance into bodies.

Furthermore, Origen does not believe that Paul is affirming predestination here but interprets this passage in light of Paul's statements elsewhere. Origen makes the fundamental assertion that Paul does not contradict himself. He reasons that since in other passages Paul says we are responsible for our actions, he would not deny free will here. For example, in 2 Corinthians 5:10 he tells us that in the "judgment" after death, everyone receives according to "what has been done in the body." Would Paul have said this if he truly believed that we are predestined, some to "honor" and some to "dishonor" or even some to "special use" and others to "ordinary use"?

Origen cites Timothy as also stating that we can change the nature of our "vessels" (ourselves) and thus our destinies. (Origen believed that Paul wrote Timothy. See chapter 15, note 4 for discussion of authorship of Epistles.) Second Timothy 2:20, 21 says that these "vessels" can "purge" themselves and become "prepared unto every good work." Again, this denies predestination. Thus Origen concludes that Paul is not asserting predestination but rather telling us that God makes "vessels of honor" out of those who have purged, or cleansed, themselves (of karma?) and that those "who allow themselves to remain unpurged" become "vessels of dishonor."

Whether a soul is made "unto honor" or "dishonor," Origen tells us, depends on "causes older than the fashioning of vessels." In other words, God's choice to make some people "special" and others "ordinary" is based on causes that predate the forming of their bodies. *On First Principles* 3.1.21, Butterworth, pp. 202, 203, 204.

Origen's explanation of Paul seems to make good sense.

8. Origen, *Homilies on Genesis and Exodus,* trans. Ronald E. Heine, The Fathers of the Church, vol. 71 (Washington, D.C.: Catholic University of America Press, 1982), p. 1.

9. See Clement of Alexandria, *The Instructor* 2.1, 2.3, 3.2, in *The Ante-Nicene Fathers,* 2:237, 248, 273.

10. See Robert M. Grant, "Early Alexandrian Christianity," *Church History* 40 (June 1971): 135–44.

11. Origen, *Commentary on John* 5.8, quoted in Joseph Wilson Trigg, *Origen: The Bible and Philosophy in the Third-Century Church* (Atlanta: John Knox Press, 1983), p. 82.

12. Origen, *On First Principles* 4.1.17, quoted in Robert Payne, *The Fathers of the Eastern Church* (1957; reprint, New York: Marboro Books, Dorset Press, 1989), p. 53.

13. See Irenaeus, *Against Heresies* 3.23, 5.23, in *The Ante-Nicene Fathers,* 1:455–58, 551–52; and Jon F. Dechow, *Dogma and Mysticism in Early Christianity: Epiphanius of Cyprus and the Legacy of Origen,* Patristic Monograph Series, 13 (Macon, Ga.: Mercer University Press, 1988), pp. 334–47.

14. Augustine, *City of God* 12.10, in *Nicene and Post-Nicene Fathers,* 1st ser., 2:232.

15. See Gerald Bostock, "The Sources of Origen's Doctrine of Pre-Existence," in Lothar Lies, ed., *Origeniana Quarta* (Innsbruck: Tyrolia-Verlag, 1987), pp. 259–64.

Origen may have had something to add to the question of whether the Jews believed in reincarnation. In his treatment of the John-as-Elijah passages in his *Commentary on John,* he tells us that the Jews' question to John, "Art thou Elijah?" suggests "that they believed in metensomatosis [transmigration], as a doctrine inherited from their ancestors, and therefore in no way in conflict with the secret teaching of their masters." He also tells us that a Jewish tradition said that one Phinehas, the son of Eleazar, "was to have been Elijah." Perhaps Origen had access to secret Jewish teachings outside of the Gospels. *Commentary on John* 6.7, quoted in Jean Daniélou, *Gospel Message and Hellenistic Culture*, trans. John Austin Baker, vol. 2 of *A History of Early Christian Doctrine before the Council of Nicaea* (London: Darton, Longman and Todd, 1973), pp. 493–94.

16. Clement does discuss the preexistence of souls, which forms the basis for reincarnation. He supports the idea of the preexistence of Christ and man in his work *Exhortation to the Greeks*. And in his *Stromateis*, he discusses reincarnation, but he does not make a clear statement in its favor. However, the ninth-century Church scholar Photius tells us that Clement taught reincarnation. See Henry Chadwick, *Early Christian Thought: Studies in Justin, Clement, and Origen* (Oxford: Clarendon Press, 1966), pp. 48–49. See also Henri de Lubac, introduction to *Origen: On First Principles*, p. xxxi.

17. Origen, *On First Principles* 2.9.8, Butterworth, pp. 137, 136.

18. Origen, *On First Principles* 1.8.1, quoted in Daniélou, *Gospel Message and Hellenistic Culture*, pp. 418–19.

19. Origen, *On First Principles* 1.8.1, Butterworth, p. 67.

20. Thomas Aquinas, *On the Power of God (Quaestiones Disputatae De Potentia Dei)*, trans. English Dominican Fathers (London: Burns, Oates and Washbourne, 1932), 1:165.

21. Origen, *Commentary on John* 6.7, in *The Ante-Nicene Fathers*, 10:358.

22. Origen denies reincarnation during a discussion of whether John the Baptist was Elijah come again. Yet he clearly had one eye on the bishops when he did it. His denial reads: "In this place it does not appear to me that by Elijah the soul is spoken of, *lest I should fall into the dogma of transmigration, which is foreign*

to the church of God, and not handed down by the Apostles, nor anywhere set forth in the Scriptures" (emphasis added).

Origen here rejects reincarnation on the grounds that it does not fit in with the Christian idea of the final judgment. How could there be an end, he asks, if souls are continually committing acts for which they must return to earth and atone? He concludes that the concept of an end would "overturn the doctrine of transmigration." *Commentary on Matthew* 13.1, in *The Ante-Nicene Fathers,* 10:474, 475.

However, Origen had previously tried to harmonize the idea of an end with the idea of continuing opportunity through reincarnation. While affirming an end when the world would be "all in all" (1 Cor. 15:28), he also predicted that "after the dissolution of this world there will be another one." *On First Principles* 3.5.3, Butterworth, p. 239.

After reading Origen's half-hearted rebuttal of reincarnation, one has to wonder if he is not using double-talk to dodge his enemies. Especially since in the very same commentary he goes on to *again* suggest preexistence as a way of defending God's justice. He does it while commenting on the parable of the vineyard in Matthew 20, in which the workers hired at the end of the day are paid the same as those who have been working all day. Origen suggests that preexistence would explain God's apparent unfairness. The workers hired at the end of the day might have earned their wages in a previous existence. See *Commentary on Matthew* 15:35, cited in Trigg, *Origen,* p. 213. The most logical conclusion we can draw from Origen's denial of reincarnation yet contradictory support for preexistence is that his denial was a deliberate attempt to mislead his enemies and that he continued to teach reincarnation secretly.

23. Origen, *Commentary on Matthew* 10.6, in *The Ante-Nicene Fathers,* 10:416.

24. Origen, *On First Principles* 4.2.7, Butterworth, p. 283.

25. R. P. C. Hanson, *Origen's Doctrine of Tradition* (London: SPCK, 1954), p. 79.

26. Jerome, *Ep. ad Avitum* 14, quoted in *Origen: On First Principles,* p. 325 n. 1.

27. Origen, *On First Principles* 3.5.4, Butterworth, p. 241.

28. Origen, *On First Principles* 2.1.2, quoted in Daniélou, *Gospel Message and Hellenistic Culture,* pp. 420–21.

29. Jerome, *Apology in Answer to Rufinus* 2.12, in *Nicene and Post-Nicene Fathers,* 2d ser., 3:508.

30. Butterworth, introduction to *Origen: On First Principles,* p. lvi.

31. Phil. 2:12.

32. Trigg, *Origen,* p. 117.

33. 2 Cor. 3:17 KJV.

34. Origen, *On First Principles* 2.9.6, quoted in Daniélou, *Gospel Message and Hellenistic Culture,* p. 416.

PART 4 | *The Church Rejects Reincarnation*

CHAPTER 17 The Mystery of God in Man

Opening quotation: Bishop Alexander, quoted in Robert C. Gregg and Dennis E. Groh, *Early Arianism—A View of Salvation* (Philadelphia: Fortress Press, 1981), p. 63.

1. Arius, quoted in Socrates Scholasticus, *Ecclesiastical History* 1.5, in *Nicene and Post-Nicene Fathers,* 2d ser., 2:3.

2. Robert C. Gregg, "Arianism," in *The Westminster Dictionary of Christian Theology,* ed. Alan Richardson and John Bowden (Philadelphia: Westminster Press, 1983), p. 40.

3. Arius to Eusebius, Bishop of Nicomedia, quoted in Theodoret, *Ecclesiastical History* 1.4, in *Nicene and Post-Nicene Fathers,* 2d ser., 3:41.

4. Clement of Alexandria, *Protreptikos* 10 (*Exhortation to the Greeks* 10), quoted in Payne, *The Fathers of the Eastern Church,* p. 29.

5. Origen, *On First Principles* 4.4.10, Butterworth, p. 327. Origen is quoting an ancient version of Gen. 1:26.

6. Origen, *On First Principles* 3.4.2, Butterworth, p. 233.

7. Origen, *Commentary on Romans* 1.18, quoted in *Origen: On First Principles*, p. 233 n. 1.

8. Tatian, *Address to the Greeks* 13, in *The Ante-Nicene Fathers*, 2:71.

9. Gregory of Nyssa, *The Creation of Man* 29.3, quoted in Tresmontant, *The Origins of Christian Philosophy*, p. 88.

10. Jerome, *To Pammachius against John of Jerusalem* 22, in *Nicene and Post-Nicene Fathers*, 2d ser., 6:434.

11. See, for example, Irenaeus, *Against Heresies* 2.10, in *The Ante-Nicene Fathers*, 1:369–70.

12. Tertullian, *Apology* 17, quoted in Stringfellow Barr, *The Mask of Jove: A History of Graeco-Roman Civilization from the Death of Alexander to the Death of Constantine* (Philadelphia: J. B. Lippincott Co., 1966), p. 469.

13. Tresmontant, *Origins of Christian Philosophy*, p. 95.

14. *New Catholic Encyclopedia*, s.v. "Creation" (emphasis added).

15. Clement of Alexandria, *Exhortation to the Greeks* 10, quoted in Payne, *The Fathers of the Eastern Church*, p. 30.

16. Gregg and Groh, *Early Arianism*, p. 50.

17. Rom. 8:17.

18. Origen, *Commentary on John* 2.17–18, quoted in Gregg and Groh, *Early Arianism*, p. 109.

19. Athanasius, *Orationes contra Arianos* 3.17, quoted in Gregg and Groh, *Early Arianism*, p. 48.

20. John 1:1, 3, 14 KJV.

21. Philo, quoted in David Fideler, *Jesus Christ, Sun of God: Ancient Cosmology and Early Christian Symbolism* (Wheaton, Ill.: Theosophical Publishing House, Quest Books, 1993), p. 41.

22. Clement of Alexandria, *Exhortation to the Greeks* 10, quoted in Fideler, *Jesus Christ, Sun of God*, p. 42.

23. 1 Cor. 11:24 KJV; Matt. 26:26; Mark 14:22; Luke 22:19.

24. Origen, *Contra Celsum* 3.28, quoted in von Balthasar, *Origen, Spirit and Fire*, p. 123.

25. Origen, *On First Principles* 1.2.6, Butterworth, p. 20.

26. *The Life of Saint Issa* 4.3, 4, in Prophet, *The Lost Years of Jesus,* p. 217.

27. John 10:30 KJV.

28. See Origen, *Dialogue with Heraclides,* in John Ernest Leonard Oulton and Henry Chadwick, trans., *Alexandrian Christianity,* vol. 2 of The Library of Christian Classics (Philadelphia: Westminster Press, 1954), pp. 439–40.

29. John 5:17 KJV.

CHAPTER 18 God in Man's Image

Opening quotation: Constantine to Alexander and Arius, in Eusebius, *Life of Constantine* 2.69, in *Nicene and Post-Nicene Fathers,* 2d ser., 1:517. All subsequent references to Eusebius' *Life of Constantine* are to this translation.

1. Michael Grant, *Constantine the Great: The Man and His Times* (New York: Charles Scribner's Sons, 1994), p. 212.

2. Eusebius, *Life of Constantine* 4.63.

3. *Pagan* here simply means those who adhered to any of the Greco-Roman religions rather than converting to Christianity. Today *pagan* can refer to someone who is hedonistic, materialistic or even a practitioner of magic. However, in its original connotation, it described a broad spectrum of people—from simple peasants who brought gifts to the Greek and Roman gods to erudite philosophers or initiates of the mystery religions.

4. Grant, *Constantine the Great,* p. 109.

5. Porphyry, cited in Christos Evangeliou, "Plotinus's Anti-Gnostic Polemic and Porphyry's *Against the Christians,*" in Richard T. Wallis and Jay Bregman, eds., *Neoplatonism and Gnosticism* (Albany: State University of New York Press, 1992), p. 124.

6. Constantine to Alexander and Arius, in Eusebius, *Life of Constantine* 2.68, 70, 65, 69.

7. Eusebius, *Life of Constantine* 3.4.

8. *Constantine's Address to the Council,* in Eusebius, *Life of Constantine* 3.12.

9. Mark 13:32.

10. Athanasius, *Orationes contra Arianos* 3.42, 43, in *Nicene and Post-Nicene Fathers,* 2d ser., 4:416–17.

11. John 17:11.

12. I am indebted here to Robert C. Gregg and Dennis E. Groh for their excellent discussion in *Early Arianism—A View of Salvation,* p. 60.

13. Alexander, *Ep. ad Alexandrum,* quoted in Gregg and Groh, *Early Arianism,* p. 50. Although the Church later decided that men can be adopted as sons, it took pains to distinguish this sonship from that of Jesus. The catechism still affirms that Jesus is the only person to unite God and man in one being and, as such, he is "the one and only mediator between God and men." See *Catechism of the Catholic Church* 2782, 2783, 480–81.

14. Athanasius, *De Decretis* 31, quoted in Gregg and Groh, *Early Arianism,* p. 70.

15. Athanasius, *Orationes contra Arianos* 1.39, quoted in Gregg and Groh, *Early Arianism,* p. 48.

16. Prov. 8:22 Septuagint, quoted in Theodoret, *Ecclesiastical History* 1.5, in *Nicene and Post-Nicene Fathers,* 2d ser., 3:42.

17. Nicene Creed, in *Nicene and Post-Nicene Fathers,* 2d ser., 14:3.

18. George Leonard Prestige, quoted in Pelikan, *The Emergence of the Catholic Tradition,* p. 202.

19. Apostles' Creed, in *Catechism of the Catholic Church,* p. 49.

20. See Funk, Hoover, and the Jesus Seminar, *The Five Gospels,* p. 33.

21. Constantine to the Churches, in Eusebius, *Life of Constantine* 3.20.

22. *Constantine's Edict against the Heretics,* in Eusebius, *Life of Constantine* 3.64, 65.

CHAPTER 19 The Stream Goes Underground

Opening quotation: "The Anathemas against Origen," in *Nicene and Post-Nicene Fathers,* 2d ser., 14:318.

1. See Dechow, *Dogma and Mysticism in Early Christianity*, pp. 405–7.

2. Ibid., pp. 19–20, 390.

3. Jerome, *Comm. in Esaiam, praefatio*, quoted in Elizabeth A. Clark, *The Origenist Controversy: The Cultural Construction of an Early Christian Debate* (Princeton: Princeton University Press, 1992), p. 14. This excellent work by Elizabeth Clark contributed to the structure of the arguments in this chapter.

4. Epiphanius, *Ancoratus* 58, cited in Clark, *The Origenist Controversy*, p. 88.

5. Methodius, *De resurrectione* 1.55, cited in Henri Rondet, *Original Sin: The Patristic and Theological Background*, trans. Cajetan Finegan (Staten Island, N.Y.: Alba House, 1972), p. 86.

6. Jerome, *Ep.* 84.6, quoted in Clark, *The Origenist Controversy*, p. 176.

7. Theophilus, quoted in Clark, *The Origenist Controversy*, p. 45.

8. Dechow, *Dogma and Mysticism in Early Christianity*, pp. 412–13.

9. See Chadwick, "The Domestication of Gnosis," pp. 14–15.

10. Plotinus, quoted in Maria Dzielska, *Hypatia of Alexandria*, trans. F. Lyra (Cambridge: Harvard University Press, 1995), p. 48.

11. Dzielska, *Hypatia of Alexandria*, pp. 90–91.

12. "The Anathematisms of the Emperor Justinian against Origen," in *Nicene and Post-Nicene Fathers*, 2d ser., 14:320.

13. See Hans-Georg Beck for an excellent discussion of Justinian's moves against Origenism, in Karl Baus et al., *The Imperial Church from Constantine to the Early Middle Ages*, trans. Anselm Biggs (New York: Crossroad, 1986), pp. 445–56.

14. "The Anathemas against Origen," attached to the decrees of the Fifth Ecumenical Council, A.D. 553, in *Nicene and Post-Nicene Fathers*, 2d ser., 14:318.

15. Restoration, or *apokatastasis* in Greek, means to restore to a previous state. To Origen it meant a restoration to pure spirituality. As Jean Daniélou puts it, "This restoration *(apokatastasis)* extends to all spiritual creatures, for all have fallen from

their first estate as pure spirits, and all have to be reestablished in that condition." *Gospel Message and Hellenistic Culture,* p. 422. This theory entails reincarnation since it says that souls journey through a series of incarnations until they return to the state they enjoyed before the Fall. This meaning, which was also used by Neoplatonists in the early centuries after Christ, is explained in the following definition of restoration: "the repeated entry of the immortal soul into the mortal body through reincarnation, with the object of thus being cleansed from matter and reattaining its original condition." Colin Brown, ed., *The New International Dictionary of New Testament Theology* (Grand Rapids, Mich.: Zondervan Publishing House, 1978), s.v. "Reconciliation, *apokatastasis.*"

Several of the other anathemas attached to the decrees of the council describe such a restoration, with the clear implication that it takes place through reincarnation. They say that this restoration is a future time when spirits will return to the pre-Fall state. Anathema number XIV tells us that this restoration is a time in which bodies will no longer exist but "spirits only... as it was in the feigned pre-existence." Thus we can see the anathematization of anyone who believes in this restoration as an indirect curse upon the belief in reincarnation. *Nicene and Post-Nicene Fathers,* 2d ser., 14:319.

16. *The Catholic Encyclopedia,* s.v. "Origen."
17. Martin Luther, *Table Talk,* vol. 54 of *Luther's Works,* ed. and trans. Theodore G. Tappert (Philadelphia: Fortress Press, 1967), p. 47.

CHAPTER 20 **A New Explanation for Human Misery**

Opening quotation: James Joyce, *A Portrait of the Artist as a Young Man,* rev. ed. (1964; reprint, New York: Penguin Books, 1976), p. 236.

1. Augustine, *City of God* 15.1, in *Nicene and Post-Nicene Fathers,* 1st ser., 2:285.
2. *Catechism of the Catholic Church* 389, p. 98.

3. Augustine, *On Free Choice of the Will* 3.18, quoted in T. Kermit Scott, *Augustine: His Thought in Context* (New York: Paulist Press, 1995), pp. 136–37.

4. Elaine Pagels, *Adam, Eve, and the Serpent* (New York: Random House, 1988), p. 112.

5. According to Augustine, sexual desire, even that which leads to procreation, is evil. Lust and death entered the world at the same time, Augustine believed. Adam would never have died if he hadn't sinned. And the punishment for his sin was not only to grow old and die but also to experience uncontrollable lust. Sexual desire was thus the direct result of this Fall.

   Augustine believed that all of Adam's descendants are tainted by his lust. As he put it, Adam's "carnal concupiscence" (lust) corrupted "all who come of his stock." In other words, one man's lust makes all babies sinners. *On the Merits and Forgiveness of Sins, and on the Baptism of Infants* 1.10, in *Nicene and Post-Nicene Fathers,* 5:19.

   Through this teaching comes the idea that marriage, procreation and babies themselves are tainted by original sin. By telling us that we are born sinners because we are conceived through the sexual act, the Church is putting every one of us under a weight of condemnation. This guilt affects us at subconscious levels and burdens many Catholics and former Catholics whom I have counseled, not to mention some Protestants who absorbed it through the thought of Martin Luther and John Calvin, leaders of the Protestant Reformation.

   When the Church exempts Jesus from original sin, it distances him even further from the rest of us. By saying that we are sinners and that Jesus never was, it robs us of our potential to become Sons of God as we walk in the footsteps of Christ.

   The sexual act by which a person was created does not deprive him of the ability or right to attain sonship, neither does it make mothers, fathers and children corrupt. Our bodies are temples of God and when we bear children, we are instruments of God.

6. Augustine's view on sexuality may be a twisted interpretation of Manichaeism. This religion, named after its founder, Mani, synthesized Christian, Gnostic, Buddhist and Zoroastrian beliefs. Mani, a contemporary of Origen, was born in 216 in Babylonia to a family of Jewish Christian Baptists. After about thirty-six years of preaching, Mani was executed and his head was impaled over the Babylonian city gates. His followers carried his beliefs east to China and west into the Roman Empire, where they influenced Augustine.

   Mani's version of the creation story was similar to that of the Orphics and Gnostics. The Creator used a mixture of good and evil in creating the world. Man, as a part of the world, also contains a mixture of good and evil. God created the world as a place for separating the principles of Good and Evil. Souls are meant to return to their original condition of complete Good by separating themselves from the body and the "material soul," which are melted to the true soul like copper amalgamated with silver.

   In their complicated myth of the creation of man, the Manichaeans believed that some of God's light had been trapped in the bodies of demon-animals. This light was passed on to Adam and Eve, tainted by the passions of the demon-animals. And thus, according to scholar Hans-Joachim Klimkeit, it also passed on "greed, the lust for procreation, envy, hate, and other evil qualities. . . . These negative aspects together form what is called the 'dark' or 'material soul,'" which overlays the true soul.

   The soul itself, of divine origin, is destined to shake off these evil qualities and "be restored to its pristine beauty, purity, and integrity."

   The key point here is the Manichaean system of salvation, which includes reincarnation. The Manichaeans taught that there were different classes of believers—the "elect" and the "hearers." The elect were capable of returning to God in their current life. They were required to follow a rigid code as they struggled to separate all elements of the demon passions. The other group, the hearers, were given less strict commandments and could expect to be reborn as elect. Thus the hearers could expect a second chance at salvation since they were not destined to make it in this life. Like many sects of their day, the Manichaeans were exclusive. Everyone who was neither a hearer nor an elect was headed for damnation.

The elect were vegetarians and, like Hindu ascetics, were forbidden meat, alcohol or sexual activity. Their attitude toward sex may have influenced Augustine. They believed, as Klimkeit writes, that they must detach themselves from all forms of lust or greed since, in their creation myths, "sexual lust led to the creation of man and his fall." Thus, the "mixed" state of good and evil that we live in today is "perpetuated by the lustfulness associated with procreation."

Augustine was a hearer, not an elect, so the requirement of celibacy did not apply to him. Nevertheless, he struggled with his sexuality all his life, perhaps initially out of hopes of becoming an elect. When he left the Manichees, he discarded reincarnation. But he took with him the sense of sin attached to sexuality. In Augustine's hands, Manichaeism without reincarnation became the ultimate fatalism. See Klimkeit, *Gnosis on the Silk Road: Gnostic Texts from Central Asia* (Harper-SanFrancisco, 1993), pp. 6, 15, 18, 20, 252.

7. See T. Kermit Scott, *Augustine: His Thought in Context,* for an excellent discussion of the evolution of Augustine's concept of God.

8. Rom. 5:12, quoted in Pelikan, *The Emergence of the Catholic Tradition,* p. 299.

9. Augustine, *City of God* 13.14, in *Nicene and Post-Nicene Fathers,* 1st ser., 2:251.

10. Augustine, *Against Julian,* 3.3, trans. Matthew A. Schumacher, The Fathers of the Church, vol. 35 (Washington, D.C.: Catholic University of America Press, 1957), p. 113.

11. Augustine, *City of God* 13.14, in *Nicene and Post-Nicene Fathers,* 1st ser., 2:251. See also Rev. 21:8.

12. Augustine, *On the Merits and Forgiveness of Sins, and on the Baptism of Infants* 1.39, 3.7, in *Nicene and Post-Nicene Fathers,* 1st ser., 5:30, 71.

13. Peter Brown, *Augustine of Hippo* (1967; reprint, New York: Dorset Press, 1986), p. 385.

14. See the discussion on John Chrysostom in Pagels, *Adam, Eve, and the Serpent,* pp. 108–9.

15. Augustine, *On Free Choice of the Will* 3.20, quoted in Scott, *Augustine,* p. 136.

16. Pelagius, *ad Demetriadem* 17, quoted in Brown, *Augustine of Hippo,* p. 352.

17. Clark, *The Origenist Controversy,* pp. 196–97, 207.

18. Augustine, *Against Julian* 3.4, Schumacher, p. 115.

19. Augustine, *Against Julian* 3.4, 3, Schumacher, pp. 115, 113.

20. Augustine, *Against Julian* 2.1, Schumacher, p. 56.

21. Augustine, *Against Julian* 3.5, 6.10, Schumacher, pp. 116, 339.

22. Augustine to Jerome, "On the Origin of the Soul," in Saint Augustine, *Letters,* vol. 4 (165–203), trans. Wilfrid Parsons, The Fathers of the Church, vol. 30 (Washington, D.C.: Catholic University of America Press, 1955), p. 30.

23. Augustine, *To Simplician—On Various Questions* 2.17, quoted in Scott, *Augustine,* p. 212.

24. Augustine, *On the Merits and Forgiveness of Sins, and on the Baptism of Infants* 1.31, in *Nicene and Post-Nicene Fathers,* 1st ser., 5:26–27.

25. Augustine, *To Simplician—On Various Questions* 2.16, quoted in Scott, *Augustine,* p. 212.

26. Augustine to Sixtus, *Letter* 194, quoted in Scott, *Augustine,* p. 214.

27. Scott, *Augustine,* p. 214.

28. Ibid., p. 147.

29. *The Catholic Encyclopedia,* s.v. "Limbo."

30. Andrew M. Greeley, *The Great Mysteries: An Essential Catechism* (New York: Seabury Press, Crossroad Book, 1976), pp. 58, 64.

31. John Dillenberger and Claude Welch, *Protestant Christianity* (New York: Charles Scribner's Sons, 1954), pp. 279, 280.

32. Telephone interview with Dr. Gerhard Forde, Luther-Northwestern Theological Seminary, 30 June 1989.

33. Peter De Rosa, *Christ and Original Sin* (Milwaukee: Bruce Publishing Co., 1967), p. 17.

34. *Catechism of the Catholic Church* 390, 403, pp. 98, 102.

35. *Catechism of the Catholic Church* 405, p. 102.

36. Origen, *On First Principles* 2.1.1, Butterworth, p. 77.

37. Ibid.

38. Augustine to Pope Innocent I, *Letter* 175, Parsons, p. 89.

39. See Brown, *Augustine of Hippo*, p. 358.

40. Scott, *Augustine*, p. 57.

41. Brown, *Augustine of Hippo*, pp. 235–37.

42. John Chrysostom, *On the Priesthood* 2.3, quoted in Pagels, *Adam, Eve, and the Serpent*, p. 103.

CHAPTER 21 **Smoke Rises from Montségur**

Opening quotation: *Collection Doat* 35, Inquisition Records, quoted in Jean Duvernoy, *La Religion des cathares,* rev. ed. (Toulouse, France: Privat, 1990), p. 94.

1. See Henry Charles Lea, *A History of the Inquisition of the Middle Ages,* 3 vols. (New York: Harper and Brothers, 1887), 2:36.

2. Zoé Oldenbourg, *Massacre at Montségur: A History of the Albigensian Crusade,* trans. Peter Green (1961; reprint, New York: Dorset Press, 1990), p. 335.

3. *Collection Doat* 22, quoted in Oldenbourg, *Massacre at Montségur,* p. 336.

4. See Yuri Stoyanov, *The Hidden Tradition in Europe* (London: Penguin Books, Arkana, 1994), p. 160.

5. Pope Innocent III, *Epistles,* quoted in Oldenbourg, *Massacre at Montségur,* p. 53.

6. Bernard of Clairvaux, *Epistles* 241, quoted in Walter L. Wakefield and Austin P. Evans, *Heresies of the High Middle*

Ages: Selected Sources (New York: Columbia University Press, 1991), p. 122.

7. See Anne Brenon, *Les femmes cathares* (Paris: Librairie Académique Perrin, 1992), pp. 122–35.

8. William de Puylaurens, quoted in Oldenbourg, *Massacre at Montségur,* p. 18.

9. Bernard of Clairvaux, *Epistles* 365, quoted in Oldenbourg, *Massacre at Montségur,* p. 84.

10. Saint Dominic, quoted in Oldenbourg, *Massacre at Montségur,* p. 95.

11. Pope Innocent III, quoted in Oldenbourg, *Massacre at Montségur,* p. 1.

12. See Steven Runciman, *The Medieval Manichee: A Study of the Christian Dualist Heresy* (Cambridge: Cambridge University Press, 1960), pp. 158–59.

13. Wakefield and Evans, *Heresies of the High Middle Ages,* p. 44.

14. *Collection Doat* 25, quoted in Duvernoy, *La Religion des cathares,* p. 94.

15. Jacques Fournier, quoted in Duvernoy, *La Religion des cathares,* p. 94.

16. See Stoyanov, *The Hidden Tradition in Europe,* pp. 154–59; and Malcolm Lambert, *Medieval Heresy: Popular Movements from Bogomil to Hus* (New York: Holmes and Meier Publishers, 1976), pp. 12–14, 18–19.

17. See Anne Brenon, *Le Vrai Visage du catharisme,* rev. ed. (Portetsur-Garonne, France: Editions Loubatières, 1994), pp. 139–50. See also Wakefield and Evans, *Heresies of the High Middle Ages,* pp. 139, 172–73.

18. See Ioan P. Couliano, *The Tree of Gnosis: Gnostic Mythology from Early Christianity to Modern Nihilism,* trans. H. S. Wiesner and the author (HarperSanFrancisco, 1992), pp. 226–29; also Duvernoy, *La Religion des cathares,* p. 99.

19. See Brenon, *Le Vrai Visage du catharisme,* pp. 28–29.

20. Duvernoy, *La Religion des cathares,* p. 98. The Cathars' spiritual marriage strongly resembles that of the Gnostic *Gospel of Philip.*

21. See Jacques Madaule, *The Albigensian Crusade: An Historical Essay,* trans. Barbara Wall (New York: Fordham University Press, 1967), p. 45. Since the Cathars taught that those who received the *consolamentum* must afterwards live as perfects and avoid meat and sexual intercourse, many of them chose to wait until their death to receive it. At some point, Catharism may have inflated the power of the *consolamentum* until it was equal to the Christian belief in the power of baptism or the last rites. The annals of the Inquisition are filled with questions about who gave the blessing and under what circumstances. They tell us that Cathar believers went to great lengths to receive the *consolamentum* before death.

22. See the Cathar text *The Secret Supper,* in Wakefield and Evans, *Heresies of the High Middle Ages,* p. 464; also Duvernoy, *La Religion des cathares,* p. 99.

23. Robert G. Hall, "Isaiah's Ascent to See the Beloved: An Ancient Jewish Source for the *Ascension of Isaiah?" Journal of Biblical Literature* 113 (1994): 477, 483.

24. *The Vision Which Isaiah the Son of Amoz Saw* 8:15, 7:23 in Charlesworth, *Old Testament Pseudepigrapha,* 2:168, 167.

25. Oldenbourg, *Massacre at Montségur,* pp. 111–12.

26. Ibid., p. 119.

27. David Roberts, "In France, an Ordeal by Fire and a Monster Weapon Called 'Bad Neighbor,'" *Smithsonian* 22 (May 1991): 44. Casearius of Heisterbach is the chronicler who is the source for this sentence. His original words, quoted in Walter L. Wakefield, *Heresy, Crusade and Inquisition in Southern France 1100–1250* (London: George Allen and Unwin, 1974), p. 197, were "Kill them! The Lord knows those who are his own."

    Wakefield, commenting on the quote, says: "This is probably the best-known anecdote of the crusade. It has often been called apocryphal..., but there is an echo of it in the *Annales sancti Albini Andegavensis,* which states that when the crusaders captured Carcassonne and other places, they slaughtered many Catholics as well as heretics, because they could not tell them apart." Wakefield, p. 199.

28. Oldenbourg, *Massacre at Montségur,* p. 184.
29. See Lea, *History of the Inquisition,* 2:1–3.
30. Ibid., 2:10.
31. Brenon, *Le Vrai Visage du catharisme,* p. 256.

PART 5 | *Jesus' Secret Teachings on the God Within*

CHAPTER 22 Your Divine Image

1. See the excellent discussion of heavenly journeys by James D. Tabor, *Things Unutterable: Paul's Ascent to Paradise in Its Greco-Roman, Judaic, and Early Christian Contexts.*
2. Ezekiel the Tragedian, *Exagoge* 73–82, in Charlesworth, *Old Testament Pseudepigrapha,* 2:812.
3. Philo, *On the Birth of Abel and the Sacrifices Offered by Him and by His Brother Cain* 9 and *On the Life of Moses* 1.158, Yonge, pp. 95, 474 (emphasis added).
4. Philo, *On the Life of Moses* 1.159, Yonge, p. 474.
5. 1 Enoch 90:37–39, in Charlesworth, *Old Testament Pseudepigrapha,* 1:71.
6. Alan F. Segal, *Paul the Convert: The Apostolate and Apostasy of Saul the Pharisee* (New Haven, Conn.: Yale University Press, 1990), p. 46.
7. 2 Baruch 51:3, 10, 12, in Charlesworth, *Old Testament Pseudepigrapha,* 1:638.
8. 2 Cor. 12:2–4 Revised Standard Version.
9. Segal, *Paul the Convert,* p. 38.
10. C. R. A. Morray-Jones, "Paradise Revisited (2 Cor. 12:1–12): The Jewish Mystical Background of Paul's Apostolate: Part 2: Paul's Heavenly Ascent and Its Significance," *Harvard Theological Review* 86:3 (1993): 283.
11. 2 Enoch [A] 22:6, 8, 10, in Charlesworth, *Old Testament Pseudepigrapha,* 1:139.
12. 2 Cor. 5:1, 2, 4.
13. 2 Cor. 12:2 KJV; 1 Cor. 15:22; Rom. 12:5; 2 Cor. 5:17.

14. Segal, *Paul the Convert,* p. 64.
15. Ibid., p. 42.
16. Eph. 2:4, 5, 6.
17. 2 Cor. 4:11.
18. Gal. 2:20.
19. Rom. 8:29 JB.
20. Segal, *Paul the Convert,* p. 41.
21. 2 Cor. 3:18.
22. 1 Cor. 15:45, 49.
23. *Gospel of Thomas,* saying 22, Meyer, p. 35.
24. 1 Cor. 13:12 KJV.
25. Gal. 1:12.
26. Gal. 2:9.
27. Segal, *Paul the Convert,* p. 37.

CHAPTER 23 The Original Christian Mystic

1. John 3:18.
2. John 3:16.
3. John 1:12 KJV.
4. See James H. Charlesworth, *Jesus within Judaism: New Light from Exciting Archaeological Discoveries* (New York: Doubleday, 1988), p. 152. Those who believe that Jesus did call himself God's Son point to Jesus' use of the word *Abba* to address God (Mark 14:36). *Abba* is an Aramaic word that is a familiar form of Father and can be translated as "Daddy" or "Papa." Some scholars believe that the use of *Abba* goes back to the historical Jesus. It is unlikely that Jesus would have used this more intimate form of address if he did not consider himself to be at least *a* son of God.

   In the parable of the vineyard (which we discussed in chapter 11), the owner of a vineyard, clearly meant to be God, sends two servants and finally his son to collect rent from farmers, who then kill the son. In this allegory, Jesus appears to be casting himself in the role of God's Son. Scholar James Charlesworth argues that indeed Jesus did see himself as the son in this parable. See Charlesworth, pp. 148–49.

5. 4Q246, quoted in John J. Collins, "A Pre-Christian 'Son of God' among the Dead Sea Scrolls?" *Bible Review,* June 1993, p. 37.

6. Sirach 4:10.

7. Ezekiel the Tragedian and *Testament of Levi* 4:2, quoted in Charlesworth, *Jesus within Judaism,* p. 150.

8. b.*Zera'im Berakot* 17a, quoted in Charlesworth, *Jesus within Judaism,* pp. 150–51.

9. Gal. 4:5 JB.

10. Christians acknowledge the concept of adoption of sons but do not consider that it confers the same kind of sonship Jesus possesses. *The Catholic Encyclopedia* tells us that "the correct interpretation of the Scriptural concept of our adoption must...locate itself midway between the Divine Sonship of Jesus on the one hand, and human adoption on the other—immeasurably below the former and above the latter." It tells us that there is an "infinite distance" between our adoption and Jesus' sonship (s.v. "Adoption, Supernatural").

11. For further reading on this subject see Funk, Hoover, and the Jesus Seminar, *The Five Gospels;* John Dominic Crossan, *The Historical Jesus: The Life of a Mediterranean Jewish Peasant* (HarperSanFrancisco, 1992); and Borg, *Meeting Jesus Again for the First Time.*

12. See chapter 11 note 26.

13. The view of Jesus as Cynic is popular among more liberal scholars. Scholar John Dominic Crossan, who supports the Jesus-as-Cynic view, points to similarities between Jesus and the Cynic preachers who were a common sight in the first century.

Although *cynical* has come to mean sarcastic and doubting, *Cynicism* has a much broader meaning. The prototype for the Cynics, Diogenes of Sinope (fourth century B.C.), held that true freedom was achieved by rejecting traditional values such as wealth, pleasure and family responsibilities. The Cynics sought to become self-sufficient by reducing their needs and wants. It was a sort of Greco-Roman version of the hippie ethic. You are most happy and free when you have no possessions, cares or responsibilities.

Supporters of the Jesus-as-Cynic view focus on the social implications of many of his sayings. They see Jesus as primarily a critic of the establishment, an advocate of social reorganization. Like the hippies, Jesus challenged the established social order. Crossan points to Jesus' glorification of the poor and denigration of wealth. For example, he called the poor blessed but said it was difficult for a rich man to enter heaven (Mark 10:23–27; Luke 18:18–27).

According to Crossan, Jesus is attacking the family, a pillar of Jewish society, when he tells a follower not to bury his father but to "let the dead bury their own dead" (Luke 9:60) and says that only those who hate their fathers and mothers can be his followers (Luke 14:26). Crossan terms this "an almost savage attack on family values."

He also sees a reference to Cynicism in some of Jesus' sayings. The Cynics were known for the standard belongings they carried: a bag, or knapsack, and a staff. Jesus told his disciples not to carry even a "bag...or sandals, or a staff" or money (Matt. 10:9, 10). Although Crossan admits "we have...no way of knowing for sure what Jesus knew about Cynicism," he finds the picture of Jesus as a peasant Jewish Cynic a tempting one. *Jesus: A Revolutionary Biography,* pp. 58, 122.

Jesus also seems to mirror the Cynic philosophy when he tells his disciples not to be concerned about the future: "Do not worry about your life, what you will eat, or about your body, what you will wear" (Luke 12:22).

The Stoic-Cynic philosopher Epictetus advises his student to cultivate a spirit of "patient endurance" and to "love the men who flog him." Quoted in Crossan, pp. 120, 121. This invites the obvious comparison to Jesus' "Bless those who curse you" (Luke 6:28) and his instruction to offer the other cheek to someone who hits you (Luke 6:29). The Cynics even had a view of kingship and ruling that resonates with some of Jesus' sayings about the kingdom of God.

The Jesus-as-Cynic theory is useful. But it doesn't pass the crucial test for any theory since it doesn't account for all the data. It is undeniable that some of Jesus' teachings are similar to those of the Cynics. Jesus may have agreed with certain elements of Cynic philosophy. But he went beyond it. By telling his disciples not to carry even a knapsack and staff as the Cynics did, was he telling them to out-Cynic the Cynics?

Cynicism does not explain the mystical side of Jesus. He dealt with unseen things. He told people to store up "treasure in heaven" (Luke 12:33), he had divine visions, he spent hours in prayer and he healed people. Cynics did not cast out demons or make lame people walk or see God's Spirit descending "like a dove" (Luke 3:22). Jesus had a profound spirituality that was able to attract and hold followers. The best explanation for these elements is that Jesus was a mystic who absorbed them from the tradition of Jewish rabbi sages.

14. Borg, *Meeting Jesus Again for the First Time*, p. 36.

15. If Jesus was connected with the first-century Jewish sages, it would seem that he could read and write. However, Crossan and most members of the Jesus Seminar have concluded he was illiterate. They discount the evidence in the Gospels, which portray Jesus reading and quoting scripture. They argue that a group of Jesus' literate followers must have inserted anything in the New Testament that quotes from or refers to the Hebrew scriptures.

For a moment let us examine the controversy about whether Jesus was literate. I believe he could read and was familiar with Jewish scriptures and mystical teachings as well as Greek speculations.

Most of us have assumed that Jesus was literate, conjuring up images of first-century Jewish boys going to synagogue and learning the Torah. There is some archaeological and literary evidence for first-century synagogues. Enough for scholar Marcus Borg, a member of the Jesus Seminar, to conclude that it is likely that Jesus "went to school in the synagogue in Nazareth, where the emphasis would have been on reading and writing, with the Torah as the primary text." *Meeting Jesus Again for the First Time.* p. 26.

However, other scholars disagree. They doubt whether the synagogues and schools that were established in later Judaism existed in the first century. They prefer to focus on Jesus' position in society and to argue that he was illiterate because he came from a class that was, statistically, illiterate.

Crossan is one of the chief proponents of this view. He bases his argument on the fact that, as artisans, carpenters were among the lowest strata of Jewish society, below the peasants and just barely above the "expendables" such as beggars and slaves. Crossan concludes that "since between 95 and 97 percent of the Jewish state was illiterate at the time of Jesus, it must be presumed that Jesus also was illiterate."

The socio-economic evidence for Jesus being illiterate seems weak at best. If Jesus was simply an illiterate peasant, how could he have gone on to make such an impact on first-century Judaism in his short, three-year ministry? And furthermore, how could he have managed to attract literate and educated followers? Secondly, we do know of other poor first-century Jews who became literate.

Crossan, while arguing that Jesus was illiterate, suggests that his brother James managed to break out of his class and become literate. (Jesus was probably not an only child but had at least four brothers and two sisters as stated in Mark 6:3.) In his book *Jesus: A Revolutionary Biography,* Crossan suggests that James became literate after Jesus' death.

He bases this supposition on a reference by the Jewish historian Josephus, who tells us that the high priest Ananus the Younger brought before the Sanhedrin "a man named James, the brother of Jesus who was called the Christ." James was sentenced to death by stoning for "having transgressed the law." This offended some inhabitants of Jerusalem, who complained to King Herod Agrippa II, who deposed the high priest.

James was prominent enough that his death led to the downfall of the high priest. Therefore, "James must have had powerful, important, and even politically organized friends in Jerusalem," writes Crossan. Although acknowledging that his speculation is tentative, Crossan asks, "Did [James] leave Nazareth long before [his execution] and become both literate and involved within scribal circles in Jerusalem?" *Jesus: A Revolutionary Biography,* pp. 25, 134–35.

My follow-up query would be: If James could leave Nazareth and become literate, why could not Jesus have done the same? Jesus wouldn't have been the first Jewish religious teacher to have become literate after emerging from a lowly background.

Rabbi Akiva, one of the founders of rabbinic Judaism and the foremost scholar of his age, started life as a shepherd and did not learn to read until late in life, probably around age forty. Yet after thirteen years of study, he was accepted as an equal by the great Talmudic sages.

Another example of someone who managed to bridge class lines and become literate is Epictetus, the first-century Stoic-Cynic philosopher. Although he was born a slave, his master allowed him to study philosophy and eventually freed him. Epictetus became one of the best-known exponents of the Cynic lifestyle.

Even though, as far as we can tell, Jesus never wrote anything, his teachings on the kingdom of God betray a familiarity with Jewish wisdom writings, apocalyptic literature and the type of mystic speculation engaged in by Philo of Alexandria. Therefore, I conclude that he was both literate and well versed in the theological arguments of his day.

16. Hillel, quoted in Adin Steinsaltz, *The Essential Talmud,* trans. Chaya Galai (New York: Basic Books, 1976), p. 26.

17. *Avot* 2:7; *Sukkah* 53a, quoted in Yitzhak Buxbaum, *The Life and Teachings of Hillel* (Northvale, N.J.: Jason Aronson, 1994), p. 62.

18. Acts 22:3.
19. Matt. 17:1; Mark 9:2.
20. Luke 9:34.
21. Mark 9:7 KJV.
22. *Bat kol,* literally "daughter of a voice" in Hebrew, is a heavenly voice that was believed to deliver God's decisions to man. The Jews believed that a *bat kol* could be received by one person or a group of people. It was, as scholar Geza Vermes describes it, "the only substitute instrument of revelation recognized by rabbinic teaching, an instrument expressly described as having succeeded prophecy." *Jesus the Jew: A Historian's Reading of the Gospels* (Philadelphia: Fortress Press, 1981), p. 92. The Talmud tells us, "After the death of the last prophet the holy spirit left Israel; but even now the Divine Word may come through a Bath Kol." *Yoma* 9b, quoted in *The Universal Jewish Encyclopedia,* s.v. "Bath Kol." The reports of a heavenly voice speaking at Jesus' baptism and transfiguration would have alerted Jews of his time that here was a teacher who had been confirmed by this accepted method of divine revelation.
23. Acts 1:9.
24. Morton Smith, "Ascent to the Heavens and the Beginning of Christianity," *Eranos Jahrbuch* 50 (1981): 416.
25. Ibid., p. 429.
26. John 3:13.
27. Smith, "Ascent to the Heavens," p. 418.
28. See Matt. 8:20, for example.
29. Dan. 7:13–14 KJV.
30. John 10:30 KJV.
31. Smith, "Ascent to the Heavens," p. 417.
32. John 14:6 KJV.

CHAPTER 24 **Where Is the Kingdom?**

Opening quotation: Julian of Norwich, *Revelations of Divine Love* 67, in Karen Armstrong, *Visions of God: Four Medieval*

Mystics and Their Writings (New York: Bantam Books, 1994), p. 218.

1. *Psalms of Solomon* 17:21, in Charlesworth, *Old Testament Pseudepigrapha,* 2:667.

2. *Testament of Moses* 10.9, in Charlesworth, *Old Testament Pseudepigrapha,* 1:932.

3. *Catechism of the Catholic Church* 1042, 1047, pp. 272, 273.

4. Wisd. of Sol. 6:17, 18–20.

5. Prov. 8:23.

6. Wisd. of Sol. 3:8.

7. *Aramaic Levi* (4Q213 [4QTLevi ar]), frag. 5, cols. 1, 2, in Florentino García Martínez, *The Dead Sea Scrolls Translated: The Qumran Texts in English,* trans. Wilfred G. E. Watson (Leiden: E. J. Brill, 1994), p. 268.

8. Philo, *On Dreams* 2.243, 244, quoted in Crossan, *The Historical Jesus* (HarperSanFrancisco, 1992), p. 288.

9. Philo, *On Abraham* 261, quoted in Crossan, *The Historical Jesus,* p. 289.

10. See Philo, *Every Good Man Is Free* 19, 20, Yonge, p. 683.

11. Epictetus, *Discourses* 3.22, quoted in Crossan, *Jesus: A Revolutionary Biography,* p. 119.

12. Philo, *Every Good Man Is Free* 159, Yonge, p. 697.

13. See Philo, *Every Good Man Is Free* 121–24, Yonge, pp. 693–94.

14. *Sentences of Sextus* 309–11, in Robinson, *Nag Hammadi Library,* pp. 504–5.

15. Luke 13:18–21, quoted in Burton L. Mack, *The Lost Gospel: The Book of Q and Christian Origins* (HarperSanFrancisco, 1993), p. 79; *Gospel of Thomas,* sayings 20, 96.

16. *Gospel of Thomas,* saying 113, in Kloppenborg et al., *Q–Thomas Reader,* p. 154.

17. Luke 17:20–21, in Miller, *The Complete Gospels,* p. 157.

18. Heb. 12:28.

19. Heb. 12:27. See Smith, "Ascent to the Heavens," p. 417.

20. *Gospel of Thomas,* saying 3, in Kloppenborg et al., *Q–Thomas Reader,* pp. 129–30.

21. *Book of Thomas* 9:7, in Meyer, *The Secret Teachings of Jesus,* p. 51.

22. *Pistis Sophia* 96, MacDermot, p. 465.

23. *Gospel of Thomas,* saying 82, in Kloppenborg et al., *Q–Thomas Reader,* p. 148.

24. *Gospel of Thomas,* saying 108, in Kloppenborg et al., *Q–Thomas Reader,* p. 153.

25. Stevan Davies, "The Christology and Protology of the *Gospel of Thomas,*" *Journal of Biblical Literature* 111 (1992): 665.

26. *Gospel of Thomas,* saying 18, quoted in Stevan L. Davies, *The Gospel of Thomas and Christian Wisdom* (New York: Seabury Press, 1983), p. 59.

27. *Gospel of Thomas,* saying 24, in Kloppenborg et al., *Q–Thomas Reader,* p. 136.

28. *Gospel of Thomas,* saying 77, quoted in Davies, *Gospel of Thomas and Christian Wisdom,* p. 87.

29. *Gospel of Philip* 61.20–34, in Layton, *The Gnostic Scriptures,* p. 337.

30. Rom. 8:29.

31. See Sharpe, *David Bohm's World,* pp. 39–44; see also Peat, *Einstein's Moon,* pp. 131–36, 156–57.

32. See David Bohm, "Hidden Variables and the Implicate Order," in B. J. Hiley and F. David Peat, eds., *Quantum Implications: Essays in Honour of David Bohm* (London: Routledge and Kegan Paul, 1987), pp. 33–45.

33. Peat, *Einstein's Moon,* pp. 133–34.

CHAPTER 25 Breaking the Chain of Rebirth

1. *Sayings of the Fathers* 18, 12, quoted in Bernard McGinn, *The Foundations of Mysticism,* vol. 1 of *The Presence of God: A History of Western Christian Mysticism* (New York: Crossroad, 1992), p. 137.

2. Vladimir Lossky, *In the Image and Likeness of God,* ed. John H. Erickson and Thomas E. Bird (Crestwood, N.Y.: St. Vladimir's Seminary Press, 1985), p. 67.

3. 3 Enoch 15:1, quoted in Gilles Quispel, "Transformation through Vision in Jewish Gnosticism and the Cologne Mani Codex," *Vigiliae Christianae* 49 (1995): 189.

4. *The Prayers of Catherine of Siena,* ed. Suzanne Noffke (New York: Paulist Press, 1983), p. 104.

5. See Nicholas Heller, *The Exemplar: Life and Writings of Blessed Henry Suso,* trans. M. Ann Edward (Dubuque, Iowa: Priory Press, 1962), p. 14.

6. Matt. 24:27.

7. Blaise Pascal, *Pensées and Other Writings,* trans. Honor Levi (Oxford: Oxford University Press, 1995), p. 178.

8. William James, quoted in F. C. Happold, *Mysticism: A Study and an Anthology* (Baltimore: Penguin Books, 1970), pp. 135–36.

9. For further teachings on the violet flame see Mark L. Prophet and Elizabeth Clare Prophet, *The Lost Teachings of Jesus,* Book 4, chap. 13; *The Science of the Spoken Word.* Elizabeth Clare Prophet, *The Astrology of the Four Horsemen,* chaps. 39, 40; *Saint Germain and Violet Flame Decrees,* videocassette; *On the Violet Flame and the Chakras,* videocassette. *Save the World with Violet Flame! by Saint Germain 1–4,* audiocassettes of decrees and songs. *Violet Flame for Elemental Life—Fire, Air, Water and Earth 1* and *2,* audiocassettes of decrees and songs. *Saint Germain, Send Violet Flame!* CD of decrees. *Saint Germain's Violet Flame for the Age of Aquarius: Meditations for the Purification of the Seat-of-the-Soul Chakra,* audiocassette of songs. *Hail, Freedom Flame! For the Liberation of the Oppressed Peoples of the World,* audiocassette of songs. For information and to order the publications and cassettes listed here, contact Summit University Press.

10. See Plotinus, *Ennead* 1.4.16.

11. Matt. 5:48; 1 Cor. 2:6 KJV. In 1 Corinthians of the King James Version, Paul said, "We speak wisdom among them that are perfect"—translating the Greek word *teleios* as "perfect." Yet the New Revised Standard Version translates the same word as "mature." But if Paul used mystery terminology, as we have

demonstrated, when he used *teleioi,* we can only assume that he meant "initiates," comparing Christians to initiates of the mystery religions.

12. Origen, *Homily on Jeremiah,* quoted in von Balthasar, *Origen, Spirit and Fire,* p. 279.

13. Origen, *Homily on Ezekiel,* quoted in von Balthasar, *Origen, Spirit and Fire,* p. 279.

14. See "Cana of Galilee," bk. 7, chap. 4, in Fyodor Dostoevsky, *The Brothers Karamazov,* trans. Richard Pevear and Larissa Volokhonsky (New York: Random House, Vintage Classics, 1991), pp. 359–61.

15. Eph. 2:8.

16. Heb. 10:10, 14.

17. Phil. 2:12.

18. Ramakrishna, quoted in Swami Prabhavananda with Frederick Manchester, *The Spiritual Heritage of India* (Hollywood, Calif.: Vedanta Press, 1969), p. 123.

19. "Amazing Grace," words by John Newton, verse 3.

20. Plotinus, *Enneads,* 4.8.4, trans. Stephen MacKenna (London: Penguin Books, 1991), p. 339.

21. Meister Eckhart, Sermon 54, in *Sermons and Treatises,* 3 vols., trans. and ed. M. O'C. Walshe (Longmead, Shaftesbury, Dorset: Element Books, 1987), 2:71.

22. Huston Smith, *The World's Religions* (HarperSanFrancisco, 1991), p. 48.

23. *A Discourse on Abba Philimon,* in *The Philokalia,* comp. St. Nikodimos of the Holy Mountain and St. Makarios of Corinth, trans. G. E. H. Palmer, Philip Sherrard, and Kallistos Ware (London: Faber and Faber, 1981), 2:348. The *Discourse* is considered to be the earliest source for this formulation of the prayer.

24. 1 Thess. 5:17.

25. *A Discourse on Abba Philimon,* in *The Philokalia,* 2:348.

26. Sergius Bolshakoff, *Russian Mystics* (Kalamazoo, Mich.: Cistercian Publications, 1980), pp. 232, 233.

27. A *Discourse on Abba Philimon,* in *The Philokalia,* 2:349.

28. See Mark L. Prophet and Elizabeth Clare Prophet, *The Science of the Spoken Word; The Science of the Spoken Word: Why and How to Decree Effectively,* 4-audiocassette album. Jesus and Kuthumi, *Prayer and Meditation.* Elizabeth Clare Prophet, *How to Work with Angels; "I'm Stumping for the Coming Revolution in Higher Consciousness!"* 3-audiocassette album; *The Liberating Power of the Word,* album 1, 6 audiocassettes. *Prayers, Meditations, and Dynamic Decrees for the Coming Revolution in Higher Consciousness,* sections 1 and 2. *Angels,* booklet of prayers, decrees, mantras and affirmations. *Heart, Head and Hand Decrees,* booklet. For audiocassettes of decrees given at a beginning pace, see *Devotions, Decrees and Spirited Songs to Archangel Michael; Healing Meditations; Love Meditations;* and *Fiats! Fiats! Fiats!* (also on CD). For more information and to order the books and audiocassettes listed here, contact Summit University Press.

29. Plotinus, *Ennead* 4.4.7, MacKenna, p. 291.

30. Hai Gaon, quoted in David S. Ariel, *The Mystic Quest: An Introduction to Jewish Mysticism* (Northvale, N.J.: Jason Aronson, 1988), p. 22.

Bibliography

Primary sources

Amidon, Philip R., trans. *The Panarion of St. Epiphanius, Bishop of Salamis: Selected Passages*. New York: Oxford University Press, 1990.

Butterworth, G. W., trans. *Origen: On First Principles*. 1936. Reprint. Gloucester, Mass.: Peter Smith, 1973.

Catechism of the Catholic Church. Liguori, Mo.: Liguori Publications, 1994.

Charlesworth, James H., ed. *The Old Testament Pseudepigrapha*. 2 vols. Garden City, N.Y.: Doubleday, 1983–85.

Colson, F. H., and G. H. Whitaker, trans. *Philo*. 10 vols. and 2 suppl. vols. Loeb Classical Library. Cambridge: Harvard University Press, 1929–62.

Conybeare, F. C., trans. *Philostratus: The Life of Apollonius of Tyana*. 2 vols. Loeb Classical Library. Cambridge: Harvard University Press, 1912.

Falconer, William Armistead, trans. *Cicero: De Senectute, De Amicitia, De Divinatione*. Loeb Classical Library, vol. 20. Cambridge: Harvard University Press, 1923.

Ferguson, John, trans. *Clement of Alexandria: Stromateis: Books One to Three*. The Fathers of the Church, vol. 85. Washington, D.C.: Catholic University of America Press, 1991.

Foerster, Werner. *Gnosis: A Selection of Gnostic Texts*. 2 vols.

Translated by R. McL. Wilson. Oxford: Clarendon Press, 1972.

Heine, Ronald E., trans. *Origen: Homilies on Genesis and Exodus.* The Fathers of the Church, vol. 71. Washington, D.C.: Catholic University of America Press, 1982.

Imerti, Arthur D., trans. and ed. *Giordano Bruno: The Expulsion of the Triumphant Beast.* New Brunswick, N.J.: Rutgers University Press, 1964.

Jowett, Benjamin, and J. Harward, trans. *The Dialogues of Plato and The Seventh Letter.* Chicago: Encyclopaedia Britannica, 1952.

Kaplan, Aryeh, trans. *The Bahir.* 1979. Reprint. York Beach, Maine: Samuel Weiser, 1989.

Klimkeit, Hans-Joachim. *Gnosis on the Silk Road: Gnostic Texts from Central Asia.* HarperSanFrancisco, 1993.

Kloppenborg, John S., et al. *Q–Thomas Reader.* Sonoma, Calif.: Polebridge Press, 1990.

Layton, Bentley, trans. *The Gnostic Scriptures.* Garden City, N.Y.: Doubleday, 1987.

MacDermot, Violet, trans. *Pistis Sophia.* Nag Hammadi Studies 9. Leiden: E. J. Brill, 1978.

MacKenna, Stephen, trans. *Plotinus: The Enneads.* Abridged by John Dillon. London: Penguin Books, 1991.

Martínez, Florentino García. *The Dead Sea Scrolls Translated: The Qumran Texts in English.* Translated by Wilfred G. E. Watson. Leiden: E. J. Brill, 1994.

Mead, G. R. S., trans. *Pistis Sophia.* Blauvelt, N.Y.: Garber Communications, Spiritual Science Library, 1984.

Meyer, Marvin, trans. *The Gospel of Thomas: The Hidden Sayings of Jesus.* HarperSanFrancisco, 1992.

———, trans. *The Secret Teachings of Jesus: Four Gnostic Gospels.* 1984. Reprint. New York: Random House, Vintage Books, 1986.

———, ed. *The Ancient Mysteries: A Sourcebook.* San Francisco: Harper and Row, 1987.

Miller, Robert J., ed. *The Complete Gospels: Annotated Scholars Version.* 3d ed. 1992. Reprint. HarperSanFrancisco, Polebridge Press, 1994.

Nikodimos, St., of the Holy Mountain, and St. Makarios of Corinth, comps. *The Philokalia.* Translated by G. E. H. Palmer, Philip Sherrard, and Kallistos Ware. London: Faber and Faber, 1981.

Parsons, Wilfrid, trans. *Saint Augustine: Letters.* Vol. 4 (163–203). The Fathers of the Church, vol. 30. Washington, D.C.: Catholic University of America Press, 1955.

Prabhavananda, Swami, and Frederick Manchester, comps. and trans. *The Upanishads: Breath of the Eternal.* 1948. Reprint. New York: New American Library, Mentor Books, 1975.

Roberts, Alexander, and James Donaldson, eds. *The Ante-Nicene Fathers: Translations of the Writings of the Fathers down to A.D. 325.* 10 vols. Reprint. Grand Rapids, Mich.: Wm. B. Eerdmans Publishing, 1978–81.

Robinson, James M., ed. *The Nag Hammadi Library in English.* 3d ed., rev. San Francisco: Harper and Row, 1988.

Schaff, Philip, ed. *A Select Library of Nicene and Post-Nicene Fathers of the Christian Church.* 1st ser. 14 vols. Reprint. Grand Rapids, Mich.: Wm. B. Eerdmans Publishing, 1979–80.

Schaff, Philip, and Henry Wace, eds. *A Select Library of Nicene and Post-Nicene Fathers of the Christian Church.* 2d ser. 14 vols. Reprint. Grand Rapids, Mich.: Wm. B. Eerdmans Publishing, 1978–79.

Schumacher, Matthew A., trans. *Saint Augustine: Against Julian.* The Fathers of the Church, vol. 35. Washington, D.C.: Catholic University of America Press, 1957.

Wakefield, Walter L., and Austin P. Evans. *Heresies of the High Middle Ages: Selected Sources.* New York: Columbia University Press, 1991.

Walshe, M. O'C., trans. and ed. *Meister Eckhart: Sermons and Treatises.* 3 vols. Longmead, Shaftesbury, Dorset: Element Books, 1987.

Whiston, William, trans. *The Works of Josephus: New Updated Edition.* Peabody, Mass.: Hendrickson, 1987.

Williamson, G. A., trans. *Eusebius: The History of the Church from Christ to Constantine.* New York: Dorset Press, 1965.

Wright, M. R., ed. *Empedocles: The Extant Fragments*. New Haven: Yale University Press, 1981.

Yonge, C. D., trans. *The Works of Philo: New Updated Edition*. Peabody, Mass.: Hendrickson Publishers, 1993.

SECONDARY SOURCES

Akira, Hirakawa. *A History of Indian Buddhism from Sakyamuni to Early Mahayana*. Translated and edited by Paul Groner. Asian Studies at Hawaii, no. 36. Hawaii: University of Hawaii Press, 1990.

Angus, S. *The Mystery-Religions: A Study in the Religious Background of Early Christianity*. 1928. Reprint. New York: Dover Publications, 1975.

Ariel, David S. *The Mystic Quest: An Introduction to Jewish Mysticism*. Northvale, N.J.: Jason Aronson, 1988.

Armstrong, Karen. *A History of God: The 4000-Year Quest of Judaism, Christianity and Islam*. New York: Alfred A. Knopf, 1994.

Barker, John W. *Justinian and the Later Roman Empire*. Madison, Wis.: University of Wisconsin Press, 1966.

Barnes, Timothy D. *Constantine and Eusebius*. Cambridge: Harvard University Press, 1981.

Barr, Stringfellow. *The Mask of Jove: A History of Graeco-Roman Civilization from the Death of Alexander to the Death of Constantine*. Philadelphia: J. B. Lippincott, 1966.

Baus, Karl. *From the Apostolic Community to Constantine*. Vol. 1 of *History of the Church*. New York: Crossroad, 1986.

Baus, Karl, et al. *The Imperial Church from Constantine to the Early Middle Ages*. Translated by Anselm Biggs. Vol. 2 of *History of the Church*. New York: Crossroad, 1986.

Bentley, James. *Secrets of Mount Sinai: The Story of the World's Oldest Bible—Codex Sinaiticus*. 1985. Reprint. Garden City, N.Y.: Doubleday, 1986.

Bohm, David. "Hidden Variables and the Implicate Order." In *Quantum Implications: Essays in Honour of David Bohm,* edited by B. J. Hiley and F. David Peat. London: Routledge and Kegan Paul, 1987.

Bokser, Ben Zion. *The Jewish Mystical Tradition*. Northvale, N.J.: Jason Aronson, 1993.

Bolshakoff, Sergius. *Russian Mystics*. Kalamazoo, Mich.: Cistercian Publications, 1980.

Borg, Marcus J. *Jesus in Contemporary Scholarship*. Valley Forge, Penn.: Trinity Press International, 1994.

———. *Meeting Jesus Again for the First Time: The Historical Jesus and the Heart of Contemporary Faith*. HarperSanFrancisco, 1994.

Bostock, Gerald. "The Sources of Origen's Doctrine of Pre-Existence." In *Origeniana Quarta*, edited by Lothar Lies. Innsbruck: Tyrolia-Verlag, 1987, 259–64.

Boulting, William. *Giordano Bruno: His Life, Thought, and Martyrdom*. London: Kegan Paul, Trench, Trübner, 1914.

Brenon, Anne. *Le Vrai Visage du catharisme* (The true face of Catharism). Rev. ed. Portet-sur-Garonne, France: Editions Loubatières, 1994.

———. *Les femmes cathares* (Cathar women). Paris: Librairie Académique Perrin, 1992.

Brinton, Daniel G., and Thomas Davidson. *Giordano Bruno: Philosopher and Martyr*. Philadelphia: David McKay Publisher, 1890.

Brown, Peter. *Augustine of Hippo*. 1967. Reprint. New York: Dorset Press, 1986.

———. *The Making of Late Antiquity*. 1978. Reprint. Cambridge: Harvard University Press, 1993.

———. *Power and Persuasion in Late Antiquity: Towards a Christian Empire*. Madison, Wis.: University of Wisconsin Press, 1992.

Browning, Robert. *Justinian and Theodora*. Rev. ed. London: Thames and Hudson, 1987.

Burkert, Walter. *Greek Religion*. Translated by John Raffan. Cambridge: Harvard University Press, 1985.

Buxbaum, Yitzhak. *The Life and Teachings of Hillel*. Northvale,

N.J.: Jason Aronson, 1994.

Chadwick, Henry. *Early Christian Thought and the Classical Tradition: Studies in Justin, Clement, and Origen.* Oxford: Clarendon Press, 1966.

Charlesworth, James H. *Jesus within Judaism: New Light from Exciting Archaeological Discoveries.* New York: Doubleday, 1988.

———, ed. *Jesus and the Dead Sea Scrolls.* New York: Doubleday, 1992.

Ch'en, Kenneth K. S. *Buddhism in China: A Historical Survey.* Princeton: Princeton University Press, 1964.

Clark, Elizabeth A. *The Origenist Controversy: The Cultural Construction of an Early Christian Debate.* Princeton: Princeton University Press, 1992.

Cockell, Jenny. *Across Time and Death: A Mother's Search for Her Past Life Children.* New York: Simon and Schuster, Fireside Book, 1994.

Collins, John J. *The Scepter and the Star: The Messiahs of the Dead Sea Scrolls and Other Ancient Literature.* New York: Doubleday, 1995.

———. "A Pre-Christian 'Son of God' among the Dead Sea Scrolls?" *Bible Review,* June 1993.

Couliano, Ioan P. *The Tree of Gnosis: Gnostic Mythology from Early Christianity to Modern Nihilism.* Translated by H. S. Wiesner and the author. HarperSanFrancisco, 1992.

Crossan, John Dominic. *Jesus: A Revolutionary Biography.* HarperSanFrancisco, 1994.

———. *The Historical Jesus: The Life of a Mediterranean Jewish Peasant.* HarperSanFrancisco, 1992.

Crouzel, Henri. *Origen.* Translated by A. S. Worrall. San Francisco: Harper and Row, 1989.

Daniélou, Jean. *Gospel Message and Hellenistic Culture.* Translated by John Austin Baker. Vol. 2 of *A History of Early Christian Doctrine Before the Council of Nicaea.* London: Darton, Longman and Todd, 1973.

Davidson, John. *The Gospel of Jesus: In Search of His Original*

Teachings. Shaftesbury, Dorset: Element Books, 1995.

Davies, Stevan. "The Christology and Protology of the Gospel of Thomas." *Journal of Biblical Literature* 111 (1992): 663–82.

———. *The Gospel of Thomas and Christian Wisdom.* New York: Seabury Press, 1983.

Dechow, Jon F. *Dogma and Mysticism in Early Christianity: Epiphanius of Cyprus and the Legacy of Origen.* Patristic Monograph Series, 13. Macon, Ga.: Mercer University Press, 1988.

De Conick, April D. "The *Dialogue of the Savior* and the Mystical Sayings of Jesus." *Vigiliae Christianae* 50 (1996): 178–99.

———, and Jarl Fossum. "Stripped before God: A New Interpretation of Logion 37 in the *Gospel of Thomas.*" *Vigiliae Christianae* 45 (1991): 123–50.

De Rosa, Peter. *Christ and Original Sin.* Milwaukee: Bruce Publishing, 1967.

Dillenberger, John, and Claude Welch. *Protestant Christianity.* New York: Charles Scribner's Sons, 1954.

Duvernoy, Jean. *La Religion des cathares* (The Cathar religion). Rev. ed. Toulouse, France: Privat, 1990.

Dzielska, Maria. *Hypatia of Alexandria.* Translated by F. Lyra. Cambridge: Harvard University Press, 1995.

Edinger, Edward F. *The Eternal Drama: The Inner Meaning of Greek Mythology.* Edited by Deborah A. Wesley. Boston: Shambhala Publications, 1994.

Fideler, David. *Jesus Christ, Sun of God: Ancient Cosmology and Early Christian Symbolism.* Wheaton, Ill.: Theosophical Publishing House, Quest Books, 1993.

Filoramo, Giovanni. *A History of Gnosticism.* Translated by Anthony Alcock. Cambridge: Basil Blackwell, 1990.

Fisher, Joe. *The Case for Reincarnation.* New York: Carol Publishing Group, Citadel Press, 1992.

Fowden, Garth. *Empire to Commonwealth: Consequences of Monotheism in Late Antiquity.* Princeton: Princeton University Press, 1993.

Franck, Irene M., and David M. Brownstone. *The Silk Road: A*

History. New York: Facts on File Publications, 1986.

Friedländer, Paul. *Plato.* 3 vols. Translated by Hans Meyerhoff. 2d ed., rev. Bollingen Series 59. Princeton: Princeton University Press, 1969.

Frith, I. *Life of Giordano Bruno, the Nolan.* Rev. ed. London: Trübner, 1887.

Fujita, Neil S. *A Crack in the Jar: What Ancient Jewish Documents Tell Us about the New Testament.* New York: Paulist Press, 1986.

Funk, Robert W., Roy W. Hoover, and the Jesus Seminar. *The Five Gospels: The Search for the Authentic Words of Jesus.* New York: Macmillan, Polebridge Press, 1993.

Gallup, George, Jr., with William Proctor. *Adventures in Immortality.* New York: McGraw-Hill, 1982.

Gershom, Yonassan. *Beyond the Ashes: Cases of Reincarnation from the Holocaust.* Virginia Beach, Va.: A.R.E. Press, 1992.

Godwin, Joscelyn. *Mystery Religions in the Ancient World.* London: Thames and Hudson, 1981.

Goodenough, Erwin R. *By Light, Light: The Mystic Gospel of Hellenistic Judaism.* 1935. Reprint. Amsterdam: Philo Press, 1969.

Goodman, Hananya, ed. *Between Jerusalem and Benares: Comparative Studies in Judaism and Hinduism.* Albany: State University of New York Press, 1994.

Govinda, Lama Anagarika. *Insights of a Himalayan Pilgrim.* Berkeley, Calif.: Dharma Publishing, 1991.

Grant, Michael. *Constantine the Great: The Man and His Times.* New York: Charles Scribner's Sons, 1994.

Grant, Robert M. "Early Alexandrian Christianity." *Church History* 40 (June 1971): 135–44.

Greeley, Andrew M. *The Great Mysteries: An Essential Catechism.* New York: Seabury Press, Crossroad Book, 1976.

Gregg, Robert C., and Dennis E. Groh. *Early Arianism—A View of Salvation.* Philadelphia: Fortress Press, 1981.

Gruenwald, Ithamar. *Apocalyptic and Merkavah Mysticism.* Leiden: E. J. Brill, 1980.

————. *From Apocalypticism to Gnosticism: Studies in Apocalypticism, Merkavah Mysticism and Gnosticism*. Frankfurt am Main: Verlag Peter Lang, 1988.

Guthrie, Kenneth Sylvan, comp. and trans. *The Pythagorean Sourcebook and Library: An Anthology of Ancient Writings Which Relate to Pythagoras and Pythagorean Philosophy*. Grand Rapids, Mich.: Phanes Press, 1987.

Guthrie, Shirley C. *Christian Doctrine*. Rev. ed. Louisville, Ky.: Westminster/John Knox Press, 1994.

Hall, Robert G. "Isaiah's Ascent to See the Beloved: An Ancient Jewish Source for the *Ascension of Isaiah?*" *Journal of Biblical Literature* 113 (1994): 463–84.

Hanson, R. P. C. *Origen's Doctrine of Tradition*. London: SPCK, 1954.

Hardon, John A. *The Catholic Catechism*. New York: Doubleday, 1981.

Harley, Brian, and Glenn Firebaugh. "Americans' Belief in an Afterlife: Trends over the Past Two Decades." *Journal for the Scientific Study of Religion* 32 (1993): 269–78.

Harrison, Jane. *Prolegomena to the Study of Greek Religion*. 3d ed. 1922. Reprint. New York: Meridian Books, 1955.

Hengel, Martin. *Judaism and Hellenism: Studies in Their Encounter in Palestine during the Early Hellenistic Period*. 2 vols. Translated by John Bowden. London: SCM Press, 1974.

Horowitz, Irving Louis. *The Renaissance Philosophy of Giordano Bruno*. New York: Coleman-Ross, 1952.

Howe, Quincy, Jr. *Reincarnation for the Christian*. Wheaton, Ill.: Theosophical Publishing House, Quest Book, 1974.

Kamenetz, Rodger. *The Jew in the Lotus: A Poet's Rediscovery of Jewish Identity in Buddhist India*. HarperSanFrancisco, 1994.

Kannengiesser, Charles. *Arius and Athanasius: Two Alexandrian Theologians*. Hampshire, Great Britain: Variorum, 1991.

Kerényi, Carl. *Eleusis: Archetypal Image of Mother and Daughter*. Translated by Ralph Manheim. Bollingen Series 65. 1967. Reprint. Princeton: Princeton University Press, 1991.

Koester, Helmut. *Ancient Christian Gospels: Their History and Development*. Philadelphia, Trinity Press International, 1990.

Küng, Hans, et al. *Christianity and the World Religions: Paths of Dialogue with Islam, Hinduism, and Buddhism*. Translated by Peter Heinegg. Garden City, N.Y.: Doubleday, 1986.

Lambert, Malcolm. *Medieval Heresy: Popular Movements from Bogomil to Hus*. New York: Holmes and Meier Publishers, 1976.

Langley, Noel. *Edgar Cayce on Reincarnation*. New York: Warner Books, 1967.

Layton, Bentley, ed. *The Rediscovery of Gnosticism*. 2 vols. Leiden: E. J. Brill, 1980.

Lea, Henry Charles. *A History of the Inquisition of the Middle Ages*. 3 vols. New York: Harper and Brothers, 1887.

Lightner, Robert P. *The Last Days Handbook*. Nashville: Thomas Nelson Publishers, 1990.

Lohse, Bernhard. *A Short History of Christian Doctrine*. Translated by F. Ernest Stoeffler. 1966. Reprint. Philadelphia: Fortress Press, 1978.

Lossky, Vladimir. *In the Image and Likeness of God*. Edited by John H. Erickson and Thomas E. Bird. Crestwood, N.Y.: St. Vladimir's Seminary Press, 1985.

Louth, Andrew. *The Origins of the Christian Mystical Tradition: From Plato to Denys*. 1981. Reprint. Oxford: Clarendon Press, 1983.

Luce, J. V. *An Introduction to Greek Philosophy*. New York: Thames and Hudson, 1992.

MacGregor, Geddes. *Reincarnation in Christianity: A New Vision of the Role of Rebirth in Christian Thought*. Wheaton, Ill.: Theosophical Publishing House, 1978.

Mack, Burton L. *Who Wrote the New Testament? The Making of the Christian Myth*. HarperSanFrancisco, 1995.

———. *The Lost Gospel: The Book of Q and Christian Origins*. HarperSanFrancisco, 1993.

MacMullen, Ramsay. *Constantine*. New York: Dial Press, 1969.

Madaule, Jacques. *The Albigensian Crusade: An Historical Essay.* Translated by Barbara Wall. New York: Fordham University Press, 1967.

McGinn, Bernard. *The Foundations of Mysticism.* Vol. 1 of *The Presence of God: A History of Western Christian Mysticism.* New York: Crossroad, 1992.

McIntyre, J. Lewis. *Giordano Bruno.* London: Macmillan, 1903.

Meyers, Eric M., Ehud Netzer, and Carol L. Meyers. *Sepphoris.* Winona Lake, Ind.: Eisenbrauns, 1992.

Modrzejewski, Joseph Mélèze. *The Jews of Egypt: From Rameses II to Emperor Hadrian.* Translated by Robert Cornman. Philadelphia: Jewish Publication Society, 1995.

Moody, Raymond A., Jr. *Life After Life: The Investigation of a Phenomenon—Survival of Bodily Death.* New York: Bantam Books, 1975.

_____, with Paul Perry. *The Light Beyond.* New York: Bantam Books, 1988.

Morray-Jones, C. R. A. "Paradise Revisited (2 Cor. 12:1–12): The Jewish Mystical Background of Paul's Apostolate: Part 1: The Jewish Sources" and "Part 2: Paul's Heavenly Ascent and Its Significance." *Harvard Theological Review* 86:2, 3 (1993).

Nash, Ronald H. "The Notion of Mediator in Alexandrian Judaism and the Epistle to the Hebrews." *Westminster Theological Journal* 40 (1977): 89–115.

Nikam, N. A., and Richard McKeon, eds. and trans. *The Edicts of Asoka.* 1959. Reprint. Chicago: University of Chicago Press, Phoenix Books, 1966.

Oldenbourg, Zoé. *Massacre at Montségur: A History of the Albigensian Crusade.* Translated by Peter Green. 1961. Reprint. New York: Dorset Press, 1990.

Oulton, John Ernest Leonard, and Henry Chadwick, trans. *Alexandrian Christianity.* Vol. 2 of Library of Christian Classics. Philadelphia: Westminster Press, 1954.

Pagels, Elaine H. "The 'Mystery of Marriage' in the *Gospel of Philip* Revisited." In *The Future of Early Christianity,* edited by Birger

A. Pearson. Minneapolis: Fortress Press, 1991, 442–54.

———. *The Gnostic Paul: Gnostic Exegesis of the Pauline Letters.* Philadelphia: Trinity Press International, 1975.

———. *The Gnostic Gospels.* New York: Random House, 1979.

———. *The Johannine Gospel in Gnostic Exegesis: Heracleon's Commentary on John.* 1973. Reprint. Atlanta: Scholars Press, 1989.

———. *Adam, Eve, and the Serpent.* New York: Random House, 1988.

Patterson, Stephen J. *The Gospel of Thomas and Jesus.* Sonoma, Calif.: Polebridge Press, 1993.

Payne, Robert. *The Fathers of the Eastern Church.* 1957. Reprint. New York: Marboro Books, Dorset Press, 1989.

Pearson, Birger A. *Gnosticism, Judaism, and Egyptian Christianity.* Minneapolis: Fortress Press, 1990.

Peat, F. David. *Einstein's Moon: Bell's Theorem and the Curious Quest for Quantum Reality.* Chicago: Contemporary Books, 1990.

Pelikan, Jaroslav. *The Emergence of the Catholic Tradition (100–600).* Vol. 1 of *The Christian Tradition: A History of the Development of Doctrine.* Chicago: University of Chicago Press, 1971.

Perkins, Pheme. *Gnosticism and the New Testament.* Minneapolis: Fortress Press, 1993.

Philip, J. A. *Pythagoras and Early Pythagoreanism.* Supplementary volume 7 of *Phoenix: Journal of the Classical Association of Canada.* Toronto: University of Toronto Press, 1968.

Prophet, Elizabeth Clare. *The Astrology of the Four Horsemen: How You Can Heal Yourself and Planet Earth.* Livingston, Mont.: Summit University Press, 1991.

Prophet, Mark L., and Elizabeth Clare Prophet. *The Lost Teachings of Jesus 1–4.* 1986. Reprint. Livingston, Mont.: Summit University Press, 1988.

———. *The Science of the Spoken Word.* 1974. Reprint. Livingston, Mont.: Summit University Press, 1991.

Quispel, Gilles. "Transformation through Vision in Jewish Gnosticism and the Cologne Mani Codex." *Vigiliae Christianae* 49 (1995): 189–91.

Raphael, Simcha Paull. *Jewish Views of the Afterlife.* Northvale, N.J.: Jason Aronson, 1994.

Ring, Kenneth. *Life at Death: A Scientific Investigation of the Near-Death Experience.* New York: Coward, McCann and Geoghegan, 1980.

————. *Heading toward Omega: In Search of the Meaning of the Near-Death Experience.* New York: William Morrow, 1984.

Roberts, David. "In France, an Ordeal by Fire and a Monster Weapon called 'Bad Neighbor.'" *Smithsonian* 22 (May 1991): 40–51.

Rondet, Henri. *Original Sin: The Patristic and Theological Background.* Translated by Cajetan Finegan. Staten Island, N.Y.: Alba House, 1972.

Rousseau, John J., and Rami Arav. *Jesus and His World: An Archaeological and Cultural Dictionary.* Minneapolis: Fortress Press, 1995.

Rudolph, Kurt. *Gnosis: The Nature and History of Gnosticism.* San Francisco: Harper and Row, 1987.

Runciman, Steven. *The Medieval Manichee: A Study of the Christian Dualist Heresy.* Cambridge: Cambridge University Press, 1960.

Sandmel, Samuel. *Philo of Alexandria: An Introduction.* New York: Oxford University Press, 1979.

Schiffman, Lawrence H. *Reclaiming the Dead Sea Scrolls: The History of Judaism, the Background of Christianity, the Lost Library of Qumran.* Philadelphia: Jewish Publication Society, 1994.

Scholem, Gershom. *On the Mystical Shape of the Godhead: Basic Concepts in the Kabbalah.* Translated by Joachim Neugroschel. Edited by Jonathan Chipman. New York: Schocken Books, 1991.

————. *Jewish Gnosticism, Merkabah Mysticism, and Talmudic Tradition.* 2d ed. New York: Jewish Theological Seminary of America, 1965.

————. *Major Trends in Jewish Mysticism.* New York: Schocken Books, 1946.

Schwartz, Howard, ed. and comp. *Gabriel's Palace: Jewish Mystical Tales.* New York: Oxford University Press, 1993.

Scott, T. Kermit. *Augustine: His Thought in Context.* New York: Paulist Press, 1995.

Sedlar, Jean W. *India and the Greek World: A Study in the Transmission of Culture.* Totowa, N.J.: Rowman and Littlefield, 1980.

Segal, Alan F. *Rebecca's Children: Judaism and Christianity in the Roman World.* Cambridge: Harvard University Press, 1986.

———. *Two Powers in Heaven: Early Rabbinic Reports about Christianity and Gnosticism.* Leiden: E. J. Brill, 1977.

———. *Paul the Convert: The Apostolate and Apostasy of Saul the Pharisee.* New Haven, Conn.: Yale University Press, 1990.

Shanks, Hershel, ed. *Christianity and Rabbinic Judaism: A Parallel History of Their Origins and Early Development.* Washington, D.C.: Biblical Archaeology Society, 1992.

———. *Understanding the Dead Sea Scrolls: A Reader from the Biblical Archaeology Review.* New York: Random House, 1992.

Sharpe, Kevin J. *David Bohm's World: New Physics and New Religion.* London: Associated University Presses, 1993.

Singer, Dorothea Waley. *Giordano Bruno: His Life and Thought.* New York: Henry Schuman, 1950.

Smith, Morton. *The Secret Gospel: The Discovery and Interpretation of the Secret Gospel According to Mark.* Clearlake, Calif.: Dawn Horse Press, 1982.

———. "Ascent to the Heavens and the Beginning of Christianity." *Eranos Jahrbuch* 50 (1981): 403–29.

Spampanato, Vincenzo. *Documenti della vita di Giordano Bruno.* Florence: Leo S. Olschki Editore, 1933.

Spanos, Nicholas P., et al. "Secondary Identity Enactments during Hypnotic Past-Life Regression: A Sociocognitive Perspective." *Journal of Personality and Social Psychology* 61 (1991): 308–20.

Spencer, Sidney. *Mysticism in World Religion.* 1963. Reprint. Gloucester, Mass.: Peter Smith, 1971.

Stanton, Graham. *Gospel Truth? New Light on Jesus and the*

Gospels. Valley Forge, Penn.: Trinity Press International, 1995.

Stead, Christopher. *Philosophy in Christian Antiquity.* Cambridge: Cambridge University Press, 1994.

Stearn, Jess. *Edgar Cayce—The Sleeping Prophet.* Toronto: Bantam Books, 1968.

Steen, Gareth L., ed. *Alexandria: The Site and the History.* New York: New York University Press, 1993.

Steinsaltz, Adin. *The Essential Talmud.* Translated by Chaya Galai. New York: Basic Books, 1976.

Stevenson, Ian. *Children Who Remember Previous Lives: A Question of Reincarnation.* Charlottesville, Va.: University Press of Virginia, 1987.

———. "A Case of the Psychotherapist's Fallacy: Hypnotic Regression to 'Previous Lives.'" *American Journal of Clinical Hypnosis* 36 (January 1994): 188–93.

———, and N. K. Chadha. "Can Children Be Stopped from Speaking about Previous Lives? Some Further Analyses of Features in Cases of the Reincarnation Type." *Journal of the Society for Psychical Research* 56 (January 1990): 82–90.

Stoyanov, Yuri. *The Hidden Tradition in Europe.* London: Penguin Books, Arkana, 1994.

Tabor, James D. *Things Unutterable: Paul's Ascent to Paradise in Its Greco-Roman, Judaic, and Early Christian Contexts.* Lanham, Md.: University Press of America, 1986.

Tarazi, Linda. "An Unusual Case of Hypnotic Regression with Some Unexplained Contents." *Journal of the American Society for Psychical Research* 84 (October 1990): 309–44.

Terian, Abraham. "Had the Works of Philo Been Newly Discovered." *Biblical Archaeologist* 57 (1994): 86–97.

Tresmontant, Claude. *The Origins of Christian Philosophy.* Translated by Mark Pontifex. Vol. 11 of the *Twentieth Century Encyclopedia of Catholicism.* New York: Hawthorn Books, 1963.

Trigg, Joseph Wilson. *Origen: The Bible and Philosophy in the Third-Century Church.* Atlanta: John Knox Press, 1983.

VanderKam, James C. *The Dead Sea Scrolls Today.* Grand Rapids,

Mich.: William B. Eerdmans Publishing, 1994.

Vermes, Geza. *Jesus the Jew: A Historian's Reading of the Gospels.* 1973. Reprint. Philadelphia: Fortress Press, 1981.

Von Balthasar, Hans Urs. *Origen, Spirit and Fire: A Thematic Anthology of His Writings.* Translated by Robert J. Daly. Washington, D.C.: Catholic University of America Press, 1984.

Wakefield, Walter L. *Heresy, Crusade and Inquisition in Southern France 1100–1250.* London: George Allen and Unwin, 1974.

Walbank, F. W. *The Hellenistic World.* Rev. ed. Cambridge: Harvard University Press, 1993.

Wallis, Richard T., and Jay Bregman, eds. *Neoplatonism and Gnosticism.* Albany: State University of New York Press, 1992.

Weatherhead, Leslie D. *The Christian Agnostic.* Nashville: Abingdon Press, 1965.

Wells, Amber D. "Reincarnation Beliefs among Near-Death Experiencers." *Journal of Near-Death Studies* 12 (1993): 17–31.

Whitton, Joel L., and Joe Fisher. *Life between Life: Scientific Explorations into the Void Separating One Incarnation from the Next.* 1986. Reprint. New York: Warner Books, 1988.

Williams, Stephen, and Gerard Friell. *Theodosius: The Empire at Bay.* 1994. Reprint. New Haven: Yale University Press, 1995.

Winston, David. *Logos and Mystical Theology in Philo of Alexandria.* Cincinnati: Hebrew Union College Press, 1985.

Yates, Frances A. *Giordano Bruno and the Hermetic Tradition.* Chicago: University of Chicago Press, 1964.

Picture Credits

P. 70 *Persephone carried off by Pluto,* wall painting from the Tomb of the Nasonii, later 3rd century A.D., copyright British Museum.

P. 73 *Orphic signet ring,* gold ring, 5th century A.D., copyright British Museum.

P. 80 *Philo of Alexandria,* courtesy of Bibliothèque Nationale, Paris.

P. 87 *Gandhara Buddha Head,* 3rd–4th century A.D., copyright British Museum.

P. 98 *Elijah on the Fire Chariot* by Alessandro Franchi, marble inlay from pavement, Duomo, Siena, Italy, Scala/Art Resource, N.Y.

P. 126 *Christ Preaching and Bystanders* by Perugino and Pinturicchio, detail from the *Baptism of Christ* fresco, Sistine Chapel, Vatican Palace, Vatican State, Alinari/Art Resource, N.Y.

P. 128 *Cliffs of Jabal al-Tarif, Nag Hammadi, Egypt,* Institute for Antiquity and Christianity, Claremont, California.

P. 131 *Nag Hammadi Codex II,* Institute for Antiquity and Christianity, Claremont, California.

P. 153 *The Last Judgment, Resurrection of the Dead,* c. 1210, detail from the Ingeborg Psalter of Denmark, Musée Condé, Chantilly, France, Giraudon/Art Resource, N.Y.

P. 175 *The Birth of Jacob and Esau* by Benjamin West, Bob Jones University Collection.

P. 183 *Origen of Alexandria* by Michael Burghers, Art Resource, N.Y.

P. 200 *The Institution of the Eucharist* by Nicolas Poussin, Louvre, Paris, Scala/Art Resource, N.Y.

P. 207 *Head of Constantine,* Musei Capitolini, Rome, Alinari/Art Resource, N.Y.

P. 211 *Council of Nicaea* by Cesare Nebbia, fresco, 16th century, Biblioteca Apostolica Vaticana, Vatican Palace, Vatican State, Scala/Art Resource, N.Y.

P. 227 LEFT *The apple, symbolizing the Fall of man,* Rare Book Department, Free Library of Philadelphia.

P. 227 RIGHT *Christ the Redeemer lifts the burden of original sin,* Rare Book Department, Free Library of Philadelphia.

P. 232 *Saint Augustine* by Simone Martini, reproduction by permission of the Syndics of the Fitzwilliam Museum, Cambridge, England.

P. 247 *Saint Dominic and the Albigensians* by Pedro Berruguete, Museo del Prado, Madrid, Scala/Art Resource, N.Y.

P. 256 *Saint Dominic Presiding over an Auto da Fé* by Pedro Berruguete, Museo del Prado, Madrid, Alinari/Art Resource, N.Y.

P. 261 *Castle at Montségur,* Graham Finlayson/Colorific!

P. 281 *Transfiguration* by Fra Angelico, fresco, Museo di San Marco, Florence, Scala/Art Resource, N.Y.

P. 317 *Dante and Beatrice,* illumination by Giovanni di Paolo for Dante's *Divine Comedy,* by permission of the British Library.

Other titles from
SUMMIT UNIVERSITY PRESS

The Lost Years of Jesus

The Lost Teachings of Jesus
BOOK 1 *Missing Texts • Karma and Reincarnation*
BOOK 2 *Mysteries of the Higher Self*
BOOK 3 *Keys to Self-Transcendence*
BOOK 4 *Finding the God Within*

Saint Germain On Alchemy:
Formulas for Self-Transformation

Forbidden Mysteries of Enoch

Dossier on the Ascension

The Science of the Spoken Word

Prayer and Meditation

The Answer You're Looking for Is Inside of You

FOR MORE INFORMATION

Summit University Press titles are available directly from
the publisher or from fine bookstores everywhere, including
Barnes and Noble, B. Dalton Bookseller, Borders and
Waldenbooks.

For a free catalog or for information about conferences,
workshops or cable TV programs in your area, contact
Summit University Press, Dept. 458, Box 5000, Corwin
Springs, Montana 59030-5000 U.S.A. Telephone 1-800-245-
5445 (outside the U.S.A., 406-848-9891). Fax 1-800-221-8307
(outside the U.S.A., 406-848-9866). Or visit our Web site at
http://www.tsl.org

ELIZABETH CLARE PROPHET is a pioneer of modern spirituality. She has written such classics of spiritual literature as *The Lost Years of Jesus, The Lost Teachings of Jesus* and *Forbidden Mysteries of Enoch.*

Since the 1960s, Mrs. Prophet has been lecturing throughout the United States and the world on spiritual topics, including angels, the aura, soul mates, prophecy, spiritual psychology, reincarnation and the mystical paths of the world's religions. Her lectures are broadcast on more than 200 cable TV stations throughout the United States.

She has been featured on NBC's "Ancient Prophecies" and has talked about her work on "Donahue," "Larry King Live," "Nightline," "Sonya Live" and "CNN & Company."

Mrs. Prophet lives in Montana at the Royal Teton Ranch, home of a spiritual community where she conducts conferences and workshops.

ERIN L. PROPHET is a freelance writer based in Livingston, Montana. She earned a journalism degree with honors from the University of Southern California.